Regulation is supposed to protect
the interests of consumers, workers,
and the general public—according to
the traditional justification. Yet much
of the research on regulation finds
that it sometimes worsens the performance of markets or ends up serving the interests of the very producers
it was intended to control. The papers
in this book examine the political
and organizational causes of these
outcomes and how they might be
avoided or ameliorated. Among
many valuable insights, this volume
advances our understanding of why
regulatory agencies sometimes perform poorly and suggests fruitful
paths of reform.

Roger G. Noll is Professor of
Economics at Stanford University.

D1503074

Regulatory Policy and the Social Sciences

California Series on
Social Choice and Political Economy

Edited by Brian Barry and Samuel L. Popkin

HD
3616
.U47
R144

Regulatory Policy and the Social Sciences

Edited by
Roger G. Noll

UNIVERSITY OF CALIFORNIA PRESS

Berkeley   Los Angeles   London

BNA O.A. 12-17-85 #31.50

University of California Press
Berkeley and Los Angeles, California

University of California Press, Ltd.
London, England

© 1985 by
The Regents of the University of California

Library of Congress Cataloging-in-Publication Data

Main entry under title:
Regulatory policy and the social sciences.

    Based on papers presented at the Conference on
Regulation and the Social Sciences, held at Reston, Va.,
Jan. 1982, and sponsored by the National Science
Foundation's Regulation and Policy Analysis Program.
    Bibliography: p.
    1. Trade regulation– United States–Congresses.
2. Social sciences– Research– United States–Congresses.
I. Noll, Roger G.   II. Conference on Regulation and the
Social Sciences (1982: Reston, Va.)   III. Regulation
and Policy Analysis Program (National Science Foundation)
HD3616.U47R144   1985   338.973   85-16515
ISBN 0-520-05187-4 (alk. paper)

Printed in the United States of America

1   2   3   4   5   6   7   8   9

Contents

Preface

A considerable amount of congressional and executive branch government activity consists of creating public policy to redistribute income and to protect or use resources efficiently. Of the many ways available to achieve these objectives, governments frequently chose one despite evidence suggesting that it is not only unlikely to accomplish the objectives but is even liable to create an inefficient use of resources. I refer to regulation—governance by command and control. The study of this phenomenon has become a virtual subdiscipline, especially within economics but also within political science and law.

The ubiquitous use of regulation raises questions that are the province of study for many behavioral and social sciences. Why do organizations, especially governments, choose regulation instead of other options that employ incentives and disincentives? What behavioral reactions does regulation induce? How does government organize to effect regulation, and how successful are its organizational modes? What alternatives to regulation may accomplish the objectives more efficiently?

It is easy to recognize that these questions concern not only economic behavior but political, social, cultural, and psychological behavior as well. Yet contributions to the literature on regulation are mostly from economics. Thus, the purpose of the Conference on Regulation and the Social Sciences, held at Reston, Virginia, in January 1982, was to seek out knowledge from disciplines other than economics and to encourage more direct research on the subject of regulation. This undertaking was founded on the belief that contributions of theory, method, and tools from many disciplines will continue to enliven the study of regulatory phenomena as a legitimate, discrete field of scholarly inquiry. Thus, the National Science Foundation's Regulation and Policy Analysis Program was delighted to fund the conference and the preparation of this book, which is a synthesis of the findings of that conference.

In this volume leading scholars of anthropology, law, political science, psychology, and sociology describe and analyze the phenomenon of regulation from the perspective of their own discipline and also contrast work in their discipline with that in economics. The volume contains individual studies and proposes research agendas for each of the represented disciplines to pursue.

The volume begins with Roger Noll's introduction and brilliant review and analytic synthesis of the multidisciplinary literature on regulation. These chapters prepare for the rest of the book by describing the work of economists on regulation in reference to that of scholars from other disciplines.

Three chapters in the volume are concerned with the definition and characterization of regulation from the perspectives of different disciplines. Laura Nader and Claire Nader apply the anthropologists' holistic approach to understanding regulation in complex industrial societies. They view government regulation in the context of the private and governmental, social and cultural organization of American society. Theodore Lowi explores the political science of policy analysis by identifying and characterizing public policies as four types: regulatory, distributive, redistributive, and constituent. He analyzes the organic statutes creating government agencies in the United States and France to classify each agency according to his scheme. Lowi argues that the form of an agency and of its regulations is dependent on the type of legislative rule it enforces. Lawrence Friedman develops the theme that regulation operates through the law and that the legal system is a reflection of the social and moral beliefs of society.

The volume also contains studies of particular aspects of regulation that illustrate the contributions of political science, psychology, and sociology. Morris Fiorina extends a model of the political incentives that lead legislators to delegate regulatory powers to administrative bodies. He finds that a model maximizing pecuniary and nonpecuniary net benefits to a legislator's district satisfactorily describes the decision processes resulting in regulatory delegation. Examining three agencies that have "deregulated," Martha Derthick and Paul Quirk search for the reason these agencies made policy changes toward less regulation even before congressional legislation mandated the reform. Their findings give weight to the force of "prevalent ideas."

Paul Slovic, Baruch Fischhoff, and Sarah Lichtenstein explore the applications to regulation of research in two areas of cognitive psychology: the limits of human intellectual ability, and the perception of risk. The authors believe that research on intellectual ability sug-

gests that the rationality assumption of economics is not a good pre-
dictor of behavior and needs modification. Research on risk suggests
the need to consider social issues in setting safety standards.

Theodore Caplow reports on six interview and questionnaire
studies of organizations subject to large amounts of regulation. He
studies the relation of organizational structures and functions to the
management of perceived conflicts between regulations. The study
advances a number of interesting explanatory hypotheses and rec-
ommends an agenda for further research. Mitchel Abolafia examines the case of self-regulatory behavior and motives in commodity
futures exchanges. He advances the view that self-regulation may be
pro-competitive in reducing transaction costs to all parties and that
cartelizing activities are held in check by the threat of government
intervention.

The book concludes with a thought-provoking series of commentaries by three leading scholars of regulation: Bruce Ackerman (law);
James Q. Wilson (political science); and Philip Selznick (sociology).

I hope readers find that the book has merit in its own right and
that it stimulates more good research on regulation as a social, cultural, political, and legal phenomenon as well as an economic one.

The National Science Foundation thanks all the conference participants for the effort and interest that made this project a success. Special thanks are due to Roger Noll for creating and structuring the conference, carrying it to a successful conclusion, and then contributing
to and editing this volume.

Laurence C. Rosenberg

National Science Foundation

Acknowledgments

Several organizations helped support the preparation of this book, and I am grateful to each. The Regulation and Public Policy Program of the National Science Foundation provided financial support for preparation of the papers, the conference on which they were based, and the refereeing process. Final editing was completed while I was in residence at the Center for Advanced Study in the Behavioral Sciences, supported by a fellowship from the John Simon Guggenheim Memorial Foundation and by the Center's institutional grant from the National Science Foundation. The remaining costs associated with the final preparation of the manuscript were financed by the Energy Policy Studies Program of the Caltech Environmental Quality Laboratory.

During the process of completing the book, I received able assistance from some excellent people. Kathryn Kurzweil performed with dedication and dispatch the numerous secretarial and administrative tasks necessary to coordinate and prepare the final text. Susan Davis, with her amazing administrative talent, organized the conference and assisted me in coordinating the process by which the papers were refereed and revised for publication. Jane-Ellen Long performed the small miracle of editing the manuscript, sometimes quite heavily and always with skill, without offending a single author! Finally, I want to thank Robyn and Kimberlee for their understanding and support as they spent a highly constrained summer vacation in Mammoth Lakes watching me edit this book.

Roger G. Noll

April 1984

PART I

An Overview of Social Science Research on Regulation

1

Introduction

Roger G. Noll

Government regulation of business is a ubiquitous feature of the American economy. Originating in attempts by state government to establish political control of infrastructural industries such as railroads and grain elevators, the concept of creating a government bureau to constrain business activities has mushroomed into a complex, multiagency, and multijurisdictional system that touches every commercial and nonprofit organization in the country.

Not surprisingly, the growth of regulation caused its size and scope to become a major political issue in the 1970s. Two successive successful presidential campaigns—Carter's in 1976 and Reagan's in 1980—included regulatory reform and selective deregulation as principal campaign issues. Certainly this political prominence is a far cry from the political invisibility that scholars and regulators in the 1950s claimed made reform of regulatory policy difficult. The new-found political salience of regulatory policy has led to widespread changes in regulation since the mid-1970s: deregulation in several spheres of the economy, various forms of mandatory impact analysis in social regulatory agencies that are part of cabinet departments, and new approaches to monitoring regulatory decisions by Congress and the courts.

Research by social scientists has played an important role in the reform of regulatory policy. Perhaps the best evidence that scholarly research has affected regulatory policy is that several scholars whose reputations were built, at least in part, upon their research on regulatory policies have been appointed to important government positions in regulatory affairs. Notable examples are Alfred Kahn, Elizabeth Bailey, and Michael Levine at the Civil Aeronautics Board; Paul MacAvoy, Murray Weidenbaum, and George Eads at the Council of

3

Economic Advisers; Stephen Breyer as the staff person who organized the investigations by Senator Edward Kennedy that led to airline deregulation; Darius Gaskins at the Interstate Commerce Commission; and James Miller and George Douglas at the Federal Trade
Commission.

All the social sciences contain some research on regulatory policy;
however, only in two—economics and political science—has the
work been sufficiently extensive to constitute a subfield of the discipline. Moreover, a fair assessment of the impact of this work is that
research by economists has been by far the most influential in the
policy process. Again, evidence in support of this proposition is the
dominance of economists in the roster of scholars who have occupied
important positions in regulatory affairs since the wave of reform
began in the mid-1970s.

The purpose of this book is to explore the scope of research on
regulation in social science disciplines other than economics. The
premise of the book is that research on regulatory policy in disciplines other than economics can be of both intellectual and practical
value and ought to be encouraged. In political science, of course,
there is already a body of interesting scholarship; however, with few
exceptions it has lacked practical focus and has had little influence
on policymaking.

Although research on the economics of regulation is both powerful and useful, its focus does not include the full range of social
scientific questions that could have important practical significance.
Economics is especially useful for analyzing the effect of institutional
arrangements on economic efficiency. With respect to regulation,
the principal contribution of economics has been to show theoretically and empirically how regulatory policies alter the incentives of
businesses and how changes in incentives in turn affect the efficiency
of the markets in which the regulated businesses operate. Economists have also analyzed the effects of regulation on income distribution. This work has been especially useful in three respects. First, it
has identified instances in which regulation achieves little more than
protecting a narrow special interest in a manner that creates substantial inefficiencies, and thereby it has provided the informational
foundation for extensive deregulation in energy, transportation,
communications, and financial institutions. Second, it has identified
alternative approaches to command and control regulation when
the purposes of intervention can be accurately characterized as economic in character. The impact of this work has been less sweeping
than the effects of the work supporting deregulation but has sometimes led to important policy reform—notably, in the movement to-

ward greater use of incentives in environmental regulation. And third, this work has been sufficiently influential to cause its approach to be institutionalized in most regulatory agencies by the development of mandatory benefit-cost analysis and by the creation of economic analysis groups that play an important role in developing policies and priorities in regulatory agencies.

As important as this work has been, it does not provide a solid intellectual foundation for rationalizing all aspects of regulatory policy. To the extent that regulatory policy serves objectives that are not narrowly economic in character, analysis that focuses exclusively on technical efficiency and income distribution will not constitute a complete, comprehensive basis for policy actions. In its broad sense, economic efficiency can incorporate all the values normally assumed to be missing from economic theory: fairness, justice, equity, altruism, legitimacy, etc. Efficiency arguments in economics turn on the ability of the economic system to do the best possible job in serving individuals as final consumers. If individuals are willing to sacrifice more narrowly economic objectives in order to gain these other values, economic theory can incorporate this phenomenon in a rather straightforward way. But practically speaking, theory and measurement are vastly better developed for analyzing prosaically economic activities and objectives of members of a society. Presumably, scholars whose research focus is on these noneconomic aspects of life know best how to incorporate these aspects into a broader view of the regulatory process.

Research on the economics of regulation has also paid relatively little attention to the problem of designing maximally effective organizations for promulgating regulatory policy. Again, the problem is not that in principle economics has nothing to say about designing organizations: economists have played an important though not dominant role in the development of organization theory, especially concerning the internal incentive structure of organizations. But little of this work has found expression in research on regulation, just as relatively little work in organization theory from other disciplines has focused on problems of designing regulatory agencies. Consequently, the scholarly community has been able to provide little useful advice on how reorganizing agencies or restructuring the relationships among agencies, courts, and the legislature might affect regulatory decisions. If the primary issue is whether to have regulation at all (if, for example, the most important question is whether to deregulate or whether to switch to another instrument of public policy such as taxation, subsidization, or a new form of tradeable and enforceable property right), the application of organization theory to the design of regulatory agencies is not very important; however, wherever regulation is the preferred policy instrument, organization theory becomes the primary lever for improving performance and hence assumes great importance.

Another set of research questions arises from the tendency of nearly all research on regulation by economists to assume a strong form of economic rationality. On questions relating to decisionmaking in environments characterized by substantial uncertainty, the theory is more normative than positive, in that its emphasis is on characterizing the nature of a rational approach to decisionmaking rather than describing how people actually behave. This work provides useful techniques for decisionmakers who are faced with uncertainty, and it provides a means of evaluating the quality of decisions in any given decisionmaking environment. But other interesting issues remain. One is how to educate decisionmakers to behave more rationally when facing complex decision problems characterized by incomplete and probabilistic information. Another is how to construct decisionmaking environments so that people are likely to make rational decisions—or at least how to avoid situations in which people systematically make bad mistakes in dealing with uncertainty.

Finally, economic research alone cannot be relied upon to illuminate the process by which regulatory policy is adopted and promulgated. Again, the problem is not that economists have nothing, or only incorrect things, to say about the connections between economic policy and political processes: economists have played an important role in the development of explanations of how narrow economic interests influence the political process. The difficulty is that there is ample evidence that there is more to regulatory politics than this. The deregulation movement of the 1970s and the concomitant influence of economists in reforming regulatory policies were certainly not predictable from purely economic models of the political process. There is some irony in the fact that in the act of demonstrating the emptiness of a public-interest theory in many areas of regulation, several influential economists played a major role in causing a pronounced shift to serving what most would regard as the public interest in those very areas. An important question is how and why many poorly performing regulatory policies were turned around in the late 1970s, and what if anything can be done to the structure of government to insure that this is not a temporary phenomenon.

The purpose of this book is not to provide the last word on any of these questions. Instead, it is to assemble papers that suggest in some detail promising avenues of policy-relevant research on regulation in disciplines other than economics. The book is addressed to two audiences: research scholars who might find useful ideas that will influence their future research, and government officials who might gain a greater comprehension of the potential contribution of social science to understanding and improving the regulatory process.

The genesis of the book was an interest on the part of the National Science Foundation in expanding the scope of its Regulation Program. To this end, the Regulation Program provided financial support for a conference to explore what useful research on regulation might be done by scholars in such disciplines as political science, psychology, and sociology, as well as possible social-scientific perspectives in legal scholarship. Scholars in each of these disciplines were told the purpose of the conference and asked to write papers that would explicitly identify valuable research questions. Two forms of papers were solicited: articles reporting the results of a research project as an example of a general category of useful research for scholars in social science, and essays that explained how a research literature in social science not directly focused on regulatory policy might usefully be applied to studying regulation.

To provide background and coherence to the collection of papers, before they began work on their papers all the authors were supplied with two monographs. One was a survey by Paul Joskow and me (1981) of the economics literature on regulation. The other was an earlier version of Chapter 2 of this book. Chapter 2 addresses the problem of building a theory of the regulatory agency based not only on what scholars in the social sciences have had to say specifically about the regulatory process, but also on the more general literatures on political processes, bureaucracy, organization theory, and the law.

First drafts of all the commissioned papers were discussed at a conference in January 1982. The formal discussant of each paper was a scholar from the same discipline as the author. In addition, conference participants, including several economists, were invited from government agencies and universities. (A complete list of participants is given in the Appendix.) The purpose was to address regulatory research in a multidisciplinary fashion, giving authors maximal opportunity to profit from the knowledge of practitioners and scholars in other fields. Each paper was then revised—most, substantially so—on the basis of the discussion at the conference. Each paper except Chapters 2 and 11 was then submitted for review by an anonymous referee who is a distinguished scholar in the same discipline as the author. The referees were asked to evaluate the papers according to the standards of leading journals in their fields. Finally, two additional referees were asked to review the entire manuscript. In a few cases, the refereeing process led to another revision.

Part I provides the framework for the book by explaining its origins and providing a unifying structure in which the remaining chapters can be placed. Part II contains essays that examine how regulation fits into a broader pattern of social institutions and values. Part III focuses on the politics of regulatory change: political actors' motives in writing regulatory legislation and how politics affect the decisions of the agencies. Part IV contains detailed studies of specific issues in regulatory policy. The examples are the use of research in cognitive psychology in developing regulatory policies to deal with risk; the use of organization theory to shed light on the problem of conflicting regulations—how it arises and how it can be ameliorated; and the use of organization theory to understand self-regulation—why it develops and how it can be used for valid social purposes without leading to cartelization. Part V contains three general statements about promising lines for future research on central questions about regulatory processes.

2

Government Regulatory Behavior
A Multidisciplinary Survey and Synthesis

Roger G. Noll

Government regulation is a pervasive feature of the American economic system. It is a uniquely American approach to the political control of market processes. The purpose of this chapter is to review the range of theories to explain the development and direction of regulatory policy and to point out lines for further research.

First, a definition of regulation is in order. All levels of government attempt to control some private-sector economic decisions to which the government is not a party. One such method of control is to assign to a government agency the responsibility of writing rules constraining certain kinds of private economic decisions, using a quasi-judicial administrative process to develop these rules. This process has two key features. First, the job of the agency is to channel and to alter the direction of an economic activity that is generally regarded as desirable to society. Second, because private ownership of property and its exchange through markets are protected constitutional rights, the agency must satisfy elaborate procedural and evidentiary

Part of the financial support for preparing an earlier version of this essay was provided by the National R&D Assessment Program of the Natural Science Foundation, grant DA 39495. Research assistance was supplied by John Allen, Marcia Bencala, Maryly Crutcher, and Barry Weingast. Especially helpful comments on an earlier draft were provided by Ross Eckert, Paul Joskow, Kai Lee, Michael Levine, and Charles Perrow.

9

rules if it seeks to constrain market activities. These rules give rise to the quasi-judicial process by which the agency develops its policies and means of controlling economic activities within its sphere of responsibility. The bureaus organized to undertake such tasks are herein referred to as *regulatory agencies,* a definition that is developed and defended in Noll (1980). Included in this classification are agencies that control aspects of transactions such as the price or the quality of the good transacted, that mandate certain features of the production process such as emissions-control methods and worker-safety requirements, or that control entry, as by licensing. Excluded are agencies that are public enterprises in that their primary function is either to procure private goods or to produce government goods, that try to prevent certain types of behavior or transactions rather than manage them, that manage government financial affairs such as tax collection or control of the money supply, or that try to alter market behavior by subsidy or by placing conditions on government procurement when the government is an important but not the sole entity on the demand side of the market.

The reason for this focus on regulation is more practical than theoretical. It may well be the case that the theory of regulation is very close to the general theory of government policy, but regulation is a distinct kind of policy that has spawned a distinct theoretical and empirical literature; indeed, in economics and political science its study has been elevated to the status of a subdiscipline. Moreover, because the state of knowledge about the development of the character of public policies is still rather primitive, the focus at this stage should be on specific kinds of policies.

Regulatory agencies come in many sizes and forms. Some are headed by commissions—a group of coequal heads who make decisions by voting on formal proposals, much like a legislature—while others have a single administrative head. Some are independent agencies technically outside the President's administrative control, while other are lodged in executive branch departments. Some are what amounts to the first court in the judicial system, with the power to fine regulated firms or even to ban them from markets, while others must achieve their ends by fighting regulated firms in the federal courts. Some have very narrow responsibilities, such as the appropriately named Packers and Stockyards Administration or the Commodities Futures Trading Commission. Others, like the Occupational Health and Safety Administration, regulate every business in the nation.

Despite their variety, all regulatory agencies make many decisions that, in principle at least, affect economic efficiency. The economics

literature as well as regulatory law emphasizes the effects of regulation on static efficiency—that is, the effect of regulatory decisions on
costs, prices, and product quality, given unchanging technology and
consumer tastes. By controlling prices, profits, entry, and the attributes of products or processes, regulators directly alter the net economic benefits derived from the regulated industry. To the extent
that regulatory rules counteract market imperfections, they contribute to economic efficiency; to the extent that they reduce production
efficiency or confer monopoly market positions on regulated firms,
they reduce efficiency.

In addition, the policies of regulatory agencies also effect the dynamic efficiency of regulated markets, that is, whether the rate and
pattern of technological change in regulated industries are economically efficient. In some cases, agencies have an explicit mandate to
influence technology, either by subsidizing research and development (as was the case with the Atomic Energy Commission prior to
1974) or by imposing technical requirements intended to improve
the performance of a particular industry (as was the case in the promotion of UHF television by the FCC [Webbink, 1969]). More commonly, agencies play a relatively passive role, approving or disap-
proving adoption of new technology on the basis of other policy
mandates (Ackerman and Hassler, 1981; Capron, 1971; Peltzman,
1974; Warford, 1971). Finally, agencies make decisions on matters
not directly related to the choice of technology but that, perhaps
unexpectedly to the agency, indirectly influence technological
change. Thus, regulatory lag—the time required for regulators to
change regulations in response to changed conditions—may change
the incentive of regulated firms to innovate, and rate-of-return regulation may bias innovation of regulated firms in favor of more capi-
tal-intensive technologies (Westfield, 1971).

The research literature on the effects of regulatory agencies on
economic efficiency reaches generally harsh judgments. Government agencies are pictured as ineffective in dealing with market-fail-
ure problems such as environmental externalities or monopolistic
control of markets, while they generate serious liabilities by protecting business against competition, thwarting warranted technological
and economic changes, and imposing significant costs on consumers
without producing many benefits.

This chapter does not evaluate the empirical literature on the undesirable economic effects of regulatory agencies (for a review of this
work see Joskow and Noll, 1981). Instead, it presumes that agencies
do have such effects. The purpose here is to examine the literature
on government processes and bureaucratic organizations in search

of plausible explanations of the selection of regulatory policies. In principle, theories of government policymaking behavior could provide some basis for evaluating proposals to reorganize a regulatory agency, to redesign its mandate, or to replace regulation with some other form of government policy, and for predicting the likely long-term effect of a regulatory agency.

Let us examine an illustration. During the first term of the Nixon Administration, the President's Advisory Commission on Executive Organization (1971)—the Ash Council—proposed a sweeping reorganization of the executive structure of the federal government. The council's report on regulatory agencies contained numerous proposals motivated in part by the perception that independent regulatory authorities create economic inefficiency. The proposals included transferring the agencies to the executive branch, replacing commissions with single administrative heads, streamlining the decisionmaking process, and combining regulatory agencies with related responsibilities into single agencies. A relevant question is whether existing knowledge concerning the operation of government bureaucracies provides support for the notion that these organizational changes would significantly improve the policies of regulatory institutions and the performance of regulated firms.

Dissatisfaction with the performance of a regulated industry can lead to reform proposals of four types.

1. *Reorganization.* The theory underlying reorganization proposals is that the location of regulatory responsibility within the governmental hierarchy and the organizational structure of the agency significantly affect policy outcomes. Since the early 1970s, this has been a particularly popular category of reform. Some examples are:

    Moving an independent commission into an executive department. For example, the Federal Power Commission, an agency responsible for regulating natural-gas prices both at the wellhead and in pipelines, interstate wholesale sales of electricity, and hydroelectric projects, was renamed the Federal Energy Regulatory Commission (FERC) and placed in the Department of Energy when the latter was created in 1978.

    Combining several offices with related responsibilities into a new agency (perhaps with additional powers and responsibilities). Two examples are the creation of the Consumer Product Safety Commission out of a product-safety office in the Food and Drug Administration and a hazardous-product labeling responsibility at the Federal Trade Commission, and the creation of the Environmental Protection Agency largely by taking some responsibilities from the Department of the Interior.

Changing the internal structure of an agency. One way is by creating new administrative subunits. In the early 1970s, the Federal Communications Commission (FCC) created the Cable Television Bureau and the Office of Plans and Policy, the latter a group that undertakes economic analyses of the effects of proposed changes in regulation. Another structural reform is to change the number of administrative leaders of an agency. In the early 1980s, the number of commissioners at the Interstate Commerce Commission (ICC), which regulates surface transportation, and the FCC were reduced from eleven and seven, respectively, to five apiece.

Reshuffling policy responsibilities among agencies. One example is the transfer of the program for subsidizing the maritime industry from the independent Federal Maritime Commission (which also regulates the industry) to the Department of Transportation. Another is the move of oil-pipeline regulation from the ICC to the FERC.

2. *Procedural Reform.*   Administrative law, legal precedent, and the operating rules adopted by agencies determine the flow of information into administrative proceedings and, in principle, constrain the decisionmaking power of agencies. A common complaint is that these procedures slow agencies' decisionmaking and limit their flexibility, particularly in adjusting policies to changing external circumstances. Another complaint is that agencies systematically give insufficient weight to some types of information. Reform proposals include changing the rules of evidence, relaxing the requirement that decisions take account of all evidence submitted but of no other factual material, imposing deadlines on agency decisions, and requiring benefit-cost analysis.

Since the early 1970s, a series of laws and executive orders have imposed more comprehensive reviews of regulatory decisions in and out of agencies. Beginning with the National Environmental Policy Act in 1970, regulatory agencies have faced an ever-expanding array of requirements to perform benefit-cost analysis. Presidents Ford, Carter, and Reagan, in somewhat different ways, all assigned to a special staff in the Executive Office of the President the responsibility of reviewing the economic impact of major new regulations.

3. *Changing the Mandate.*   Another locus of criticisms of the regulatory process centers on the objectives, methods, and powers given to agencies by Congress through legislation and, to a lesser degree, by the President through executive order. If agencies adopt bad policies or overlook key issues, one possible solution lies in

clarifying or correcting the mandate (Friendly, 1962). Another solution is to use a method other than regulation to achieve the same objectives, such as taxes (Mills and White, 1978) or tradeable permits (Hahn and Noll, 1982) to control pollution.

Like the agencies themselves, regulatory legislation varies widely in the precision with which its policy directives are stated and the powers granted to the agency. Many agencies have been told that their purpose is to serve "the public interest, convenience, and necessity"—whatever that may mean—or have been given a wish list of conflicting objectives with no guidance about how to make trade-offs among them. Other regulatory laws are far more explicit. For example, when Congress decided to regulate the fuel economy of automobiles, it enacted legislation that contained explicit standards for the first few years and that gave the regulators the responsibility to devise a way to measure fuel efficiency accurately and to enforce the regulations, as well as to develop further standards for future years not covered by the standards in the law.

4. *Altering the External Environment.*   If the interactions among an agency, a particular industry, other groups with a stake in the industry's performance, the courts, and Congress produce unsatisfactory results, one approach to reform is to restructure these external institutions so that the agency is better able to produce the desired performance. For example, the single-entity proposal for international telecommunications (Peck, 1970)—that the companies providing international telephone service be merged— was based on the presumption that the FCC could regulate the introduction of satellite technology more effectively if the industry were monopolized, rather than if a single satellite company, Comsat, were competing with several companies that owned only transoceanic cables. At the other extreme, the antitrust case that successfully sought the dissolution of the American Telegraph and Telephone Company (AT&T) was based in part on the belief that the size, wealth, and political power of AT&T made it essentially unregulatable. Public ownership is another alternative arrangement for the managed industry. Other reforms of this type include proposals to create a special type of court to review regulatory decisions, to create a special agency to participate in regulatory decisions as the representative of consumer interests, and to reorganize the congressional oversight process.

All four types of proposals rest on theories concerning the behavior of government agencies, private organizations, and elected political officials. Yet the proponents of reform rarely justify their proposals by reference to explicit theories and empirical observations of the interactions among these groups. Nor is much thought normally given to the organizational problems of structuring an effective agency at the time that the legislation is adopted establishing a new regulatory role for the government.

A useful theory of regulatory policy would provide empirically verifiable propositions on the relationships among structure, responsibility, powers, and performance of a regulatory agency. It would provide subsidiary propositions about how private organizations influence policy design and cope with the particular government regime that is established. It would predict the capacity of an agency to control various aspects of private market behavior and would identify optimal choices of agency organization, procedures, and policy instruments for a given policy objective and a given structure of the private market to be managed. A useful theory would explain why an agency responds favorably to some technological innovations and unfavorably to others, and the extent to which an agency's response is affected by controllable characteristics such as structure, procedures, powers, methods, and responsibilities.

The remainder of this chapter examines the existing literature relating to the behavior of regulatory agencies in search of generalizations that are useful in the sense described above. While substantial work has been done in recent years on the theory of regulatory agencies, the results are still fragmentary. Consequently, most of the literature surveyed here is not addressed specifically to the question of regulatory policy. Some is very general, addressed to the properties of all government policymaking processes or even all decision-making organizations. Some is more specific but is addressed to organizations other than regulatory agencies. Indeed, most research on the public policy process and the behavior of government officials has not dealt explicitly with regulation. Consequently, any attempt to suggest in a comprehensive fashion how work in most of social science might enhance our understanding of the regulatory policymaking process must extract inferences from research that was undertaken for other purposes.

The analysis of the behavior of regulatory agencies can be usefully divided into two parts. The first deals with organic theories of regulatory behavior: theories that characterize a regulatory agency as a coherent whole, having objectives that it rationally pursues. The second focuses on structural theories: explanations of regulatory performance that are based on analyzing agencies as collections of individuals with conflicting objectives whose behavior is coordinated by the selection of operating rules, hierarchies and methods of communication.

Organic Theories

One approach to studying the behavior of organizations is to adopt the metaphor of an organization as a rational actor having explicit objectives and choosing among alternative actions on the basis of their expected contributions to organizational goals. This approach abstracts from the influence the structure of the organization and the experiences of its members may have on organizational outcomes. It also abstracts from the problems of managing the behavior of members of an organization so that their performance will be consistent with organizational objectives.

The appeal of so-called rational-actor models lies in the powerful, empirically testable hypotheses that can be derived from their simplistic motivational assumption. The power of organic theorizing is best demonstrated by the microeconomic theory of the firm, which assumes that private businesses are single-mindedly devoted to the maximization of some index of their financial success, such as profits or sales. From this simple assumption, plus characterizations of technological possibilities, the demand for a firm's product, and the supply of resources used by the firm, microeconomic theory has produced a variety of testable hypotheses about how firms respond to various changes in market conditions, when they decide to invest in new facilities, and whether the firm, if unregulated, will be efficient.

Goal-directed theories are not universally accepted, especially outside of economics. Before proceeding with a detailed discussion of them, a few remarks about the critics of these theories are in order.

Most criticisms of rational-actor theories are essentially commentaries on the failure to consider: (1) how goals are formulated; and (2) how structural phenomena affect behavior. In principle, both points could be important. If one observed considerable differences among organizations engaged in the same general type of activities, more powerful theoretical predictions might be obtained by incorporating goal-formulation and structural features into a model of organizational behavior. In the following discussion, the process of goal formulation and emendation is accorded attention in several of the expositions of various organic theories, while the issue of the relationship between structure and performance is examined at length in the next section. In the end, whether one should abandon the simplicity of the model by incorporating these features rests on the empirical success of the simple model in providing good predictions about organizational behavior.

Another criticism of organic theories is that the concept of organizational goal lacks meaning and therefore should not be an admissible assumption in organization theory. Furthermore, such theories are said to be normatively inadmissible on the grounds that because they incorrectly assume the presence of an organizational goal, researchers necessarily find all organizations inefficient since they inevitably uncover some output of the organization that is inconsistent with the goal presumed by the researchers (Etzioni, 1960).

The alternative approach proposed by such critics is that the objectives of the organization should be regarded as whatever the organization is currently doing and, according to its members, would like to do now and in the future. The normative standards for judging organizational effectiveness should be: (1) whether it can do whatever it now does or wants to do more effectively or efficiently by reallocating its resources (Etzioni, 1960); and (2) whether it is succeeding in obtaining sufficient resources to do most effectively what it is now doing (Yuchtman and Seashore, 1967).

The alternative formulation offered by Etzioni and his followers has very little merit. It is useful for predicting and explaining organizational actions only if it is converted to a rational-actor theory (Mohr, 1973). Once one has observed organizational outputs and learned from its members what else they would like to do, one has a multidimensional goal for the organization. Moreover, this information is useful only if one presumes regularity in goals through changes in time and conditions. If the Etzioni approach makes an assumption of regularity, then it boils down to an argument that better predictions will be made if the goal of the organization is stated more carefully. If these regularities do not occur, there is little point from an explanatory perspective in defining the original goal, because each observation on organizational performance will be associated with a different, randomly selected objective.

From a normative point of view the two criteria offered by Etzioni and his followers raise legitimate questions, but there is no reason to exclude others. In particular, citizens and government officials outside a specific bureau can legitimately choose to judge an agency's performance by standards other than those the bureau might use for self-evaluation. From the perspective of an analyst, it is a scientific, not a normative, issue to inquire whether the behavior of an agency is consistent with a particular objective. The Etzioni model explicitly disallows questions about whether the organization is doing the wrong things. From the standpoint of policy formulation and evaluation, then, such a model is essentially useless.

The remainder of this section discusses several different organic, rational-actor theories of regulatory agencies. The key element of a rational-actor theory is specification of the organizational objective.

The number of organizational goals that have been hypothesized is nearly as large as the number of organization theorists (for an interesting survey of the problem of defining organizational goals, see Mohr [1973]). But, with respect to regulation, organic theories are usually based on some form of one of three assumptions about the motives of regulators: they seek to serve the public interest, implicitly maximizing some—usually undefined—measure of national welfare; they try to serve the interests of particular client groups, often by creating a legally enforceable cartel arrangement in an industry that would otherwise be competitive; or they attempt to maximize their own economic rewards or some measure of the success of their bureau.

Serving the Public Interest

A useful point of departure in a catalogue of theories of bureaucratic behavior is to consider models based on the straightforward assumption that government agencies seek to maximize social welfare or the public interest. Numerous conceptual models of government bureaucratic behavior are based on this assumption. These models differ according to their descriptions of how government officials develop perceptions of the public interest they seek to serve. Of course, two related paradoxes in economic theory cast grave doubts on the existence of a well-defined, consistent public interest.

One is the controversy surrounding the compensation principle (Hicks, 1939; Kaldor, 1939; Scitovsky, 1942). The original proposition was that a public policy ought to be adopted if the beneficiaries of the policy could fully compensate the losers and still be better off if the policy were adopted. This principle underpins the use of benefit-cost analysis as a means for evaluating public policies. The paradox that was revealed in subsequent work was that the compensation principle can produce indeterminate results. If a policy passes the compensation test, its very enactment can change income distribution and relative prices in such a way that repeal of the policy would then also pass the compensation test.

The second paradox is found in the literature on social choice theory, beginning with the possibility theorem (Arrow, 1951). The principal lesson of this work is that majority-rule voting to select a winner among a set of mutually exclusive policies does not, in general, have a unique equilibrium. Indeed, the outcome of majority-rule voting depends on procedural rules such as whether defeated proposals can be reintroduced, the order in which proposals are considered, and the number of proposals that can be introduced before voting stops.

The shaky foundation for a "public interest" as a clear, identifiable concept does not imply any fundamental error in public-interest theories of bureaucratic behavior. As long as officials believe that a public interest has been defined for them and act to serve it, the fact that the public interest they perceive lacks interesting normative properties is inessential to the theory of their behavior. The key issue is what they believe the public interest to be, not whether their beliefs are correct or theoretically well-founded.

Traditional public-interest theories—those that were in general acceptance until around 1960—in economics, political science, and sociology, while emphasizing different aspects of the social process, are quite similar in their basic conceptualization of bureaucratic behavior. Although the traditional view is no longer widely shared, it is a good place to begin. Traditional theory provides a benchmark for investigating other theories, many of which have roots in the traditional approach.

Traditional sociology, developing from the ideas of Max Weber (1946), made few distinctions between public and private organizations. It viewed society as requiring the performance of certain functions for its survival. Society creates institutions or structures to perform these functions (Parsons, 1960). Bureaucratic institutions, with formal and impersonal rules carried out by professionals whose employment is based on expertise and other objective measures of competence, are the most effective mechanism for performing essential functions (Weber, 1946).

Traditional political scientists, focusing on government institutions, emphasized the natural separation of functions among the branches of the government. Through the workings of the democratic process, legislation worked out by compromise and bargain among elected representatives reflected the public interest, while the development of a career civil service based on expertise provided objectivity and freedom from partisanship in policy implementation (Bernstein, 1955).

Economists, interested in the microeconomic aspects of policy mandates, viewed government agencies as devices for correcting inefficiencies. The implicit theory of the state in much of the work on the economics of regulation is that the purpose of government is to correct for various kinds of market imperfections. Three general kinds of market failure have been widely analyzed: seller concentration or monopoly, which is inefficient because high monopoly prices lead to underconsumption of the monopolized product; external effects—when some of the benefits and costs of producing and consuming a product fall on people who neither make nor purchase it (e.g., air pollution from autos); and imperfect information, which prevents either buyers or sellers from making efficient market decisions. Strangely enough, the costs of government intervention to correct these market imperfections have been systematically examined by economists only relatively recently (Arrow, 1970; Breyer and Mac-Avoy, 1974; Williamson, 1970), despite the discipline's characteristic concern for costs and efficiency.

Consider, for example, the best-developed current theoretical literature in economics on the costs of regulation, concerning the so-called A-J effect (Averch and Johnson, 1962; Baumol and Klevorick, 1970). This literature analyzes how economic regulation that limits firms' profits on invested capital—that is, rate-of-return regulation—makes them inefficient in their choice of production technology. This theory, though focusing on costs, is otherwise traditional in approach. It assumes that the regulatory process is adequately described as simply limiting the profits of a firm that possesses market power, that the costs of determining and enforcing the regulatory constraint can be ignored, and that conditions of demand and technical change are sufficiently static that the principal effect of profit regulation on a firm's efficiency is through a bias in the selection of long-term capital investments.

As a second example, consider the literature on optimal-pricing policy for a regulated natural monopoly that is sustainable, e.g., the technical characteristics of the monopoly's production process make it possible for the monopoly to set prices that cover its total costs without inducing competitive entry (Panzar and Willig, 1977). Optimal pricing theory proposes two solutions to this problem. The first-best solution is a two-part tariff: set the prices of each of the monopoly's outputs equal to its marginal costs, and then charge each customer a fixed "hook-up" charge to raise whatever additional revenue is necessary in order to cover total costs. If all customers are charged a hook-up fee sufficient to cover total costs exactly, some are likely to cancel service who would have been willing to continue to be customers at a lower hook-up charge that would have made some contribution to paying total costs. Hence, because the customers of the monopoly are likely to vary considerably in the intensity of their demand for the monopoly's outputs, and because it is inefficient to set a group's hook-up charge so high that they elect not to become customers, the fixed charge will probably have to differ among groups of consumers. The second-best pricing rule, to be employed when it is not possible to charge a hook-up fee or, indeed, to engage in any policy other than setting a single price for each output, is Ramsey pricing (Baumol and Bradford, 1970). Here prices are set above marginal cost for each output, with the magnitude of the departure depending on the elasticity of demand—that is, prices are higher as the effect of price on total quantity sold becomes smaller. If customers can be segmented into groups and trades between groups can be prevented, Ramsey pricing involves price discrimination among customers for the same output: charge groups different prices for the same product, with people who have less opportunity to find substitutes being charged a higher price.

Both these optimal-pricing theories make a number of questionable assumptions about regulatory processes. Like A-J theory, the optimal-pricing literature assumes that costs and demand elasticities can be measured sufficiently precisely and that pricing rules can be sufficiently rigorously enforced that optimal pricing is a practical option for a regulatory agency. In addition, both pricing rules involve price discrimination: collecting different amounts of money from different people who are buying the same thing. Indeed, price discrimination will generally be required even if all groups impose the same costs and are objectively similar in their socioeconomic status—or, in some cases, even if the policy involves setting higher prices for some groups that are generally regarded as otherwise socioeconomically disadvantaged. The issue is not just that some people might find such pricing systems morally repugnant, it is a matter of political theory: if such value judgments are widespread they may well make efficient pricing politically unfeasible. If so, failure to adopt such a policy is hardly a valid basis for criticizing regulatory policy.

As these examples illustrate, the assumptions used in normative economic analyses of regulation are often traditional in character. They presume a clean separation of the value-laden choice of a policy objective (e.g., control natural monopoly) and the technical implementation problem to be undertaken by experts, presumably economists (e.g., set optimal prices), and they ignore the direct and indirect costs of implementing alternative policies. For the most part, the exceptions to this generalization can be found in the research on environmental economics, where the problems of administrative feasibility and implementation costs have received more attention (Dales, 1968; Hahn and Noll, 1983). In addition, a few studies on optimal taxation, a topic that is very similar to optimal pricing in utilities, have dealt with the problems of administrative costs (Heller and Schell, 1974; Polinsky and Shavell, 1982; Stern, 1982). But for the most part, the assumptions of normative economic analysis in both regulation and taxation are remarkably similar to the characteristics of sociological structural-functionalist theories, which economists have severely criticized (Harsanyi, 1969; Olson, 1970). They oversimplify the social function of an organization, ignore the relationship between its responsibilities and its costs, and give scant attention to the manner in which it establishes and adjusts policies in light of perceptions of the response of its environment to its actions and to other sources of change (Joskow, 1974; Burness, Montgomery, and Quirk, 1980a).

Combining the traditional views of all three disciplines, the following characterization of regulatory policy emerges. An essential function of a capitalist society is to limit the inefficiencies arising from certain imperfections that can arise in private markets. One purpose of democratically elected legislatures is to detect serious market imperfections and to establish administrative agencies to ameliorate those imperfections. Because these agencies can, by their decisions, cause a substantial redistribution of wealth, they are potential targets for corruption. Hence, they must be placed in the hands of experts who are removed from partisan politics and made subject to decisionmaking rules that protect the process from bribery. When administrative policy fails, the causes can be found among the following: the administrators are poorly selected, being either corrupt or inexpert (Bernstein, 1955; Cary, 1967); the legislative mandate is faulty, either because it lacks clarity or because subsequent events have outdated it (Friendly, 1962); the agency has too few resources to implement its policy directive effectively (Cary, 1967); or the agency has been given a combination of objectives and powers that are incommensurate—a mismatch of means and ends (Breyer, 1981). Solutions include: better appointments, which may require giving the agency more prestige or greater insulation from corrupting influences; clear legislative mandates that are regularly reviewed, such as by including an expiration date in all legislation that creates an administrative agency; and increases in agency budgets.

The traditional approach to the behavior of regulatory agencies has many weaknesses which are sufficiently obvious that they need not be elaborated. But those that stand out as particularly important should be emphasized.

First is acceptance of the possibility of making a clear separation between policymaking and policy implementation, the former by political actors and the latter by experts. The need for expert policy implementation arises from the difficulties of establishing causal connections between policy actions and performance outcomes (March and Simon, 1958). To the extent that expert judgment is relied on for estimates of the relationships between actions and outcomes, policymaking authority resides at least in part in the expert

(Bendix, 1968; Etzioni, 1959). The experts' control over information and access to sophisticated analytic techniques enables them to vitiate, to some degree, any attempt to alter policy objectives through clarifying and tightening the mandate. In fact, judging from the language of the laws that establish regulatory agencies, it is apparent that Congress often does no more than set loose guidelines within which policy will be formulated by the agency (Lowi, 1969). In general, agencies are admonished to serve an undefined public interest and are given a conflicting set of general policy directions. To the extent that expert judgment is an essential ingredient in rational policy formulation, such behavior from Congress is to be expected and is not really a sign of failure.

At the same time, Congress does not fail to demonstrate interest in specific cases involving important constituents. Because Congress controls the budget and legislative authority of the agency, it can and does override expert judgments by the agency (Green and Rosenthal, 1963, re the AEC; Scher, 1960, re the NLRB; Weingast and Moran, 1983, re the FTC). And, as mentioned above, it sometimes writes very detailed regulations on its own.

Second, the traditional theory provides no logical foundation for the presumption that governmental organizations are inherently efficient (Blau and Scott, 1962). In economics, the assumption that the internal structure of the firm can be overlooked rests on the argument that under competition, only efficiently organized firms will survive. Economists have recognized that the assumption of internal efficiency may not be satisfied in imperfectly competitive markets, and Leibenstein's (1966) empirical work argues for the presence of considerable internal inefficiency, which he called X-inefficiency and which other social scientists would call organizational slack. By the same logic, the monopolistic position enjoyed by most agencies (rarely do two agencies perform the same service) could lead to the same type of organizational slack. The insulation of agencies from markets for their outputs or equities should leave them with less incentive than a private monopolistic firm has to operate efficiently. Moreover, the interests of legislators in providing ombudsman services to constituents as a means of securing reelection can lead the legislature purposely to create excessively bureaucratic processes that provide opportunities for intervention by legislators (Fiorina and Noll, 1978). For example, the legislation establishing the Consumer Product Safety Commission appears designed to produce an inefficient process (Cornell, Noll, and Weingast, 1976). At best, Weber's criteria for effective bureaucratic organizations are no more than necessary conditions for efficient operation.

In order for the public-interest theory to be viable, it must have
two components that are lacking in the traditional theory. It must
include a model of how an agency comes to perceive the public interest, and it must identify the source of an agency's motivation to pursue that objective with some degree of efficiency. Part of the motivational argument rests on the limitations for improving personal
welfare in government service. Much of the literature in public administration contends that the income, status, and rate of advancement of government employees, particularly in higher policymaking
jobs, are largely determined by tenure in office, not by performance
(Bendix, 1949; Warner et al., 1963). If so, secondary motivations, of
which only one possibility is identifying and serving some public-
interest objective not associated with personal well-being, can dominate decisionmaking even by individuals who are normally driven by
rational self-interest (Tullock, 1965).

Comanor and Mitchell (1972) have supplied one such motive.
They contend that the Federal Communications Commission regards itself as an economic planning agency, basing their argument
upon the generality of its legislative mandate. As a theory, however,
their model is tautological because it lacks an explanation of how
public-interest planning objectives are discovered. Because it would
be impossible for an administrative agency to have absolutely no effect on resource allocation—even if it were totally ineffective, resources would still be devoted to operating it—the assertion that
agencies engage in economic planning is incapable of disproof unless
the purpose of the plan is specified. Once again, the two essential
ingredients of a theory are missing.

The obvious places to look for sources of a perception of the public
interest are in the institutions that in American society have some legitimate claim to speak for the public: elected representatives, the
press, the courts, and leaders of broadly based organizations. We will
return to these external sources of objectives at the end of this section.

Capture-Cartel Theories

In contrast to the traditional view that bureaus attempt to
serve the general welfare are theories that view bureaus as servants
of some well-defined interest, either because the agency was set up to
serve that client (the cartel theory) or because, through the years,
agencies are vulnerable to being taken over by some special interest
(the capture theory). The special-interest group that the organization serves is usually identified as the producers in the market that

the agency regulates. Another candidate is a professional elite, such as lawyers in agencies with cumbersome procedures or physicists in the case of the old Atomic Energy Commission. A third possibility is an especially powerful group of customers, such as gas utilities in the regulation of natural-gas prices by the FPC and then the FERC.

Marxist Theories. The Marxist perception of politics, which vests political control in the hands of those who control economic production, provides the simplest cartel theory. It sees American government as an instrument for protecting capitalist interests, with revolution being the only means of creating a government interested in the welfare of the working class. It follows without further argument that regulatory agencies are agents for increasing the wealth of producers, usually by establishing a legally enforceable cartel.

The Marxist argument has been used to explain the birth of the Interstate Commerce Commission and the regulation of railroads (Kolko, 1965, whose Marxism is explicit; and MacAvoy, 1965, whose analysis is not explicitly Marxist but is consistent with Kolko's). The argument here is not without controversy, however; whereas regulation may have benefited railroads by establishing a cartel, it imposed costs on another corporate sector—manufacturing—and probably benefited rural agriculture and consumers (Spann and Erikson, 1970). Similar though more complicated cases have been made regarding regulation of banking and airlines (Davis and North, 1970) and professional licensure (Stigler, 1971).

Unfortunately, the Marxist cartel theory has several fatal flaws. It can provide no explanation for the few instances when regulation has been imposed on an industry against its will, such as government controls on coal-mine safety, automobile safety and emissions, toy safety, pay television, the siting of electric power generation facilities, and performance standards for medical instruments. Nor does it provide an explanation for the cases where industries have tried but failed, at least to date, to obtain an effective cartel, such as commuter airlines, wholesale and retail trade, and hospitals. It offers no explanation for agency policies that clearly run counter to producer interests in industries in which regulation is nevertheless generally favored. Railroads, for example, have favored innovations that were blunted or delayed by the ICC (Gellman, 1971). Moreover, some have argued that the principal beneficiaries of the regulation of several industries—notably construction and trucking—have been employees, not ownership.

Marxist theory also has nothing to say about administrative agencies that referee conflicts among producer groups, such as FERC regulation of the field price of natural gas, FCC regulation of the prices charged by telecommunications companies for interconnecting television networks, or Bureau of Land Management control of the uses of public lands. Finally, it cannot explain the deregulation of the 1970s in airlines, surface transportation, banking, securities, and communications, in which anticompetitive policies were abandoned over the objections of most people in the industry.

The flaws in the Marxist cartel theory arise from its simple dichotomization of society into two interest groups, capitalists and workers. Only by adopting a model of society as a complex combination of numerous interests can one explain the diversity of regulatory institutions. Because more often than not regulatory agencies deal with policy issues having far more complexity than a straightforward conflict between capitalists and workers, Marxist theory is not really appropriate for examining and explaining their behavior.

The Market for Regulation. Another cartel theory applies the economists' model of a market to the supply and demand of regulatory institutions (Stigler, 1971; Peltzman, 1976). The presumption is that all producer groups stand to benefit from institutionalized protection from competition. The magnitude of the potential benefit creates maximum payment the group is willing to make to legislators in order to obtain the institution. On the other side, legislators, seeking reelection, would like to confer benefits on voters and potential campaign contributors that would increase their reelectability. They are therefore willing to confer institutionalized protection from competition on the interest group only if the political costs of reducing competition are offset by political benefits flowing from the group's purchase of the institutional change. The currencies for this transaction are numerous: they may be direct payments in campaign contributions, or—if the group is large enough to matter—in votes, or they may be indirect, through improvements in service quality or the provision of uneconomic services to designated constituents of key legislators (Posner, 1971).

Political scientists have often thought of legislators as engaged in conferring private benefits on selected constituents (Mayhew, 1974; and Fiorina, 1977), and numerous empirical studies provide support for this view (Arnold, 1980; Ferejohn, 1974; Scher, 1960). The political science view is more dynamic than the economists' version. The latter formally presents only a theory of the establishment of an agency, implicitly presuming that agencies behave as originally intended—the common presumption that the regulatory process is perfectly controlled and efficient, despite its insulation from a market test. The political science view takes into account the steady stream of pressure from legislators for favors.

Although few political scientists subscribe to Stigler's approach, their work on the role of private favors in legislative activities is consonant with it and can be used to make Stigler's theory more dynamic. The result is a description of the regulatory process along the following lines. A producer group transmits a continual flow of requests to key legislators, usually those in the relevant subcommittees, who in turn pressure a regulatory agency to provide more institutionalized protection from competition. The legislator applies the pressure if the group agrees to certain other direct or indirect political conditions. The agency, responding to the directions of the legislator, obliges.

The preceding explanation of regulatory behavior has several problems. One is that it is tautological: it assumes its conclusion by presuming the existence of suppliers, demanders, and an equilibrium between the two. It is impossible to conceive of a market managed by a regulatory agency that is as efficient as either a perfect cartel with legally enforceable rules or a perfectly competitive industry. Because everything else can be construed as a willful redistribution of income that stands at the intersection of institutional demand and supply, the theory is incapable of disproof. To escape the tautology the theory must include an explanation of why certain groups receive benefits as successful purchasers of institutional protections while others receive no benefits at all but bear some costs through the economic inefficiencies of administrative management, and it must describe the factors that determine the relative sizes of these amounts. This explanation inevitably reduces to a theory of the emergence of political issues relevant to regulatory policies and of the relationship between interest-group characteristics and the effectiveness of groups in the political decisionmaking process. An explanation of why these factors lead to cartelization is not to be found in the cartel-theory literature except in the oversimplification of Marxist theory.

Another problem is that it is not a theory of regulation, but a theory of government policy. Indeed, in Stigler's original paper almost all policies are called regulation, and his approach is really to view legislation as a kind of commodity that is sold to the highest bidder. The theory has not developed as a systematic analysis of why an interest group picks regulation as its source of public assistance.

Goal-Deflection in Bureaus

The goal-deflection model of agency capture stands between the other capture-cartel theories and the traditional public-interest view. It postulates a concern within agencies to serve a broad public purpose but predicts goal deflection as the agency builds up relations with external clients and as the agency, through experience, comes to rely on certain types of professional employees.

Conflict-Avoidance and Producer Capture.   Goals become deflected in favor of producer interests, according to this theory, because agency personnel develop a symbiotic relationship with their principal client group. The usual explanation for the development of a symbiosis lies in the desire to avoid conflict.

Administrative agencies see in producers potential allies in dealing with government budgeters (Wildavsky, 1964) or, what amounts to the same thing, potential threats to the survival of the organization (Thompson and McEwan, 1958). Or perhaps both sides just prefer to avoid conflict with those with whom each is in constant contact (Gouldner, 1959). In any case, the result is a compromise of objectives between organizations. Neither organization remains as free to pursue its original objective, but in return both achieve regularity and predictability in their relationship along with a reduction in conflict.

The feature of this theory that goes beyond the public-interest theories is the value it assigns to regularization of interorganizational relationships. In the goal-deflection theory the existence of the original goal, like original sin, is accepted as an act of faith, much as in traditional theories of administrative behavior. But acts to reduce conflict and tension represent a factor not derivable from the public-interest theories. An agency, according to this theory, will consciously alter its objectives to regularize relationships, perhaps because an agency can function more efficiently in the absence of conflict. Similarly, client organizations will bend their own actions to accommodate agencies, to some degree abandoning their profit orientation.

The most persuasive statements of this theory are in the context of two-way relationships. The importance of conflict-avoidance in a more complicated environment in which an agency is interposed between opposing organizations with unavoidable and perpetual conflicts of interest is less persuasively argued and certainly has yet to be established empirically.

Internal Goal-Deflection and Lawyer Dominance.   The second type of goal-deflection theory sees organizational goals being bent according to the interests and values of an elite group in the organization. Perrow (1963) hypothesized, based on the observation that doctors tend to dominate policy decisions in hospitals, that an internal group will control an organization if the services of its members are crucial to the success of the organization and if the group is the most-skilled, highest-status, most-difficult-to-replace occupational group in the organization. Such a group is called a key factor, a reference to its position in the hierarchy of factors of production (e.g., resources) used by the organization.

This theory goes beyond normal economic predictions about monopolized factor markets, such as the Pauley-Redisch (1973) hypothesis that hospitals are essentially a physician's cartel, for the theory contends that the key group will dominate organizational decisions even on matters not closely related to its own welfare. For the present, we will abstract from the monopolistic effects and deal with key-factor dominance as a determinant of organizational objectives unrelated to the welfare of particular types of organization members. While the applicability of this theory to organizations producing private goods for competitive markets is certainly subject to serious question, it nevertheless is a serious candidate for explaining some of the behavior of institutions such as government bureaus or regulated monopolies, which are insulated from competition in product markets and, therefore, can survive with considerable organizational slack (x-inefficiency).

Lawyers, who hold many key positions in regulatory agencies, clearly satisfy the conditions for key-factor dominance. Their services are essential to the operation of quasi-judicial processes. They are a highly skilled and well-organized professional elite. Members of such professional groups, according to a substantial amount of sociological research, tend to be motivated in part by the extra-organizational standards of their profession rather than by the objectives of the organization with which they are affiliated (Blau and Scott, 1962). Lawyers are trained to be concerned about the maintenance of due process, the protection of private equities, and the ability of a system to achieve consensus. These concerns are not as dominant in other professional groups, although they appear in political science. For example, Lindblom's (1959) attack on benefit-cost analysis as a government budgeting system is based on its failure to account for these values.

The desire among lawyers to adhere to professional norms and to attain peer-group approval leads to a particular kind of goal and a motive to be efficient in achieving it. Peer-group approval will depend on the extent to which the performance of the agency corresponds to the legal profession's measures of success, including winning court challenges to agency decisions. This in turn will depend on the extent to which the agency collects information and develops decisionmaking procedures that agree with the legal profession's definition of a fair process. The elements of a fair process include adherence to legal rules of evidence and the dependence of decisions on evidence.

Another motive for developing fair procedures could be that they contribute to the psychological well-being of those who stand to lose. Michelman (1967) has hypothesized that arbitrary, capricious redistributions of income impose demoralization costs on the losers— that is, they will take unproductive defensive actions against further redistributions, reduce their own productivity, or even seek revenge through destructive acts if they are not compensated. Williamson (1970) has incorporated the concept into a general model of optimal intervention into market failures, where intervention proceeds to the point at which administrative costs and inefficiencies are balanced, at the margin, with the reduction in demoralization costs they bring about. The model can easily be extended to incorporate the dimension of fairness postulated above—that demoralization effects are reduced if losers lose in a fair process rather than in an unfair, capricious one. Of course, while this is a clever and useful way to incorporate fairness into an efficiency argument, it seems to lack operational importance. Demoralization costs can rarely be measured. In the end, this analysis cannot escape the absence of a measure for comparing fairness and economic efficiency.

A system will be inefficient in the economist's sense of the term if it places value on decisionmaking processes having certain procedural characteristics that are not related to the outcome of the process. The reason is that a process that satisfies the lawyer's conception of fairness may not be the least expensive method for achieving the same policy outcome. This is not to argue that lawyers are indifferent to the procedural costs of decisionmaking, although there may be an element of this—where an economist perceives a procedural cost a lawyer sees income. But even if lawyers who run administrative agencies attempt to achieve a given degree of institutionalized protection of private equities and of procedural fairness for the minimum feasible cost, the performance of the regulated market will still fail a test of economic efficiency.

To the extent that lawyers seek to preserve private equities through institutional protections rather than through direct financial compensation, regulatory policy leads to economic inefficiency in the performance of the regulated market. For example, the adoption of a new technology may be delayed while the agency determines its impact on each of the buyers and sellers of the service and develops a procedure for adopting the new method gradually so as to reduce the losses of those with investments in the old method. This creates an incentive to produce innovations that avoid the regulatory process or that do not threaten the existing distribution of wealth. While in terms of economic efficiency these effects may generate far greater costs than benefits, in terms of legal efficiency—the extent to which private equities are protected and high procedural standards are maintained—the process may be exemplary.

A lawyer-dominated system also creates problems of selective representation of interests in the decisionmaking process (Noll, 1971a). Among the characteristics of a procedural system that meshes with the values of lawyers are decisions based on formal evidence admitted only according to strict rules, among them the right to rebut opposing arguments in an adversary process. Participation in such a process is expensive. Hence, the effectiveness of a group in having its private equities preserved depends on the resources it has available to represent it in the decisionmaking process. Not all private equities of equal size will have equal representation. Generally, the smaller the group, the higher the per capita stake of the group members in the issue, and the more dependent the success of the group on the participation of each member, the greater is the likelihood that the group will become organized to represent its interests (M. Olson, 1965; Becker, 1983).

To the extent that decisions depend on the information derived from the regulatory process, uneven representation of interests will lead to uneven concern for private equities (Noll and Owen, 1983) and a bias against change—new policies, new organizations, new technologies—in agency decisions. Because of the uncertainties attendant upon a proposed change, some potential beneficiaries are likely to be unaware that they stand to gain from it, and consequently will not be as well organized as other groups with equal stakes. Some private equities will not be represented at all. Furthermore, the rules of evidence will downgrade conjectural information about the potential benefits of change in comparison with more certain information about established methods and institutions and the equities depending on their continuation. And, because the interests of consumers are widely diffused, they are also less likely to be effectively represented in the adversary process. This is a further bias against change, insofar as its potential benefits in the end derive from consumer demand for the products affected by the innovation.

Perhaps the most important effect of lawyer-dominated agencies is the response they engender in private organizations. The more a private organization finds itself involved in regulatory proceedings that strongly influence its well-being, the more likely are lawyers to dominate that organization. In the extreme case in which agencies are willing to insulate a private organization from competition, success in dealing with government officials can be a far more important factor affecting the firm than is the efficiency of its operations. For industry, development of legal strategies becomes the most important business activity, and persons who are especially adept at executing these strategies rise to the top of the firm. For society as a whole, the effect is to increase the demand for lawyers, thereby sucking off a share of the most intelligent, creative minds into what is essentially an economically unproductive activity—the care and feeding of government regulators.

The lawyer-dominance theory leaves many questions unanswered. Most important is the issue of its significance. Presumably this could be estimated at least qualitatively by comparing the performance of lawyer-dominated agencies and industries with those that appear not to be lawyer-dominated, such as institutions that manage medical care, agricultural production, and atomic energy. The Atomic Energy Commission, for example, appears to have been controlled primarily by scientists and engineers. The objectives of the agency appear to have been related to the key role of scientists. Its promotion of peaceful uses of atomic energy increased the demand for scientists and engineers and helped to assuage lingering doubts in the scientific community about its participation in the development of atomic weapons. Also, procedures and private equities were less important concerns at the AEC than at other independent commissions until the rise of the environmental movement introduced serious conflict into AEC proceedings.

Another important issue is the cause of lawyer dominance. Some attention to legal process is necessary, of course, because of constitutional protections of private property, guarantee of due process, and provision for the right to petition for redress of grievances. But agencies differ in the formality of their process, and some agencies are not dominated by lawyers. Hence, the question arises whether lawyer dominance is systematically related to some other feature of policy responsibility. Perhaps lawyer dominance happens to be built into most agencies simply because Congress includes many lawyers, and the exceptions are anomalies. Or perhaps lawyer dominance is an

effect of environmental factors that influence an agency's development over time. Lawyers may be observed to attain a dominant position in an agency because its responsibilities include resolving conflicts among several well-represented interests, leading it to adopt
procedures and objectives that generate a demand for lawyers' skills
in key policymaking positions (Eisenstadt, 1958). The absence of
lawyer dominance for two decades in the AEC, for example, may
have been a result of the fact that until the late 1960s there were
really no significant private equities to be preserved in the nuclear
energy business nor any serious conflicts over the technology. The
removal of AEC regulatory powers to a specialized agency, the Nuclear Regulatory Commission, may have served to cut off some technical personnel from these policies, leaving the field easier for lawyers to dominate. Simultaneously, the industry grew in size and
controversiality, making the skills of lawyers more germane.

The Bureau as Enterprise

Another major theoretical approach to an organic theory of
administrative behavior pictures an agency as having motivations
similar to those of a private entrepreneur.

Budget-Based Theories.   The most common approach is to
assume that the agency attempts to maximize its budget (McKean,
1964; Niskanen, 1971; Wildavsky, 1964). From this assumption, two
general types of conclusions have been reached.

One set of conclusions follows from the observation that the
budget-maximizing agency is roughly equivalent to a sales-maximiz-
ing private enterprise, so that theoretical implications of the latter
have counterparts in the theory of the former. The firm that maximizes total revenue, subject to the condition that its profits not fall
below some minimum level, will, from the standpoint of economic
efficiency, produce too much output if it exhibits diseconomies of scale
and operates in a market that is not perfectly competitive (Baumol,
1967). Such a firm increases output to the point where price equals
average cost—which, incidentally, is the objective normally assumed
for public utility regulation (Baumol and Klevorick, 1970)—whereas
optimal pricing from the standpoint of economic efficiency depends
on the relationship between price and marginal costs (Baumol and
Bradford, 1970; Dixit, 1970). By similar argument, the conclusion is
reached that a budget-maximizing bureau will, in the presence of decreasing returns, produce more service and obtain a larger budget
than is economically efficient (Niskanen, 1971).

This conclusion depends on the assumptions made about the relative bargaining power of an agency compared to budget decisionmakers. As Niskanen points out, a bureau is normally a monopolistic supplier of its service, but the legislature is a monopsonistic demander. If the legislature is totally passive, exploiting none of its bargaining power, the revenue-maximizing bureau will expand until the social value of the agency, as measured by the legislators' demand, is zero; that is, it extracts sufficient budget from the legislature so that the latter is as willing to abolish the agency as to continue it at its current cost. If the agency and legislature have roughly equal bargaining strengths, one possible result is the one that would prevail under competition—an agency of optimal size.

The second set of theoretical conclusions is derived from assumptions about the factors that influence the relative bargaining strengths of agencies and budgeters. In general, these ideas constitute arguments in support of the proposition that agencies have greater bargaining power than budgeters and hence are likely to be too large. They fall into five general categories.

1. *Budget Complexity.*   The budget of the entire government must be considered by budgetary decisionmakers, while an agency considers only its own budget. Because the overall complexity of the budget is so great, budgeters can devote little attention to the particulars of the budgets of most agencies. They respond by developing automatic rules-of-thumb for most budget items, examining only a few with care in any budget cycle (Wildavsky, 1964; Woll, 1963).

2. *Building a Clientele.*   Recognizing the sensitivity of legislators to special-interest lobbies, an agency can increase its bargaining strength by creating wealth among some well-defined, organized group whose well-being will be linked to the size of the agency budget (Somers, 1965; Wildavsky, 1964). Conversely, the best strategy for a private organization is to work out a symbiotic relationship with its monitoring agency.

3. *Control of Information.*   Agencies are expert on their own activities and control the flow of most of the information relevant to evaluating their budgetary requests. This allows subjective opinions to be masqueraded as objective facts and gives an agency the opportunity to present a restricted list of alternatives that make the policies they propose appear more desirable (Danziger, 1974; March and Simon, 1958; Wildavsky, 1964).

4. *Private Favors.*   A legislator normally desires special favors for his constituents. An agency can increase its budget by working

out special favors for those who support its overall budget request (Ferejohn, 1974; Wildavsky, 1964).

5. *Competition for Control.*   The agency normally possesses a monopoly in its service, but Congress and the executive may compete for
control of agency policy; to curry favor, the executive may approve
a budget it does not expect Congress to approve; for similar reasons, Congress may exceed the executive request (Sayre, 1965).

While these arguments all establish plausible independent effects,
they do not sum to proof that the agency has superior bargaining
power. For example, the argument about the diffused budget process can cut both ways. Each agency budget is reviewed in Congress
by at least two budget, two authorization, and two appropriation
committees, the first and last with more broadly based financial responsibilities that lead them to have relatively greater concern for
overall spending. Furthermore, the sequential process of budget determination still yields one final budget figure, not separate contributions from different committees for different purposes. In such a
decisionmaking process, the distribution of all voting individuals
among the various committees considering the proposal and the sequence in which committees vote can have a major effect on the outcome (Shepsle, 1979). The fact that for most agencies the appropriations stage produces the binding figure probably reduces the
bargaining power of the agency. This is consistent with the general
belief that budgets are higher in programs with back-door financing,
that is, programs in which the appropriations committees have little
influence because the authority to commit federal funds is granted
prior to appropriations (Plott, 1968).

Competition between executive and legislative branches for control could lead to higher budgets, but it will occur only when both
branches find it worthwhile to control the agency. But, for reasons
given in point (1), agencies may not be carefully scrutinized by Congress or the Executive Office of the President, in part because there
is little to gain politically from controlling them (Cary, 1967).

Another feature of the theory that is open to serious doubt is its
presumption that the proper characterization of the budgetary process is conflict resolution between agencies and Congress. If Congress,
too, likes to build alliances with client groups through regulatory provision of private favors, the desire of the agency for larger budgets
meshes with the desire of Congress to provide favors. In this milieu the
budget becomes a competition among agencies for developing client
groups, regardless of the function of the agency. Assuming that the
specific identity of the source of votes and campaign contributions
does not affect their value, the tendency to assign functional responsi-

bilities monopolistically among agencies may be without operative significance—particularly in a process in which the budgets are, in general, determined by appropriations committees who will be in a better position than authorizations committees to trade the interests of one functional client group for the favor of another.

The welfare implications for the budget-maximizing bureau that parallel those for the revenue-maximizing firm are also subject to question. Welfare implications of price and output behavior in private markets are based on the derivation of supply-and-demand analysis from actual resource costs and consumer preferences. Advocates of the budget-maximization theory point out that the state of knowledge about the true resource costs of programs is obscure at best and may even be intentionally clouded as part of rational bureaucratic behavior (Wildavsky, 1964). But advocates of the theory have not fully realized that on the demand side, too, the connection between congressional willingness to budget and voter welfare is tenuous. Legislator prerogatives, or agreements that within limits certain personal favors can be accorded each legislator without peer review, make the acquisition of some favors of zero cost to legislators, so that the value of an increment in expenditures on favors need not equal that for other public services (Ferejohn, 1974). Furthermore, because of the nature of collective-choice institutions, the stability and regularity of political outcomes do not require the attainment or even the existence of a normatively interesting political equilibrium. Consequently, the presumption that the expressed preferences of a legislature reveal information about the relative benefits at the margin of alternative public and private goods is without theoretical foundation (Plott, 1972). This means that the difference in output between a budget-maximizing and a profit-maximizing bureau has, by itself, no normative significance.

The budget-maximization hypothesis yields several predictions about the behavior of regulatory agencies that do not depend on its questionable assumptions about the behavior of budget decision-makers, the bargaining process, and the welfare implications of the model. In general, a budget-maximizing agency should react favorably to possibilities for expanding its sphere of control. In particular, opportunities to expand the number of regulated markets should be regarded with favor, because they increase the workload of the agency and increase the number of clients. One would also expect budget-maximizing agencies to prefer to regulate competitive industries. A larger number of firms means that administering market behavior requires more resources. And more firms means a more loyal clientele, because competition creates greater dependence of the industry on regulation to generate profits that exceed the normal earnings of competitive firms.

The actual behavior of regulatory agencies does not appear to fit these predictions.

Agencies have often opposed proposals to expand their responsibilities: examples are the Federal Power Commission and natural-gas field prices, and the Food and Drug Administration and toy safety. Agencies appear to prefer fewer firms rather than more: for example, the promotion of mergers by the Civil Aeronautics Board and ICC, the receptive attitude of the Department of the Interior to joint ventures in oil production on federal lands, and the initial opposition of the FCC to pay television, cable television, and spectrum reallocation, all of which provided opportunities to expand broadcasting. Historically, extensions of authority have often been a reluctant response to the emergence of an unregulated, competitive threat to the structure of an industry that the agency has created, such as the movement of the FCC into cable-television regulation because it threatened the agency's plans for broadcasting (Noll, Peck, and McGowan, 1973). Of course, because inefficiency attracts competitive entry, agencies find that expanding their responsibilities is a continuing necessity (McKie, 1970).

The budget-maximization theory also predicts that administrative agencies will tend to adopt formalized, lengthy procedures for reaching decisions, because these, too, raise the costs of performing administrative tasks. But this leads to a dilemma. If Congress permits expenditures to grow in order to finance adversary procedures only when an agency is often called upon to resolve conflicts among represented groups, then agencies should have an incentive for creating conflict. This conclusion is at variance with the findings of most of the sociological research on bureaus and the observation of economists that agencies generally oppose new entrants with new technology. On the other hand, if Congress does not evaluate the necessity for formalized procedures on the basis of the existence of conflict, the presence of formalized procedures should not vary systematically with the existence of conflict among agencies—the former will be sought regardless of the relevance of a conflict-resolution system. In fact, formalized procedures are highly correlated with the presence of conflict. At the FCC, for example, no formal inquiry into the pricing of interstate telecommunications prices was held for over thirty years, while during the same period elaborate procedures were developed and continually amended with respect to competitive hearings for broadcast licenses. Procedures are less legally formalized for licenses that are not limited in number or that are merely sold through competitive bidding, such as certifications that qualify housing for FHA or VA loan-guarantee insurance, rights to log in national forests, or CB and amateur radio licenses at the FCC.

The strength of budget-based theories depends in part on their ability to characterize accurately the budgeting process—the focus of most of the criticisms above—and in part on the validity of the simplifying assumption that budget is all that matters or is close enough to being all that matters to allow the simplified theory to make accurate predictions (Niskanen, 1971).

In the case of regulatory agencies, the theory just does not seem to work. These agencies have relatively small, stable budgets and very little programmatic responsibility. This sets them apart from super-agencies such as the Department of Defense or the Department of Health and Human Services, which are the sort of agencies that authors such as Niskanen (1971) and Wildavsky (1964) have in mind when theorizing about the budgetary process. Perhaps differences in agency purposes—buying or producing a service versus regulating a private market—give rise to different modes of behavior.

Some of the inadequacies of budget-based theories might be overcome if revenue maximization were replaced by a more direct measure of the elements of a budget that an agency regards as important to its welfare (Miqué and Bélanger, 1974). Suppose that agencies maximize their discretionary budget—or at least a weighted sum of budgetary components that favors discretionary funds—where discretionary funds are the parts of the budget that the administrators of the agency are free to spend on themselves. Because administrators normally have salaries fixed by office and tenure, opportunities for increasing salary income are small. But administrators can receive other types of income: a travel budget, a chauffeured car, a large staff, a beautifully appointed office, and a fund to spend on friends through advisory groups, conferences, consultantships and so forth. When an agency has the opportunity to expand the domain of its authority, it might react according to the expected difference between the increase in revenues and the added costs associated with the new activity. Included in the calculation would be the costs that might be incurred if the old client group were adversely affected by the new responsibility, either because its interests might conflict with those of the new client or because its affairs might receive less attention if the new responsibility were added.

The Venal Administrator.   Another approach to viewing the agency as an enterprise is the theory that agencies are operated to maximize the permanent income of administrative heads. In some instances this is taken to mean that commissioners are simply bought and paid for by the industries they regulate (Schwartz, 1959). But, because the amounts of money involved in most of the famous regulation scandals are so small, it seems unlikely that payoffs cause a commission to favor a particular group; they are more likely to be simple expressions of gratitude among friends of long standing.

A more subtle version of this theory involves analysis of the career opportunities of administrators. Because opportunities for increases in income while in the federal service are limited, career-minded regulators may view an agency as a vehicle for obtaining better employment in the private sector. A high-level official of a regulatory agency develops specialized skills that are highly valued by regulated firms. Hence, regulatory officials, when their on-the-job training is complete, will take positions with the firms whose behavior they formerly regulated or with professional firms (law, consulting, engineering) who assist the regulated firms in representing themselves in regulatory proceedings. Their behavior while in the service of the agency will be oriented toward obtaining these more lucrative private-sector positions, leading administrators to devote considerable effort to developing cordial relations with regulated firms (Eckert, 1972). While this behavior falls short of capture—obviously, some independence of mind and show of integrity is necessary to appear as an attractive future employee—the predicted result is an agency operated primarily to serve the interests of the regulated industry.

This prediction does not necessarily follow from the assumption that regulators are ultimately seeking outside employment that uses their expertise. Specifically, serving the interests of regulated groups is not necessarily as good a strategy as writing complicated regulatory rules or otherwise dramatically changing the environment of regulated firms in a way that only the regulatory officials fully understand. Indeed, regulators who participated in the regulatory reforms of the 1970s, over the objections of regulated firms, were quite successful in acquiring good posts in the industry. For example, Michael Levine, chief of staff at the CAB when it deregulated the airlines, became an airline executive, and Darius Gaskins, chairman of the ICC when it introduced more competition into surface transportation, found a similar post with a railroad.

The empirical support for the theory resides mainly in demonstrations of the free flow of personnel between administrative agencies and firms in the managed industry (Eckert, 1972; Noll, Peck, and McGowan, 1973; U.S. Senate Committee on Governmental Affairs, 1978). What has yet to be demonstrated is the predicted connection between the observed employment pattern and the decisions made by regulatory officials. For example, only one study has sought to find systematic differences in voting behavior among commissioners in a regulatory agency according to their employment histories (Gormley, 1979). It found that the two former full-time broadcasters were substantially more likely to cast pro-broadcaster votes at the FCC than were other commissioners; however, it found political affiliation to be still more important.

Probably the most interesting prediction derived from the permanent-income theory relates to the planning horizon of the agency. Because officials expect to find greener private pastures before long, it is argued that they are only interested in the immediate results of agency policies. Decisions that resolve an issue temporarily or a lengthy procedure that postpones a decision until after the official's expected term of office will be more attractive than they would be if the official expected to face deferred consequences of present actions.

In practice, the tenure of administrative officials is, on the average, very short (President's Advisory Council, 1971). This could explain why regulatory agencies tend to focus on short-run problems related to current prices and profits rather than on long-term planning and technological change. Once again, though, this hypothesis has never been tested by examining the records of regulators with varying lengths of tenure. Conceivably, short tenure could simply transfer more authority to permanent bureaucrats, who would thus become indispensable to agency operations, since top-level administrators would lack expertise (Perrow, 1961b).

In any event, one does not need the permanent-income theory to predict that regulatory agencies will be oriented toward the short run. The behavior of a rational elected official will be heavily influenced by the necessity of winning the next election, producing pressures from Congress and the political officials in the executive to deal with short-run problems. And postponing unpleasant decisions will always be appealing unless the likely unpleasantness of the decision grows more rapidly than the rate at which the decisionmaker discounts the future. Here the existence of fixed tenure of office provides an additional incentive, regardless of future employment, to postpone a decision that will inevitably create problems for the agency beyond an official's term of office. In fact, the permanent-income theory might actually yield the hypothesis that officials will be somewhat more concerned about long-term consequences of decisions because their expected jobs in the regulated sector give them a stake in the operation of the industry that extends beyond their tenure of office.

More generally, the principal deficiency of the permanent-income theory is its low predictive power. While it predicts a tendency to favoritism toward producer groups, it offers only a qualitative judgment. And in conflicts among producer groups, it does not yield predictions of behavior. At best, it points to one of many ways in which represented interest groups influence regulatory outcomes.

External Signals

The last organic theory considered here is an eclectic one, combining many features of the preceding theories. The discussion that follows is intended to outline the rudiments of a general theory of regulation, not to be a comprehensive statement of the theory, The latter requires much additional work, especially of a more formal nature. The underlying hypothesis of the external-signal theory is that agencies try to serve the public interest but have difficulty identifying it, because the public interest is such an elusive concept. Consequently, they judge the extent to which their decisions satisfy the public interest by observing the responses of other institutions to their policies and rules.

The external signals of agency performance are numerous. Agencies regularly perform in what I have somewhat pompously labeled theaters of external judgment, institutional settings in which someone outside the agency with some control over its policies and/or budget passes judgment on the agency's performance (Noll, 1971a). Among these sources of performance indicators are the courts; congressional committees that decide upon the budget and legislative program of the agency; the relevant budget examiners in the Office of Management and Budget or corresponding state or local government agencies; the press, whose primary locus of concern is the regulated industry and who may criticize the agency if performance there deteriorates; and the constituent interest groups participating in agency procedures, who, if dissatisfied with an agency decision, can appeal to the courts or can take their case to the politicians or the press.

From each theater of external judgment—courts, Congress, constituents, executive branch budget process, and press—the agency receives a flow of success indicators: actions that express approval or disapproval of the agency's decisions. It is plausible that agencies will view the public interest as being served if the success indicators show approval: budget requests and legislative proposals are generally well received by OMB and the overseeing congressional subcommittees; encounters with Congress, whether in private or at open congressional hearings, are free of serious conflict; agency decisions are rarely appealed to the courts, and when appeals are made the courts normally uphold the agency decision; and the performance of regulated firms is sufficiently good that journalistic inquiries into the agency's policies are rarely made. Behaviorally, an agency may actively seek to maximize the extent to which its feedback is positive, or it may more passively seek to avoid negative feedback or to receive positive signals to some satisfactory extent. Downs' theory sees government bureaus as passing from the active to the passive mode as they grow older (Downs, 1967). The satisfying model may be most relevant for relatively small, unimportant agencies that normally escape notice (U.S. Bureau of the Budget, 1950). Bernstein's (1955) life-cycle theory of regulatory agencies constitutes an argument for this view.

The three sources of signals that most plausibly could be interpreted by an agency as representing the public interest are the courts, elected political officials, and the general public (including the press in all agencies except the FCC, where the press is a constituent). Since the courts' retreat from substantive due process in the early decades of the twentieth century, their primary role has been to signal procedural fairness and a rational basis for agency decisions. The role of political leaders is more complex. To the extent that a politician uses regulatory policy to further reelection aims, he or she may seek to provide favors to specific constituents, to respond to political swings in the electorate, or even to act as a political entrepreneur or leader by creating a new salient issue with which he or she can be identified (Noll and Owen, 1983). If the latter two, the purpose of regulation among the general population is important to the extent that the democratic process succeeds in leading to the election of political officials whose opinions reflect the center of public sentiment on salient issues. This public rationale for regulation can be one of several possibilities: to correct market imperfections, to effect a redistribution of wealth from sellers to buyers (e.g., controls on residential rents or fuel prices), or to avoid markets in cases in which consumers do not like negotiating or want to increase the stability of prices and production (Owen and Braeutigam, 1978).

Whether the general voting population is a consideration to politicians depends on the salience of regulatory policy, that is, whether at any given time regulation, either in general or a specific part of it, is important enough in relation to other issues that voters will give it significant weight in making voting decisions (Noll, 1983). This depends in part on whether markets (regulated or not) are perceived to be performing poorly, as well as on the state of affairs in other policy areas such as foreign relations, public services, or the overall state of the economy.

Direct citizen participation in regulatory affairs is relatively rare. When it does occur, it usually parallels a rise in the political salience of regulatory issues. But one form is probably not sensitive to politics: the activities of the academic policy-research community in helping to fill the "garbage can" of government organizations (Cohen, March, and Olsen, 1972). The presence of academic research critical of ineffective or inefficient regulatory policies played a key role in the 1970s battles over deregulation of cable television (Besen et al., 1977) and airlines (Breyer, 1981).

Research can affect regulatory policy in three ways. First, it can be used as a weapon by interest groups in agency, court, and congressional processes. The advantage of this pathway is that decisionmakers are forced to consider it in making decisions; the disadvantage is that its scientific objectivity is highly suspect. Second, it can suggest to political entrepreneurs possibilities for gaining recognition by successfully raising a new salient public issue. The lead role played by Senator Edward Kennedy in airline deregulation illustrates this pathway (Breyer, 1981). The problem here, of course, is the rarity of its occurrence. Third, to the extent that public officials regard themselves as serving a deeper public purpose than creating institutionalized protection for special interests, they will be interested in scholarly work evaluating their performance and will respond to it if it is regarded as of high quality. This pathway is illustrated by the role of research in reversing the policy of the FCC on cable television deregulation. This pathway is in some sense the purest and has the greatest aura of scientific objectivity. While it appears somewhat more trodden than the second path, its major disadvantage is still its rarity. Obviously, a necessary condition is that the research be known to the agency. This in turn requires that the agency include some people—usually, high-level professional staff—who keep abreast of research in pertinent areas or that the research community play an active role in making its results known to policy officials. Until the mid-1970s the former was rare among regulatory agencies, and few academics have pursued the latter course; hence the situation, uncomfortable to academics, that the first pathway predominates (Noll, 1973).

Playing a ubiquitous role in the provision of signals to the agency are the interest groups who are organized to participate in agency information-gathering processes, to challenge agency decisions in the courts, and to lobby politicians. The sensitivity of government policy in a representative democracy to pressures from interest groups has long been recognized. James Madison in *Federalist 10* understood that a key constitutional problem was how to build a democratic government that protected individual rights but was not controlled by special interests. Madison's solution was to construct a legislature in which all important interests were likely to be represented but each was unlikely to have much power. Regulatory agencies, because of their single-purpose mission and relatively small size, do not have this Madisonian protection when undertaking their quasi-legislative functions; hence their susceptibility to dominance by special interests.

Although the role of interest groups has long been known, until the 1960s relatively little attention had been given to the process by which interest groups are formed and become politically effective. The theory of interest-group mobilization is an important part of the theory of agency behavior because it enables us to predict the kinds of signals an agency will receive both through its own processes and from legal and political sources. Economists have formalized this theory, although its predictions are still largely qualitative (Olson, 1965; Buchanan, 1965; Davis and North, 1970; Becker, 1983). According to this point of view, an interest will be represented in a political process if it expects to gain more from representation than its participation will cost and if it can avoid the problem of free-riding among its members.

Being represented in a regulatory proceeding can be very expensive. When an important issue is at stake, agencies can take years to reach a decision, and all the while a represented group must retain the services of high-cost professionals—lawyers, engineers, economists. After an agency has announced its decision, court appeals and political lobbying may still be necessary. In order to be represented effectively, an individual or a group whose members share an economic interest must be willing to pay these costs plus any costs of organizing and maintaining the solidarity of the group.

In general, the larger and more diverse the group, the greater are the expenses of becoming organized, deciding upon policies and strategies, and obtaining effective representation. And a firm or individual is more likely to associate with a group to secure representation the higher is its stake in the outcome and the more important to achieving its objectives is its own participation in group activities. An individual is not very likely to join an extremely large organization that seeks ends that are not seen as especially important or that is likely to achieve its goal even if the individual does not pay a fair share of the costs. As a result, a group will commit more resources to being represented in the regulatory process the higher is the per capita stake of the members in the issue. If the sum of the economic stakes in an issue for all members is the same for two groups, the smaller group, with lower group organization costs and a higher per capita stake, will be more effectively represented.

The economic model of interest-group representation leads to the prediction that the information and success indicators flowing to the government will be biased in favor of small groups with large per capita stakes in political issues and against large, diverse groups whose members individually have little stake in the outcome but, because of the greater number of members, may have a larger total stake. Agency capture is predicted as a special case that occurs when (a) only one interest group has sufficient per capita interest in the issue to be effectively represented, and (b) only interest-group pressure (not, for example, the press or Naderesque intervenors) can activate politicians, other bureaus, or the courts to affect agency decisions (Weingast, 1981). Until the 1970s, most regulated monopolies typically fell into this category and, predictably, were not significantly affected by regulation (MacAvoy, 1970, 1971; Moore, 1970). Another illustration of the importance of condition b is argued in an interesting comparative study of four government agencies that support basic research (Weiner, 1972). Apparently, independent bureaus facing only budgetary examination (NSF, NIH) are far more likely to exhibit capture than agencies that are part of larger, mission-oriented bureaus (ONR, OSR), even though in all four cases the research community is the only external group in significant contact with the agency.

The external-signal theory provides an explanation of the conditions under which Congress and the executive will engage in effective oversight of agencies. As discussed above, some attribute poor regulatory performance to a persistent tendency of political leaders to ignore regulatory policy. The problem with this view is that on occasion Congress or the executive decides to play a major role. Sometimes Congress does so by writing regulations (the Coal Mine Safety Act of 1967; the fleet fuel efficiency standards for automobiles; the Delaney Amendment to the Food, Drug, and Cosmetic Act; the new source performance standards for coal-fired electricity-generation facilities). Other times it does so by signaling its aims in the oversight process. The executive branch sometimes deals with agencies only by appointing to them people who deserve political rewards. But sometimes it selects appointees very carefully for a well-developed policy purpose, and sometimes it institutionalizes its own oversight, such as by creating a regulatory review bureau in the Executive Office of the President. The deeper question is why the executive and Congress sometimes become extraordinarily active. External signals provide an answer. When the clients of an agency are happy and the agency is not receiving public attention, there is no reason for extensive political oversight. But when agencies are in conflict, appeals are made to the political system and regulatory policy becomes salient (McCubbins and Schwartz, 1982). And agencies that are always a focus of political conflict ought systematically to receive more political attention than their more placid siblings. This is borne out by the turbulent politics of the regulation of natural gas (Sanders, 1981) and broadcasting. Even better evidence is the transition of telecommunications regulation from relative political obscurity to extensive political attention in the 1970s. Decisions by the FCC to allow new firms into telecommunications as satellite operators or specialized common carriers created an organized interest in opposition to AT&T in the late 1960s. By the early 1970s, the executive branch had created the Office of Telecommunications Policy (later the National Telecommunications and Information Administration) and Congress had reinvigorated the subcommittees overseeing the FCC.

The external-signal theory provides a similar explanation for the tendency of some agencies to develop cumbersome procedures and to exhibit excessive concern for the preservation of the most important private equities, which are the motivational assumptions of the lawyer-dominance, goal-deflection model. These tendencies are an agency's natural response to attempts by competing organized groups to influence agency decisions.

The protection of private equities is in part caused by Constitutional protection of rights and property, but it also arises out of the nature of the representation process. A group that has become organized to represent itself in the deliberations of the regulatory agency may also appeal the agency's decision to the courts, may lobby congressmen about the error of the agency's ways, and may wage a public-relations campaign in support of policies contrary to those established by the agency. An agency attempting to avoid negative feedback from the providers of success indicators will seek to protect the equities of the organized groups in order to avoid the negative feedback the groups can trigger.

An agency will also develop complicated decisionmaking procedures for reasons related to representation. First, they will enable the agency to gauge the stake of the represented groups in the issue at hand and thereby to make better estimates of the probability that each one will appeal any particular decision. Second, they will make participation in the process more expensive, which will reduce the number of groups entering the process. This in turn reduces the amount of information the agency must process and the number of threats to appeal agency decisions. Third, they will give outsiders the impression that the agency has behaved fairly in gathering information and listening to divergent points of view. Because courts review agency decisions almost exclusively on the basis of procedural issues, the chance that the agency will win an appeal to the courts is greatly enhanced by the adoption of complex procedures (Woll, 1963). Fourth, an agency truly interested in serving the public interest will want to formalize procedures as a mechanism for depersonalizing information so as to mitigate subconscious subjectivity in evaluating information from wealthy, prestigious sources. The import and even the perceived validity of information may depend upon its source. In part this is due to the possibility that only information from well-represented groups is likely to be used in legal, political, or public-relations attacks on the agency. But in part the reason may be sub-conscious. Psychologists have found that judgments about purely physical characteristics of objects such as weight and size, as well as recall of events, depend on the value of the object used in the experiment and the demeanor and status of those offering opinions (Asch, 1955; Bruner and Goodman, 1947; Sherif, 1935).

Unfortunately, formal procedures cannot be wholly successful in dealing with the problem of obtaining objective, complete information. The sources of relevant information are normally the private organizations participating in the process. To the extent that information affects outcomes, firms have an incentive to use information strategically (Owen and Braeutigam, 1978). While selectivity in introducing information into regulatory proceedings is one possibly productive strategy, especially in uncontested processes, other more subtle strategies are also available. One such strategy is information overload. When a firm profits from delay in decisions, it can benefit itself by introducing so much information into the proceedings that the agency cannot assimilate it quickly. Another strategy is to organize the regulated firm in such a way that certain types of information that might be damaging are never collected or are evaluated and dealt with at a low, probably undetectable level in the organization. Normally a private business would find information about customer complaints of value; however, in the context of economic or safety regulation, such data could damage the enterprise. A firm, in making certain that damaging information is kept unavailable, reduces the chances that its opponents will succeed in challenging an agency policy that the firm finds beneficial.

The extent of observed lawyer dominance in a regulatory agency is, according to the external-signal theory, a consequence of the extent to which the clients of the agency are well organized, have mutually conflicting interests, and are likely to appeal to the courts rather than to politicians or the press to reverse decisions that threaten their interest. For example, Elling's (1963) case study of hospital planning describes a decisionmaking process that sought to balance conflicting, well-organized interests and was extremely slow in reaching decisions, but, because the principal theaters in which pressures were exerted were political and economic, did not exhibit lawyer dominance. Similarly, the agricultural sector is diffuse and rather weakly organized, and its chief mechanisms for generating feedback to the agency are through the press and Congress, rather than by appeals to the courts. Only in rare instances are representatives of other organized interests participants in making agricultural policies, and when they are so represented the process appears to exhibit more lawyer dominance—the Packers and Stockyard Administration and the Commodity Exchange Authority operate in much the same fashion as the independent regulatory commissions that have similar responsibilities, in comparison to the far less open and structured process by which agricultural prices, acreage allotments, and marketing quotas are decided (Bonnen in Noll, 1971b). Finally, the decisionmaking structure in Sweden concerning health and safety regulation—less formal, less adversarial, and probably more effective than its U.S. equivalent—corresponds to a situation in which court appeals are essentially foreclosed (Kelman, 1981b).

The loosely organized scientific community would be expected to dominate the Atomic Energy Commission's decisionmaking process only until the agency succeeded in creating a commercial nuclear-energy industry. The prospect of widespread commercial use of atomic power creates large private equities that conflict with the interests of scientists and of other groups: witness the debate about the safety and environmental implications of nuclear electric-power facilities. This generates a demand for the special skills of lawyers at building and operating systems to resolve conflict in an equitable manner. And as the importance of lawyers increases, scientists are transformed from the dominant force in setting agency objectives to one of the weaker interest groups represented in an adversary process that reflects the values of lawyers. The consequence is a slower, more costly process but one that is more likely to address a range of political issues broader than the purely technical (Cohen, 1980).

The preceding suggests an inherent dilemma in the regulatory process. Agency procedures will be most conducive to the timely adoption of policies favored by producers if only the producers are represented in the process and if their principal threat to the agency is through political and public relations appeals, rather than appeals to courts. But this type of regulatory environment will not be favorable for otherwise desirable policies that the principal producer group perceives as opposed to its interests, such as when the policy would allow more competition or, as is often the case, when the only effect of a policy change is an improvement in product or worker safety, reduction in the environmental damage associated with producing a product, or even reduction in costs under certain methods of price and profit regulation, such as was offered by the unit train (MacAvoy and Sloss, 1967). These types of changes might receive more favorable attention if those who would benefit by them were given representation in the proceedings, such as by creating an agency to advocate the interests of consumers or nongovernmental public-interest lobbying organizations (Terris, 1971). But when the regulatory agency becomes the adjudicator of conflicts among divergent, represented groups who threaten court appeals of agency decisions, lawyer dominance results in retarded rates of adoption of all changes, not just the ones opposed by the regulated industry. In similar fashion, more diverse representation makes agencies more likely to exercise effective control over producers and thereby to ameliorate market imperfections, but by the same token it will increase the delay and the costs of adopting economically warranted changes in technology or market structure that are supported by producers.

This dilemma provides an argument against proposals to combine agencies with overlapping responsibilities in related industries. The purpose behind these proposals is to promote rational planning: only by having control of all policy areas affecting a particular sector can an agency be expected to adopt efficient policies. For example, the creation of the Department of Energy, a superagency including nearly all existing regulatory and other agencies with responsibilities in managing the energy sector, was defended because it would produce policy that was more sensitive to the interactions among separate energy industries, that contributed to a better-balanced development of alternative sources of energy, and that was better able to weigh the benefits and costs of alternative policies concerning the safety and environmental effects of new institutions and technologies. Similarly, the Ash Council proposed that the regulatory agencies responsible for various components of transportation—the Interstate Commerce Commission, the Civil Aeronautics Board, and the Federal Maritime Commission—be combined so that cross-model effects of policies would be given more weight.

The counterargument to these proposals is that agencies who must adjudicate disputes among conflicting, well-represented interests assign a low priority to the very purpose of establishing a comprehensive agency—the economically efficient operation of the sector over which it has authority. In principle, DOE could have become a comprehensive energy-planning agency. In practice, it structured itself into quasi-independent, technology-based bureaus each serving a particular constituency in the energy sector. In principle, the ICC certainly is better able to implement a rational multimodal surface-transportation policy than would be a collection of agencies, one for each surface transportation industry. In practice, rational intermodal planning never occurred, because the ICC exhibited little concern for economic efficiency, basing decisions about prices and route structure almost totally on preserving the relative private equities in the national surface-transportation system (Friedlaender, 1969). And, because the ICC was not particularly interested in efficiency, it should be no surprise that, as time passed, the regulated firms lost some of their zeal for efficient operation.

The possible escapes from the Hobson's choice of which type of progress to retard all involve fundamental changes in the regulatory environment. One approach is to merge the opposing interests in order to reduce the number of conflicts an agency must settle. The rationale for the single-entity proposal in international communications was that only through merging the international carriers would the Federal Communications Commission and the industry make a rational choice between technologies—cables versus satellites (Peck, 1970). Of course, such a merger improves producers' ability to represent themselves effectively, but it also reduces the agency's control over the regulated market. Moreover, if some groups remain unrepresented, the result is a coalition against the unrepresented groups. For example, Ackerman and Hassler (1981) argue that a coalition of Western environmental groups and the Eastern coal industry led to the adoption of stack-gas scrubbers as mandatory for new coal-fired electricity-generation facilities. Both groups wanted to avoid the development of a Western coal industry, and the regulation eliminated the incentive to use low-sulphur Western coal. The nascent Western coal industry and Eastern environmentalists were poorly organized and not well represented, and hence lost out.

Another approach is to replace institutionalized protection of private equities with direct compensation. The disappearance of the CAB's subsidies of domestic airlines did not result in the bankruptcy of inefficient carriers or the abandonment of subsidized routes; rather, the direct subsidies were replaced by the use of price regulation to protect high-cost firms and to create cross-subsidization—the transfer of excess profits on some routes to offset losses elsewhere within the same firm—or, in Posner's (1971) term, taxation by regulation. Because institutionalized protection causes loss of production efficiency, direct compensation should be a cheaper way to obtain subsidized services. Direct compensation would, in several instances, have led to more rapid adoption of new technologies that were retarded or prevented because of their likely effect on the existing distribution of equities: piggyback truck-rail shipping (Gellman, 1971) and cable television (Noll, Peck, and McGowan, 1973) are cases in point. Of course, direct compensation is not without costs. It requires a complicated procedure for determining equity losses and blunts incentives for efficiency and innovation: if competition proves too tough, compensation awaits. Whether these costs outweigh the costs of institutionalized preservation of equity remains to be determined; certainly, a definitive study of the effects of the abandonment of trunk airline subsidies in the 1950s would contribute to that end.

A third approach is to break away from the model of regulation by expert judgment. One possibility is to free regulators from formal rules of procedure but to make their decisions only advisory to the legislature, putting policy responsibility on the shoulders of politically accountable officials. Another possibility is direct election of regulatory authorities or referenda on regulatory policies, either of which would add a direct signal from the electorate to the other signals received by the agency. In some states, public utility commissions are directly elected, and in these states regulation appears to be more consumer-oriented (Mann and Primeaux, 1982). A study of local urban-renewal authorities provides a similar finding: a requirement to pass a referendum on an urban-renewal plan substantially reduces the extent to which an urban-renewal authority designs projects to suit special interests (in particular, developers) (Plott, 1968). In both cases, however, the direction of causality in these findings is unclear: states and localities in which general public interests are better represented and more effective may also, for independent reasons, be more likely to use direct elections and referenda.

In any case, these more political approaches raise new problems. Most obviously, because it is not clear that agency policies stray from the intent of Congress, the effect of making policies more directly related to politics could be minimal. An election-referendum system, given the extent of regulation, would lead to a horrendously complicated ballot. States in which referenda and initiatives are relatively easy to place on the ballot have proverbial bedsheet ballots that require considerable voter sophistication if the results are to be valid indicators of preferences, particularly given the incentives for rational ignorance in a multi-issue, multichoice, large-electorate election (Downs, 1957). An alternative to direct election is a collegial body of representatives of different constituencies, such as is sometimes used in establishing water-basin planning authorities and, in Illinois, the state air-pollution-control agency. These are attempts to conserve on the limited attention span of voters in direct elections by creating decisionmaking subsets of the electorate that will somehow be representative of the divergence of views on the issue. Of course, in this type of body, the voting rules and the distribution of voting strengths among constituencies have very important, and very complicated, effects on outcomes (Haefele, 1973; Dorfman and Jacoby, 1970; Levine and Plott, 1975).

Concluding Observations on Organic Theories

One principal conclusion to be derived from the discussion of organic theories of regulatory agencies is that simple analogies to the theory of the firm and markets do not appear to be very powerful in explaining processes in which the outcome is determined by interest-group aggregation. This is due in part to important differences between decentralized and collective decision processes and in part to the nature of administrative jobs. The American federal service is a remarkably effective device for turning agencies away from objectives based solely on financial measures such as personal income and agency budget (Tullock, 1965; Warner et al., 1963). This feature strengthens the case for a perceived public-interest model of decisionmaking like the external-signal theory. Harsanyi (1969) has speculated that one axiom of individual-preference theory should be low-cost objectivity, that is, an individual has to have a significant stake in an issue before behavior becomes motivated by self-interest. If so, when decisionmakers have little direct financial stake in any single issue, an attitude of detachment and objectivity results. Combined with the uncertainties and informational problems faced by agencies, as emphasized by March and Simon (1958), public-interest orientation seems to lead inevitably to an external-signal behavioral system. This, in turn, requires connecting the theory of regulation to the behavior of voters, legislators, courts, and other groups besides clients that can influence an agency.

Another general conclusion is that regulation does not have an immutable tendency to create cartels. Indeed, a captured agency is a predictable result of a specific set of political conditions, just as is an agency that focuses primarily on economic efficiency or an agency that is primarily interested in preserving historical relationships among different categories of suppliers.

The final conclusion is that a general theory of regulatory activity is a promising possibility. In particular, positive political theory, built on the rational-actor hypothesis, provides falsifiable propositions about the sources of changes in regulatory policy. Moreover, these propositions appear to explain a great deal of regulatory history. Of course, much work remains to establish this conclusion firmly; the alternative view that there is no general political theory of regulation, defended most strongly by James Wilson (1980), cannot yet be dismissed.

Structural Theories

An enormous literature—far more extensive than the literature on organic theories of agency behavior—has developed on how and why organizations become structured as they do, and what differences structure makes in an agency's performance. Yet almost none of this literature is focused on regulation per se.

Determinants of Structures

No rigorous, formal theory of the structural development of organizations has been developed. Instead, the literature on the topic consists of a series of partial, single effect/single cause conjectures. Most are based, at least implicitly, on a rational-actor conception of organizational structure, that is, the idea that organizations develop as they do because it is efficient for them to do so. Of course, because much of the relevant theorizing is by sociologists, the rational-choice process is rarely made explicit, a notable exception being Blau (1970).

A major line of theoretical inquiry has been directed toward justifying Weber's unproven assertion about the optimality of bureaucratic structures, which he described as having the following key characteristics: functional specialization of jobs; formal rules to make decisions impersonal; a hierarchical authority structure for communication and control; and employment based on objective measures of competence and qualification.

One body of theory (Blau, 1970; Blau and Schoenhen, 1971) derives from the following set of assumptions: organizations are goal-directed and attempt to achieve efficient operation; individuals have limited capacity for receiving communications and controlling subordinates; and, echoing Adam Smith, increasing specialization of jobs leads to increasing worker productivity. As an organization grows, then, it will have ever-expanding opportunities for engaging in division of labor but ever-increasing problems in monitoring and controlling individual performance. In order to sacrifice as little division of labor as possible while retaining control, an organization will have specialized subunits as numerous as is consistent with communication and control capabilities, and the number of hierarchical levels will depend on the size of the organization and the degree of division of labor. Furthermore, to increase the ability of superiors to control subordinates, parallel hierarchical structures will be split along functional lines so that the subordinate group of any superior is relatively homogeneous. In organizations with diverse activities, as the organization grows the number of administrators required to control specialized associates may increase more rapidly than the total number of employees (Aiken and Hage, 1968; Blau, 1970; Terrien and Mills, 1955).

To increase the ability of superiors to control subordinates and to reduce communications per organization member, as much as possible of the activity of the organization will be made routine through formal rules. Formal rules can be consulted by subordinates without communication with the superior and can be used to communicate changes. Hence, as an organization grows, both the number of parallel hierarchies and the number of hierarchical levels increase, and its operations become more formal, impersonal, and routine.

The extent of hierarchical development and functional grouping of increasingly narrower tasks depends on the nature of the organization's activities (Blau and Scott, 1962). In communicating performance information upward and commands downward through hierarchical levels, at each stage some information and some control are lost. The optimal extent of hierarchical development will, therefore, depend on the extent to which coordination, information, and instruction are needed: units along an assembly line, for example, require far more coordination, and hence a better information-control system, than departments in a retail store. Conversely, the greater the gains from division of labor, the greater is the optimal degree of hierarchical structure.

Another body of theory derives from the observation that organizations develop for the purpose of finding solutions to problems that no single individual could solve. It is based on the view that part of the process of solving a problem is to develop alternatives from uncertain information about cause and effect and about the environment in which the organization operates (March and Simon, 1958). Organizations will divide insoluble problems into manageable components, with those responsible for each subproblem attempting to reduce informational uncertainties and find acceptable, but not necessarily optimal, partial solutions. The ultimate solution to the problem, still based to some extent on uncertain information and on a marriage of acceptable solutions to component problems, will depend heavily on the initial factoring of the problem and the sequence in which information and subproblem solutions are generated. The organization learns by experience which methods of factoring problems and generating information tend to produce desirable results, and will employ those methods regularly (Cyert and March, 1963). By this process the functional divisions within the organization are developed.

Another line of theory derives from assumptions about the reaction of an organization to its environment. If the organization is threatened by external groups, it will alter its structure to ease the threat. One mechanism is to set up substructures that permit the external client group to influence the organization (Selznick, 1943; Thompson and McEwen, 1958). This structural response causes debureaucratization in the sense that those at the bottom of the structure, because they interface with the potentially threatening client, transmit the client's policy wishes up the hierarchy (Aiken and Hage, 1968; Corwin, 1972). Another possible structural response is to develop protective relations with other client groups that offset the threat of the first client group (Blau and Scott, 1962). A third structural response is to develop regularized relations with external organizations to reduce uncertainties about the outcomes of alternative courses of action (Cyert and March, 1963). In this instance the other organization is not so much a threat as a presence whose behavior is unpredictable unless some sort of normalized relationship can be developed by connecting the organizational structures. All these possibilities apply equally to agencies and to the organizations with which they deal. The symbiosis grows upward in both organizations from the point of contact, making it especially difficult to undo through changes at the top—for example, by appointing new administrators.

Structure and Performance

The development of causal conceptual models of the structure of organizations inevitably led to the discovery of costs as well as benefits in Weber's ideal bureaucratic structure. Most of these ideas have appeared in the literature of sociology; however, they have not been particularly well developed, owing to an inexplicable abandonment of the presumption of rational development once a potential cost is identified. This criticism will become more apparent as the various theoretical ideas are explored.

Division of Labor.   One consequence of division of labor into homogeneous groups with specialized tasks is the creation of clusters of organization members who possess expertise and technical skills. Their technical sophistication makes them more difficult to monitor and control, for their superiors in the organization become unable to comprehend the requirements of the job they are performing. By originating the upward flow of information, these groups can deflect organizational objectives (Blau and Scott, 1962; Eisenstadt, 1958).

By a similar argument, the development of structures for dealing with external threat creates a specialized, expert group with control over an important block of information. This group, too, has a perception of identity. Because of its close association with the external group, its mandate to build working relations with it, and its unusual ability to translate policy upward through the hierarchy, it can have its own objectives and, through its control of information and partial policymaking authority, direct the operation of the organization toward serving some combination of its own welfare and that of its external client (Eisenstadt, 1958).

The preceding model has serious problems when applied to competitive, profit-oriented enterprises, because it abstracts from the participation of the firm in factor and product markets, and hence from the variables that determine the amount of slack in the organization and the bargaining strengths of superiors and subordinates. When applied to regulatory agencies and regulated firms, it makes more sense. Agencies deal with ambiguous problems involving substantial technical expertise, and the firms are partially protected from competition, so inefficiency is possible. The issue boils down to an empirical one: do superiors receive sufficient information from subordinates to judge the performance of the subordinates and to make rational decisions?

Kaufman and Couzens (1973) asked exactly this question in examining information flows in nine government agencies. They found that in seven cases the information received by the agency decision-makers was accurate enough, complete enough, and digestible enough (it was neither impossibly voluminous nor excessively technical) that administrators did know what subordinates were doing and how to alter their behavior. The study concluded that subordinate behavior inconsistent with publicized agency policy was either desired by the administrator or of too little consequence to generate compensating action.

These findings should not be surprising, for they are consistent with the theoretical model that led to the predictions of how structure would develop. The argument that structural differentiation of responsibilities proceeds along rational, goal-directed lines should lead to the conclusion that among the costs entering the decisions about structure will be whatever loss of control the administrator must face under alternative structural regimes. If a structure is created that gives substantial discretionary authority to a particular subgroup of the organization, it is because that structure seemed to produce more desirable results than the alternatives. In particular, if the substructure organized to deal with a threatening client gains ascendency, it seems sensible to consider the threatening client, not the resulting substructure, to be the causal influence. Arnold Weber's (1973) discussion of the decision to create an independent price control authority indicates awareness, at the highest level of the executive, of precisely the factors discussed here. In any event, a rationalistic structural theory based on the benefits of divided labor and the costs of maintaining coordination and control is not logically consistent with the assumption that the administrator ignores the costs of creating an organizational subgroup with autonomous power.

When applied to regulation, the principal implication of this theory is that regulatory agencies will tend to structure themselves by creating separate hierarchies for each client group. An example is the creation of the Cable Television Bureau at the FCC after the agency asserted jurisdiction over cable and began to regulate it. A second implication is that these functional divisions will develop close associations and even a merged identity with their related clients, and will grow into powerful influences on agency policy from the bottom up. This provides an explanation for a capture theory of regulation that does not depend on the nature of appointments at the top of the agency or on the delivery of favors by elected politicians, except insofar as administrators or politicians consciously structure agencies for such reasons. A third implication is that in some circumstances the structuring process leads to reform. Specifically, when client groups conflict, so do their bureaus. Hence, the creation of a cable bureau guaranteed that conflicts between broadcasting and cable eventually had to be faced squarely by the FCC.

Formalized Rules.   Another set of arguments relating structure and performance focuses on the effects of formalized rules. The impersonal and communications-conserving features of formalized rules may generate benefits of the kind described above, but they may have undesirable side-effects as well. First, being based on minimum acceptable performance, they weaken incentives for better performance by more able workers (Gouldner, 1954) and promote conformity of behavior among workers and through time (Thompson, 1965). Second, rules initially designed to bring subordinates under better control develop into a statement of the rights and duties of a class of workers. As such, their maintenance becomes an objective of its own, creating inflexibility and rigidity in the organization (Merton, 1936). Both are examples of what Merton calls false generalization: a procedure that works once is permanently adopted, with unanticipated counterproductive long-term consequences.

The same argument could be applied to rules and procedures concerning the relationship between an organization and its clients. What is originally designed as a mechanism for acquiring information and exercising control may become a right that is valued by clients as they adjust their behavior to accommodate the system (Dill, 1962).

The generalization of the preceding argument is that there is a factor that retards organizational adaptability, a kind of structural inertia. It is somehow more expensive to change existing structures and patterns of relationships than to construct new ones, so that when a structure becomes outdated due to external changes it is inhibited in its ability to adjust. Otherwise, when an administrator observed performance standards and procedural rules leading to diminishing productivity, he would simply alter the structure, rules, and procedure. In short, rules and procedures create valuable property rights for those who enforce or are protected by them. Hence, a group is created to defend them that did not exist—and therefore, of course, did not work for them—at their creation.

Perhaps a fruitful theoretical path in developing a model of organizational inertia would follow from the concept of learning by doing (Arrow, 1962). Individuals schooled in an old structure may have to go through a period of unlearning old rules and methods before they can master the new. This would occur if, as some have found, formal rules lead to a reduced ability to cope with unusual events and a mechanical reliance on established methods (Shepard, 1967; Warner et al., 1963). Without job tenure, organizational structures could freely change, but with job tenure it could be more costly to change to a new system and live through the unlearning process than to start the system from scratch.

Arguments predicting long-term rigidities in an agency cannot be readily dismissed by appeals to the rational-choice model of structuring. Given the presence of a discount rate or of a planning horizon fixed by tenure of office, long-term consequences of present structural and procedural decisions are likely to be given little weight. The problem is aggravated to the extent that the administrators face a situation of bounded rationality in which more problems clamor for attention than can ever be solved and in which the future is uncertain.

The key empirical prediction of this theory is that formalized organizations such as regulatory agencies are resistant to change. This should lead regulatory agencies to try to solve new problems with old methods and could account for the shortsightedness in decisionmaking mentioned in the discussion of the permanent-income theory. In the case of a new policy issue, old practices may be applied inappropriately and thereby prevent or retard response. Furthermore, because many of the formalized rules and practices apply to relations between the agency and its client, they are likely to retard policy changes in client organizations as well. This offers an alternative explanation to the one based on preservation of private equities for bias in the rate and pattern of innovation and change in regulated industries. It also leads to the prediction that established firms will fare relatively poorly after they are deregulated.

The structural-inertia theory suggests that an apt characterization of the life history of a regulatory agency is that, as a result of a short-term planning horizon arising from rational individual behavior by administrators, performance is relatively efficient in the beginning but then deteriorates steadily. An organizational structure is thus quite similar to a very long-lived capital asset with high disposal costs—for example, a central city whose large buildings were designed according to rational comparison of the net value of alternatives, based on calculations many decades ago that gave virtually no weight to disposal problems. Present problems of replacing these capital assets, whether nineteenth-century buildings or outmoded organizational structures, can be viewed as an inevitable outcome of decisions arising from individual rational-choice processes.

Some ideas have been offered on how to structure organizations so that they are more flexible and adaptable. Generally, the most important result is that structures that do a relatively good job in dealing with recurring problems do relatively poorly when faced with a new problem requiring creative, adaptive behavior, and vice versa (Burns and Stalker, 1966; Shepard, 1967; Thompson, 1965). Adaptive behavior requires looser, less hierarchial, more informal arrangements, which reduce the extent to which behavior can be controlled from above (Aiken and Hage, 1968; Hage and Aiken, 1967; Weiner, 1972). This suggests that a regulatory agency will be better prepared to deal expeditiously with changes in the regulated industry, such as those created by technological advances, if one of its functional divisions is a planning and research staff with minimal formal responsibilities and some real authority.

Most agencies, especially in response to the wave of enthusiasm over cost-effectiveness analysis that swept through Washington in the 1960s, have created planning offices along the lines the theory suggests (Schultze, 1968). Regulatory reform at the CAB and FCC in the 1970s, for example, began with the creation of first-rate offices for policy analysis, staffed primarily by economists. Of course, while this creates a potential source of adaptive responses to changing external conditions, it does not guarantee responsiveness by the agency, as those who have filled planning roles can attest (Joint Economic Committee, 1969). Creation of a planning institution does not give administrative leaders more motivation to consider the long-term consequences of their actions. In order for agencies to develop more flexible policies, they must possess the incentive as well as the ability to do so (Mohr, 1969; Weiner, 1972).

Several proposals to provide an incentive for long-term planning have been made. Agencies could be required to submit to the legislature regular multiyear plans for future policy (Cary, 1967). Congress could include an expiration date (sunset) in the legislation establishing administrative agencies that would lead to periodic review of the agency's purpose and performance (Friendly, 1962). Tenures of administrative policymaking positions might be lengthened, perhaps to lifetime appointments as with Supreme Court justices, and salaries increased to make them competitive with top jobs in the private sector, not only to increase independence through job security but to lengthen the planning horizon of the decisionmaker (Bernstein, 1955). Whether these changes can overcome the short-term focus of the political system remains unproven. Also unproven is how much the active resistance to change by regulatory agencies is accounted for by these structural explanations and how much by the sensitivity to private equities in the status quo hypothesized in the external-signal theory. The more important the latter, the less is the likelihood that structural changes will matter.

Fuzzy Output. Another structural explanation of deteriorating performance arises from the difficulty of defining and measuring the output of most government agencies. A hypothesized first law of public administration is that measuring the output of public activities is systemically more difficult than measuring output in private production, leading to an especially great difficulty in attaining technical efficiency in a public agency (Olson, 1973). Nevertheless, for both external and internal reasons, agencies must develop performance measures and standards. The more ambiguous the product of the agency, the further removed is the performance measure from a true index of the product the agency is designed to produce and the greater is the likelihood that the agency will, over time, assign increasingly greater weight to the measurable component of output (Cohen, 1965; Perrow, 1961b).

This tendency is certainly observable in some regulatory agencies. One example is the enormous attention paid by the Federal Trade Commission during the 1960s to its rather mundane responsibilities in textile and fur labeling (Noll, 1971b). Another example is the set of procedures adopted by the Federal Power Commission to measure its activity (namely, specific price decisions) and the result— thousands of meaningless cases (MacAvoy, 1971). Still another is the attempt of the FCC to establish criteria for assessing the extent to which an applicant for a broadcast license was likely to serve the public interest (M. Spitzer, 1979). Attention to these measurable components may also influence technical decisions in regulated firms as both regulator and producer become oriented toward suboptimizations of an incomplete characterization of industry performance.

As with the other partial theoretical observations, this argument has not been established to have a great quantitative significance in terms of regulatory behavior. It stands as an addition to the file of potential costs to be considered when establishing a regulatory agency.

Observations on Structural Theories

The overriding characteristic of all these structural arguments is that empirical tests are woefully lacking, particularly with respect to regulatory agencies. In order for structural theories to be treated seriously in the public policy process, the literature must be extended beyond the current status of essentially wise musings about partial, *ceteris paribus* effects. Cases of structural change in agencies should be studied with an eye to estimating the significance of the structural effects on agency policies and producer performance, not only in the short run—which tends to pick up primarily Hawthorne effects (Blau and Scott, 1962; Roethlisberger and Dickson, 1939)— but also in the long run.

Common Themes

Several consistent themes run through the numerous conceptual models of administrative behavior. To a significant degree the theoretical models are alternative explanations for the phenomena which, in all disciplines, scholars have generally come to agree are characteristic of regulatory policies.

First, to the extent that a consistent majority opinion in the electorate exists and can be characterized as representing a definition of the public interest, delegation of decisionmaking to regulatory agencies leads to policies that drift from this position. This suggests a loss of public control through successive delegations—to Congress to subcommittee to agency to lower hierarchical levels in the agency. Furthermore, for a given agency and policy the drift grows larger until performance is bad enough to recreate political salience to the regulatory policy.

Second, capture by clients is common. The direction of drift from the hypothetical majority opinion is in the direction of the welfare of the particular groups in greatest contact with the regulatory agency and is most pronounced in agencies with very narrow responsibilities that have contact with few interest groups.

Third, regulatory agencies are inflexible and rigid, too slow to adapt policies to changing external conditions. Decisions tend to be based excessively on short-run considerations and on the preservation of the existing socioeconomic structure, which leads agencies to retard technological advancement and to resist new sources of competition unless they can be shown to leave the existing institutional system and distribution of wealth largely unchanged.

Fourth, regulation causes changes in client organizations that detract from their efficiency and perhaps even from their viability in an unregulated environment. It affects the selection of leaders by private organizations, placing premiums on personnel who can deal effectively with government officials and legal processes rather than on those who best perform the primary function of the organization. It deflects resources and attention to a fundamentally unproductive activity, participation in formalized processes. And it sacrifices some warranted innovations and other economic changes by raising the costs of creativity and the wages of inefficiency through protecting established ways of doing business.

Fifth, cures may lie in two general directions: reducing the advantage of small, well-organized groups in political and regulatory decisionmaking, and making more flexible the various organizational structures through which authority is delegated. Among proposals that might accomplish these objectives are: (1) public-interest lobbyists that would give representation to less well-organized groups having a large aggregate stake in a regulatory issue; (2) greater insulation of the political process from organized interests, such as by changing the method of financing political campaigns and by requiring complete financial disclosures by candidates; (3) changes in the congressional committee structure, such as finding an alternative to the divisions of responsibility among subcommittees according to agencies and functions; (4) greater politicization of regulatory decisions by making offices elected, by allocating positions to constituencies, or by making decisions advisory to political bodies; (5) simplifications in agency procedures that would make participation in the process by outsiders less expensive and that would free agencies from formal rules of evidence; (6) alterations in the structure and nature of the participants in the regulated market, as by nationalization, dissolution of large firms, mergers of small firms, or legal redefinition of property rights; or (7) formalization of a long-term planning process by creating a permanent, well-staffed, non-hierarchical planning group within each agency, by requiring regular submission of long-term policy plans, and by including expiration dates in regulatory laws.

A conventional economic argument against incentive systems for promoting any particular kind of behavior is that they are insufficiently selective, that is, the decisions that will not be affected by the incentives are nevertheless subsidized or taxed. The folk wisdom on regulatory agencies suggests that the regulatory solution has its own problems, which may tip the efficiency balance the other way. Specifically, regulatory agencies can come to represent the interests of their clients. The key to wise choice among instruments of public policy—regulation versus incentives versus reorganization of firms—is to be able to characterize accurately the conditions that are more or less conducive to effective regulation.

Unfortunately, more definite specification of the causal relationships between policy actions and performance is not justified on the basis of the current state of knowledge about regulatory decision-making. The theory of regulatory behavior is rudimentary and fragmentary, although it is promising and progressing. Empirical work is almost nonexistent on the kinds of issues of interest to policymakers.

Certainly the most productive scholarly research at this stage would be detailed studies of how regulatory agencies actually work and what factors influence their performance. In order to understand how, if at all, regulatory processes can be improved, scholars must start investigating the empirical importance of political and organizational influences on decisions.

Many more case studies of agencies and policies must be undertaken to begin sorting out which theoretical models actually work best. Examples of the kind of work that needs to be done are Weingast and Moran (1983) on congressional control of the FTC and Cohen (1980) on the process of nuclear safety regulation. It is no longer enough for a researcher to identify some egregious example of regulatory malfeasance; that agencies create significant inefficiencies is well established. What is now required is some insight into how this performance can be improved. This requires more studies of the relationships among private sector performance, the decisionmaking process within the agency, and the nature of the political process.

PART II

Regulation in the Larger Social Setting

3

The State in Politics
The Relation Between
Policy and
Administration

Theodore J. Lowi

Anyone who studies political systems today must be struck by the presence of the state in all avenues of life. Yet, American political science has not fully integrated this fact. Although political science is rich in theories that help give meaning to political experience, none of these has tried to construct a politics on the basis of the state and its functions.

A state-centered theory of politics is based on a simple assumption—that every type of state, or regime, creates a politics consonant with itself. But one can look in vain for the state. What one generally sees are rules—actual rules, or actions emanating from rules—rules that are highly formal and explicit or rules that are implicit in uniforms or other official paraphernalia. The most important and formal rules are called by many names, such as laws, statutes, decrees, regulations. Most recently, the general category is referred to as policies, or public policy.

To extend the line of reasoning, the state, although an abstraction, can be experienced through the policies pursued by institutions that possess political authority. And, if policies are the state in action, then, if properly classified, they are types of regimes, each of which is likely to develop its own system of politics. This line of reasoning involves a considerable shift in theoretical perspective, from the assumption that politics causes policy to the assumption that policy causes politics. In operational terms, the causal arrows run from a policy proposal to its formulation to its implementation, and back again through group reaction to policy and administrative adaptation. The policy becomes the boundary conditions within which political action takes place. In brief, the theory requires the following analytic procedure: first, to identify and categorize public policies in their most formalistic and legalistic terms—literally as types of state or regime; second, to attempt to understand, explain, and predict political patterns, with politics defined as everything in the political system *except* the formalistic, legalistic policies. That is, the independent variables are the policies, properly categorized; the dependent variables are all other phenomena thought of as politics (again assuming that they are properly defined).

The larger purpose of this effort is to develop a political science of policy analysis—a politics rather than an economics of public policy, indeed, a politics of economics rather than an economics of politics. Up to now, political science has had very limited success in the theoretical or practical side of policy analysis. Many political scientists have become important political advisers, but aside from their skill in polling and in aggregate electoral data analysis, their success has come from good personal instincts more than from direct application of knowledge and theory drawn from political science and applied to public policy. In the area of policy evaluation, political scientists have been limited to helping politicians get votes for the passage of a bill through Congress or have played second chair to biologists, engineers, geologists, economists, and many others in the evaluation of actual impact of policies on the society. Political science may best make its pro rata contribution to good government on the basis of its ability to help define what government is, for purposes of analysis, and to evaluate the significance and impact of each form of government action *on the political system itself.* The reasoning is as follows. It takes many years for a policy to have an effect on the society, and once enough time has elapsed to warrant an evaluation of this effect, it is extremely difficult for even the most skillful analyst to isolate the particular contribution of the policy from the many other factors that could explain the outcome. In the meantime, however, each policy choice will have an almost immediate effect on the political environment. This important area is one in which political scientists are presumed to have expertise. Thus, if there is more than one policy approach to a given problem, political scientists ought to be able to advise policymakers on which approach would have the most desirable or the least undesirable effect on political institutions.

State into Policies: The Problem and Purpose of Classification

Once policies are appreciated as outward manifestations of the state, they cannot be adequately defined by mere designation of the subject matter with which each policy deals. Such designations as agricultural policy, educational policy, or industrial policy are, at best, indications of the interests of citizens and groups seeking something from governments. A proper definition of policy must be built not in terms of the interests of citizens but in terms of the forms of state action and the formally expressed intentions of the state. In the long run, state actions and private interests cannot remain far apart. Most policies are responses to interests or to demands made on the basis of interests. But policies are not themselves mere interests; they are state interests. If individual perceptions, interests, and organizations are made part of the definition of policy, there would be no way to explore the relationships between the two. A definition of policies must therefore be divorced from all interests other than those of the state itself.

A divorce of policy from all other aspects of politics requires two elements: the language of law and the techniques of control. Since the highest and most lasting forms of state action are expressed in legal language, so too must the definition of policy be expressed in that language. This is not merely a matter of vocabulary. The content of policies is law or law-like. Rulers—no matter what their number, the nature of their selection, or their methods of policymaking—must delegate much of their power to agents. If the agents are not to become the rulers themselves, the delegation of authority must be made in language clear enough so that the delegates follow the intentions of the rulers and not their own. Consequently, the essential problem of active rulership is how to use language to maintain some connection between the intent of the rulers and the actual implementation by agents. In an important sense, the language *is* the policy.

Thus, the policy must intend—and it must address—a future state of affairs for a class of cases or actions. But if it is a public policy, it will also contain a coercive element. Coercion, following Weber, is basic to all state action. Unlike private institutions, the institutions of the state are not merely actors in their environment. State institutions have the right and the obligation to improve the probability that the future will resemble the intent of the original policy. A great part of the ultimate success of a public policy may be attributable to the mere statement of the preferred future state of affairs. The purpose of good citizenship is to make public policies virtually self-executing. But most policies are accompanied by explicit means of imposing their intentions on their environments, and in all policies some techniques of control are implicit.

A policy, then, is a rule formulated by some governmental authority expressing an intention to influence the behavior of citizens, individually or collectively, by use of positive and negative sanctions. This definition closely resembles the accepted definition of *rule* in jurisprudence. According to Roscoe Pound, a rule is a "legal precept attaching a definite detailed legal consequence to a definite detailed statement of fact" (quoted in Friedman and Macaulay, 1977, p. 855). Friedman and Macaulay see this as breaking down into two parts: the statement of fact and the statement of consequences. A third part is implicit: Friedman adds, "within some normative order or system of governmental control" (ibid.). In other words, the third part of the definition amounts to a provision for implementing the intention and imposing the consequences. Today, that usually means a government agency. It is this third part of the definition that so often creates problems, because rules must be formulated in such a way as to provide standards and guidelines for these agencies. In the modern age of large government, laws, or legal rules, rarely communicate directly to citizens but, rather, to administrators.

A policy defined as a legal rule with these characteristics is obviously different from a specific decision or order, which derives from a rule but is not the rule itself. It is also different from a sentiment, which may express a desired end but embodies no rule. The preambles to statutes, full of important rhetoric, are often mistaken for policies. Finally, policy defined this way is obviously not intended to include observed changes in actual citizen behavior (such as increased savings or reduced racial discrimination), which, though they may have been the intent of the policy, are not necessarily attributable to that policy.

As clear and simple as the definition is, it does not locate a single, homogeneous class of phenomena. There is more than one type of policy, because there is more than one way the state can express an intention and more than one way the state can use its coercive powers through administrative agencies.

An important case in point is regulation, or regulatory policy. In his constitutional law treatise, Tribe (1978, ch. 18) tends to equate regulation with government control and state action. He leaves open the question of what follows regulation, or what regulation is not. Thurow (1980) is probably typical of economists in taking regulation as a concept that needs no definition and then dealing theoretically and empirically with the impact of regulation on society. Regulatory policies raise the incomes of some people and lower the incomes of others. But there is no concern for forms of government action other than regulation and therefore no opportunity to clarify the concept for purposes of political theory.

Others, including some political scientists, make some worthwhile distinctions among types of regulatory policy but fail to define regulation itself. In an important article, Wilson (1979) indicates, without explicitly stating, that there is a threefold distinction among government policies—government regulation, government ownership, and deference to the private sphere. He then presents a more systematic scheme that becomes the center of an important part of his book, *Political Organizations.* This scheme is concerned with the variations in political patterns within the various types of regulatory agencies according to whether the policy concentrates or disperses costs and benefits. Although very interesting, this does not sharpen the distinction between regulation and other types of state action.

Roger Noll (1980) devoted an entire essay to the question of "What Is Regulation?" and was only able to come up with a clearer distinction between regulatory and nonregulatory public policies. First, the regulatory authority is not a party to the transactions it regulates but is a referee of transactions between other parties. (By contrast, the cost-reimbursement formulas for Medicare or Medicaid are not regulatory, because they are written by the purchaser of the service.) Second, regulation operates by cases and procedural rules. There are some problems with the second characteristic, but this definition gets closer than any other to a formal definition of regulation that is clean and clear of the many political and social variables one might wish to study in relation to the policy.

Nonregulation, however, remains merely the residual category. This is an important substantive issue. If we are to study regulation in any sense other than the technical one of the cost-effectiveness of particular agencies, we must have clear categories of comparison.

Some legal theorists help pierce through the dense atmosphere of the nonregulation sphere of public policy. The less they are directly concerned with regulation itself, the closer they seem to come to theoretically helpful formulations. Summers and Howard (1972) provide a fivefold categorization of the nature of law, which can be taken as virtually synonymous with state action: (1) law as a grievance-remedial instrument; (2) law as a penal instrument; (3) law as an administrative-regulatory instrument; (4) law as an instrument for ordering governmental conferral of public benefits; and (5) law as an instrument for facilitating and effecting private arrangements. The first three categories include parts of what others often consider regulation, the first being court-made law for tort action; the second mainly legislative laws for conduct deemed evil in itself; and the third mainly legislative-administrative law for conduct deemed evil only in its consequences. The fourth category is a mixture of subsidy and welfare benefits, and the fifth concerns laws that distribute powers between the public and the private sphere. Summers's categories are asymmetrical, and he does not provide a logic for the distinctions or for their significance. But his scheme is rich in distinctions, and is a step toward defining areas of state action that are nonregulatory.

The logic absent from Summers's categorization can be found in the work of legal theorist H. L. A. Hart (1961). Hart begins with a critique of the traditional Austinian definition of *law* as "a rule that imposes an obligation and then applies a sanction for noncompliance." It is "criminal in form." He criticizes traditional jurisprudence for adhering to such a one-dimensional definition and identifies a second basic type of rule whose distinction from the first will immediately appeal to anyone who has examined legislation. Hart refers to the first or classical definition as a Primary Rule and then distinguishes it from a Secondary Rule, which fulfills Roscoe Pound's definition of a legal rule yet imposes no duties directly upon citizens. Rather, it confers powers or facilities on them. As an example of Secondary Rules, Hart suggests laws on marriage. This is a particularly good example, because some laws on marriage are Secondary Rules and some are Primary Rules. Marriage laws that confer facilities and processes to make marriage, marriage contracts, and marriage records available are examples of Secondary Rules. Laws that oblige husband and wife to observe the provisions of the contract, such as to refrain from adultery or bigamy, are examples of Primary Rules. Here we can see clearly the distinction between two basic types of laws or policies and at the same time can see the weakness of trying to distinguish among policies according to subject matter. That is to say, "marriage policy" is not a meaningful category.

Yet, powerful though Hart's dichotomy is, it does not appear to exhaust all the possibilities, especially when considering legislation instead of the judge-made law with which students of jurisprudence tend most to concern themselves. For example, some policies may appear at first to fit the definition of the Primary Rule in that they are involuntary, but they fall outside the definition in that they do not attempt to impose obligations directly on individuals. That is to say, some patently coercive rules do not seem to work through individual conduct but instead seek to influence the individual by working through the environment of conduct. This distinction between individual conduct and the environment of conduct is more easily recognized in the study of legislation than in the study of judge-made law, because judge-made law tends to work through individuals in individual cases (except when appeals courts review legislation). For example, a change in tax law can influence individuals without any concern for specific individual conduct or even the identities of individuals. Indeed, some provisions of the tax law are pure Primary Rules (regulatory)—for example, the obligation to file a return. But some tax provisions are clearly *not* regulatory, in that they deal with some aspect of the environment of conduct—for example, the definition of taxable income, the rate structure itself, general categories of deductions, general categories of exemptions, general statuses such as marriage and dependence. (Tax law also contains examples of still other types of policy, but these categories have not yet been identified.)

The concept of environment of conduct is not simply a third category to go along with Primary and Secondary Rules. It introduces an entirely separate dimension. This obviously breaks Hart's dichotomy into a four-celled typology, as indicated in Table 1. Simply put, this gives us two kinds of Primary Rules and two kinds of Secondary Rules, summarized as follows.

Regulatory policy.   Primary Rules are regulatory when they work directly through individual conduct, where identities and questions of compliance and noncompliance must be involved. Regulatory rules impose obligations and sanctions. They are criminal in form. If effectively implemented, they may create an environment of conduct conducive or nonconducive to compliance. That, however, is a behavioral hypothesis about the political or societal impact and has nothing to do with the definition of the legal rule itself.

Redistributive policies.   These are Primary Rules: they impose something on the private sphere but work through the environment of conduct rather than directly upon conduct itself. Rules impose classifications or statuses; individual membership in a classification is involuntary and by definition (i.e., categoric).

Distributive policies.   These are Secondary Rules: they work through individual conduct but do not impose obligations. Patronage and subsidies are Secondary Rules in that they confer privileges or facilities. They are a special type of Secondary Rule because they make privileges or facilities available on a personal, individualized basis. People approve or disapprove of such policies according to their judgment or hypotheses about the cumulative

74   THEODORE J. LOWI

Table 1   *Categorization of Public Policies*

FORM OF EXPRESSED INTENTION	FORM OF INTENDED IMPACT	
	Works through Individual Conduct	*Works through Environment of Conduct*
Primary Rule (imposes obligations or positions)	*Regulatory policies:* Rules impose obligations; rules of individual conduct, criminal in form	*Redistributive policies:* Rules impose classification or status; rules categorizing activity
	Synonyms: police power, government intervention	*Synonyms:* fiscal and monetary policy, overall budget policies
	Examples: public health laws, industrial safety, traffic laws, antitrust	*Examples:* income tax, Federal Reserve discount rates, Social Security
Secondary Rule (confers powers or privileges)	*Distributive policies:* Rules confer facilities or privileges unconditionally	*Constituent policies:* Rules confer powers; rules about rules and about authority
	Synonyms: patronage, subsidy, pork barrel	*Synonyms:* overhead, auxiliary, government organization
	Examples: public works, agricultural extension, land grants	*Examples:* agencies for budgetary and personnel policy, laws establishing judicial jurisdiction

effect of these privileges. Such judgments and hypotheses are part of the politics or economics of policy analysis and should not be included in the definition itself.

Constituent policies.   These are Secondary Rules: they work through the environment, either by making services and facilities generally available or by conferring powers or jurisdictions. These are referred to as rules about powers or rules about rules.

An operational definition of each of the four categories of policy is developed in detail below, but one further point should be made here.

Because this approach is based on a formal concept of the functions of the state, the classifications here deal only with the formal language of the statute (or other formal expression of policy). They are in no way concerned with the actual impacts of policies on the society, polity, or economy. If the classifications (which we are taking as the independent variables) were to include such elements, any theory developed from them would be circular. To avoid this, the definitions self-consciously avoid any elements of politics about which later hypotheses may be formed. Thus a statute can be classified, say, as redistributive even if after twenty years of operation no actual redistribution has taken place as a result of the statute. The labels adopted for each of the four categories may be unfortunate if they are taken to imply hypotheses about impact. The strong caveat here is that the reader avoid such interpretations: classification and the ensuing analysis require that the categories of public policy, that is, the independent variables, be understood as efforts to grasp the intentions of rulers as expressed in the established formal language of government.

Policy Classifications and Agency Missions

If the initial assumption—that each type of public policy, i.e., regime, tends to develop its own distinct political structure and process—is to govern the analysis, then it follows that four distinguishable types of policy ought to produce four distinguishable *arenas of power*, that is, four identifiable clusters of political characteristics. This is the route from classification to theory.

The U.S. Congress has been explored on the basis of this scheme, using two different kinds of data. First, a reanalysis of seventeen published case studies of the formulation of important legislation revealed dramatic differences in the way the legislative process operates, depending on whether the bill in question is regulatory, redistributive, distributive, or constituent (Lowi, 1972). For example, distributive (pork-barrel) bills show Congress as an institution dominated by its committees, with the floor and the parliamentary dimension playing a very passive and uncreative role. The typical regulatory bill shows the committee system much less dominant and the floor far more active and creative. Second, by use of statistics developed from the frequency of floor amendments of committee bills, a quantitative study of committee-floor relationships strongly confirmed the patterns of variation developed by reanalysis of the published case studies. These not only confirmed predicted variations in the internal workings of Congress but showed consistent patterns of relationships between Congress and the executive branch (R. Spitzer, 1979).

Among all the opportunities available for empirical exploration of the relationship between the state and its political environment, the concern here is with administrative phenomena—how the data on administrative structure and process vary from one policy category to another. Administration, despite the fact that it is the core of modern government, is one of the least systematically researched areas in politics. A rich literature of description and case studies was developed between the 1930s and the 1950s. Political scientists studied agencies as units of action in their political environment. From there the jump to organization theory and decisionmaking was made without going through intermediate levels of empirical research. Nothing was done comparable to what Key and others did for the study of elections by use of aggregate data within geographical units. Most of the systematic comparative study of administrative structure has been done by sociologists from sociological perspectives. Little political content can be found there.

This is not meant as a criticism. It simply underscores the need for similar work in political science. Administration is not only politics in its most serious form, it is also the most quantifiable form. Administration has at times been defined as voluminous, routine business. No routines are more important than administrative routines. Administration not only lends itself to quantification, it provides better reality checks on itself because so much can be known about administrative agencies independent of survey data.

Thus the study of administration must be central to the study of the relation between the state and politics. Differences among bureaucracies are significant for organization theory and for political practice but are most important for political theory, because observed variations can and must be explained by reflection on the way states and regimes shape their environments.

Rationale for the Classification

The agencies chosen for analysis are located at the first operating level below the top of each department or ministry. In the United States this is called the bureau, the first level below the Secretary and a phalanx of deputy and assistant secretaries. Independent commissions are included. In France, the comparable level of agency unit is called the *direction*. Each such agency or unit, with few exceptions, operates within a jurisdiction delegated to it by a higher authority. The form of that delegation is an organic statute or similar instrument. It is usually a single statute or decree that extends, with occasional amendments, throughout the life of the agency. Because the organic statute can be taken as the mission of the agency, each agency is automatically classified once its organic act is classified. Thus, an agency is classified as regulatory if and only if its governing statute has been so classified. All personnel in the agency (if they are in the sample) are grouped according to the agency's mission, regardless of their individual tasks. What proportion of an agency's personnel is actually performing tasks directly relevant to the mission (versus auxiliary, support, or management tasks) is an empirical question, and an interesting one.

The first step, then, is to conduct an exhaustive inventory of the basic policies in each country and to concentrate on those that give agencies their mission and jurisdiction. These are then classified according to guidelines and procedures laid out below.

Classification: A Problem of Content Analysis

It is impossible to operationalize the definition of each category of policy in such a way as to make the classification task automatic. However, it is possible to minimize the inconsistencies of classification. Policies do not present problems of content analysis different in principle from those encountered in attempts to classify materials drawn from interviews of individuals. We have followed the procedure of survey researchers in setting up panels of coders to read and crosscheck each policy as it is classified. Experience so far with nearly two hundred agencies and their policies in the United States and in France has produced nearly 90 percent intra-panel agreement on policy classifications. The guideline questions for the panel are provided in Table 2. These were derived logically from Table 1 and were revised and sharpened in response to the experience with the legal language confronted in actual U.S. and French laws. Table 2 is essentially an interview schedule of policy materials.

Disagreement among two or more panel members has been dealt with according to the following procedures:

1. Some statutes are omnibus laws that combine two or more separate subjects or functions in the same official enactment. Because each subject or function is given a separate title or chapter, each such title or chapter can be classified separately. However, in a few instances separately classified policies are given over to a single agency, and in a few other instances more than one separate statute delegates an additional and separately classifiable function to an agency. These agencies are, for our purposes, multi-functional and therefore impossible to place exclusively in one of the four categories. Such an agency is dropped from the aggregate analysis and is dealt with as a single case study.

Table 2 *Guidelines for Content Analysis of Statutes*

Question	Responses, Comments
1. Does the rule of the statute (or decree) apply to persons or conducts in the private or in the public sphere?	If in the public sphere, the policy is almost certainly constituent. If private, it could be any of the other three types.
2. Does the rule set conditions or impose obligations and provide penalties for nonperformance?	If yes, the policy is regulatory. This applies even to public officials because in matters of crime and tort all persons are private citizens.
3. Does the rule set conditions without sanctions?	If yes, the policy could still be regulatory if there is an implicit sanction such as exposure or publicity. The policy could be distributive, if the policy sets a process in train or provides for a facility without setting conditions of performance for participation.
4. Does the rule pertain to individuals and deal with them by name or provide specific facilities without providing general standards from which the privileges or facilities derive?	If yes, the policy is almost certainly distributive; a clear example is a "pork barrel" act authorizing projects by name.
5. Does the rule create an agency?	If yes, the policy is constituent.
6. Does the rule provide an agency with jurisdiction over other agencies?	If yes, the policy is constituent; a clear example is a budget bureau.

7. Does there appear to be a rule without contemplation of action by public or private persons?

If the rule sets a public process in train or defines the jurisdiction of an agency, it is a constituent policy. If the rule provides for a process for all or a large, defined aggregate of persons, it is probably redistributive. (See also q. 9.)

8. Does the rule ignore individual conduct and concentrate on characteristics or properties of individuals, i.e., does the rule attempt to discriminate among defined aggregates of persons without regard to their conduct?

If yes, as in identifying all persons below a certain income or age, and if the category is invidious and involuntary, the policy is almost certainly redistributive (e.g., tax categories, welfare classification).

9. Does the rule provide for or alter a process or structure that is economy-wide?

If yes, the policy is almost certainly redistributive (e.g., Federal Reserve System; low-interest loan programs). In such cases, the entire citizenry is the category defined in the rule.

2. Some statutes are so vaguely written that very different intentions can be inferred from them, and panel disagreement is very
high. Additional materials are then collected, including, where
possible, the official legislative history. If panel disagreement per-
sists, the agency is eliminated from the aggregate analysis and is
examined intensively for effects on the agency of operating under
such vague legislative language. Vagueness in legislation is a serious problem for modern government, and it points to one of the
normative or applied aspects of this study: How widespread is the
practice of writing statutes that cannot be understood? And how
can the legal integrity of such statutes be improved? These questions are extensively examined in Lowi (1979).

The outcome of the agency classification is presented in Appendix A for the United States and in Appendix B for France. Agencies
included are only those for which personnel working in those agencies were present in the samples of the original two studies.

Initial Results

The governing empirical question follows simply and logically: do important characteristics of agencies or their personnel distribute themselves significantly differently from one category of
agencies to the next? To put the matter another way: when agencies
are arranged according to this fourfold scheme, does the distribution of their characteristics present a clearer and theoretically more
interesting pattern than groupings of agencies according to alternative classifications?

Selection of empirical materials was aided very substantially by
two major surveys of administrative personnel carried out independently in the United States (Corson and Paul, 1966) and France (Darbel and Schnapper, 1969, 1972). Reanalysis of their data produced
findings that strongly confirm the scheme.

The system in France is older and more formal than in the United
States. France has a highly unitary concept of civil service (*fonction
publique*), applying many laws and regulations to all areas, even including professors in public universities. Specialization is provided
for in a formal and orderly way through the *corps*, which tie schooling
to job specialties, careers, and status. This gives French bureaucracy
diversity as well as uniformity. The diversity may well outweigh the
uniformity, despite efforts to the contrary.

Of the various corps, as grouped in Table 3, the most significant
are the *grands corps*. In prestige, personnel of the grands corps may
appear to be a senior civil service, but they are not truly so because

Table 3 *French Corps Personnel Distributed by Type of Mission of Their Agency*

	Grands Corps (%)	Corps de Control Administrative (%)	Corps d'Administration Centrale (%)	Corps Techniques (%)	Corps des Services Extérieurs (%)
Constituent	53	43	47	40	75
Distributive	1	11	17	43	—
Regulatory	1	17	14	11	25
Redistributive	44	30	22	5	—

they are not evenly distributed across the top of all agencies. Only one percent served in the top management of regulatory agencies, and an equally small proportion served in distributive agencies, leaving 98 percent in the top management of constituent and redistributive agencies. A very different pattern obtains for the other two prestigious corps, the *corps techniques* and the *corps des services extérieurs*—not opposite in either case, but asymmetrical and very different.

The grands corps can be defined as including the career personnel in the Conseil d'Etat, the Cour des Comptes, and the Inspection Générale des Finances.[1] These corps go back generations, emerging out of the ancient *fonctions régaliens*—the king's requirements for maintenance of the realm in its civil life (accounts, records, the court itself, etc.). In farthest contrast, the corps techniques arose out of essentially military functions. They are engineers and other technicians who are responsible for roads and other public works, the post office, the mines, and so on. The prestige of these personnel is as high as that of the personnel of the grands corps. Entrance to their schools, called the *grandes écoles*, is intensively sought after by students from all classes, but especially the upper middle class. Though it is reasonable for agencies to draw staff from the grandes écoles, those high-powered trades schools, it is not so clear why graduates from the grandes écoles hold the top managerial positions. The answer cannot be merely that the tasks of such agencies are technical.

1. Darbel and Schnapper (1969), p. 126. Consensus does not exist on the definition of *corps*. For example, Sulieman (1974) defines *grands corps* to include major technical corps and the prefectoral corps. Without judging the merits of the differences, I am following Darbel-Schnapper because their data are being used.

Building a road is no more technical than designing and managing social security (redistributive), yet few technical specialists reach high management there. The contrasting distribution of services extérieurs personnel is made more interesting by the inclusion in this category of the *corps préfectoral*. Regulatory and constituent agencies delegate more policy and rule-making responsibility to the field (extérieur)—more will be said of this later.

No comparable data exist on the United States, because there is no corps tradition. However, some roughly equivalent data will be found in the center column of Table 4. Although drawn from aggregate Civil Service Commission data and one step removed from individual personnel, these data are nevertheless strongly confirming. The only agencies where substantive specialists are at all prominent in top management are distributive agencies. Moreover, although 4 percent seems a minuscule cut-off point, these figures are roughly cumulative. That is to say, any agency with at least 4 percent of each of these specialties will show over 15 percent of the combined use of the specialties in their top positions.

This pattern is further confirmed by the center column of Table 4. Only among the respondents in distributive agencies was there a strong tendency to rate outside professional training as of high value in promotion to top management.

The French data are clearly consistent with those of the United States. First, reading from Table 3, 43 percent of all corps techniques personnel in top management were in distributive agencies. The same data in a cross-cutting direction reveal that of all personnel in the top management of distributive agencies, 54 percent were from the corps techniques (versus none for corps des services extérieurs).

Table 5 is the only view offered here of variations in tasks, but it is an extremely important dimension. The task in question is that of coordinating the work of others in the agency. Coordination is the key to agency conduct and efficiency. Without effective coordination almost none of the advantages of bureaucratization can be realized. Yet there are limited methods of coordination available to policymakers, and some methods may be mutually contradictory. Only a few types of methods can be imposed on a reanalysis of the American or French data but several others are conceivable and will be identified and investigated in future research. Meanwhile, the few in Table 5 are sufficient to make the point.

Note first the prominence of overhead mechanisms in redistributive agencies in the United States and France. Close supervision is also prominent among redistributive agencies in both countries: U.S. top personnel in redistributive agencies rate supervision activities second

Table 4 Professionalism: Use and Value of Technologists in Top Management, United States and France

	UNITED STATES					FRANCE
	Percentage of agencies in which at least 4 percent of top managers are:				Average rating given to value of outside professional training (1 high, 6 low)	Percent of top managers recruited from corps techniques
	Biomedical specialists	Engineers	Physical scientists	Social scientists		
Distributive	36	50	25	21	2	54
Regulatory	11	17	6	11	6	21
Redistributive	7	14	14	14	6	6
Constituent[a]	—	—	—	—	—	19

SOURCE: Corson and Paul (1966) interview data.

[a] Analysis of U.S. categories was developed before Constituent category was analyzed.

Table 5 *Mechanisms of Administrative Control: Agencies Rely upon Different Means of Coordinating Agency Conduct*

	UNITED STATES				FRANCE			
	Distributive	*Regulative*	*Redistributive*			*Distributive*	*Regulative*	*Redistributive*	*Constituent*
Overhead mechanisms Agencies in which over 10% of the top personnel are in budgeting and accounting	7%	17%	43%	Top personnel drawn from the two major overhead corps	6%	13%	45%	24%
Close supervision Executives rank supervision activities as important (1) to unimportant (6) in a typical week's work	6	5	2	Top personnel required to report to three or more superiors	15%	24%	24%	19%
Bureaucratism (1) Rank on bureaucratism scale (promotion within rank, etc.)	4th	2nd	1st	Top personnel drawn from corps de services extérieurs	0%	21%	0%	16%
(2) Rank on procedure scale (typical week involved staffing, negotiating, or representing)	1st	1st	3rd	Top personnel who spent no time in field (services extérieurs)	61%	58%	71%	63%
Hierarchy Agencies in which at least 15% of HQ personnel are G315 and above	32%	72%	50%	Numbers of separate units or divisions within each direction	1–9	10–21	21+	1–9
Agencies in which 40% of top personnel are in the field	11%	39%	21%	Personnel who have departed from precedent or introduced an innovation	55%	51%	44%	49%

in importance; and in France the respondents in redistributive agencies reported the narrowest span of control, an almost certain indication of relatively close supervision. Redistributive agencies also rate high on coordination through what (for lack of a better term) we have called *bureaucratism,* i.e., building careers strictly within the agency, with entry at the bottom, promotion through the ranks, and the internalization of norms and policy preference. Although no directly comparable data were available for the French, the French did demonstrate a consistent tendency to recruit top management in redistributive agencies fairly strictly from headquarters careers. This would tend to give the managers common values and also push them to rely still more heavily on overhead and direct supervisory methods (and precedent—note percentages for field control).

Some contrasts with coordination patterns in other agencies are visible. Regulatory agencies rely far more heavily on procedural and authority mechanisms. Not only do regulatory agencies rely heavily on proper procedure for coordination, they also structure these agencies so that there are both relatively high proportions of rank at headquarters and high proportions of rank in the field, serving presumably as policymakers and as direct supervisors.

Syntheses and Hypotheses

On the basis of these and a few other data, rough models of administrative structure can be constructed. The task is akin to primitive archeology, where whole creatures were reconstructed from a few bone fragments and fossils. Though later refinements of theory and measurement exposed a great range of error in the original reconstructions, those first guesses provided the rationale for the hypotheses and the guidelines used to eliminate the errors.

The Regulatory Agency Model

Regulatory agencies are responsible for implementing the classic control policies of government, formulating or implementing rules imposing obligations on individuals, and providing punishment for nonconformance. This requires at a minimum that administrators know the main rules and share interpretations about how and when to impose them. Others, including courts, may be ultimately responsible for applying the sanctions, but only after the administrators have set the process in train by finding the individual, deciding that the conduct is contrary to the rule, and bringing that individual, by arrest or exposure, to the attention of the sanctioning authority. Interpretations of rules of conduct are passed along as operating rules of the agency officials, incorporating their reading of the statute with their understanding of legislative intent, court rulings, or executive orders. Other operating rules come from previous cases. Use of precedents produces a kind of common law in regulatory agencies. The fact that direct controls and punishments of individuals are involved creates an environment in which citizens will compare agency decisions for consistency and fairness. This leads to stress on rights, formal procedures, and a standardized relationship with higher authorities through rules and additional formal procedures. Although each regulatory decision is an individual case, the cases are tied by reference to one or more rules or precedents. Thus, although regulatory policies work through individual conduct (see Table 1), they cannot be disaggregated to the level of single individuals, each taken as a separate unit. That is a feature of distributive, not regulatory, policies.

Regulatory agencies will, then, show distinctive organizational features, some of which can be found through examination of the special distributions of personnel data. Regulatory agencies should be the most rule-bound (rather than tradition-bound, authority-bound, status-bound, or hierarchy-bound). Thus, for example, only one percent of all the top management in regulatory agencies in the French data were drawn from the grands corps, while 46 percent were drawn from the middle-status corps d'administration centrale and 21 percent each from the corps techniques and the corps des services extérieurs. The latter means primarily the prefectoral corps, whose members are more likely to be experts on process and procedure than on substance. Add to that the earlier data showing the heavy emphasis in regulatory agencies on coordination by procedure. Add also the practice of placing top managerial personnel directly in the field. Surely this is an expression of the need to maintain a balance between two conflicting requirements: to give ample discretion to workers on the line to decide which individuals are not conforming, and to maintain some appearance of consistency with rules and precedents. Sometimes high-ranking field officers are there to supervise the discretion of lower-ranking officials—for example, captains of police over patrolmen. At other times high-ranking officials are put in the field to make the decisions themselves, as in the United States is the case for hearing examiners, who in recent years have had their status upgraded (or finally recognized) with the new designation *administrative law judge*.

Table 6 suggests a few other hypotheses logically derived from this line of thought in dimensions of agency life for which data at present do not exist but could fairly easily be collected. For example, because citizen conduct is being controlled and sanctioned by rules, regulatory agencies should tend to be more specialized by units than by individual job specialties.[2] One case in point: a separate unit might be highly specialized, working only on rate charges or toxic substances while within each unit all employees may be doing the same kind of work. By the same logic, control-oriented, rule-laden regulatory agencies are likely to have the most intense and unstable relationships with their larger political environment (see Table 6). Intense involvement with organized interest groups should produce enhanced efforts at mutual cooptation and exploitation which should take the form of lateral entry, i.e., a tendency to recruit personnel from the outside directly into upper-middle and upper ranks. Lateral entry should tend to be practiced in distributive agencies also; however, these lateral entrants would be subject specialists (engineers), whereas in regulatory agencies they would tend to be process and procedure specialists (lawyers). To summarize, regulatory agencies are hierarchical but the hierarchy is flatter and more truncated than in Weber's model. They have large proportions of high-ranking managers, many of whom are in the field carrying policy responsibilities, and many horizontal linkages among lower units as well as vertical linkage to headquarters and the courts.

The Distributive Agency Model

In mission, distributive agencies are almost the opposite of regulatory agencies. Although like regulatory agencies in being responsible for policies that work directly on or through individuals, the relationship is one of patron and client rather than controller and controlled. Consequently, distributive agencies can operate in their political environment almost as though they had unlimited resources. There are no integrative rules of conduct, only rules designating facilities, which do not require elaboration of intermediate rules or standards for agency decisions. Consequently, these agencies can respond to political conflicts by disaggregation. That is to say, they can take each decision or facility, each unit of output, and treat it as separate and distinct from all others. Few criteria or precedents tie decisions together or provide a direct basis of comparison, espe-

---

2. Note in Table 5 that in France redistributive agencies outrank regulatory agencies on unit differentiation. This could be true, but it is likely to disappear when agency size is controlled for. Since regulatory agencies tend to be smaller, the ratio of units to members is likely to be a great deal larger.

Table 6 *Guidelines for Hypotheses*

Organizational Characteristic or Concept	Definitions, Indexes, and Comments	Hypotheses: Examples and Comments
A. Formal Structure		
Specialization (of labor): Unit differentiation	Controlling for size of agency, how many distinguishable work units are there, and in how many distinguishable layers? Are units divided by jurisdiction, or process or area? Some measures of "shape" are being considered.	Logic and experience suggest that regulatory agencies will rate highest on measures of unit specialization, with constituent agencies also high.
Specialization: Task specialization, division of labor	How many formally indentified tasks are there? (See definition of occupational families—aggregate data). How much pre-training and how much certification are required? How many different tasks (and what kinds) do senior administrators perform in a typical week?	Distributive and redistributive agencies will be highest in measures of task specialization, but since this is true for different reasons, more specific hypotheses will be framed to capture the different measures of specialization.
Organizational dispersion	What proportion of the agency's personnel are in field rather than HQ units? What percentage of top management have had field experience prior to HQ? What percentage of senior managers are serving in field units? What is the normal chain of command between field and HQ—e.g., between functional specialists, or strictly from unit chief to agency chief?	Distributive and regulatory agencies ought to show highest, and constituent agencies lowest (with concentration at HQ). But regulatory agencies should also show highest in average civil service ratings serving in the field.

		Redistributive agencies ought to show highest on any measures of chain of command.
Chain of command (operational centralization and decentralization)	What kinds of rules are there, and how strictly observed are they, pertaining to communications between layers and units, superiors and subordinates? Are horizontal linkages discouraged in favor of vertical linkages? How formalized and specific are requirements to notify and to record communications (e.g., to initial, to send carbons, etc.)?	
Delegation of authority (policy centralization and decentralization)	How much responsibility is delegated to field units? How carefully and explicitly do agency rules circumscribe discretion? How much freedom of action do personnel at different levels feel they have? How closely tied are these rules to the statute (and legislative intent)? How closely tied are procedures to decisions?	Most extreme general policy decentralization should be found among distributive agencies, least among redistributive agencies. But different types of delegation must be allowed for—e.g., there is broad delegation in regulatory agencies, but it tends to be accompanied by general guidelines and more procedural limits. Constituent agencies are also broad.

B. Distribution of Responsibilities

Coordination (types of centralization and decentralization)	What methods and devices does the agency rely upon most heavily to coordinate work? Overhead controls? Direct supervision? Formal clearance? Committees? Professional norms and common schooling? Explicit rules ascribing work, status, interdependence, etc.? How narrow or broad is the span of control (as measured by superior-subordinate ratios)?	One of the most important findings of the pilot study is that these various coordinating devices are inconsistent and often inversely related. Hypotheses concern not whether but which devices are used, and in what combinations. The findings tend to produce different types as well as degrees of centralization for each category of agency.

Table 6 *Guidelines for Hypotheses (continued)*

Organizational Characteristic or Concept	Definitions, Indexes, and Comments	Hypotheses: Examples and Comments
Internal accountability	How does the agency review responsibility for decisions and their outcomes? Are rewards and punishments meted out explicitly for performance? To what extent do personnel feel that promotion is tied to good decisions or good performance? Are there routines for monitoring individual performance?	Central substantive review would most likely be found among regulatory agencies. Performance and expenditure review more likely among redistributive agencies. Least surveillance among distributive agencies.
External accountability (formal)	How much departmental oversight is there? To what extent through agency chief or functional specialists? How much and what kind of congressional oversight is there? Is it budgetary or substantive? What level or status is permitted to deal directly with the department? With Congress and committees? With the public? How litigious is the agency? What kind of judicial review does it get, and how frequently? How strict and extensive are procedural rules? Do they apply only to individual cases? To public participation in policymaking? How hard or easy is it to get information from the agency? How often are Freedom of Information Act requests dealt with, and to what result?	Here again the type of external relationship is as important as the degree. Constituent agencies are likely to rate highest on formal relations with virtually all governmental agencies, but regulatory agencies tend to rate highest on requirements to relate to nongovernmental groups and to congressional committees. Lowest on formal (but high on informal) should be distributive agencies. Lowest on formal relations should be redistributive agencies.

Environmental relationships (informal)	Without regard to agency rules, what percentage of each level of agency reports direct contacts with the department? With congressional committees? Individual members of Congress? Interest group representatives, etc.? What percentage of top personnel entered laterally? Vertically through the agency? If laterally, from what source (e.g., other federal agencies, private sector, state government)? How active are top personnel in their professional association? In political parties or interest groups or major clientele firms or groups (present or former)?	Constituent agencies expected high here too, for governmental units, but tend to be low on lateral entry. Regulatory agencies higher in lateral entry and in various other informal relations, especially the practice of lower administrators having direct relations with outside. (Distributive agencies rate high here too.)
Management style	What percentage of the managers are from subject specializations? What percentage from more general administrative occupations and careers? What percentage had direct field experience? How important is specific management training? Do agency heads tend to be agency careerists or lateral entrants? How public has the career of the head or top echelon been — e.g., in newspapers, Who's Who?	Distributive agency personnel tend to rate highest in preference for subject specialists in top management, regulatory lowest. Constituent agency personnel tend to come from higher social statuses and from more general career categories. Lateral entrants in top management least likely among redistributive agencies.

cially across regions of the country. For example, the typical public works (pork-barrel) statute is composed of dozens of individual authorizations to build, design, or inquire into proposals for specific, named projects. The only connection among the projects and proposals is the agency authorized to take the actions. These agencies can make peace with their constituencies because agency constituencies correspond to congressional constituencies, which can be placated by adding authorizations for further projects. Even when expansion is not possible, conflict can be bought off by subdividing existing units, particularly of commitments to run studies and cost-benefit analyses on proposals that could later become authorizations. In contrast, losers and winners are closer together in the regulatory agency environment, and rules or standards of conduct provide a basis for comparing agency decisions, thereby inhibiting the agency from disaggregating decisions into separate units.

Once again, organizational consequences ought to flow from the peculiarities of mission. Distributive agencies, while not the precise opposites of regulatory agencies, are likely to be far apart on a number of important characteristics. Organizations are too complex to be put on a single continuum, but it is possible to say at least that the absence of responsibility for imposing authoritative rules affects distributive agencies. The absence of rules is compensated for in large part by professionalism. Most hypotheses about these agencies will revolve around these and related characteristics.

We have already noted the heavy use of corps techniques personnel in the top management of French distributive agencies. Similar data were found in U.S. agencies, and further confirmation is expected in future studies. Professionalism is partly a solution to the problem of consistency without rules and partly a solution to the problem of coordination. Common schooling, common texts, common "cookbook" formulas, equations, techniques, and computer programs help give these personnel the same premises, so that when confronted with the same problem they are likely to make the same decision despite the absence of policy guidelines. Even though professionals may enter top management laterally, they presumably can fall right into step.

Like regulatory agencies, distributive agencies delegate a great many responsibilities to the field, but along functional rather than management (generalist) lines. To deal with this functional decentralization, more specialists are likely to be elevated to top management positions (see Table 6). Procedure is also likely to be as heavily stressed as in regulatory agencies—but, again, it is of a far different kind. Here are to be found fewer formal legal procedures and less due process, but a far greater number and variety of decision rules such as letting decisions rest on cost-benefit ratios, outcomes of environmental impact statements, or citizen participation.

A visualization of the hierarchy of typical distributive agencies would show them relatively flat, like regulatory agencies. But there the resemblance would end. The hierarchy is not truncated but integrated along functional lines. Professional discretion is permitted in the field, but horizontal linkages among field units are expected to be minimized while vertical linkages are maximized. The vertical linkages here are quite distinctive, passing through professional norms on the one hand and congressional committee oversight on the other. In contrast, vertical linkages in redistributive agencies are more likely to be internal and hierarchical (see Table 6). The relatively flat hierarchy has a double apex corresponding to the dual administration of functional and managerial authority.

The Redistributive Agency Model

Redistributive agencies maintain and manipulate categories of human beings. Their rules or the rules for which they are responsible affect society on a larger scale than any others. And although it is true that all rules discriminate, rules of redistributive agencies discriminate along broad class lines. As a matter of formal policy as well as informal politics, redistributive rules discriminate between the money providers and the service demanders, e.g., rich versus poor, young and employed versus old and unemployed, savers versus consumers.

This responsibility for making or maintaining rules that cut broadly along class lines ought to be a determining factor in the organizational structure of redistributive agencies. The general political environment of these agencies is likely to be stable, but for reasons far different from those stabilizing distributive agencies. Redistributive agencies have the stability of careful balance of organized conflict among major class interests, where small changes at the margins threaten large shifts of advantage in the economy (e.g., a fraction of a percent in the discount rate; the change of a word in the definition of eligibility; a change of one item in the composition of the CPI). These factors contribute to a declassing of the agencies. Great stress is placed on having the best management at the top, including people and professions of high social status (e.g., high proportions of grands corps in French agencies), coupled with tight control on entry and conduct throughout the agency. These agencies are, relatively speaking, severed from society by heavy stress on recruitment at the bottom, low lateral entry, and internal, bureaucratic careers. Internal career life is emphasized even more by the practice of promoting to top management people who have had experience only at headquarters. Virtually every type of coordination will be utilized to keep the field units working consistently with central policies: these agencies are expected to be as rule-bound as regulatory agencies and as professionalized as distributive agencies, but as a result of internal careers, not common schooling. In addition, very narrow spans of control will be maintained: many units within divisions and bureaus, close supervision, few subordinates per superior, stress on record-keeping and clearance, and so on (see Table 6). In addition, there will tend to be heaviest stress on overhead methods, including pre-audit, post-audit, performance, and efficiency reports.

A picture of redistributive agencies would come closest to the classic, narrow, high-peaked pyramid. The sharpness comes from narrow spans of control, where one superior has a minimum number of subordinates. Rules keep discretion to a minimum, and the concern for consistency with the rules produces strong vertical linkages plus efforts to discourage horizontal linkages. The American pattern will have to be adjusted for the federalistic structure of its welfare programs, where state agencies may be operating as local units. In these agencies, even more stress is put on overhead controls. And, although they fail in real-world situations, top management in Washington is likely to produce a lot of evidence of effort to maintain vertical linkages and to discourage horizontal ones.

The Constituent Agency Model

Although least has been done empirically on constituent agencies, some patterns can be drawn from the logic of the scheme, from contrasts with the three other types, and from case studies in the published literature. The missions of these agencies come closest to maintenance of sovereignty, what the French call *agences régaliens*. There is minimal responsibility for making or implementing rules that pertain directly to citizen conduct or status. Rules of these agencies apply to other government agencies, whether these are rules of jurisdiction or operating rules about budgeting, purchasing, recruiting and promoting personnel, or writing contracts or conditions for payment and nonpayment of contracts.

For reasons of both function and tradition, agencies with constituent missions are most likely to live by the older ideal of the good administrator as a person of good breeding, good general education, and the ability to make decisions. Almost everything happens at headquarters, and there is not likely to be much hierarchy, although these agencies support hierarchy in all other agencies (see Table 6). And although managers in these agencies are given a great deal of discretion, there are strong vertical linkages. The difference is that these are less likely to be superior-subordinate linkages than ones of collegiality and trust extending beyond the agency chiefs to cabinet and chief executive. A pictorial rendering yields no pyramid: there are too many generals and too few privates. An approximation would be a diamond shape with lines of authority and communication indicating a network rather than a hierarchy. The network includes linkages to the other three types of agencies, over which constituent agencies hold their special type of authority either directly through their ability to withhold resources or indirectly through their special access to the chief executive and others at the highest political levels.

Conclusions: Comparative Studies of Policy and Administration

Let it be said forthrightly that these findings and hypotheses, being based on reanalysis of data produced from old and independent studies, are intended to serve only as the groundwork for a large new comparative study. These fragments of bone and fossil were sufficient as long as they permitted extension of the original argument that regimes through their established policies make their own politics. But extension to other phenomena as well as further confirmation of patterns already observed is essential if progress is to be made along theoretical, empirical, or practical lines.

As many as half the questions in the Darbel-Schnapper and Corson-Paul studies can be replicated. This means that the original surveys can be used as a pre-test as well as a basis for longitudinal analysis covering nearly twenty years. (The original interview schedules for both studies are available from the authors.)

It should be clear from earlier data and from the survey questions that the variables and methods to be utilized in such a study are simple and direct. Because the conventions of systematic empirical analysis of bureaucracy are not well established and the impressionistic work is very rich, it is essential that the variables stick close to sensory experience. For the same reason, the methods ought to be simple. And what makes simplicity possible is the presence of a theory. The most dynamic and relevant aspects of the analysis are inherent in the policy categorizations themselves. The arenas-of-power scheme has been widely utilized in the political science literature, and at the same time it has been criticized even by some of its users as being too difficult empirically. Much progress has in recent years been made on the definitional aspects of the theory, which should make it more useful empirically. No theory in political science has ever received more thorough published discussion and testing than this one prior to its application to systematic research. The time is ripe for application. Moreover, though the theory itself is closed as to its categories and the general nature of the hypotheses the research project is quite open to other approaches. The data drawn from the country surveys will be useful to political sociologists who are interested in mobility and the social backgrounds of modern functionaries. The data will be valuable to students of organization who approach them without an explicit theory. The data will be even more valuable to those who approach public agencies with a different policy theory or different sets of policy categories. One obvious comparison to make is between regulatory agencies and all others, ignoring any systematic distinction between the two. Another might be a comparison of characteristics as they are distributed between agencies that deal only in domestic policy and those that deal in foreign policy or foreign and defense policy. Within the broad area of regulatory policy, another set of comparisons can be made between departmental and independent regulatory agencies. The analytic possibilities, though not infinite, are certainly numerous enough to satisfy a wide variety of interests and, we hope, are valuable enough to justify foundation support in the United States and abroad.

APPENDIX A

Bureaus or Services in the Federal System Arranged According to Policy Area

Distributive Agencies

Department of Agriculture

Agricultural Research Service (Regulatory Division, Research Division)
Economic Research Service (Market Analysis, Low Income Program, Agricultural Economics)
Farmer Cooperative Service
Federal Crop Insurance Corporation
Federal Extension Service
Forest Service
National Agricultural Library
Office of Rural Areas Development
Rural Electrification Administration
Soil Conservation Service

Department of Commerce

Area Redevelopment Administration
Bureau of International Commerce
        Bureau of Public Roads
Bureau of Standards
Business and Defense Services Administration
Coast and Geodetic Survey
Maritime Administration
Office of Business Economics
Patent Office

97

Small Business Administration (Office of Investment, Office of Procurement and Technical Assistance, Office of General Counsel, Office of Economic Adviser)
Weather Bureau

Department of Health, Education and Welfare

National Institutes of Health
National Library of Medicine
St. Elizabeth's Hospital

Department of the Interior

Bureau of Commercial Fisheries
Bureau of Land Management
Bureau of Reclamation
National Park Service

Department of Labor

Bureau of Labor Standards
Bureau of Labor Statistics
Women's Bureau

Independent Agencies

Smithsonian Institution

Regulatory Agencies

Department of Agriculture

Agricultural Marketing Service
Commodity Exchange Authority
Stabilization and Conservation Service

Department of Health, Education and Welfare

Food and Drug Administration

Department of Justice

Antitrust Division
Bureau of Prisons
Frauds Section
Internal Security Division

Department of Transportation

Federal Aviation Administration

Department of the Treasury

Bureau of Narcotics

Independent Agencies

Civil Aeronautics Board
Federal Maritime Commission
Federal Power Commission
Federal Trade Commission
Interstate Commerce Commission
National Labor Relations Board
National Mediation Board
Securities and Exchange Commission
Subversive Activities Control Board

Redistributive Agencies

Department of Agriculture

Farm Credit Administration
Farmer's Home Administration

Department of Health, Education and Welfare

Bureau of Federal Credit Unions
Social Security Administration (Bureau of Hearings and Appeals, Bureau of
Old Age and Survivor's Insurance)
Welfare Administration (Children's Bureau, Office of Welfare Commissioner)

Department of Housing and Urban Development

Federal Housing Administration

Department of Labor

Bureau of Employment Security

Department of the Treasury

Bureau of Public Debt
Internal Revenue Service (Field Offices, National Office)

Independent Agencies

Federal Home Loan Bank Board (Division of Federal Home Loan Bank
Operations)
Veterans Administration

Constituent Agencies

Department of Agriculture

Departmental Administration (Office of Management Services, Office of
Information)
Office of Budget and Finance
Office of the General Counsel
Office of the Secretary
Statistical Reporting Services

Department of Commerce

Bureau of the Census
National Capital Planning Council
Office of the Assistant Secretary for Administration
Office of the General Counsel
Office of the Secretary
Undersecretary for Transportation (Research Office)
U.S. Travel Service

Department of Health, Education and Welfare

Bureau of State Service
Office of Education
Office of the General Counsel
Office of the Secretary
Office of the Surgeon General
Vocational Rehabilitation Administration

Department of Housing and Urban Development

Compliance Division
Office of Metropolitan Development
Office of Program Policy
Regional Director
Urban Renewal Administration

Department of the Interior

Office of the Secretary

Department of Justice

Lands Division (Indian Claims Section)
Office of the Deputy Attorney General
Office of Legal Counsel
Office of Pardon Attorney
Office of the Solicitor General
Tax Court of the U.S.
Tax Division (Assistant for Civil Trials)

Department of Labor

Executive Assistant to the Secretary
Office of the Solicitor

Department of the Post Office

Bureau of Facilities
Bureau of Finance
General Counsel
Office of the Deputy Postmaster General

Department of the Treasury

Bureau of Accounts
Bureau of Customs
Engraving and Printing
Office of the Secretary
Office of the Treasurer of the U.S.

Executive Office of the President

Bureau of the Budget (Office of Legislative Reference)

Independent Agencies

Civil Service Commission (Regional Director, Bureau of Recruiting and Examining, Bureau of Programs and Standards)
Commission on Civil Rights (Program Division)
General Services Administration (National Archives and Records Service, Transportation and Communications Service, Office of Finance and Administration)
Tariff Commission (Technical Service)

APPENDIX B

Ministries and *Directions* in the Government of France, Classified by the Mission of Each *Direction*

Constituent Agencies

	No. in Sample	
Cabinet (PM)		4
Corps d'Insp. et de Contrôle (PM)		1
Serv. rattachés au Cabinet (PM)		11
Dir. Gén. de l'Ad. (PM)		2
Sec. a l'Inf. (PM)		3
Cabinet (Outre-Mer)		4
Dir. du Personnel et des Serv. (Fin)		7
Comm. Con. Centrale (Fin)		1
Dir. du Budget (Fin)		16
Dir. des Relations Econ. (Fin)		17
Dir. de la Comptabilité (Fin)		8
Cabinet (Fin)		5
Cabinet (Ed)		2
Serv. rattachés au Sec. (Ed)		3
Dir. des Ens. Supérieurs (Ed)		5
Dir. de la Péd. des Ensei. (Ed)		5
Dir. du Pers. d'Ensei. (Ed)		4
Corps d'Insp. et de Contrôle (Ed)		27
Cabinet (Ag)		1
Dir. Gén. des Etudes (Ag)		8
Corps d'Insp. et de Contrôle (Ag)		2
Cabinet (PTT)		1
Dir. du Personnel (PTT)		1
Dir. des Bâtiments et des Trans. (PTT)		7
Corps d'Insp. et de Contrôle (PTT)		5
Cabinet (Soc)		2

NOTE: This listing is for agencies in 1966–67. It is not an up-to-date guide to French national government.

Serv. rattachés au Cabinet (Soc)	5
Dir. de l'Admin. Gén. (Soc)	3
Cabinet (Vets)	3
Dir. de l'Admin. (Vets)	3
Serv. de la Pro. Civile (Int)	1
Serv. des Transmissions (Int)	3
Dir. Gén. des Affaires (Int)	8
Dir. Gén. des Collectivités (Int)	11
Cabinet (Int)	5
Corps d'Insp. et de Contrôle (Int)	3
Cabinet (Eq)	2
Serv. des Affaires Econ. (Eq)	1
Serv. de Cooperation Tech. (Eq)	1
Dir. du Personnel de la Compta. (Eq)	1
Dir. des Aménagements Fonciers (Eq)	3
Cabinet (Trsp)	6
Dir. du Pers. et de l'Admin. (Av)	1
Services rattachés (Av)	2
Serv. des Affaires Econ. (TrPu)	2
Dir. des Ports Maritimes (TrPu)	2
Cabinet (Loge)	2
Dir. de l'Admin. Gén. (Loge)	1
Dir. de la Lég. et du Con. (Loge)	2
Corps de Contrôle d'Insp. (Loge)	9
Cabinet (Ind)	2
Dir. de l'Admin. Gén. (Ind)	1
Dir. des Mines (Ind)	9
Dir. des Carburants (Ind)	7
Dir. du Gaz et de l'Elec. (Ind)	4
Corps d'Insp. et de Contrôle (Ind)	6
Cabinet (Etr)	1
Cabinet (Jus)	7
Serv. Judiciares (Jus)	5
Admin. Gén. et Equip. (Jus)	10
Conseil d'Etat (Jus)	28
Cabinet (J&S)	2
Administration (J&S)	1
Dir. Gén. de la Recherche (Ref)	3

Distributive Agencies

Dir. de la Documen. (PM)	1
Radio–TV (PM)	3
Dir. Gén. des Arts et Lettres (Cult)	1
Dir. de l'Architecture (Cult)	2
Dir. des Musées de France (Cult)	3

Inst. Nat'l de la Statistique (Fin)	40
Dir. de l'Equip. Scolaire (Ed)	2
Dir. Gén. de la Production (Ag)	11
Dir. de l'Espace Rural (Ag)	7
Office Nat'l des Forêts (Ag)	4
Dir. Gén. de l'Enseign. (Ag)	6
Dir. Gén. des Postes (PTT)	4
Dir. Gén. des Télécomm. (PTT)	9
Dir. de l'Equip. San. (Soc)	2
I.N.S.E.R.M. (Soc)	2
Dir. des Statuts et Services (Vets)	6
Dir. des Routes (Eq)	2
Dir. des Ports et Voies Navi. (Eq)	1
Dir. des Bases Aériennes (Av)	3
Dir. des Indus. du Fer (Ind)	2
Dir. des Indus. Chimiques (Ind)	5
Dir. des Indus. Diverses (Ind)	1
Dir. des Indus. Mécaniques (Ind)	3
Equipement (J&S)	2

Regulatory Agencies

Centre Nat'l de la Cinéma (Cult)	1
Dir. des Assurances (Fin)	12
Dir. des Affaires Commerciales (Fin)	1
Dir. du Commerce Intérieur (Fin)	12
Dir. de la Sûreté Nat'l (Int)	9
Dir. des Transp. Aériens (Av)	5
Dir. de la Naviga. Aérienne (Av)	3
Dir. de l'Admin. Gén. (MM)	1
Dir. des Pêches Maritimes (MM)	2
Dir. de la Construction (Loge)	5
Dir. de la Propriété Ind. (Ind)	4
Dir. des Affaires Criminelles (Jus)	5
Admin. Pénitentiaire (Jus)	7
Educ. Surv. (Jus)	5
Dir. des Sports (J&S)	1
Corps d'Insp. et de Contrôle (Soc)	5
Dir. des Routes et de la Circ. (TrPu)	2
Dir. de Transp. Terr. (PTT)	6

Redistributive Agencies

Dir. des Territoires (OM)	5
Comm. du Plan d'Equipe (Ref)	9
Dir. du Tresor (Fin)	15

Dir. de la Dette Publique (Fin)	3
Dir. de la Prévision (Fin)	9
Corps d'Insp. et de Contrôle (Fin)	57
Dir. Gén. des Impôts (Fin)	22
Dir. Gén. de la Population (Soc)	3
Dir. Gén. de la Sec. Soc. (Soc)	6
Dir. des Pensions (Vets)	2

Multifunctional Agencies (Unclassifiable)

Dir. des Douanes et Droits (Fin)	4
Dir. Gén. du Travail (Soc)	5
Dir. de la Flotte de Comm. (MM)	2
Dir. des Affaires Civiles et du Sceau (Jus)	4
Serv. de la Jeunesse et l'Educ. (J&S)	1

COMMENT: *John Ferejohn*

I am of the generation of students of political science who grew up with Lowi's maxim that policy causes politics, and I have spent a fair amount of time trying to classify policies according to various schemes proposed since Lowi's initial effort almost twenty years ago. Like many in my cohort, I found Lowi's idea attractive and the classification scheme provocative but could never really decide where to draw the lines separating the categories. Besides, the agencies that were of most interest to me (especially the older ones) always seemed to administer several different types of policy. However, Lowi's theory does seem to contain an important perspective on public policy formation, even if many of us have trouble applying this perspective.

Since I do not pretend fully to understand all the arguments made in the paper, I will start with a statement of my comprehension of it. In fact, my grasp is weakest right at the start. I do not really see the sense in which modern political science can be said to be stateless or to ignore the state. There are, to be sure, perspectives that have risen out of Marxist or sociological theories which take state action to be determined completely by economic or social structure. Such approaches, not surprisingly, are characteristic of a variety of interlopers to political science, from Floyd Hunter to Gary Becker. Political scientists have resisted these perspectives with some degree of success, and I suspect that if there is a disciplinary consensus, it is that political institutions possess a good deal of autonomy at least in the short run. Indeed, if there is one major theme of studies of American policymaking institutions since *Who Governs,* it is that the scope for political leadership is broad and that leaders possess a great deal of discretion within the institutional structures of decision. This is, in fact, thought by some to be a source of our failures in predicting and explaining the behavior of political leaders. I do not know whether the complex of policymaking institutions constitutes a state. But, at the very least, these institutions and the social processes that evolve within them appear to possess powerful internal dynamics that inhibit their direction by external social or economic forces.

Lowi is saying more than that governmental action is at least partly determined by internal institutional dynamics. He claims that the choice of type of governmental activity in some way determines the resulting evolution of the political and administrative structures that grow up around the activity. In other words, regulatory politics is different from distributive politics just because of the differences between the tasks. He has gone even further in this paper: the structure of a regulatory agency, he says, is likely to be predictably different from the structure of an agency engaged in distributive policy, for the same reasons. In other words, the structure of institutions is determined at least in part by characteristics of the policies they administer. By now, no doubt partly due to the impact of Lowi's own work, this point is widely accepted in political science. Without much prior explanation, scholars of politics have been writing books and articles with titles like "The Politics of Regulation" (or Distribution or Redistribution). The implication is that a policy area carries its unique politics with it.

One might think that at this point Lowi would attempt to give an argument (or a theory) about the logic of these connections. He does not, at least not here. Instead, his method is empirical. He tries to classify agencies in France and the United States according to his (somewhat expanded) scheme and then tries to see what regularities emerge. He then moves from these observations to formulate hypotheses about the effects of policy on agency structure.

The salient characteristics of policies are supposed to be two: whether the principal actions of the agencies are Primary or Secondary Rules; and whether these rules work on individual agents (people or firms, etc.) or through the environment of conduct. I confess to being vague on these distinctions but they appear to mean the following: Primary Rules impose obligations on actors under threat of sanctions; Secondary Rules confer power or wealth. If the rules work on individual agents, they either regulate behavior or distribute benefits; if they work on the environment of conduct they either require that agencies recognize certain classes of rights or statuses of individuals or they require that certain agencies recognize certain rights or statuses of other agencies. Table 1 is intended to summarize this idea.

Lowi's thesis is that agencies that are in the business of administering regulatory policies (Primary Rules imposed on individual conduct) will tend to take on particular structural and behavioral characteristics. For example, they will tend to have highly specialized subunits, to have high-status administrators, not to have a strongly defined chain of command, and to exhibit central substantive review. These propositions and others like them are supposed to have logical connections and not merely to be gleaned from historical experience, even though they were apparently arrived at inductively.

This is the point at which the paper seems sketchiest. When Lowi asserts that a certain type of agency ought to exhibit a certain characteristic, I can usually see some reasons—after the fact—why this might be the case. But I do not know how to use the theory on my own. I do not understand how to deduce from policy characteristics to agency structure or behavior, or to the structure of politics. He presents an argument that has connective statements of the following form: "This requires at minimum that . . ." (p. 85) and "This leads to . . ." (p. 86). I understand the words, but I just do not understand what they mean.

The remainder of the paper is dedicated to arguing that it is possible to categorize agencies by their organic statutes. I remain somewhat skeptical about the possibility of doing this in a convincing way, for several reasons. First, at least in old agencies, the mission may well have changed. For example, for the first 130 years of its existence the mission of the Corps of Engineers was to promote navigability of inland waterways. It has had that mission enlarged a number of times to include flood control, wildlife preservation, and outdoor recreation, among other purposes. In addition, it has sometimes been given regulatory powers to enforce pollution legislation. Second, I am confused by some of the operational procedures. For example, in Table 2 Lowi says that if a statute creates an agency it is necessarily constituent. But many organic statutes create agencies which would be classed elsewhere using other criteria in the scheme. In fact, Table 2 does not seem to define a partition of statutes or agencies: the categories appear to be neither mutually exclusive nor collectively exhaustive. On the other hand, the proof of the pudding is in the

108   JOHN FEREJOHN

eating, and Lowi says that the scheme has been successfully applied to the classification of French and American organic statutes. While I might have some quibbles with certain aspects of the classification, it may be that some people with enough training (or just enough intelligence) will be able to classify agencies reliably.

As I indicated at the beginning of my remarks, I am attracted by Lowi's theory. I believe that it captures important aspects of political behavior that are missed by other schemes and that it forces us to pay close attention to the fact that when a government decides what policies to pursue it is, in a sense, remaking itself and the political forces that surround it. This valuable insight is missed by those coming from the neo-Marxist orientation and by many economists. Another way to make the same point is to say that if government is large and relatively inert, nongovernmental units will tend to take it as a part of the natural environment and adjust their own structures and behaviors to it rather than conversely.

But two further questions arise. First, given that the choice of policy has a variety of structural and political implications, why (and how) does a government decide to undertake a specific policy? Second, when the state decides to undertake a policy, does it specify enough about the means by which that policy is to be pursued to entail the classification of the agency in Lowi's scheme?

The first question is, to me, most fundamental. I argued earlier that political scientists largely accept Lowi's maxim at present. I suspect that a great many thoughtful political actors would as well. I think it is quite likely that congressmen are aware that enacting a regulatory statute is characteristically and predictably different from passing an appropriations bill to distribute subsidies. They see different sorts of people in the two settings, and different sorts of concerns are expressed. But if they are aware of at least part of the connection between policy and politics, do they take it into account in any way in choosing how to treat a particular problem? If these effects are anticipated, Lowi's argument about the exogeneity of policy may be rather seriously compromised.

One example that comes to mind is that of water pollution control. The 1972 Water Pollution Act embodied two distinct approaches to pollution control: one was regulatory and the other involved the use of subsidies (construction funds for treatment plants and sewage transport). Interviews with participants indicated that characteristic legislative patterns emerged in the debate on this legislation and that political actors were fairly well aware that the different parts of the program would confront different political realities. As is well known, the Senate was interested mostly in the regulatory approach to pollution control, while the House focused mostly on enacting a subsidy program. I suspect that members of the two bodies anticipated some of the implications of the two different programs and that their preferences may have been systematically determined.

Lowi's theory, then, seems to have implications about what sorts of activities the state will undertake which he has not tried to work out. If he were to agree that political actors anticipate the relationship between policy and politics, state action could no longer seem to be entirely exogenous. Unless Lowi believes that political actors are unusually insensitive to the consequences of their own acts, I believe that he should be prepared to accept this implication.

My second point is somewhat more narrowly focused. If Congress decides that a certain problem (say, water pollution) required a federal approach, to what extent does its action determine the policy instruments to be employed in treating the problem? To be sure, the 1972 Water Pollution Act ran to 200 pages and was very specific as to which tasks the agency should undertake, what deadlines were to be imposed, and what criteria should be applied. Other legislation is less specific. Congress sometimes confers a mission on an agency in such a way that the specifics of the approach are left completely open. And even when this is not the case, agencies sometimes try to redefine their missions in ways that allow them to make use of regulatory instruments (if they are subsidy-oriented to start with) or subsidies (if they are regulatory). One example of this can be seen in the attempts of the Corps of Engineers to gain control over the regulation of land use in flood plains. If Lowi's theory is correct, these agency attempts might very well have significant effects on the subsequent political environment within which the agency must operate and on the structure of the agency itself. And, to repeat my previous point, these effects may be anticipated, with varying consequences, by agency leaders.

These remarks are not intended to suggest that Lowi's approach to the study of agency structure is without promise. On the contrary, I believe that there may well be systematic differences among agencies that fall in different parts of Lowi's classification, and I think it is important to understand these differences. I have, however, tried to point out that some very great problems of implementation may be entailed in this approach. The problems are of two general sorts: first, it may not be possible to perform the classification (either of agencies or of statutes) in a satisfactory manner; second, and more fundamentally, to the extent that the proposition is true (that policy determines politics/structure/behavior), this may tend to be taken into account by actors in such a way that the composition of state activity can no longer be thought of as autonomous in any serious sense.

Lowi's scheme promises to allow us to say some things about the characteristics of the politics and administration of regulation. It suggests that there may be some lawlike connection between the type of policy entrusted to a particular agency and the structure of the agency itself. Then, via the maxim that who wills the end wills the means, we may discern a connection between the state's choice of activities and its political and administrative characteristics.

4

On Regulation and Legal Process

Lawrence M. Friedman

Regulation means different things in different contexts. Without straining the English language, it can cover all attempts by authority to control behavior. In this sense, laws that set minimum ages for voting, getting married, or owning a gun are examples of regulation. The trouble with so broad a definition is that it makes regulation more or less coextensive with the whole legal system—an unwieldy topic. But at the core of public debate about regulation is concern with regulation of business or, put less narrowly, economic behavior.

Regulation, even in this reduced sense, is not the same as administrative law or administrative process. An important point to remember is that an economic activity can be regulated by a court, a policeman, the President, or a mayor, just as it can be regulated by an administrative agency. It is also important to remember that the modern state has much more than business under its regulatory control. Welfare administration (not usually called regulation) is a tissue of rules about economic activity (or inactivity). So is the law of theft, for that matter.

In practice, debates about regulation involve discussion of administrative law. This is because detailed, continuous monitoring of economic processes is beyond the capacity of legislatures (at least according to the legislatures themselves), and implies, in the modern world, boards, agencies, and commissions of some sort to do the work.

Regulation is, in general, a matter of rules. The rules come from various sources, take various forms, and operate at various levels. Both the form and the level can be important. A used-car dealer has

The author wishes to thank Roger Noll, Paul Brest, and Robert L. Rabin for their very valuable comments on an earlier draft.

a better crack at influencing zoning practice in Omaha than at influencing the FTC. Civil rights lawyers attacked segregation in federal court, not on the level of the city council of Jackson, Mississippi.

Presumably, form can also change the effect of a rule. There are rules that are flat and objective; others are broad, vague statements of principle. Some are narrowly detailed, others are sweeping and general. The Food and Drug Administration's regulations about frozen cherry pie, for example, allow no more than 15 percent of the cherries in any pie, by actual count, to be "blemished with scab, hail injury, skin discoloration, scar tissue or other abnormality"; skin discoloration is a "blemish" if it has "an aggregate area exceeding that of a circle nine thirty-seconds of an inch in diameter."[1] On the other hand, the original Interstate Commerce Act of 1887 laid down the rule that all fares and freight charges had to be "reasonable and just," with no definition of these terms.[2]

Generally speaking, broad, general rules are more likely to be found in governing statutes than in administrative regulations. Congress often sticks to basic commands and leaves it to the boards and commissions to put flesh on the bones. The Pure Food and Drug Act, for example, talks about food that is misbranded or adulterated; the FDA must fill in details. On the other hand, in many cases a good deal of detail comes prepackaged in the statutes. Congress, for example, does not leave it to the FDA to decide how to label foods that contain saccharin. The statute sets out the exact words to be put on the label (but the Secretary of HHS may revise the label if "necessary to reflect the current state of knowledge about saccharin").[3] Behind these choices of form and the level at which detail is inserted into general command, lies, in each case, a particular conflict of interests or principles. The user of the rule, or the person subject to it, may not much care at what level it became specific, or whether it came from a statute, executive order, act of Congress, or regulation. Sometimes, though not always, the source does make a difference: it affects the way the rule is administered or the influence users have over its application.

The range of regulation is vast. So vast, that one wonders whether regulation (or administrative process) can really be treated as a single subject. Regulation may mean anything from control of conglomerate mergers to the number of bruises on frozen cherries. Agencies range from great Washington boards and commissions through

1. 21 CFR Section 152.126.
2. 24 Stats. 379, ch. 104, sec. 1, 1887.
3. 21 U.S.C. Sec. 343 (a) (o).

state boards that license plumbers and watchmakers all the way down to local zoning boards and school districts.

What they all have in common is the process of making or applying rules and, more generally, being part of the same legal system. Now, *legal system* itself means different things in different societies. In our society time has chiseled certain special meanings into the concept of law. For one thing, regulation is not and cannot be independent of the Bill of Rights, the Fourteenth Amendment, American federalism, or even common-law traditions. All are part of the background in this particular society.

Social notions of what the rule of law means permeate the whole legal system—most definitely including the regulatory enterprise. To understand the forms and limits of regulation we have to understand our own legal culture. Also, regulation is embedded in a system that boasts (if that is the word) an army of 600,000 lawyers. This is far more than in almost any other country, both in absolute terms and in numbers of lawyers per head. Our lawyers are all trained in much the same way, and perhaps (this is open to some question) they share certain quirks of mind, certain habits of thought, tiny synapses developed in or out of law school, which may affect how they think and work. Posner (1969), for one, blames lawyers for certain sins of the regulatory process: lawyers are ignorant of economic principles, neglect efficiency, and, because of their training, overemphasize "formal processes . . . and . . . considerations of fairness and equity." There have been even more violent attacks. Silberman (1978) goes so far as to ask whether "lawyering" is not about to "strangle democratic capitalism."

Research on this issue, as opposed to speculation, has been quite sparse. There are some enticing theoretical grounds for doubting whether lawyers can be blamed for what is wrong with the regulatory process (Friedman and Macaulay, 1977, pp. 926–31). The basic point is simple. The legal system is the product of social forces, rather than the other way around. What makes regulation—form and substance—is pressure: pressure groups, political and economic activity. Lawyers are at most responsible for details. They are only middlemen, servants of power and authority.

But the army of lawyers is a national fact. Another fact is the system of courts, which plays a major role in producing law and in monitoring regulation—its forms, its processes, its limits. By and large, the language of law, lawyers, and the courts is not economic; rather, it is moral, ideological, and procedural. To this extent Posner is correct. But the ideology is a mirror of social thought, not the naked construction of lawyers.

The subject of law and regulation is depressingly large; there is no way I can do it justice. I will confine myself to a few points which will,

I hope, shed light on the subject and which tend to get lost in the hubbub of debate. One theme is stressed: law is not merely a system for efficient allocation. It reflects all sorts of social impulses and ideas. Regulation in the United States is regulation through law or, specifically, through rules of law, and is administered by men and women of law. But law is not autonomous; it is a reflection of society. Legal control means control of the economy through social norms of justice and morality.

Law as Economics and Some Alternative Functions

The legal system is a living organism with many facets and functions. In a way, it is a gigantic rationing system, one of society's ways to allocate goods and resources (Friedman, 1975). The system issues commands, grants and withholds benefits, and tells people what they can and cannot do. Every aspect of law is an allocation. This is even true of social control itself, the maintenance of law and order. Rules of law define rather strictly who can use force and under what circumstances. Through the legal system, the state collects money from some people and gives money to others. It may do this directly by taxing and subsidizing, or it may do it more indirectly through rules about tort liability, patent infringement, nuisance, breach of contract, will contests, and all the rest. The legal system creates and defines a free market zone and sets out limitations on that market. It explains what can and cannot be the subject of contract and of private ownership. It defines property rights, and it extends guarantees to contract and property as so defined. For example, it may outlaw gambling contracts, forbid the private ownership of giant pandas, or ban the sale of children on the open market. It establishes money, issues marriage and dog licenses, grants divorces, awards child custody, ends the destruction of historic buildings, punishes embezzlers and bank robbers, and so on. All these activities benefit some people and burden others. They set up or reinforce a social structure and regulate the ways it can change.

The allocative aspect of all this is plain, and because the economic effect of law is so palpable, it follows that one can subject the working rules of law to economic analysis and handle them with the tools of this trade. The point has not escaped either lawyers or economists. A major literature has grown up in recent years. The literature ranges over many fields of law, from antitrust to burglary (Manne, 1975; Posner, 1977), but it does have some common themes. What binds much of it together is an agreed-on standard against which to judge the legal system—its output, its impact, the doctrines that make up its body and bones. This is the standard of economic efficiency.

The results are mixed, hard to sum up, and in any event beyond the scope of this paper. There is also a large subliterature on regulation, which is by now probably big enough to fill a good-sized room. Some of it is favorable to regulation, but much is hostile, expressing the notion that regulation, in general, is inefficient, wrongheaded, and wasteful, that the free market is on the whole vastly preferable. A typical example is Michael E. Levine's article on air transportation (1965): "Is Regulation Necessary?" The answer (with regard to ticket prices in particular) is an emphatic no. The political system ultimately came to agree.

Other papers in this collection will pursue this theme further. I am more concerned with explaining the nature of the beast than with praising or blaming it or, for that matter, killing it. To this end I make two general points.

First, the legal system, though it is a rationing or allocative system, is also part and parcel of a political system. Its structure and process cannot be disentangled from the sticky gum of politics. This much is obvious. Second, law is part of the normative system of society. It is indelibly stamped with what people think about right and wrong. In every society laws are wrapped up in cultural and ethical values, and there is no way to disengage law from morals and traditions any more than from politics. This, too, is obvious. Yet it is surprising how often and how easily we lose sight of the obvious.

In a society like ours, laws are made in a noisy, shouting, crowded way. They are born in a kind of mad bazaar, with groups crying out and demanding to be heard. Generally speaking, these groups assert two different kinds of claim. Some are claims that they consider claims of *right*. Other demands call for actions which would increase wealth but which are not pressed forward as rights. We can call these claims *interests*. (A right, of course, can also involve money.) The difference between rights and interests is not a real-world difference but a difference in the way arguments are framed (and sometimes, too, in the way people feel about them). It is a good argument against a claim of interest that it costs too much or that the costs outweigh the benefits. These are not good arguments against claims of right.

Of course, the two kinds of claims overlap quite seriously. Almost any claim of right can be rephrased as a claim of interest. Economists specialize in doing just that, but lawyers are paid to dress interests in the clothing of rights. Nevertheless, there is no point in being completely cynical about the differences between the two. For now, it is enough to note that moral and political arguments constantly compete with economic ones for attention. This is the daily bread of government and the raw material of policy.

To a weary policymaker it must seem all but impossible to reach rational decisions, with all the noise and the shouting, the grabbing and posturing. And for a long time it struck many thoughtful people as a grave failing that politics should interfere with the solution of technical questions, especially in the management of so delicate and immense a machine as the economy. Anyway, politics is for many people a dirty word. Early in the twentieth century and through the days of the New Deal, this attitude was reflected in the dreams of the technocrats: the hope of divorcing process from politics. Allied to this was the idea that legislatures were incapable of dealing consistently and continuously with complicated problems. They had to be handled administratively (Gellhorn, 1941; Landis, 1938). If one must regulate the economy at all, experts and specialists should do it coolly and rationally. Lay down general principles—which can be political—and then let those who know the field, whose judgment is scientific and impartial, carry them out. In this way the public interest will be served. These general ideas were basic to the philosophy of public administration, and they helped legitimate the administrative state.

For a long time there was deep faith in administrative process. Indeed, regulation in this form seemed a natural response to social change and new technology. Agencies, as Gellhorn (1941, p. 5) put it, were not created "to satisfy an abstract governmental theory, but to cope with problems of recognized public concern." He cites an early federal example, steamboat inspection (1838), and reminds us that the "growth of steam navigation," not a "predisposition toward administrative agencies," lay behind it.

In the last hundred years or so, regulation through administrative agencies has grown dramatically. The Interstate Commerce Commission Act (1887) was a landmark. Other agencies followed in due course—the Federal Trade Commission, for example, in 1914. During the New Deal there was a great leap forward. The Securities and Exchange Commission, the National Labor Relations Board, and many others got their start in this period.

This eruption of government by commission did not go unchallenged. There was vigorous legal debate over whether it was good to delegate so much power to the President and his agencies. In the great case of *Schechter Poultry Corp.* v. *United States*,[4] for example, the

4. 295 U.S. 495, 1935.

Supreme Court struck down the National Industrial Recovery Act of 1933, which it denounced as delegation run riot.

In its struggles with the New Deal, the Supreme Court won a battle or two but lost the war. Roosevelt carried forty-six states in 1936, and it was clear that the New Deal was no flash in the pan. The President's infamous court-packing plan never got off the ground; nonetheless, the Supreme Court shifted slightly to the left and ceased to raise objections to New Deal programs. The key case was *National Labor Relations Board* v. *Jones & Laughlin Steel Corp.*[5] Here the court, speaking through Chief Justice Hughes, upheld the National Labor Relations Act of 1935 and its creature, the National Labor Relations Board. Roosevelt replaced dying and retiring justices in the next few years. Never again during the New Deal nor for years beyond did the Court stand in the way of delegation to agencies. Only recently has the nondelegation doctrine revived ever so slightly.[6] Essentially, since 1937 there has been no serious legal barrier to economic regulation in scope or substance, and no serious barrier to the expansion of administrative law. On this basic point there is still no turning back.

Regulation in a complex society is necessarily part of a political process. The New Deal came and went. Much of what it set out to do was done and appears to be permanent. But its own successes undermined some of the premises on which it was built. Our generation has no memory of the struggle to pump power into a weak central government. We have lost most of our zest to curtail or kill private markets or to rein in big business, which once seemed so blind, so inhuman, so arrogant a force. To many people the government is just as bloated and arrogant, if not more so. The struggle *for* federal power seems as archaic as Andrew Jackson's war against the Bank of the United States or the tariff disputes that bored generations of college students. Moreover, people who grew up after World War II are not frightened by stories of the Great Depression. They are not afraid that breadlines and Hoovervilles will come back or that veterans will sell apples on the street if the federal government loses power.

This change in attitude has enormous effects on the politics of regulation and hence on its *legal* structure. It makes regulation more vulnerable and also more complicated. This is because it was faith in administrative process, faith that agencies were sensible, fair and skilled in their jobs, that insulated the agencies from gross political process. Present-day administrative regulation is once more in the thick of politics. And this inevitably carries with it exposure to legal process—to court cases, for example.

5. 301 U.S. 1, 1937.

6. See, e.g., Rehnquist concurring in *Industrial Union Dpt., AFL–CIO* v. *American Petroleum Institute,* 488 U.S. 607, 686–87, 1980.

The movement to get government off our backs and to deregulate does not necessarily bring about less regulation. Government, in the aggregate, keeps right on growing, and the number of rules grows along with it. Congress has neither time, patience, nor will to decide how battered a cherry has to be before it is labeled blemished. That is and will continue to be a question for the FDA. But the FDA cannot simply lay down rules and make them stick. There is a long road of process in between. With regard to some other kinds of agency decisions, neither at the beginning nor at the end are there flat rules. Rather, the agencies have to decide whether this or that is within vague guidelines or, all things considered, in the public interest. More and more this comes to mean that the important decisions are made at the end of the chain of process and that many steps along the way mix politics, legal process, and technical know-how. Consider, for example, how an agency would handle the question of where to put a dam, jetport, or power plant: notices, hearings, reports, and the rest, ending, often, in protracted litigation. This is not the administrative process that was envisioned in the thirties.

Businesses and consumer groups always lobbied and jockeyed for position before administrative agencies. There was always some threat of action: pressure, argument, logic, litigation, emotion, and votes were always called into play. Never did actual administration measure up to the technocratic dream. In the years since the 1930s, however, the process has gotten more and more wound up in procedures. This tends to convert regulation into nearly the opposite of what it was originally intended to be. Administrative regulation is no longer the way to make plans and decisions more quickly and efficiently than court or legislature could. Rather, the process is in some ways the reverse—not out of sloth, to be sure, but in the name of participation, access, and fairness.

In other words, the regulatory process was once conceived of as an objective, effective way to fix problems caused by imperfections in the market. It once meant removal from politics. This was the New Deal style of regulation: technocratic, insulated from Congress and free from judicial meddling (Ackerman and Hassler, 1980). After all, Congress and the courts were amateurs, technically speaking. What did they know about industrial relations, securities markets, unemployment insurance, or unfair competition? The commissioners and their staffs would have the know-how. As for the courts, they were political in a hidden, tricky way, and conservative to boot.

Now in the new, finer grade of political consciousness, nothing can be done without notices and hearings, without the public's voice or the voice of those who act in its name. The administrative process has become, more and more, a method for fixing *political* imperfections, that is, a form of governing which is more open to public participation than elected bodies or bureaucracies would normally be. And the process includes more judicial meddling, not less. Obviously, there are many reasons for this change. But surely one of them is a general loss of faith in government, experts, and technocracy. If we trusted city hall and legislatures, if we trusted the agencies and their experts, we would not need to go over these issues time and again. Between the New Deal and today something happened to public trust. Maybe government lied once too often; maybe experts claimed too much and delivered too little. At any rate, there are enough cynics, doubters, and militants around to guarantee a constantly boiling pot of protests, class-action suits, injunctions, and other legal moves.

Fairness and Morality

Curiously enough, while faith in something called government has declined, there is still a great deal of faith in the courts and in the idea of law. Indeed, judicial review presupposes this faith. The courts will do justice even when nobody else will, and their brand of justice will be free from the grosser forms of politics and economic calculation. Scholars may call these ideas myths, but they are pervasive nonetheless.

This brings us to a second theme which will also strike most observers as obvious, yet somehow it too is often lost in the shuffle: legal arrangements carry moral weight. I am not referring here to philosophical assessments of the wisdom, justice, and value of arrangements. Rather, I mean what people who use and have a voice in the system think about its fairness and good sense. It is a fact that people consider certain arrangements fair and others unfair. It is hard to get an accurate account of these facts, but they are facts all the same and must be contended with.

The point is a general one. The legal system codifies a set of norms. These norms can be analyzed in terms of their actual impact; they can be assessed as efficient or inefficient. But norms are more than bearers of allocative outcomes. They have symbolic meanings (Gusfield, 1967). They come up out of a deep sense of right and wrong. The entire legal system is a concretization of the normative structure of society. The regulatory part of it is no exception.

To begin with, different psychological and moral labels attach to different structural arrangements. The labels are extremely important, both politically and legally. Take, for example, the infamous

Brannan Plan, hatched during the Truman administration. Truman's Secretary of Agriculture conceived the plan as a way out of a particular nightmare. Agricultural price supports encouraged overproduction; many tons of commodities went into storage. Meanwhile, the consumer paid inflated prices for food. Why not let the market set prices and buy off the farmers with direct cash payments whenever the market price did not give him a fair return? This seemed a reasonable solution, all things considered. But farm organizations screamed and yelled. Perhaps some of them suspected that it would be easier politically to get rid of the payments than to end price supports (which might be true). Yet they also used such scare words as *socialism* and *subsidization* (Truman, 1956). Farmers did not want welfare or government handouts. Of course, price supports were just as much handouts or welfare or subsidies as the Brannan Plan payouts. But there was a crucial difference in the feeling attached to the programs. The Brannan Plan foundered and sank in a storm of protest.

Every major Western society is a welfare state, yet nobody likes to be on welfare. Nothing seems to be more critical, oddly enough, than the label attached to programs of benefits. Thus the popularity of social insurance: programs which people at least think they are paying for. For farmers, there was a world of difference between earning a fair price and getting welfare. This difference was what killed the Brannan Plan.

As many economists see it, business regulation in its present form tends to be highly inefficient. Society as a whole would be better off with less regulation; some agencies ought to be abolished, others drastically modified. Yet getting rid of inefficient regulation is no easy task. Why is this so? Joskow and Noll (1981) give one answer, which is essentially structural. But, as the Brannan Plan shows, there is still another reason.

According to Joskow and Noll, if we change an arrangement, some people are bound to lose in the process, even when, on balance, there will be more gains than losses. Thus the public should be ahead if we get rid of price supports. Farmers will be worse off and will resist. In theory, there is a remedy. If gains exceed losses, gainers should be able to pay off losers and still show a profit. Everybody will be better off and the losers will not resist the change in arrangements. It is when no provision is made for payoffs that losers fight back to avoid losing. Legislatures naturally try to ameliorate these losses, even if it means forfeiting the chance to achieve an efficient long-run equilibrium.

Joskow and Noll have put their finger on an important structural barrier to deregulation. It is hard to contrive the right compensation scheme for paying off losers. The structural problem is soluble in theory but quite sticky practically in a wide range of situations. Payoffs, in other words, do not work.

The second objection goes beyond structure. Payoffs may be morally objectionable as well as difficult to administer. Two arrangements can be economically exact equivalents but socially distinct. This is the lesson of the Brannan Plan. The problem there was deeply political. But the politics, in part, flowed out of norms not easily accounted for in ordinary economic analysis. To explain them we have to look at the social meaning of legal arrangements.

The legal system, reflecting (perhaps influencing) common, deep-seated ways of looking at the world, is organized in terms of rights and duties. Many rights are inalienable in theory or (more important) in the way people think about them. Congress could not possibly pass a law auctioning off the right to kill an innocent person, no matter how high the price. This is an extreme case. But a good deal of what economists regard as efficient, the public finds immoral. There is resistance to the idea of buying the right to pollute or giving out a license to pollute. The director of OSHA, Thorne G. Auchter, with a mandate to devise cost-effective rules, felt compelled to say that he would not "put a dollar value on human life," though of course there is no way to avoid it.[7]

A good example of the point lies in the history of the military draft. During the Civil War it was possible to buy one's way out of the army. Under a law of 1863 a man liable to be drafted could pay money instead or furnish an acceptable substitute.[8] If it is worth $5,000 to me to stay out of the army, and you are willing to go in at that price, arguably we are both better off if we make such a deal. This seems elementary, yet the old draft system has been totally abandoned; it is utterly unthinkable today. Why? Because it is "unfair." Mostly, the poor would serve in the army and the rich would buy their way out. So sharp a division between life and death, so crassly bought and sold, does not sit well in this century. Of course, we allow all sorts of social inequalities. The rich can buy much that the poor cannot. But modern war is total war; it requires general mobilization, a spirit of patriotism, and at least the appearance of universal sacrifice. Governments feel, rightly or wrongly, that war demands a kind of national spirit. Under these circumstances the old system is too immoral to survive. Of course the draft in the World Wars, in the Korean War, and in Vietnam was in its own way profoundly unfair. But the inequities were less blatant and overt, more carefully legitimated.

7. *New York Times*, 13 July 1981, p. 8, col. 1, National Edition.
8. 12 U.S. Stats. 731, 733, ch. 75, Section 13, Act of 3 March 1863.

The moral climate of society is an inescapable fact of life for administrative agencies, too. Agencies do not work in a vacuum. Elsewhere in the present volume (Chapter 2), Noll stresses how agencies respond to external signals, cues from the outside that tell the agency how the world judges their performance. He uses the striking phrase "theatres of external judgment." This refers to courts, legislative committees, budget examiners, the press, and the general public—all the audiences whose opinions matter. The cues from outside, of course, are largely economic; they have mostly to do with cold, crass money interests. But not all of them can be analyzed this way. An agency wants approval and prestige from the outside world, or at least it wants to stay out of trouble.

Scandals are particularly unwelcome. After all, the audiences in theatres of external judgment are mostly drowsing in their seats. Publicity usually means bad publicity. This leads agencies to take special pains to avoid or get rid of abuses. An agency will go after abuses, even when the cure for an abuse flunks cost-benefit tests. What is rational for the agency may be irrational for the economy. Picture an agency head, sitting uneasily in front of a congressional subcommittee whose members are hungry for headlines, the TV cameras spinning away. There is cheating and chiseling in his agency or in the field he regulates. Does the commissioner dare admit he plans to do nothing, because enforcement costs ten dollars for every dollar saved?

When the pressure is on, agencies rush into unwise areas. When angry letters fill their mailbags and the switchboard lights up with angry calls, they take costly and foolish steps. Scandal sets off a volcanic eruption of public opinion. It changes, temporarily at least, the arrangement of policies and tactics that are best, most rational, and safest for the agency—or for the economy (Krier and Ursin, 1977). There are innumerable examples in administrative history. Scandal is at the very heart of the story of economic regulation. Railroad scandals helped pave the way for the ICC; stock fraud, for the SEC. The history of the food and drug laws and of meat inspection laws is one long story of response to scandal, beginning with the uproar around the turn of the century over embalmed beef and Upton Sinclair's novel *The Jungle*, published in 1906. The thalidomide episode was another case in point. This does not mean, of course, that regulation that comes out of scandal is less efficient than other kinds of regulation; indeed, one could argue the opposite.

Outbursts of opinion that follow scandal do not necessarily relate to issues of morality. Self-interest is, as always, richly represented. Nobody wants to eat poisoned food or give birth to deformed babies. Upton Sinclair wrote *The Jungle* to convert his audience to socialism.

It had a quite different effect. He described how rats were ground into sausage and (in one shocking passage) how a workman's body dissolved in a vat and was processed as Durham's Pure Leaf Lard. This frightened and nauseated the public. Sinclair aimed, he said, "at the public's heart" but "by accident" he "hit it in the stomach" (Friedman and Macaulay, 1977, p. 613). But this was no accident at all. The stomach is the seat of self-interest; the heart is a more elusive political organ.

Still, heart is not unknown in regulatory history. Often it gives us valuable clues to understanding the mysteries of regulation. Heart explains why certain paths or procedures are not taken even when they make so much sense to economists. Often it is because some part of the public rejects an efficient solution as immoral or, putting it the other way around, treats the inefficient solution as better for reasons of fairness or morality. Morality is particularly important in judging money subsidies or rewards in general. Money should go only to those free of ethical taint. Crime control through incentives and subsidies instead of punishment and deterrence is almost inconceivable; we cannot buy off criminals. Prisons cannot be country clubs. And so on.

The same considerations are at work in housing law (Friedman, 1968). The housing code is a dense thicket of rules enforced by local boards and inspectors, with a heavy dose of criminalization. More and more rules with higher and higher standards are enacted. Cities rarely address cost or cost-effectiveness. The idea is that slumlords make huge, mysterious, obscene profits and must be forced to bring their houses up to code. The plain fact is that the worst houses *cannot* be brought up to code—not profitably, at any rate. The state is willing to subsidize urban homesteaders—ordinary people who fix up their own homes—and other deserving types, but one cannot give a break (overtly) to slumlords any more than one can tackle the drug problem by giving away heroin.

Economists (and other social scientists) are often uncomfortable with factors that are hard to build into their usual models. But in principle there is no reason why theory should not take moral preferences into account, just as theory takes account of other sorts of social fact. Tastes in morality, fairness, ethical standards, and the like do vary from society to society and from period to period. But so do tastes for products. Price theory is not refuted by the fact that one country's meat is another country's poison.

Preferences among various forms of legal structure are also variable. These preferences derive from the normative structure of society. Our society, for example, likes the market system in general but refuses to let the market decide every question. It is not the market—or not solely the market—that decides who gets into Congress, the army, or MIT. The reasons for sidestepping the market are not mysterious and can certainly be expressed in general terms. Fuchs (1976), for example, has sketched out some reasons why country after country chose national health insurance despite the gross misallocation of resources that economists saw in these plans.

Normative considerations pop up in bits and pieces in the literature on legal arrangements and on regulation. Michelman (1967), in discussing eminent domain and just compensation, introduced the concept of demoralization costs. This was an attempt to make something systematic out of that old (but real) chestnut, the sense of fairness. Demoralization costs are made up of two components. First there are "disutilities" which "accrue to losers and their sympathizers specifically from the realization that no compensation is offered." Second, there is the value of "lost future production" arising either out of "impaired incentives" or from "social unrest" caused by the "demoralization" of "uncompensated losers, their sympathizers and other observers disturbed by the thought that they themselves may be subjected to similar treatment on some other occasion" (Michelman, 1967, p. 1214).

The general idea, then, is that society may pay a heavy price if it does not deal with people in a way they consider fair. This does not take us very far, although the basic idea seems sound. Williamson (1970) tried to formalize the concept a bit and apply it to a concrete case. One factor that both Michelman and Williamson talk about is relevant to regulation and administrative process: the psychological value of fair procedure. This again is a familiar point, but it deserves whatever emphasis it can get. Due process and legal procedures in general are valuable in spreading a sense of fairness and also of participation. In this way process helps overcome feelings of powerlessness or injustice. Hence, the expansion of administrative process may bring important benefits. The explosion of access slows down the pace of administration, but its benefits might well offset these costs.

Unfortunately, the benefits are difficult to show and impossible to tag with numbers. Costs, on the other hand, have a disarming clarity. One way of summing up the package of benefits is to bring them together under the heading of legitimation. Legitimacy is the glue that binds society together. Without legitimacy, a regime either turns to repression or rapidly disintegrates. In general, in Western societies legitimation is heavily freighted with procedural values (Luhmann, 1975). If due process is the pillar of legitimacy in American society (and in the West in general), the value of fair procedure, in administration as well as elsewhere, is absolutely incalculable.

Nobody doubts the importance of legitimacy, and nobody doubts that it has a procedural element. The critical questions are: *how* important is it, and *how* big is the procedural element? Some scraps of research suggest that procedural legitimacy is a bit overrated (Friedman, 1975; Jacob, 1971). An innocent man, condemned to die, is not likely to accept his place on death row simply because the trial was fair. (Of course, we, the observers, may feel quite satisfied.) For the most part people seem to value outcomes, not procedures. At any rate, we badly need more research on this point. One thing is clear: we should discard any notion that the legal system, and legality in general, is some kind of constraint, insofar as that word carries with it the flavor of a drag on the system. After all, constraints make the difference between tyranny and a decent society.

Fairness is an idea that goes far beyond procedure. It is not only people or governments who are or can be unfair. We often say a situation is unfair, even when there is nobody to blame it on. We say it is unfair when a tornado wrecks one person's house and spares his neighbor's. It is characteristic of the modern state and modern law to try to do something about this kind of unfairness, too. Michelman (1967, pp. 1216–17) draws a distinction between a "visible risk of majoritarian exploitation" and the "ever-present risk that accidents may happen." He suggests that these two have very different disincentive effects. To put the point more bluntly, people are more demoralized when done in by other people (or by their government) than when fate does them in.

This is, of course, an empirical proposition. My guess is that the distinction is tending to blur. In the age of big government pure accidents become rarer and rarer. An earthquake is an act of God. But it is not an act of God that nobody enforced an ordinance against overhanging cornices or that emergency services were badly organized. A flood is also an act of God, but it is easy to blame somebody for the failure of dams, levees, and warning systems (before the fact) or the failure of disaster relief (afterward). The apparatus of government is geared to preventing and mitigating disaster. The Reagan Administration fulminates against entitlements but uses the phrase *safety net* to describe an untouchable package of programs. These represent the social minimum that keeps people from starving and softens the impact of other calamities. There is broad agreement in society about these safety nets. It is not even important whether victims brought on their own misery. A tightrope walker who falls has only himself to blame; still, we prefer him to use the net (Fuchs, 1976).

Social insurance is a basic idea in the welfare state. A vast body of law establishes and maintains the social safety net of financial, medical, even psychological services. This net is not just for the poor. The middle class may in fact benefit even more. The point is to insure against calamities of every kind. The insurance notion is important politically: the programs are not welfare but insurance, which carries no stigma. Whether they are "really" insurance (economically speaking) is politically irrelevant.

Social insurance includes old-age pensions, unemployment compensation, workmen's compensation, and disaster relief. Many other types of business regulation contain a social insurance aspect—safety provisions, for example. The idea is to avoid calamity. Some economists (Peltzman, 1975; Oi, 1977) have argued that safety regulation often does more harm than good. People are lulled into risky behavior, thinking they are safe, thus bringing about more injuries instead of fewer. This idea seems rather dubious. And there is no doubt, first, that most people do not want to break their necks and, second, that safety regulation is politically and socially popular.

In any event, there is no turning back. This is most definitely not a society that tells people to take their medicine. We used to hear the complaint that people preferred security to risk (as if that were bad). People do want security. More than that, they dread irreversibility. The age of safety regulation is also the age of bankruptcy laws. Bankruptcy laws have two main points: fairness to the creditors as a group but also, very notably, a clean slate and a fresh start for the debtor. If Mr. and Mrs. Smith open up a pizza parlor and it goes broke (as most of them do), we feel (as they do) that they ought not to be ruined for life. American education (unlike some continental systems) is built on the theory of second (third, fourth) chances, even for late bloomers, for kids who frittered away their high school years. Criminal justice is full of second chances: first offenders get probation, juvenile records are sealed and later destroyed.

These are all in their fashion safety nets. We assume that people can be reckless and misguided. We know that accidents happen. If possible, mistakes and catastrophes should not become irreversible calamities. The legal system, reflecting dominant opinion, tries to mitigate consequences (as in the bankruptcy laws) or prevent the worst follies by removing danger from various settings. Whether these regulations are good or bad for society in the long run is debatable. But they are social facts and reflect widespread social attitudes.

Regulatory Law: Origins and Background

The literature on regulation also deals with the political origin and background of regulation. This literature is probably smaller than the one on regulatory impact. Economists are most at home studying impact. They have a model against which to measure results: the free market. Often enough, they conclude that regulation does worse than the market, and that repeal would benefit us all.

There is no model, however, for political origins. Yet regulation is simply an aspect of the general legal system. Getting rid of regulation means changing law—repealing or amending a statute, repealing or transforming regulations. Like it or not, this brings us back to origins and background—in a word, back to politics. If regulation has political roots, so must deregulation. All legal arrangements are stages in the never-ending process of politics.

What do we know about the political roots of regulation? We know quite a bit about interest groups, and there is a sizable literature on lobbying. There is also some agreement on basic propositions, mostly about interest group behavior. Regulation and other legal arrangements tend to favor strong, tight groups, the special interests that put all their eggs in one basket. One narrow interest is unusually strategic: politicians, whose interest is in staying in office. Some theorists also argue that state action tends to favor the middle classes and disfavor both the rich and the poor (Stigler, 1970).

These theories are only starting points. A small but intense interest group gets its way, theoretically, when the force it exerts on political structures outbalances the force on the other side. A bill to license plumbers will be intensely favored by plumbers and ignored, chances are, by everybody else. We predict, then, that such a bill will pass. It has more social force going for it than against it. In this situation energy is exerted in small doses. The general mass of political force is latent, dormant. Most of us are indifferent to plumbing. To succeed, the bill must tiptoe past the general public. Any sudden squall changes the whole political complexion. Public opinion, a sleeping giant, can rise up and overwhelm the plumbers, in the wake of scandal or crisis. Headlines produce rapid, sudden change in equations of political force.

A bill backed by a coalition of forces is sturdier than one backed by a single group. The plumbers have a better chance if they get themselves allies. In the legislature this takes the form of logrolling, explicit or implicit (Buchanan and Tullock, 1962; Ferejohn, 1974). It can happen outside the legislature, too. It is especially likely if the plumbers convince neutrals that their self-interest lies in backing the plumbers. Hence all the arguments about public health and safety. We should not dismiss these out-of-hand as hypocritical mumbo-jumbo, as disguises and masks for self-interest. These arguments may be serious bids for allies, attempts to recruit the broader public. The public would give the plumbers whatever they wanted if this were necessary to ward off pollution and plague. But they have to be convinced.

Successful regulatory politics comes about, in the main, when proponents with strong economic interests gather up coalition partners who have quite different aims. It is a shade too cynical, for example, to see the ICC as nothing but a railroad plot (Kolko, 1965); to dismiss Sunday laws as labor-union policy masquerading as religion; to expose child-labor laws as tricks to raise wages for adults. There is some truth an all of these revisionist charges. They describe the motives of some but not all the coalition partners. A mixture of motives always went into the pot.

This brings us again to the moral basis of law. Some coalition partners are in hot pursuit of naked self-interest. They are joined by others in hot pursuit of ideals. It is incorrect to explain away poverty programs by looking for some group with cynical self-interest. But many scholars try (if all else fails, the desire of elites to stave off revolution is a convenient catchall way to explain progressive programs). Why not admit that some people act out of moral and religious conviction? It is a question of striking the right historical balance.

To explain the movement for free public schools in New York, E.G. West drags in the self-seeking of teachers and administrators (West, 1967; Marvel, 1977, presents a somewhat similar brand of revisionism on English factory legislation). But if we consider West's thesis carefully, we have to ask why teachers and administrators were so persuasive in this respect? Free public education must have sounded appealing to other people too. West talks about propaganda by protagonists for free common schools and gives some examples; he treats it all as the merest charade. But propaganda, like advertising, sinks without a trace unless it strikes some chord in its audience. Society as a whole was willing, even eager, to embrace public education. It cannot be only a teachers' and principals' plot. There are vested interests behind environmental protection, consumer safety, free hot lunches at schools, and welfare in general, but there must be more to the story.

Some regulatory laws float through the legislatures without much opposition. Important, visible, expensive programs do not have this advantage. Political argument and struggle lie behind all major statutes—the ICC act, for example. Passage means forming a coalition. But it is almost never true that coalition partners hold all values and interests in common. They must compromise among themselves as well as with the opposition. Even losers leave their mark on legislation. The doctors fought bitterly against Medicare and in the end they lost. Still, the act gave them much of what they wanted. Indeed, we might venture this generalization: in a political system like ours every major piece of legislation is a compromise and in every case the outcome reflects the interests of each important contending group.

The social force each group actually brought to bear on the subject matter will leave its mark on the law or bill.

There are many forms of compromise, of course; it would be too laborious to spell them out here. The ICC compromises are among the best known and the most carefully studied. They have generated a polemical literature of their own (Kolko, 1965). The Sherman Act was another kind of compromise: it made a broad, strong statement of principle but set up no mechanism to carry this into effect (Letwin, 1965). That was left to the Justice Department and the courts, which meant delegation and delay. The Internal Revenue Code is a living museum of compromises. So in its own way is the whole code of federal regulations.

All this takes place against a real background, played out in the context of living law and living society. Legal arrangements ebb and flow, not in terms of models of perfect societies or what would happen on a desert island or behind veils of ignorance, but in a messy, noisy workshop of reality. Nothing stays the same, everything is in flux, everything is moving and changing. We must not (as the literature sometimes seems to do) ignore background, history, context. We must not treat regulation as something the stork brought suddenly one night.

Administrative Regulation and Its Common-Law Background: A Case Study

In this section I will spend a little time on one rather undernoticed sample of regulation: workmen's compensation. This is not an example illuminated by close attention to moral feelings in society, though no doubt such feelings played their part. Rather, one can explain the history in fairly straight interest-group terms. Nor does workmen's compensation spring to mind as a classic example of regulation. Yet it fits the subject as well as OSHA or the NLRB. And it illustrates, rather neatly, how regulatory regimes flow out of common-law backgrounds and how they relate to those backgrounds. The pattern is recurrent enough to be worth our attention.

I have elsewhere described the history of workmen's compensation in some detail (Friedman and Ladinsky, 1967). Briefly, the story runs something like this. Before the industrial revolution, work accidents were neither common nor serious. It takes modern machines to really mangle the work force. Industrial development and, above all, the railroad changed the picture. Personal injury law—tort law—was the child of the iron horse. From 1837 on, in England and the United States, a number of striking cases established the so-called fellow-servant rule. The best-known American decision was

Farwell v. *The Boston and Worcester Railroad.*[9] The facts were as follows: Nicholas Farwell, a railroad worker, was injured on the job through the negligence of another worker. Farwell brought suit against the company. It was not an outlandish claim. In the law of agency, under the maxim *respondeat superior,* a person injured by an agent (or employee) may sue the principal (the boss). The Massachusetts court, however, denied Farwell's claim. A workman could not sue his employer if the injury arose out of the negligence of a fellow servant.

But negligent injuries in a factory, mine, or railroad yard are almost never caused by the principal (a distant figure or, more and more often, a corporate entity). The fellow-servant rule thus cut off any real chance of indemnity through law. Yet the rule struck a responsive chord in its day. Whatever its ultimate impact, it seemed valuable and sensible to people at the time. In particular, it seemed to help out infant industry. It insulated business from lawsuits and saved it from damaging claims, or so people thought.

The rule had a stormy history. At first it seemed to command wide acceptance. But as the country industrialized (and unionized) there were more and more accidents, and the rule became very controversial. It was meant to choke off litigation. Certainly many claims never got to court, because the rule prevented them. But it never worked totally. Some cases did get brought, and the courts, perhaps out of sympathy for workmen and their families, grafted exceptions onto the rule. Naturally enough, this encouraged more lawsuits. Legislatures, too, got into the act, passing statutes that added more exceptions. The result was a gigantic, complex, technical edifice of law. By 1900, industrial-accident law was perhaps the single most complicated field in the entire common-law system.

At the turn of the century, then, the situation was roughly this: a worker who had an accident on the job was usually out of luck. The fellow-servant rule barred workers from collecting damages. But sometimes workers could fit their situations into one of the many exceptions. There was heavy litigation. The contingent-fee system financed working-class litigants. Companies settled many cases, fought some, gave up on some. They went to court from time to time and were often successful—but at a price. A losing employer had to pay damages and lawyers' fees, not to mention insurance premiums and other administrative costs. Probably less than half of the money paid out actually went to injured workmen. The rest was consumed by the swarm of middlemen. By 1900, the system was unpopular, it seems, with both management and labor.

9. 45 Mass. 49, 1842.

Workmen's compensation replaced this chaotic, unpopular system. The fellow-servant rule was swept away, together with a whole flock of employer defenses. The whole fault principle itself, keystone of the law of torts, went overboard, at least as far as accidents on the job were concerned. Liability for work accidents became in essence simple and absolute. (There were a few additional wrinkles and exceptions, but these can be ignored for our purposes.) Typically, a board or commission administers the program. The worker is guaranteed recovery, but there are strict limits on amount. At the heart of a workmen's compensation statute are tables or provisions which set out two things: first, the payments (prices) for different injuries, in dollars or percentages of average wages over given periods of time; second, for workers who are disabled, a flat percentage of wages for a flat number of weeks or months. For example, in Indiana loss of the big toe brings compensation at 60 percent of average weekly wages (up to a maximum of $125 a week) for sixty weeks in addition to the time the victim is actually disabled. Also, total permanent disability brings 500 weeks of benefits.[10]

Thus the system puts a cap on liability but makes it certain. This presumably made both sides feel better off. Under the complex, costly system of tort law, a few people collected a lot, most people collected little or nothing, and administrative costs ran high. What replaced it was a public program run by a board with rule-making power. The statutes were and are (as statutes go) unusually detailed, but so is the Internal Revenue Code.

Suppose we wish to assess the wisdom of this program. We can (let us assume) address ourselves to what it costs, in dollars and cents, and what benefits it brings to workers. But against what further standard shall we measure it? Shall we compare it to a system of private labor bargains? Workmen's compensation did not replace a system of private contract; rather, it replaced a complicated, irrational, and expensive process of lawsuits and threats of lawsuits based on rules that did not closely resemble anybody's idea of a sensible program. Nor is there any reason to believe that the history of workmen's compensation is unique in this regard. For example, Jarrell (1977) has given a somewhat similar explanation of utility regulation: the electric utilities wanted state control because of a background of municipal control that utilities liked a lot less.

The story of workmen's compensation as outlined here is hard to reconcile with a body of work, some of it by economists, that takes a very positive attitude toward common-law rules. The basic proposi-

10. Ind. Rev. Stats., Sec. 22–3–10 (a) (1), (3).

tion is that these rules, generated in private lawsuits, tend toward efficiency in ways that legislation can never approach (Priest, 1977; Rubin, 1977). The arguments are quite theoretical for the most part. Posner (1977, p. 440) argues that, over time, inefficient rules will generate more litigation; therefore "less efficient rules" will tend to be "weeded out and replaced by efficient ones."

Observers who use cruder measures and who muck about in the dirt of actual history tend to doubt whether courts really get such magical results. An instructive case in point is the history of tort law (Rabin, 1981). There were Draconian rules of liability (or rather, no-liability) in the nineteenth century (the fellow-servant rule was one). Tort law then evolved over time into a baroque network of liability rules. The fellow-servant rule reached unbearable complexity by about 1900. In the twentieth century technical law on malpractice, products liability, and the like has grown tremendously. Tort law is a field of staggering bulk and complication, and all of this with little help from statutes or regulatory bodies. Growth took place almost entirely in the courts.

If the old system was efficient (whatever that might mean), the new system is almost certainly inefficient. To be sure, society has changed; what may have been efficient in the days of the horse and buggy may no longer be so. But this is not the whole story. Whatever the economic effect of particular rules of law looked at coldly and abstractly, it can hardly be efficient when the rules are very complicated, when nobody can understand them, when results of cases are hard to predict, and when all parties spend money on lawyers and other undesirables. There is no hard evidence that the common-law works itself pure; often it works itself muddy.

For many observers, tort rules today are hard to defend on logical grounds, let alone economic ones. If so, evolution brought inefficiency if it brought anything. Some scholars argue that what comes out of courts is different in kind over the long haul from what comes out of legislatures or the executive. I find this doubtful as a matter of theory. Courts, Congress, and the executive are all embedded in the same social order. They are subject on the whole to the same social forces; they breathe the air of the same culture. It would be surprising if one type of legal process (litigation) produced results radically different from the others (legislation and administrative process).

The fact is that modern tort law was molded not by some inevitable internal process but by dramatic changes in the climate of opinion. Judges (and litigants) are not immune to these changes. The inefficiencies and complications of the law of industrial accidents were not random. They came about because of genuine social controversy.

Workmen's compensation was no revolution. It was a reform that compromised interests and tried to make technical improvement.

The same principles apply today to other aspects of law. If the population became dissatisfied enough with malpractice law (the doctors certainly hate it), we would expect to find political force building up, aimed at getting rid of current rules or changing them. The normal political process would insure that any replacement would be some sort of compromise. There might be a system something like workmen's compensation but applied to doctors and hospitals. Would this be a better, more efficient system? Possibly, but to decide we would have to compare it not with the free market, not with some idealized picture of tort law, but with tort law as it is in the real world, with its bizarre liability rules and all the rest. Licensing by the FDA might be cheaper (and better) for drug companies than a free-market free-for-all followed by tort suits in which companies pay billions of dollars. Or maybe not. The question can hardly be resolved by abstract reasoning.

The last paragraph made another point, if only implicitly. Economic analysis (or sociological analysis, for that matter) is useless unless it confronts the legal system as it works in reality, not as it is described in the books. Theories about the way courts operate mean nothing unless they are grounded in studies of what happens in real life. The Coase theorem (Coase, 1960), for example, has to be handled with care. It is an important and stimulating idea, but it is not and was never intended to be a description of litigation. Coase himself thought it very unrealistic to assume that market transactions are costless. To know the impact of liability rules, we have to consider transaction costs. We must also remember that the common law frowns on contracting out of liability for negligence and on waivers of rights by consumers. It is therefore not easy for companies to adjust to certain legal rules. A cap on liability may be worth paying a price for, even when the price is regulation.

The point is not that critiques of legal rules are wrong but only that some of them could apply just as well to "regulation" through judge-made rules. Critics, however, often compare regulation to a kind of state of nature rather than to the state of the art. Enterprise liability has increased dramatically in the twentieth century. All parts of the law have shared in this development. The courts have played a major role, and legislatures have passed safety and liability laws. Perhaps we would be better off without all this legal activity—there are arguments on both sides—but one thing is clear: there are powerful impulses pushing toward enterprise liability. These impulses affect common-law rules, legislation, and administrative law. After all, the legal system is a structure within society. Social institutions can take on lives of their own, but basically society molds them. They are dependent variables—followers, not leaders, in life.

Administrative regulation is no exception. It is a subculture of the legal system. The system reacts to forces pushing from outside. This does not mean that scholars should accept all existing arrangements as inevitable. Other arrangements may be better, more efficient, and more just by some standard. Criticism may itself awaken dormant forces and lead to needed change. But criticism is most constructive when it is informed by awareness of the concrete social forces that created the structure. Economic arguments, battering against a rather weakly held fortress, apparently made a difference in the movement to deregulate airlines. Other parts of the citadel may be much less vulnerable.

A Word on Consequences

Practically speaking, how do political, social, legal, and ethical considerations affect someone who wants to frame policy or to give advice about policy? This is not easy to say. One of the main points here has been to deny that there are simple, clean criteria. But it is useful to know that political, social, legal, and ethical factors are important, that they cannot (or should not) be ignored, and that they will not magically disappear.

Policymakers may have to reframe their questions. It is good to ask: what are the best (or most efficient) policies? But it is even better to ask a more complicated question: what are the best (or most efficient) policies in the light of social constraints? It is no use protesting that some constraints are nebulous or unmeasurable. Some are, some are not. They have effects in either case. Social climate matters, tradition matters, morality matters. It would be a waste of time to show that the best and cheapest way to cope with crime would be to shoot all felony suspects. There are laws and traditions against doing this. It cannot be done, and that is that.

Legal and constitutional restraints are fairly visible, and we take some of them for granted (basic property rules, for example). At other times the legal background is more problematic. There is an unfortunate tendency to treat legal variables abstractly. There are far too many articles assessing the efficiency or fairness of this or that rule (of contract law, tort law, property law) without regard to whether the rule has any life or effect outside of law books or a few leading cases. Many rules are slippery, open-ended creatures. Again, it is good to go back to Coase (1960, p. 19): he insisted that his theorem works only if and when "the rights of the parties" are "well-defined and the results of legal actions easy to forecast." As every lawyer knows, this is a mighty big if.

Of course, scholars must make assumptions and approximations. There is no other way to approach complicated processes. Some assumptions simplify, while others falsify. The literature does not always avoid falling over the edge. Legal arrangements are much messier in the real world than in the way law schools present them. This is dangerous for students and all but fatal for social scientists. Legal arrangements in life do not present themselves as naked entities. They carry all the freight of the social order. Their history and meaning, the behaviors that have grown up about them, are part of their very nature.

Structural, moral, and political constraints are difficult for policymakers to handle, just as economic and political constraints are difficult for moralists and reformers. We have stressed the moral meanings of technical devices and the political background out of which regulation springs and in which it works. It exasperates scholars to deal with factors that apparently cannot be measured, assessed, or predicted; it is like fighting an invisible enemy. But this cannot be helped.

Are all the facts of social climate really so elusive? The social sciences are underdeveloped, but they do have a technique or two in their arsenal. Careful study, properly done, might be able to show the moral tastes of a community. It is easier to quote the price of a common stock, but ethical prices are just as real. Earlier in the paper, we referred to the history of selective service. Close observation might reveal this story as part of a larger whole; it might uncover some norms about equality of sacrifice in this society. That would at least be a start.

There is a general lesson to be learned by scholars and policymakers—and a warning, too. The lesson is to scoop up as many facts as possible, empirical and historical, about the genesis of legal arrangements and the context in which they work, even when the facts do not lend themselves to scientific treatment. This also means listening to what people say about what economic arrangements mean to them. The more ignorant these opinions, the more valuable they may be as indicators of social force. With the help of this kind of data, policy advisors might be able, perhaps, to convert unrealistic equations into realistic ones. At the very least, they will be able to raise the level of debate.

COMMENT: *James V. DeLong*

Lawrence Friedman makes a number of excellent points in his paper, and my comments are more variations on his themes than criticisms of them.

It is important to reemphasize his thesis that the legal system is basically a reflection of the social and moral beliefs of the society and that legal control of regulation means "control of the economy by social norms of justice and morality." As Stigler (1982) wrote recently, critics from other intellectual traditions, especially economics, sometimes seem to think that regulators simply have not heard their arguments against particular regulatory arrangements. This is not so. Usually the regulators, having heard the economists' analyses, have decided to take whatever action is at issue despite its inefficiency, or perhaps even because of it.

In analyzing the current conflicts over regulation, however, I do not think Friedman pushes this crucial theme of the moral foundation of the regulatory system quite far enough. As I read his paper, he views the normative impulses affecting regulation as standing in opposition to both the "dreams of the technocrats" of regulation by objective experts—the approach that characterized the Progressive Era and the New Deal—and the efficiency criticisms made by contemporary economists. He sees the revolt against expertise and the assertion of the importance of procedures and participation as the reassertion of the moral dimension of regulation in contradiction to the experts' impulse to find some bloodless mathematical optimum.

He also seems skeptical about the possibility that these rationalist criticisms will have more than marginal impact on regulation, given the importance of the normative foundation. Finally, though this may be reading too much into his analysis, he seems to regard this foundation as one of the strengths of the system, giving it legitimacy and continuity.

Even accepting the fundamentally normative mainsprings of the regulatory system, I do not think that one can draw such a clear line between the moral arguments conventionally used to justify some set of arrangements and the efficiency grounds upon which the economists criticize them. Many of the economic criticisms of contemporary regulatory policy are, at bottom, moral criticisms. They make the point that particular regulations make the community unnecessarily poorer or that they redistribute wealth in strange ways. For example, inherent in the argument that trucking regulation is inefficient is an argument that wealth is being transferred from consumers to trucking investors and employees, and that this is not simply inefficient in some abstract sense, but—unless we regard these beneficiary groups as entitled to subsidy at the expense of the rest of the people—morally wrong.

To take a different example, the argument against increasingly unrealistic housing codes, anti-slumlord agitation, rent control, and the other symbolic acts to which municipal governments are prone is a technical or efficiency argument only on the surface. Its real bite is that such measures actually decrease the stock of housing and raise its price (in comparison with what a free market would produce) and at the same time fool people into thinking that productive action is being taken.

At a general level one can argue that current, ostensibly technical critiques represent a logical response not to the fact that most arguments for regulation are phrased in moral terms—this is indeed a given—but to the explosion of moral arguments that have been given credence.

As Friedman comments, lawyers are in the business of dressing up interests "in the clothing of rights." Over the past few decades they have been very successful at this. As an obvious illustration, one of the fascinations of the last thirty years has been to watch the legal and political systems convert the fundamental and indubitable civil rights concept that the government should not treat its citizens badly on the grounds of race, origin, or sex into the idea that any group that can assert a collective identity and a colorable theory of moral entitlement should have a blank check on society's collective resources (see, e.g., Schuck, 1979). The same period has seen other interests not so closely linked to particular groups also seek and sometimes attain the status of blank-check rights; interests in health and safety, pure environments, and long-term security are all argued in these terms. And the interests of both producers and consumers are also argued in moral terms, even if not in quite such a categorical way. Furthermore, all these interests, as a part of their efforts to metamorphose into rights, have made a multifront and often successful effort to transfer resource allocation decisions from the relatively open budget process to the more obscure crannies of the regulatory system and the tax code (Salamon, 1981).

All this makes the system into a joke. Since, as Friedman notes, arguments of inefficiency or excessive costs are not valid against rights, each successful claim must be given full force as it arises, as a browse through the United States Code and the court reports will attest. But of course the various claims conflict, sometimes directly, sometimes only in the sense that resources are not infinite. This is not a new problem for the legal system, since collision at the periphery has been a characteristic of constitutional litigation as long as there has been a constitution. But differences in degree do eventually become differences in kind, and the problems of the legal and regulatory systems in this respect have grown geometrically. Eventually the conflicts among a multitude of moral claims become so numerous, and the claims themselves so qualified, that they all begin to look like interests after all.

A few years ago I heard a radio news broadcast in which Alfred Kahn, then President Carter's anti-inflation czar, was confronted by a demand that the government subsidize consumers to compensate for inflation in the prices of four essentials—food, energy, housing, and transportation, as I recall. There was a moment of total silence, then Kahn said in a rather bemused way, "But we can't all of us subsidize all of us; the system just doesn't work that way."

This typifies the problem. If a moral claim simply cannot be met, or if it cannot be met unless we give up other entitlements, then it loses its status as a transcendent imperative. It can remain as an ideal or an aspiration, but it can no longer be regarded as immune to arguments of cost or efficiency.

Thus I do not think the present criticisms of regulation should be viewed as a nonmoral technical response to moral arguments. Rather, they represent an effort to find some way of sorting out the choices and priorities among conflicting claims that are almost always presented in categorical moral terms. Not least, they represent an effort to find a language for discussing the problem. Once, when I worked for the U.S. Bureau of the Budget, my boss (an economist) looked up from a pile of agency submissions and asked, "How many 'dire necessities' does it take to outweigh 'an urgent national need'?" This problem has not lessened. To conduct the debate over national policy entirely in terms of fuzzy moral assertion is futile. Even if one agrees that the basic arguments will always be moral, sharpening the language and thus the concepts of the debate should have substantial and beneficial effects on it.

A related area in which Friedman does not push his thesis far enough is in his discussion of legitimacy. Certainly one reason that proposals to return to market solutions often fail is that the market itself lacks moral legitimacy for many people, even aside from those areas, such as the draft, in which we are reluctant to use a market at all. Markets perform three distinguishable but practically inseparable functions: (1) they allocate investment of productive resources (including human resources) to the most valued uses; (2) they distribute the rewards of the economic system; and (3) they serve as an administrative mechanism that gives signals to the participants as to what they ought to do and feedback on whether their economic judgments were correct.

While there are some dissenters, most people accept having the market perform the first of these functions as the best way to maximize wealth, though of course when a market does not work for any of the conventional reasons (see, e.g., Breyer, 1981), they want somebody to do something. People are queasy about the second because it is hard to relate the distributions that accrue to people in their capacity as economic resources to any other criteria of worth. And they would like to soften the rigor with which the market informs people of its judgments and their mistakes.

Much of the regulatory system, much of the government as a whole, exists to perform these functions where the market has lost legitimacy. And it is fair to hypothesize that the regulatory system as it developed since the 1930s started with a presumption of moral legitimacy simply by not being the discredited Darwinian free market of Herbert Spencer. As time has passed, though, it has accumulated its own barnacles of disillusionment.

Just as market systems find it hard to perform the resource-allocation function without producing unacceptable results with respect to distribution and administration, regulatory systems seem to have a hard time tempering market results in the last two areas without also damaging its performance in the first one. Since people do regard increasing wealth as a moral virtue—indeed, as a right—this failure is a serious one. In addition, many people question whether the substitution of competition in the halls of capital cities for competition in the market has resulted in a net increase in human justice. They have similar doubts about the net gains derived by replacing the brutalities of market administration with the routinized callousness of bureaucracy.

Thus while I agree with Friedman in his comments on the importance of looking at the regulatory system as a morally legitimate alternative to the market, I think he should pay more attention to the process by which that system itself is drifting into a crisis of legitimacy. For example, it is not obvious to me that there has been a loss of faith in disinterested experts as regulators. Rather, it seems to have become a matter of conventional wisdom that many regulators are not experts but political hacks and that agencies are not disinterested but are instead either the captives of the interests they are supposed to regulate or the janissaries of some special constituency (see Lowi, 1969).

Finally, I would not be quite so charitable as Friedman in exonerating the legal profession from responsibility for current problems. It may be true that the legal system's emphasis on moral argument and its distaste for economic or technocratic approaches reflect an important aspect of the national character. At the same time, though, the legal system strongly encourages this approach in its organizational structure, its doctrines, its literature, and its training. And it has actually extended a moralistic mode of analyzing public-policy problems by an imperial expansion into more and more areas of public and private decisionmaking. The Nuremberg defense does not avail.

Despite these quibbles, I believe Friedman has elaborated in a provocative way a question that must often baffle social scientists working on regulatory issues: why the system so often seems to ignore even the most cogent analysis. Perhaps over time such interchanges will lead social scientists to cast the arguments in terms somewhat more congenial to regulators and lawyers, and the latter to realize that the use of rigorous social science is not a symptom of moral degeneracy.

5

A Wide Angle On Regulation

An Anthropological Perspective

*Laura Nader and
Claire Nader*

To equate *regulation* with *formal government
regulation* is incomplete, predictably misses important variables that
influence both its substance and process, and encourages a research
focus on the effects of government regulations rather than on the
conditions that made them necessary. Rules that shape behavior in
government agencies, business firms, and professional societies, and
among these sources of organized power, and reactions to being governed by others are essential aspects of a larger regulatory picture in
society. This view brings in relevant but conventionally excluded variables such as the behavioral patterns of corporate officers and interactions between government and businesses.[1] A wide-angle perspec-

The authors thank Suzanne Bowler, Grace Buzaljko, and JoAnn Martin for their
help in the preparation of this paper. We also thank unnamed others for rescuing this
paper from the wolves.

1. In, for example, the Ford Pinto fuel tank affair: the auto industry's complaint to
the government that auto safety regulations impaired productivity, thus diverting attention from a broader definition of economic productivity that would include improved auto efficiency, reduced number of casualties and work losses, and pollution
diseconomies, and inadequate corporate management (Abernathy, 1978); and the
government's argument that the regulation fostered innovations such as fuel efficiency, which even Henry Ford has acknowledged (interview with Henry Ford on
"Meet the Press," 30 October 1977).

tive enriches our empirical understanding and suggests lines of research that could have important practical application.

Social scientists have observed that regulation is an aspect of social life in all human societies and that in any society different groups promulgate rules regulating conduct in the various spheres of kinship, politics, business, health, and war. Some formal rules meant to control, shape, or govern are produced through public or private legislative action of organized corporate bodies (e.g., Congress, regulatory agencies, or professional societies or corporations, including engineering standard-setting groups). Other more informal rules, direct and indirect, are produced within a particular field of action, such as censorship, selective hiring, promotion, gossip, or witchcraft. Anthropologists work with the assumption that socially enforceable rules in one sphere (e.g., the corporation) depend on and affect other legally enforceable sets of rules (e.g., government rules). Both kinds of rules direct behavior and reflect disparities in economic, political, and social power. In the United States, formal rules claim public legitimacy. Informal rules imply a private legitimacy that is rationalized as producing the most feasible performance or as rooted in trade secrecy or in a secrecy that covers criminal or criminogenic activity. A further assumption is that formal regulation cannot be understood apart from the wider social context.

Our examination of specific examples of regulation in government, business, and science in the United States shows that we are not dealing with a homogeneous set of materials. In this essay we attempt to apply to this problem an anthropological approach, which identifies clearly the arrangement of parts in a society and their interactions—an approach that is sometimes called *holistic*. We feel that this holistic approach may be useful in understanding the many faces of regulation in complex, industrialized societies.

As Roger Noll (1980) and others have observed, the term *regulation* has been used variously between and within disciplines.[2] Wilcox and Shepherd (1975) provide three definitions: to govern by rule, to regularize, and to make regulations. Regulation is often equated with social control, as in Malinowski's (1926) study of the Trobriand Islanders, where he describes a system of multilateral and reciprocal control. In contrast, Wilcox (1968, p. 390) says: "In its broadest sense the term regulation may be taken to comprehend all of the controls that government imposes on business of all kinds." However, in the use of *regulation* to mean only government regulation the adjective *government* itself implies that other kinds of regulation also exist.

2. Noll (1980), p. 5.

Here we are concerned with the following comparative and interactionist questions. (1) What is the difference between regulation in different spheres: in government, in business organizations, and in professional societies? (2) How does regulation in one sphere affect that in another, and what is the overall result of the interactions among regulation in these three spheres? (3) What are the problem-solving potentials of perspectives that view government regulation through a wide-angle lens?

The Multiplicity of Legal Systems

Nineteenth- and early twentieth-century scholars Otto von Gierke (1868), Eugene Ehrlich (1913), and Max Weber (1922) worked toward an explication of the concept that several legal systems may exist within a given society, but it was anthropologist Leopold Pospisil (1971, p. 99) who traced the theoretical underpinning for the workings of such multi-level systems:

> Traditionally, law has been conceived as the property of a society as a whole. As a logical consequence, a given society was thought to have only one legal system that controlled the behavior of all its members. Without any investigation of the social controls that operate on the sub-society levels, subgroups (such as associations and residential and kinship groups) have been a priori excluded from the possibility of regulating their members' behavior by systems of rules applied in specific decisions by leaders of these groups—systems that in their essential characteristics very closely parallel the all-embracing law of the society. This attitude was undoubtedly caused by the tremendous influence the well-elaborated and unified law of the Roman Empire exerted upon the outlook of the European lawyer. Had classical Greece exercised such influence over the legal minds of our civilization, our traditional concept of law might have been much more flexible and, cross-culturally speaking, "realistic."

The tendency to "dissociate law from the structure of the society and its subgroups [society's segments] has," Pospisil laments, "unfortunately persisted until the present time."

The notion that law is monopolized by the state or by society as a whole has influenced some scholarly thinking. However, the idea that systems of rules of societal segments within the state can exist side by side with state law has been accepted by researchers working on countries where legal pluralism is a fact of life because of colonialism (see Murdock [1934] on the Inca; Canter [1978] on the Lenje of Zambia; Ruffini [1978] on the Sardinians under Italian law; Van der Sprenkel [1962] and Van der Valk [1939] on China; and Burman and Harrell-

Bond [1979] for a general picture of the model of this type of legal imposition). The concept of multiplicity has also been applied by those trying to understand the system of rules of such groups as criminal gangs in our own society (see Whyte [1955] on the United States and Stark [1981] for comparable materials on Japanese gangs). As Pospisil (1971, p. 116) said about gangs, "the legal center of power is located in the gang rather than on the level of the society as a whole. Consequently, the dogma regarding the law of the state as the most powerful source of social control proves to be a myth in some instances in our Western civilization." It might even be said that the major contribution of anthropological research on controlling processes was to indicate the rather minor role of state legal systems (at least in democratic societies) compared to that of control systems in other social institutions such as religious and business organizations.

When investigators take this idea of multiplicity into the field, how their fieldwork is conducted and analyzed will be affected. Pospisil's (1958) work on the Kapauku in Papua New Guinea illustrates this, as does the work of L. Nader on the Zapotec in Southern Mexico, a people who live in an essentially egalitarian, agrarian society. Nader (1964, 1965, 1969, n.d.) studied the functions of the village law court, family moots, supernatural devices, and the principles of societal organization in controlling and regulating social action, in an attempt to understand social control as a complete societal process. For example, youngsters were rarely brought to justice, and the age for serious delinquency was between the years of 35 and 50. An explanation of this phenomenon required understanding family structure, inheritance patterns, and drinking behavior, as well as control systems outside the court.

Nader's work illustrates two points: first, that order is not solely a result of law and the enforcement of law; and second, that the operation and organization of law cannot be understood apart from the social structure out of which the law developed and within which it operates. The first finding grew out of an examination of how Zapotec village social organization works as a form of control. The second point is related to the idea of multiplicity: a comparison of dispute-settling mechanisms within a society illuminates relationships among various agencies of social control. For example, as government becomes centralized, witchcraft tends to lose strength as a controlling force; and with increased physical mobility, family authority decreases. In other words, a number of factors related to the distribution of authority affect the regulation of behavior in this Zapotec community (Nader, n.d.).

A comparable study in the United States focused specifically on how Americans deal with their complaints about products and services (Nader, 1980a). As any active consumer knows, consumer complaints are handled not only by government regulatory agencies but by elected political officials, trade associations, professional societies, independent businesses, voluntary organizations, and individuals. All these different ways for handling consumer complaints operate simultaneously and consumers often send the same complaint to several different agencies. One interesting finding of this research was that government agencies established by law to regulate corporate activities were relatively ineffective in resolving consumer complaints, while trade associations, intent on business self-regulation, effectively deflected them.

Although regulatory agencies have generated numerous rules, their power to enforce these is limited, for they are often coopted by the organizations they are supposed to regulate. In addition, the sheer numbers of government agencies have made them inaccessible to consumers with complaints (Serber, 1980). The result of research on the American complaint process which was conducted over a period of ten years (Nader, 1980a) indicates "the fallacy of the dogma that the true and most powerful type of law exists only on the society level" (Pospisil, 1971, p. 117) and suggests the correctness of Max Weber's view that in some instances there are groups whose systems of rules are stronger than those of the state (Weber, 1967).

Again the work of Pospisil (1971, p. 118) is seminal:

> In the long perspective the center of power, of course, is not a static phenomenon. The relative amount of power at the various levels within a society . . . may diminish or increase, with the result that the center of power (defined by the relative amount of control power of the various societal segments) may shift its position to another level.

This observation is useful when regulation of complaints about products and services is viewed historically (Nader, in press). For example, consumers' inability to regulate the producer by any reciprocal economic levers resulted in the intervention of the federal government. Three hundred years ago, most people living in what is now the United States were both consumers and producers, and dependency was not a critical variable. As the country's primary economic activity changed from subsistence agriculture to industrialization and the roles of consumer and producer became separated, the balance of power shifted: the absolute power previously enjoyed by consumers was diminished. A larger diversity and availability of products served to rationalize this shift of power. By the late nineteenth century, the greater power of producers could be measured by their organization of large numbers of employees and massive resources, their effective political lobbying, the number of complaints received and left unsettled, and the number of social mechanisms created to remedy the inequities in this power shift, i.e., small claims courts, regulatory agencies, and legal aid (Samson, 1980).

The separation of the roles of consumer and producer brought about by the industrial revolution created social and economic problems. At the turn of the century, some of these problems were inflation (in particular, the exorbitant rise in food prices, which had been stable between about 1840 and 1870), contaminated food, polluted water that caused typhus and typhoid, unsafe workplaces, monopolistic practices, illegal rebate, and deceptive advertising. As a result the Federal Trade Commission, the Food and Drug Administration, and other government regulatory agencies were set up (ibid.). Thus government regulation may be said to have come about due to the imbalance and abuse of power, though the regulatory authority was at times shaped also by the future regulatees who, knowing that they could not stop regulation, determined to turn it to their advantage (e.g., Kolko, 1965). It is important to distinguish cartel regulation desired by industry (as with the ICC, the Maritime Commission, and the Department of Agriculture) from health and safety regulation (see Green and Moore, 1973; Green and Nader, 1973; Winter, 1973).

By the latter half of the twentieth century, the absolute power positions of consumers, producers, and government had changed. Now, both organized producers and organized government have considerably more power than dispersed consumers, and it is an open question whether organized government is more powerful than organized business and in what areas either predominates (Lindblom, 1978). It is also open to question whether such loci of concentrated power away from consumers can still be justified or explained as a crucial precondition for a specialized complex product and service economy. Our excessive dependence on centralized and vulnerable energy systems in contrast to energy alternatives that reduce costly dependency and increase choice illustrates this point (see Lovins and Lovins, 1982).

Government regulation—public law—is, then, fairly recent in our history. The rules that regulate social behavior may emanate from government, business firms, professional societies, or other sources of organized power, but external control of these behaviors, whether this control is public and legally enforceable or private and socially enforceable, is connected to some other part of the society's network of regulatory processes. In this view, government regulation is an accumulation of social values that translate into legal mandates to redress power imbalances and the abuse of power. Under these conditions, the issue is not one of regulation per se but, rather, one of the contending conflicts and problems existing in society.

Examining government regulation as part of a society-wide network of regulatory processes reduces the insularity with which government regulation is often viewed and highlights the distinctiveness of its role. The need for laws depends quite heavily on how the private sector is organized. Cadillac owners organized to negotiate their complaints directly with General Motors may not need government intervention, may use government empowerment tools (as under the Moss-Magnuson warranty law), or at least may provide more stimulus for the issuance of government automobile standards. An industry that translates its corporate rules into government rules (as with the trucking industry and the Interstate Commerce Commission) will oppose deregulation because it shaped governmental regulatory activity to suit its purposes.

Toward an Ethnography of Regulation

We mentioned the use of comparative and interactive models in a research agenda aimed at a holistic understanding of private controls (what we chose to call "private regulation") as they relate to government regulation. The purpose of the comparative approach is to map a working outline that schematically compares the spheres of government, business, and science organizations in relation to several distinctions: (1) between self-regulation and the regulation of others; (2) between proactive and reactive behaviors; (3) between direct and indirect (or consequent) regulation; and (4) between rules that are enforced informally (not within the context of organized corporate bodies) and regulation that is conducted in the formal setting of an organized group that can be held accountable. We want to convey the sense of what it is like to study the controlling processes in government, business, and science organizations together and at a number of levels—real and ideal, formal and informal, legally enforceable and socially enforceable, manifest and latent.[3] If one were to imagine how an anthropologist from Mars would observe and study government regulation in the United States, one would catch the spirit in which this paper is being written. We are

3. Commissioner Michael Pertschuk, then of the Federal Trade Commission, presented a set of lectures at the University of California in November 1981 (Pertschuk, 1982). Such lectures on the political strategies of regulation and deregulation are among the most useful kinds of ethnographic materials for an anthropologist.

consciously simplifying what we know to be complex in order to capture a holistic perspective. The examples presented here should provide background for a discussion of how different parties to regulation manage it.

The Comparative Model

In a commencement address at Stanford University in 1978, Donald Kennedy, then head of the Food and Drug Administration, presented one view of government regulation. He told of a food company executive who had complained to him about new labeling regulations. To underline his point, the executive read a long list of ingredient names (most of them unknown outside a chemistry laboratory) taken from a package containing some bakery confection. Kennedy confessed to feeling intimidated: "So conditioned had I become to this well-rehearsed tactic of blame-placing that it never occurred to me until that night that I should have said, 'Listen, Mr. Baker, I didn't put all that stuff in your damn sweet rolls.'" Who is responsible for regulation, Kennedy asked his audience, the government or the producer? The suggestion is that if there were no chemical ingredients in foods, we would not have to regulate them. Kennedy emphasized government's function of protecting the public against the adverse consequences of corporate power. To the question of whether regulation is growing tougher, Kennedy replied: "This is one of those times at which it will pay us to pause and consider whether the eyes are moving or the world is moving. What is moving is the size, the complexity, the power of the regulated enterprise, not government." Kennedy's example suggests that in this instance government regulation is reactive and that the reason for such labeling regulations will be found in business practices at top corporate levels.

Some view government regulation as proactive. Publications of the American Enterprise Institute report that government regulations influence employment practices and workplace conditions, earnings and pensions, prices and allocations, energy and the environment, transportation and safety, product characteristics and labeling, advertising and disclosure, and many other private and public activities. Research on the consequences of proactive government regulation, of course, has illustrated its effect on the organization of numerous subgroups in our society, ranging from families to corporate businesses.

Government regulation is initiated by such executive agencies as the Federal Trade Commission, the Federal Communications Commission, the Food and Drug Administration, and, more recently, the Environmental Protection Agency, the Consumer Product Safety Commission, the Nuclear Regulatory Commission, and the Occupational Safety and Health Administration. These and similar agencies in the executive branch of government are not the only places in government where regulation appears. When Congress legislates, it is regulating. Of course, it was the legislative branch that passed the laws creating regulatory agencies. These agencies were organized in response to demand. A corporate-created disaster such as Love Canal produces public demand that government immediately mitigate the plight of victims. The Hooker Chemical Company was not expected to respond to this pressing need, although that responsibility may eventually be defined by the courts. It appears that accepting later-stage responsibility for actions by the private sector may characterize the uniqueness of government regulation. Thus, in the case of kepone poisoning of the James River, the government rather than Allied Chemical and its subsidiary company, Life Sciences, is ultimately responsible for clean-up and public health measures associated with the factory, the river, and the fish. If the function of government is to protect ordinary people against such adverse consequences of corporate practices, then responsibility, some would argue, must be accompanied by commensurate power, such as adequate authority to survey, to prevent damage, and to impose sanctions for compensation and deterrence when damage occurs.

The responsibility of business is more clear-cut in some areas. A number of institutions have evolved as business's response to threats of federal regulation. One is the Better Business Bureaus, which were established early in the century (Eaton, 1980). More recently, trade associations have become active in strengthening regulation by industry. Among these, the most well-known are the CAP organizations, the Consumer Action Panels (Greenberg and Stanton, 1980). But two other sources of regulation are less visible: the direct regulation of the corporate worker, as in regard to occupational hazards, and the effect on society of corporate organization and praxis, as in regard to environmental pollution. The latter may be categorized as indirect, consequent, latent, or unintended. When corporations force the public to accept their standards in air, water, food, clothing, and transport, the results are just as much examples of regulation as when government sets mandatory health and safety standards for business.

The picture is complicated by questions of intentionality. We can hardly say that corporations developed rules governing workers and production with the primary intention of getting Americans to con-sume an average of five pounds a year of additives in food, or that business regulates itself in such a way as to insure that a certain amount of pollution is produced in the air we breathe or in the water we drink. Nevertheless, certain corporate regulations can knowingly result in environmental pollution, and as a consequence the businesses concerned are heavily responsible, though not necessarily accountable, for what is in our air and water. If we asked people who decides on the quality of American air and who controls the amount of pollution in our water supply, many would respond by naming a large-scale organization. If they said government, they could be referring to the regulatory aspects of the Clean Water Act or the Clean Air Act. If they said industry, they could be referring to acts regulated not by government but, rather, by the way industries regulate their businesses (that is, govern according to rules).

This comparative approach to regulation could stimulate research on the following questions: (1) How does industry's regulation of its workers and its production control the quality of the environment? (2) Does government regulation control industry? In a controlled comparative study, government deregulation can be understood as decreasing regulation in the public sphere while increasing it in the private sphere. Again the broad research question here is to compare government (public) and business (private) methods of regulation. Are they mirror-images of each other, or is there a difference related to the fact that government operates within legally enforceable rules and industry under private law?

The whole process is of interest. To say that government regulates and business does not is to omit an important part of this process. A more comprehensive view of regulation is achieved if we recognize that corporate policy compels managers to show profits quarterly and that this stricture leads to their cutting corners, resulting in environmental degradation which leads in turn to public demand for government regulation—a demand that the government does not always meet.

Another example can be drawn from educational testing. The perspective that all organizations regulate leads us to recognize that the educational testing industry regulates itself in such a way (that is, according to a set of rules) that certain kinds of intelligence are favored over others and become the heavily promoted criteria by which its customers—the universities—choose the future professionals (Nairn and Associates, 1980). Objection to this channeling may lead to a demand for government regulation in the form, for example, of a Truth-in-Testing law like that on the books in the State of New York. Such examples underscore the need for research on government regulation as a response to how corporations regulate their businesses.

When business governs science, the regulation imposed is informal and indirect. Many examples of how business regulates science have been reported to indicate that though this kind of informal regulation is hard to detect, given its indirect, sometimes hidden nature, there are rules governing behavior nonetheless.[4]

The problem of understanding how science is regulated involves both government and industry. Scientific organizations regulate behavior indirectly and sometimes by omission rather than commission. Black (1976, p. 80) has described social control among scientists as "informal and decentralized, indirect, often subtle, but inescapable," and our understanding is hardly complete without continuing the research initiated by Paul Feyerabend (1978). Understanding regulation in the sphere of science requires us to understand that the most important change here since World War II is that scientists have become employees without job security. At the end of the nineteenth century and during the early part of the twentieth, most scientists were connected with university departments and they often paid for their own research. What we have now is a scientific establishment in which great numbers of scientists are working in big industrial or government laboratories, sometimes connected with universities, sometimes with large corporations. By virtue of both latent and manifest mission this situation has resulted in a considerable amount of regulation of what scientists can investigate and what they are allowed to disclose and interpret.

In short, the requirements of the workplace can have more to do with commerce, ideology, and political-economic power than with science; these confront scientists with the issues of scientific freedom and responsibility when they are faced with self-regulation or regu-

4. A group of companies that produced the birth control pill financed research at the University of Wisconsin some years ago and refused to allow the scientists to publish findings on the consequences of particular brands that were being tested (pers. comm. from one of these researchers).

Dr. Dante Picciano, Ph.D., a worker with Dow Chemical in Galveston, Texas, wanted to release information on the harmful effects of benzene on workers; he had to quit his job (March 1978) in order to do so. Officials at a brush beryllium plant in Ohio prohibited the company physician from publishing his case on beryllium poisoning in the medical literature (testimony by Dr. Hawey A. Wells before the House Select Committee on Labor, U.S. Congress, 1968; excerpted in Page and O'Brien, 1973). The cosmetic industry regulates the kind of research its scientists undertake: for example, there is little research—or at least little published—on the effects of cosmetic products such as hair dyes (see R. Nader, 1974). The auto industry restricted the area of crash safety research and the application of what was known (R. Nader, 1973). In the food industry also, there are restrictions on the flow of information and the areas of inquiry (see Turner, 1970, pp. 82–106).

lation by others (Edsall, 1981). The task of self-regulation for scientists is made more difficult by their organizational work structure, just as it is for engineers (Layton, 1971; Noble, 1977; and the account of the generally indirect nature of social control in the sciences by H. Zuckerman, 1977).

Numerous accounts tell of the managers of science regulating what scientists work on, what they find, and what is allowed to be released to the public. We say "regulating" because there are sets of rules that govern behavior in large technical organizations where they work. If scientists violate these rules, the sanctions imposed are often severe. John Goffman and Arthur Tamplin's research on radiation risks in the late 1960s directly challenged the policies of the Atomic Energy Commission; when they refused to accept AEC directives to withhold their findings from the public, they were encouraged to resign from their jobs at the commission's laboratory at Livermore (Nader, Petkas, and Blackwell, 1972). The professional scientific societies did not unequivocally support the rights of these scientists to speak freely.

The same story has been repeated elsewhere enough times to suggest that while professional societies may have norms or rules governing scientific freedom, they have not organized their considerable clout to defend such rules (Layton, 1971; Furner, 1975). The examples again are numerous[5] and clearly illustrate regulation of the scientists, both by government and by the corporations, through a variety of patterned and predictable "rules" of behavior. These include intimidation, ostracism, threat of job loss, isolation, withdrawal of research support, forced resignations, and outright firing.

Although the rules governing the internal structuring of organizations work in many cases, self-regulation in relation to external consequences is not working in business, in science, or in government, according to concerned citizens and victims of poor self-regulation (Nader, 1980a). Sutherland (1961) reported some years ago that half of the largest corporations were habitual criminal-law violators and that among these, a small number of businesses had

5. For example, Dr. Jacqueline Verrett's work at the Food and Drug Administration on cyclamates was sanctioned (Nader, Petkas, Blackwell, 1972); Morris Baslow, a marine biologist, was fired for "going public" with company documents concerning the effects on Hudson River fish of thermal effluents from power plants; Thomas Mancuso, a radiation specialist who worked on radiation levels at the Hanford nuclear facility in the state of Washington, had his support withdrawn by the Atomic Energy Commission. Other scientists who challenged the construction of ballistic missiles and who looked for biological controls of pests were also sanctioned (Von der Bosch, 1980). A government scientist who insisted on accurately reporting the connection between exposure to formaldehyde and cancer risk was fired and then reinstated (U.S. House of Representatives, 1981; see also Garwin [1983] pp. 9–11).

been responsible for a large number of violations. The absence of socially responsible self-regulation has probably caused the substantial increase in the number of government regulations. If we add to that observation the growing number of products, chemicals, and technologies that enter the market each year, there is no possibility that government regulatory agencies can meet the increasing regulatory requirements.[6]

We need to study regulation in the context of what Malinowski (1926, pp. 3–4) called *conformity behavior,* the "mechanisms whereby the individual is induced to do what people expect of him even though through selfish interest he is tempted to do otherwise." Although it was an anthropologist who so effectively drew attention to the problem, much literature that examines this conformity in American society is found in history and sociology (e.g., Erickson, 1966; Hunter, 1953; Zuckerman, 1970).

On the other side of the coin, attempts to deal with regulation, that is, to respond to others when regulation is taking place or about to take place, indicate something about the social conditions that lead to noncomformity behavior. For example, the amount of power held by individuals or groups may influence their degree of nonconformity to regulation. American automobile company executives have been observed trying to stop or to weaken production standards. The Japanese, in contrast (at least in the late 1960s and early 1970s when they were relatively insecure), met with appropriate Department of Transportation officials to gain knowledge that would help them meet the standards.

The Interactive Model

The responses to regulation that come to public notice and often contribute to the formulation of public policy are those that include extreme forms of interaction.[7] However, it must be mentioned that regulation by others is not always resisted. Corporations, for example, have welcomed exclusive licenses, subsidies, tax incentives, loan guarantees, and other economic regulations and have, indeed, actively sought them.

Let us assume that in examining interactions between corporations and government we are able to profile corporate strategies for

6. On occasion the Federal Communications Commission has admitted that AT&T was simply too big to regulate. The FCC budget for 1977 was $56.7 million, whereas for 1980 AT&T's gross revenues were $51,680,000,000 and its assets $125,451,000,000, according to AT&T's 1980 *Annual Report.*

7. See Chapter 2 in this volume for a survey of materials relevant to an interaction model.

managing unwanted government regulation, and government response to these corporate strategies. And let us also assume, for the
moment, that certain themes characterize these interactions. Corporate strategies may include denial (as in denying the danger of chemical pesticides), confrontation (as happened directly between industry and the Federal Trade Commission in the latter part of the Carter
Administration), binary opposition (the choice between worker
safety and closed plants), intimidation (as illustrated in the statement from Donald Kennedy quoted above), corporate-centered arguments (the allegation that regulation reduces productivity and increases the cost of products), and secrecy ("we cannot tell you what is
in that product because it is a trade secret"). The profile could also
include corporate managers' inattention to the impact of their own
regulation on consumers or victims, and their tendency, instead, to
view the effects of government regulation as an infringement of personal freedom or a job put at risk. This "partial story" told by corporations may be part of an overarching strategy to woo public opinion
when confronted with proposed government regulation. Such responses (which Noll, in another context, refers to as signals) result in
a dyadic confrontation on the issue of regulation, instead of cooperation among business, government, and public to resolve the problems. For example, if corporate officials in their public statements on
regulation gave equal time to the substantial benefits corporations
have derived from government programs such as the new technologies for pollution detection, a confrontational and adversary stance
could be avoided. Research using an historical perspective on how
and in what areas this adversarial posturing has developed and how
it is woven into discussions on current government regulation would
be of value.

If denial is a central feature of corporate response to government
regulation, the profile could conclude that defensiveness followed by
cooptation is the principal characteristic of government response to
corporate regulators—a fact widely reported in political science
studies. The defensiveness is not limited to corporate intrusions,
however. Government regulators also retreated in cases like those
involving recombinant DNA technology when genetic engineering
specialists objected to government action beyond the guidelines of
the National Institute of Health. Government response strategies
are often contextually determined and due to a number of variables:
whether government is taking the initiative or simply reacting to an
external force; whether government is operating independently of
corporate goals or supporting business in its actions; and whether
the government speaks in unison or is divided.

A government that takes an autonomous position responds to such corporate malpractices as environmental pollution by passing a Clean Air Act, a Safe Drinking Water Act, a Clean Water Act, or a Toxic Substances Control Act. It responds by creating such agencies as the Environmental Protection Agency to set and enforce environmental clean-up standards or the Occupational Safety and Health Administration to insure healthful conditions in the workplace.

A reactive government may be more susceptible to corporate control. In other words, when government reacts primarily to the corporate constituency, joint corporate and government regulatory actions are likely to emerge. Research on the process of cooptation would increase our understanding of why it works in some instances and not in others. When cooptation occurs, government officials readily accept corporate complaints and assumptions about regulation obstructing productivity or stifling technological innovation. A reactive government promotes the interests of producers more often than those of consumers. For example, government, the initial promoter of nuclear technology, made common cause with the nuclear industry. Government's response to the exercise of corporate power was defensive in this area—so defensive that it restrained its scientists from making health and safety information available to the public if this information was likely to undermine the industry or Atomic Energy Commission (AEC) programs. The government also reacted defensively toward citizen groups working on nuclear safety.

In the sphere of science, standards shaped by others represent an unwelcome intrusion. Scientists, like most groups, prefer complete autonomy and, indeed, argue that science cannot exist without it. Yet, scientists have now been regulated for a number of decades by the presence or absence of funds (public and private) and by connections with the military. More recently, agencies and congressional committees have become concerned with regulating how science is done. The concern with protecting human subjects in experiments is only part of the picture.

For our purposes, recombinant DNA research is a good example of how scientists have shaped regulation. In this research, scientists first expressed concern about associated biohazards—an early effort at self-regulation. Their concern led in 1976 to National Institute of Health (NIH) guidelines for tax-supported gene-splicing research. Public questioning of biohazards from recombination continued on university campuses and in communities across the country. By 1977, the recombinant DNA issue was on the congressional agenda for the purpose of extending NIH guidelines to industry through legislation. Scientists, with few exceptions, protested vigorously. They resisted any intervention, particularly if legislation defined the regulatory framework. They were more comfortable with regulation within the NIH structure. It was their agency and, indeed, they had created the guidelines and helped to form the NIH Recombinant Advisory Committee on which they also serve. This committee is presently in the process of dismantling the guidelines completely and may even recommend its own abolition, although some members recognize that the committee gives a semblance of legitimacy to their activities and thus earns a degree of public confidence (Wright, 1982).

The strategies that these scientists used are by now familiar: denial (the research is not dangerous); optimism (the benefits are greater than the potential hazards); pulling rank (the experts promoting the technology know best); intellectual productivity (scientists cannot produce without complete autonomy). Such response strategies are used by almost any group seeking to manage unwanted external regulation. Cost-benefit analysis in which costs are emphasized and benefits ignored is another common strategy. The corporate way of handling outside regulation reflects a certain uniformity and conformity. There is little internal dissent. In government, there is more variety: some agencies pursue their health and safety missions more vigorously than others. In science, also, there are differences among scientists who serve corporate objectives well and others, for example, who belong to the Union of Concerned Scientists, a Cambridge-based group that works on nuclear health and safety issues. In contrast, corporate strategies remain mostly homogeneous, not yet diversified enough to stimulate innovative solutions.[8]

How does the public respond to government regulation? On social regulation the polls have been clear for a number of years, showing that people want their government to control the contamination of their drinking water, air and soil, and unsafe products and technologies.[9]

8. A recent exception is the insurance industry's November 1981 lawsuit challenging the basis of the federal government's rescission of the rule to install air bags or automatic seat belts. It is an example of a corporate initiative that combines the interests of insurers and consumers and that, in effect, challenges the auto industry's case against automatic restraints. The insurance companies have long pushed for federal regulation requiring automatic restraints to protect people in cars, since they have an interest in reducing the number of claims. In other areas, they have argued for fewer government regulations (Barbara Fried, "Rescission of Air Bag Rule Is Hit," *Washington Post*, 25 June 1983, p. A 1; Linda Greenhouse, "Reagan Is Set Back on Airbag Decision," *New York Times*, 25 June 1983, p. 1).

9. For coverage of a recent survey by the Roper Organization, see Barringer (1981). We know little about how the public responds to government economic regulations that favor corporations. No public fuss is made by corporations over this kind of government regulation and thus few, if any, public polls are conducted about it. More-

It may be that the response to regulation reflects the structures of power, perceived or real. Individuals and groups may be not so much opposing regulation itself as the structure of power that regulation represents. For example, corporations accept much of government's economic regulation because they themselves, through lobbying and other means of influence, have shaped the regulations to their advantage. But corporations usually resist social regulation such as the imposition of health and safety standards. In the case of the genetic engineering community, scientists took the position that if there had to be government regulations, the procedure should enable them to shape the regulations and control the regulatory apparatus to their ends. In contrast, much of the government's contemporary social regulation received its stimulus from a broader base of citizens and citizen groups. Public-interest advocates of environmental and health regulation in the 1960s and 1970s advanced their views in Congress, the executive branch of government, and the courts.

The suggestion that we adopt a comparative and interactional approach to the study of government regulation is not new. But we are not suggesting a number of isolated, institutional comparisons or comparison within one sphere of social activity, say, government. Instead, we are suggesting a comparison aimed at producing a holistic rather than a partial perspective on regulation. A simultaneous examination of controlling processes in large-scale organizations may clarify the interconnections in these forms of control and who in fact is doing the controlling. It is a method of separating myths from the realities of power. These interactions reflect power structures, but the whole picture reflects the social and cultural fabric of this country and, in particular, the distribution of power. As Pospisil (1971) notes, power is not a static entity. Government regulation and government deregulation may be, among other things, signals of power passing from one sphere to another and following a cyclical pattern over the years, a pattern explainable by phenomena such as dwindling natural resources, business stagnation, and shifts in ideological paradigms. Illuminating research on government regulation and deregulation must focus on the dynamics of power and controlling processes in the society at large.

---

over, it may be that the collective effects of corporate health and safety hazards are more easily seen and understood than the consequences of economic regulations giving advantages to corporations at the expense of victims. The regulations of the Department of the Treasury or the bank agencies may appear more esoteric than those of OSHA because they have not been publicized. This is so in part because corporate strategy in areas that did not favor corporations was to go public in an effort to put the government on the defensive.

Discussion

The study of regulation in the United States is a study of the relations between the economic activities of production, distribution, consumption, and the political institutions of an industrial society such as the U.S. (MacLennan, 1980). It is also a study of the policies and internal operations of organizations and their patterns of survival. A new view of the regulation debates not only requires us to broaden the context in which regulation may be understood as a universal process, it also requires us to include in our focus the victims as well as the perpetrators of regulatory action. The life-history method in anthropology suggests possible kinds of findings.

During research on American complaints, we pursued one complaint vertically (Nader, 1980b). The idea was that if we looked at the relations between the spheres and hierarchies we have been discussing and the people experiencing the consequences of organizational behaviors, we would have an important perspective on the evolution of responsibility for health and safety in this country. The exercise would also make concrete what is often abstract in discussions of regulation.

The complaint we investigated dealt with an eight-year-old whose shirt was engulfed in flames within two to three seconds after a match touched the cloth. The surgeon could not believe that clothing so flammable that it sticks like plastic to the skin and causes third-degree burns could be marketed legally in America, and suggested that the victim's parents complain to the Consumer Product Safety Commission. Their letter to the commission asked simply: "Why did the shirt burn so rapidly?" In our field research we examined the roles of the federal flammability laws, W. T. Grant (the retailer), the National Retail Merchants Association, the American Textile Manufacturers Institute, the Senate Commerce Committee, the Cone Mills Corporation, the Department of Commerce, the White House, a presidential campaign finance chairman, the Consumer Product Safety Commission, the Federal Trade Commission, and other hierarchies organizationally related to the situation.

The three months of research on that single complaint uncovered a dense interaction among industry and government groups, with each organization intent on its own survival. The paucity of interaction between these organizations and the family affected by their actions provided a striking contrast. The answer to the parents' question, "Why did the shirt burn so rapidly?" was as complex as America itself. In tracing a case such as this one, we become aware of the constraints organizations place on their employees and the importance of direct interaction in influencing decisions. Regulatory policies must be developed in a more comprehensive framework that recognizes that many regulatory forces affect a variety of people in this society. The prevailing approach attempts to solve the problem of government regulation while leaving untouched the corporate/government/science structures that are a significant part of the problem. Thus the search for alternative ideas concerned with systemic change in the structures and cultures of organized power should be an important part of a research agenda. The federal chartering of large corporations, designed to produce socially responsive decisions early in the process, is an example of a possible systemic change—an idea that was first bruited in the Taft-Roosevelt period.

In short, policy research that questions the structures and work arrangements of powerful organizations is badly needed if regulatory innovations that contribute to social and economic problem-solving are to take root. Policies aimed at restructuring corporations to facilitate improved self-discipline or self-criticism (in order that government not be burdened by corporate regulations) will in turn require understanding more about legal and organizational structures, how corporate officials define ethics, and the meaning of organizational survival (Martin, 1980).

We also need research to help us understand organizational cultures. The question that consumers often ask is: What is the origin of the beliefs about production that have resulted in the insertion of chemicals into our food? The usual explanation—preserving the life of the product—only accounts for a portion of the materials injected into our food chain. Yet, as Kennedy has indicated, putting less junk in bakery goods would mean that the Food and Drug Administration could shorten its list of regulated substances. But the use of these materials is no more rational than other aspects of modern life. For instance, is it rational to use pesticides far in excess of the amount needed to fulfill their objective (Von der Bosch, 1980) or not to advocate a strong program to avoid the use of harmful pesticides (see Von der Bosch and Flint, 1981)? One may also question the rationality of inappropriate application of the cost-benefit technique in health and safety matters (see Green and Waitzman, 1981) or of placing the burden of proving the toxicity or safety of an industrial product on the potential victim. Such irrationalities become an integral part of the subculture of organizations, and we need to do research on these cultural phenomena if we are to understand them.

Widening the angle of our focus on the issue of regulation invites analysis of the power of informal controlling processes and the vulnerability of formal processes to pressure from the organization(s) being regulated. Such a broader view can prevent mistakes by scholars as well as policymakers in their analysis of the effects of regulation on the regulated. The dominance of the narrow-focus view by the antiregulatory critique of the late 1970s missed the strategy of troubled companies of using regulation as a scapegoat for poor management, little innovation, and indifference to consumer needs. The auto and steel industries illustrate this point (see Abernathy, 1978, on the mismanagement issue; Peters and Waterman, 1982).

Corporate regulation is a more controversial subject to analyze; it invites avoidance because corporations regularly shield themselves from critical external inquiries.[10] This type of regulation appears more indirect and invisible conceptually, and this indirect social control is very often more powerful than formal regulation and is less subject to accountability. We recommend a research agenda that examines regulation in the United States in the context of power and responsibility over time and space and through the inclusion of a number of variables. In addition, this regulation should be analyzed in the context of organizational and cultural constraints. Such an agenda may permit a scientific and predictive analysis of more than the tip of the regulatory iceberg.

COMMENT: *Carol MacLennan*

The Naders' paper begins the unique contribution anthropologists have to make to the study of government regulation. A wide-angle focus on the study of social behavior, the hallmark of the anthropological approach, can lead to asking important historical and cultural questions about a topic that often gets lost in the more specifically focused studies characteristic of other disciplines.

The task at hand is one, as the Naders point out, of reconceptualizing the regulation debate. Their paper makes a significant step in this direction by introducing three tools that enable us to ask important questions: (1) the concept of multiple systems of regulation by which societies govern the behavior of their members; (2) the concept of the interactive model of regulation; and (3) the application of

10. See statement of Russell B. Stevenson, Jr. (1976) for a thoughtful discussion of "rules governing access to information about corporations, their products, and their activities." For example, he states: *"there is nothing private about a public corporation"* (p. 59); and "economic incentives [are used] to *conceal* from their customers most information about product quality" (p. 59; Stevenson's emphasis). Stevenson cites Tibor Scitovsky (1950).

a holistic method to understanding both the formal and informal regulatory processes. The comments below attempt to use these tools to suggest new avenues for rethinking our understanding of the role of regulation in American culture.

Multiple Systems of Regulation

A broad definition of *regulation* is extremely useful in understanding the complex debate of recent years. The wide-angle approach defines *regulation* as a form of social control and recognizes government regulation as only one among multiple systems of regulation. While government regulation may be the only "legal" system of regulation operating in the United States, other powerful systems of regulation by government, by business, and by technical/scientific societies are cited extensively in the Naders' paper. Their paper shows that government regulation can be understood only in the context of a *whole* process of regulation—both formal and informal—that includes various systems of regulation of society by powerful institutions.

The concept of multiple systems is extremely useful when interpreting the changes in government regulation that have evolved over the last eighty years. Like other cultures, including pre-state societies, Americans have institutionalized both formal and informal forms of social control. Formal legal regulation began during the period of rapid industrialization in the 1890s, with the Sherman Anti-Trust Act. Looking at the emergence of regulatory activity in the United States over the century, one might argue that it has increased in response to the new phases of industrialization just at the point when some form of public control over the process is essential either to regularize it or to enable social adaptation to the social-structural transformations it brings about. Although scholars of regulation are familiar with the general history of government regulation, it is worth a brief review in the context of the multiple-system concept.

Beginning in the early 1900s, regulation of business by government became a significant mechanism by which the public exercised control over business practices that were perceived as harmful to society as a whole (Kolko, 1963, 1965). This was the period of anti-trust legislation and the birth of the Federal Trade Commission (FTC) and Food and Drug Administration (FDA). This first regulatory wave marked the end of a thirty-year period of rapid industrialization during which the corporation emerged as a new form of business organization, the transportation industry expanded rapidly, and a growing wage-labor force and shrinking farm population turned food (especially meat) processing into a sizable industry.

In the 1930s, a new wave of social control over the economic practices and patterns of the business culture spawned agencies such as the Securities and Exchange Commission (SEC). During the economic crises of the '30s and '40s regulation brought order to the chaos of the business world and to labor-management relations (e.g., the National Labor Relations Authority).

In the 1960s and '70s, social concern over the effects new chemicals and new consumer practices in communities and workplaces and in new products might have on workers' and consumers' health and safety spurred the development of new regulatory agencies including National Highway Traffic Safety Administration (founded in 1966), Environmental Protection Agency (1970), Occupational Safety and Health Administration (1970), and Consumer Product Safety Commission (1972).

Wide-Angle Perspective

A perspective on regulation that utilizes the concept of the multiple systems of social control also helps with interpretation of the current regulation debate. *Deregulation* is a relatively new concept. The pressure for regulatory reform can be viewed as a social movement just as the move toward health and safety regulation in earlier years represented the emergence of a public health movement. Deregulation began with the recession of the mid-1970s. By 1977, with the advent of the Carter Administration, the concept of deregulation was popularly understood as a movement to curtail the *cost* of regulating business. In the context of the Naders' definition of regulation as social control occurring in multiple spheres, the regulatory reform programs of the Carter and Reagan administrations are the manifestations of this new social movement.

Under the Reagan Administration informal (indirect) systems of regulation of the public sphere (regulatory agencies) by the private sphere (business interests) are apparent. This form of social control is not institutionalized by law as is government regulation, but it is nonetheless regulation in its broadest sense. Perhaps the most important point of the regulation debate is not found in its content (whether or not regulations cost too much) but in what regulation symbolizes: the shift of power from one sphere to another and from one form of social control to another.

This leads us to the second contribution of the Naders' paper: the concept of the interactive model of regulation. The study of cost-benefit analysis as an informal mechanism of control by one sphere over another illustrates how the interactive model is useful in exploring the underlying themes of the regulatory debate.

The Interactive Model of Regulation

The Naders show that if we assume the existence of multiple systems of regulation, then we can study how powerful spheres of society interact. As the paper suggests, one broad research question that needs examination is how government (the public system governed by law) and business (a system of private law) *regulate each other:* "government regulation and government deregulation may . . . be symbols of power passing from one sphere to another." The institutionalization of cost-benefit analysis during the late 1970s and early '80s illustrates this.

The movement for deregulation has been cost-conscious, based on the belief that government regulations are harmful to society because of the cost drains on companies during a period of economic distress. Cost-benefit analysis is the tool proposed to evaluate whether regulations are too costly for the benefits in health preservation that they provide, both now and in the future. Cost-benefit analysis (CBA) has both a manifest and a latent function in the regulatory process. On the surface, it is intended to be a more or less precise and unbiased tool for determining the costs of regulation to business as compared to the societal benefits gained by implementing proposed regulation. CBA is a two-step activity: the first is measurement of costs and benefits (a research function); the second is weighing the costs and benefits against each other (a policy function). Theoretically, this approach assumes that all costs and benefits are measurable (and in the same units). Agency analysts who do this work find, as one would expect, that dollars are more measurable than the more qualitatively experienced benefits (Center for Policy Alternatives, 1980; Green and Waitzman, 1981). This is especially true when CBA is applied to proposed health and safety regulations, where the costs are primarily to business, which must comply with the standards (e.g., airbags in automobiles to protect occupants in crashes automatically and scrubbers in coal-fired power plants to reduce emissions and prevent air pollution). Often the benefits are experienced by less well-defined populations (e.g., people in auto crashes or in polluted urban areas). The benefits also tend to be expressed in the qualitative terms of health protected and lives saved. In addition, benefits are often experienced years after the expenses of altering a particular product or process have been incurred. Research has been scanty on developing the mechanisms for translating health-and-life values into monetary values (see Center for Policy Alternatives, 1982).[11] In fact, some theorists argue that this may

11. There is an important distinction in CBA between assignment of dollar values to death and injury before and after the event. It is one thing to attribute dollars to loss

not be a desirable exercise because there is no agreement in American culture that health and life can be traded for a dollar value (Kelman, 1981a; Fischhoff, 1977; Rhoads, 1980).[12] In sum, cost-benefit analysis is perceived as an analytical tool that presents objective information for decisionmakers. This is its manifest function. But it may be a flawed tool.

While the debate over CBA focuses on whether there is enough information to use the tool correctly for evaluation, there appears to be little discussion of a more important question—the effect of its use. Through the institutionalization of such categories as cost and measurement of intangible values in the regulatory process, CBA serves as an indirect form of social control of the private sphere over public or government regulation. This is its latent function. An examination of what is called regulatory reform in the health and safety fields illustrates this argument.

Cost-benefit analysis is the primary means by which the executive (the White House) has secured more central control over the activities of executive branch regulatory agencies (Dickson, 1981). Centralization of decisionmaking over the regulatory process in this sphere began during the Nixon Administration. However, increasing Office of Management and Budget (OMB) involvement in early formulation of new rules through reporting and review requirements during the Ford and Carter administrations expedited the process.

The Reagan Administration's Executive Order 12291 carries this one step further: it mandates the use of cost-benefit analysis in the decision of whether a proposed rule is too costly. To some extent, the idea of CBA had already gained credibility in regulatory agencies as one form of analysis.[13] The new Executive Order, however, made ex-

---

from death and injury after the fact as a partial compensation for the loss (e.g., court settlements for auto accidents). It is a qualitatively different practice to assign dollar values to deaths and injuries before the fact (the practice in CBA). This implies the existence of a true monetary equivalent for life. Whereas in the former case, the compensation for economic loss is negotiated among the parties involved (most often through a legal process), the latter case is the result of an arbitrary assignment of value by a technical analyst.

12. The technocratic response to this criticism of CBA has been the development of more sophisticated tools of analysis of regulatory schemes, Risk Assessment being the primary one. The focus, therefore, shifts from that of weighing the costs against the benefits to a more elaborate process of weighing costs against levels of risk. The unknown factor is no longer the value of intangible benefits, but the more statistical question of determining the risk factor of a given exposure.

13. George Ead's article (1981) verifies the trend toward greater White House control over regulation through OMB rules and review processes. As an insider in the Carter Administration he has documented the hidden activities of the deregulation movement that centered in the White House.

plicit what had been relatively hidden from public view. In fact, by 1981 the concept of cost justification (the pivotal function of CBA) had been accepted by health and safety agencies to such an extent that increasing sums have been allocated to define the costs of regulation without equal amounts (or amounts commensurate with the task) devoted to isolating and defining the benefits of specific regulations. Although decisions have not necessarily been determined on the basis of cost, during the Carter years the regulatory structures in the Executive Branch rapidly shifted toward an emphasis on cost justification. During this period of stagnation and business reactions against regulation, health and safety regulation came to be viewed as a social problem rather than a social solution.

As a tool for regulatory reform that was to be used as a method of objective analysis, CBA (and later Risk Analysis) actually undermined the original congressional intent of the regulatory programs. While regulation was not directly curtailed by business interests, it was indirectly undercut by CBA, as well as through other means. Moreover, CBA is conceptually rooted in a business philosophy about how to invest capital. The focus of CBA is on the economic consequences of decisionmaking. Therefore, when applied to social programs (e.g., social regulation) the assumption is that they must use economic or business criteria for implementation. Originally, CBA was used in the 1930s by the federal government as an evaluative tool for investment decisions concerning large public work projects such as the massive dams of the West. Its application to social (health and safety) regulatory programs is an indicator of the shift of power in the executive branch away from public control over private-sector decisions that have negative public-health consequences. The overt institutionalization of CBA through executive order marks the placement of business (cost) priorities as paramount over the health and safety concerns of the wider public interest.

The De- or Non-Regulation Effect

Imposition of formal CBA has several likely consequences that indirectly create the effect of de- or non-regulation and therefore serve as a latent form of business regulation of government. First, the requirement to promulgate regulations only if the benefits exceed the costs sets the stage for extensive delay and/or revisions in standards that weaken their ability to achieve the results desired by the general public (Eads, 1981). Because proposed standards may also force technological improvements, pushing the private sector toward more effective production schemes (Center for Policy Alternatives, 1980), there is often little or no basic data on costs and benefits that will meet the qualifications of a supporting analysis required by OMB from the agencies. In fact, research in many safety and health fields (especially that involved in development of adequate test procedures) is done by the agencies themselves. It is only after introduction of a product or a procedure that an adequate picture of cost can be achieved.

A second deregulatory effect of CBA, because of the burden of proof it imposes on innovative standard setting, is to force agencies to seek nonregulatory alternatives (that are generally less direct and less effective) to achieve their goals of life and health protection. As a result, consumer education and public information campaigns have become a substitute for standard-setting. In the public health-oriented agencies this requires a radical shift in research dollars and scientific expertise toward programs that public health experts have traditionally argued will bring small returns for the amount of time and dollar investment.[14] An example of this type of policy shift is the seat-belt campaign proposed by the National Highway Traffic Safety Administration as an alternative to a regulation requiring manufacturer installation of airbags or passive belts in vehicles.

The third deregulation effect of CBA is its role in basing the context of the regulation debate on economic premises. This is a dramatic shift away from the social and health premises of the 1960s and 1970s. This shift has occurred slowly as economic analysis has become the mainstay of policy justifications and the principal factor determining which agency research projects are funded. The more elusive social or noneconomic rationales for regulation have been largely ignored. This is an important trend because of the fact that the enabling legislation that commissioned new health and safety agencies to save lives made no or only vague mention of justifying actions upon economic grounds. Historically, the focus has been on promoting the programs that have the highest probability of success in saving lives. Traditionally, public health programs have aimed to eliminate the disease-causing agent rather than to change the behavior of the entire public. In modern terms this often means attacking the technological problem rather than ~ying to reeducate all the individuals involved.

14. One side-effect of this shift in policy focus from regulation to public education is the idling of scientific expertise built up in agency research offices during the last decade. Because the solution to the health and safety problem was defined as technological, it required recruitment of engineering, chemical, biological, epidemiological, and other expertise in the construction of solutions that made scientific sense. When the solution instead requires changing the behavior of the public, scientific research on the technological innovations atrophies. As a result, scientific advancement of im-

To summarize the above discussion, CBA has both a manifest and a latent function. It is this latter function that is a key to one way informal systems of regulation interact with each other. That is to say, while government regulates business, there is a reverse process (albeit more hidden and not part of the legal system) that has significant consequences for the regulatory process. Without applying the Naders' concepts of an interactive model and informal systems, we would have difficulty explaining the current regulatory process. From this perspective we can study two of the more powerful avenues of regulation at work—legal and ideological—each operating as a system of social control, yet effective by different mechanisms.

A Holistic View of the Regulatory Process: New Questions

The third contribution of the Naders' paper, and indeed of the anthropological perspective on regulation, is the attempt to define research questions that strike at the fundamental organization of the regulatory process: the Naders "are suggesting a comparison aimed at producing a holistic rather than a partial perspective on this particular problem of control. . . . Reconceptualizing the regulation debates will require us not only to broaden the context within which regulation may be understood as a universal process, but it will require us to include in our focus the victims as well as the perpetrators of regulatory action."

Indeed, what is needed is a reconceptualization of the research on regulation. All too often, social scientists who analyze regulation get caught in the same trap in which agency staff is enmeshed: focusing on the mechanics of the regulatory process rather than on the underlying causes and consequences of the problems. For instance, with regard to automotive regulation, past debate has centered on three areas: (1) What is to be regulated—the product or the consumer? (2) What techniques—design, or performance standards? (3) How do we evaluate the costs and benefits of regulations? These issues are important, especially when the goal is to make regulation work better or to perfect the system. But their value in helping us *understand* regulation is limited. Broader concerns have been neglected, as the Naders point out. To what extent does the regulatory process mirror patterns that are characteristic of American culture at large? Why has government regulation been the preferred public option for so-

---

portance to the preservation of health and life goes unsought in both the private and public scientific communities.

lution to economic, social, and technological problems? These types of questions require a broad historical and cultural analysis, such as that proposed by the Naders.

One approach might be the study of the political culture, the belief systems out of which government regulation has emerged and flourished. In all cultures, economic and political systems are part of larger belief systems, the assumptions held by a society about how the world is or should be ordered. Regulation, like religion, is supported by a system of beliefs about economic and political activity. In particular, three belief systems stand out as relevant to this discussion.

The Public/Private Belief System. The first is probably the most fundamental: belief in the separation of private and public sectors. Formal regulation, it is assumed, is the act of public intervention in the marketplace—the private sphere. The term *intervention* implies separation between the two spheres. Regulation is essentially an elaborate set of rules by which that intervention is allowed. Deviation from these rules, it is believed, violates the sanctity of the private sector.

The logic of economic regulation assumes that state intervention in an imperfect market situation is necessary only to correct an imbalance. Anti-trust regulation is an example. Economic regulation is distinct from social regulation, which is an elaborately developed method for what is called internalizing the externalities of the marketplace. The argument is made that market transactions do not take account of societal side-effects such as environmental pollution, highway deaths, and worker accidents. The goal is to include those costs to society (or externalities) in the marketplace transaction between buyer and seller. Therefore, the cost of pollution to society is absorbed into production and the product.

From a legal point of view, regulations are limited in their ability to address social problems in any other way than as aspects of marketplace dysfunction. Yet the problems they are designed to solve are often unrelated to the market phenomenon. Unsafe vehicles (e.g., the Ford Pinto) are not market phenomena but, rather, the result of corporate decisions to use a given design in order to meet the company's economic efficiency criteria. For instance, NHTSA can regulate the automobile—influence its technology and, to some extent, its production—but it cannot regulate the corporate investment decisions that are crucial to vehicle design. The automobile is considered an appropriate focus of regulation because it is the product that is exchanged in the marketplace between buyer and seller. Corporate investment decisions do not take place in the market, therefore they are exempt from regulatory intervention.

The Technocratic (Rational) Principle.   A second belief system that directly affects regulatory process is the technocratic (or rational) principle. There exists a belief that regulatory agencies must act as a neutral (or rational) link between consumers or workers and the industries. Regulations mediate between consumer need for safe, fuel-efficient automobiles and the manufacturer's goal to accumulate capital and produce vehicles as efficiently as possible.

The view of regulation as neutral implies that specific standards can be derived by objective means. Use of tools such as cost-benefit analysis aids rational decisionmaking. Measurement becomes an important activity of regulatory agencies. As a result, professionals and their scientific methodologies become crucial to an agency's ability to perform its function and defend its results publicly.

This focus on rational decisions has a side effect. The dominance of professionals in regulatory agencies—engineers at NHTSA, scientists at EPA, toxicologists at OSHA—further removes regulation from public comprehension. Debates over regulation occur in a language only experts understand, and as a result they feed the mystique that regulation is a technical problem and that the solutions devised are rational ones.

Only when regulatory debates arise in Congress and in the media symbolized by phrases such as "free choice" or "let the marketplace determine whether safety will sell" (as with airbags) are we reminded of the fact that regulation is not a science but a part of our political culture where the issues are clearly political issues. For instance, what are the property rights of corporations versus those of consumers? When do societal goals supersede the economic goals of individual firms? And whose free choice are we talking about when we deal with questions of life and death? These are not scientific questions but, rather, fundamental cultural issues.

The Management Belief System.   The third belief system operates within the bureaucratic structure of government itself—the belief in management as the key to solving social problems, i.e., the celebration of procedure over substance, process over ideas. To construct a regulatory solution for a health-and-safety problem is more often than not to develop a procedure, a rule-making focused on one visible aspect of the original social problem. Procedures become the activities of regulatory government workers, and innovative ideas easily get lost. Tasks are divided not topically, but by steps in the procedure. As a result the intellectual division of labor defeats the original purpose of solving the problem by removing the study of the problem from holistic inquiry.[15] Regulators write environmental-impact statements, urban-impact statements, regulatory analyses, and cost-benefit analyses, and are subject to OMB approval of research techniques. Each regulator's work is continually reviewed by other fragments of the bureaucracy, each of which evaluates according to its own peculiar logic. As a result, government workers come to spend most of their time learning the rules, trying to get around them if they are too burdensome, and carefully watching the budgets that are the lifeblood of what they see as valuable work.

Conclusion

These beliefs in the sanctity of private economic power protected from public accountability, in the technocratic principle, and in the management of social problems are at the heart of American culture and reflect basic assumptions under which government is organized. Therefore a debate over regulation may appear on the surface to be about costs and benefits, about managing the budget or about rational and efficient decisions, but underneath lies a more fundamental debate over the location of power in American society.

Regulation is most fundamentally about property and human rights in an advanced industrial society. In particular, the debate over government regulation is not merely one over rules and government burden, it is about the property and human rights of consumers and workers in areas such as health and safety in opposition to the property rights of private business interests over use of capital and investment priorities. The struggle over regulation is a significant event in the evolution of the American cultural system because it is a struggle over redefinition of private-property relations in this society.

Detailed technical debates over proposed health and safety regulations might appear to the public to be about inconsequential issues, but they are really a mirror of the larger cultural issue of conflict between property rights and the human and health concerns of the general public. This is reflected in the debate over company defini-

15. Procedure has another function in government activity: it provides important protections for the public. For instance, the Administrative Procedures Act and the Freedom of Information Act allow citizens to participate in regulatory actions or initiate access to government information. However, when procedure and process overwhelm the nature and substance of regulatory initiatives or are intentionally used to obfuscate substantive issues, they create problems.

tion of trade secrets vs. disclosure of the presence of chemicals in the workplace. The debate over drug labeling is a similar example, where warnings (such as patient package inserts in prescription drugs) are perceived by the industry as diminishing the marketability of a product while the consumer claims the right to information on known hazards of a drug or product.

From a narrow view, to locate the regulatory debate in the context of property and human rights might be seen as addressing the field of constitutional law and its history. However, this would divert us from the important questions. It behooves us as social scientists to take the Naders' lead toward a wide-angle view and examine what the regulatory process in the United States tells us about the organization of our political and economic systems, their interactions, and the themes of fundamental social change behind the seemingly unimportant struggle over details of regulatory actions by government agencies.

The regulatory debate, particularly over worker, consumer, and community health and safety, involves the feasibility of protecting private economic decisions in a culture that demands increasing participation by citizens in decisions that significantly affect their lives. The Naders' paper starts us on the path toward intelligent analysis of these fundamental cultural issues.

PART III

The Politics of Regulation and Deregulation

6

Group Concentration and the Delegation of Legislative Authority

Morris P. Fiorina

The mandate for this volume specifies that the essays should demonstrate the possible contributions of social science disciplines other than economics to the study of regulatory policy. That seems an innocent enough request for psychology and anthropology, but perhaps less so for law and political science. The latter disciplines already possess large literatures on the subject of regulation. Thus, our mandate seems to imply that these literatures amount to less of a contribution than their size might suggest. The lawyers can speak for themselves—they always do—but what about political science?

Having explored the political science literature on regulation, it appears to me that political scientists too often overlook their discipline's comparative advantages. When it comes to describing the consequences of regulation, economists have an edge (though political scientists pay relatively greater homage to distributional gods), and when it comes to description of the regulatory process, lawyers versed in administrative law, sociologists knowledgeable in the ways of organizations, and journalists steeped in context all have specific strengths on which to build. Political scientists can and do learn economics, law, sociology, and journalism, but what special strength do political scientists have, especially if they reject—as some do—the notion that the larger political system exerts a systematic and significant influence on regulation? What distinctive contribution can professional political scientists, qua political scientists, make to the study of regulation?

The answer, I think, is obvious. When economists evaluate the outcomes of a regulatory program, they are judging the ultimate consequences of choices made by the elected officials who authorized the program. When lawyers, sociologists, journalists, and others observe the operation of the regulatory process, they are viewing behavior undertaken within the constraints imposed by the elected officials who set that process in motion. The first question in the study of regulation political scientists should ask is *why* we have a policy at all—an inquiry typically undertaken in blow-by-blow descriptive fashion. Next, the perhaps more interesting corollary question arises: why does the policy take the form it does? Under what conditions do legislators delegate to administrators rather than rely on judicial enforcement of statute law (the Act to Regulate Commerce of 1887 is a watershed)? A shrug of the shoulders, a sigh, and the remark, "It's all so complex nowadays," fall short of an adequate scientific explanation. Under what conditions do legislators adopt specific mandates (e.g., parts of the Clean Air and Clean Water Acts) rather than vague and platitudinous wish lists (e.g., the Communications Act of 1934)? This is the concern that Lowi (1979) has eloquently articulated. Under what conditions do legislators opt for command and control policy instruments (Schultze, 1977) rather than conceivable alternatives that are more efficient? Frustrated economists criticize such (perceived) nonoptimal choices. Questions like these suggest a natural political-science focus on regulatory origin, which in turn suggests a focus on legislatures, for regulatory origin is in great part a legislative game.

This chapter takes an initial stab at the question of delegation. What incentives lead legislators to delegate to unelected officials not only the administration but even the formulation of public policy? A variety of considerations are relevant; my focus will be on political (rather than managerial) incentives to delegate. The next section of the paper develops a simple framework in which the later discussion can be conducted.

Theoretical Framework

In analyzing legislative calculations I will build on Shepsle and Weingast's (1982) discussion of legislator objectives in a single-member district system. Their model postulates that a legislator attempts to maximize his probability of reelection, which is assumed to be a monotonically increasing function of the district net benefits function:

$$N_j(x) = b_{1j}(x) + c_{1j}(x) - c_{2j}(x) - t_j T(x) \tag{1}$$

Here $N_j(x)$ represents the net benefits to district j from a government activity, project, or program carried out at level x, where x is a vector of characteristics describing the policy; $b_j(x)$ summarizes the benefits of the government activity to district j; and $c_{1j}(x)$ summarizes direct program expenditures in district j. Note that the legislator regards these latter as benefits, i.e., c_1 costs appear with a plus sign in the net benefit function. Direct program expenditures in other districts, of course, are regarded as costs. These accrue in a total tax bill, $T(x)$, of which district j pays share t_j. Finally, c_{2j} represents the external or indirect costs of a program (e.g., compliance costs, higher prices). All benefits and costs are present-value discounted.

The preceding formulation is a generalization of analyses of distributive (i.e., particularized) policymaking (Fiorina, 1981; Weingast, Shepsle, and Johnsen, 1981). Distributive policy is a special case in which c_{2j} costs are regarded as zero by the legislator. Shepsle and Weingast (1982) suggest that regulatory policy might be treated as a special case in which the legislator regards public expenditure costs $[c_{1j}(x), T(x)]$ as negligible (Green and Nader, 1973; Weidenbaum, 1980), thus reducing (1) to the following simple formulation:

$$N_j(x) = b_j(x) - c_{2j}(x) \qquad (2)$$

If the benefit function is assumed to increase with the components of x at a marginally decreasing rate while the cost function increases at a marginally increasing rate, then (2) will be single-peaked. Moreover, if x is taken to be a scalar measure of government involvement, then Black's median dominance theorem yields a majority-rule equilibrium in the legislature, namely, the median of the individual legislators' maxima, MED$_j$ MAX$_x$ $N_j(x)$. At equilibrium, marginal benefits equal marginal costs for the median legislator, and if the net benefits functions are normalized so that the net benefits of the status quo are zero, then $b_j(x) \geq c_j(x)$ for a majority of the legislators. Though the assumption of a scalar x is very helpful in the search for legislative equilibrium, it is not necessary for an analysis of the induced preferences of individual legislators.

From a formal standpoint (2) is so simple as to appear trivial. From a substantive standpoint, however, (2) implicitly makes a number of nontrivial presumptions. First is the aforementioned district orientation: legislators evaluate government policies solely in terms of benefit and cost incidences in their districts. This assumption is probably more accurate than not, though the increasing geographic mobility of campaign resources introduces some slippage. Second, (2) assumes a retrospective voting electorate. The incumbent's probability of reelection depends not on his position vis-à-vis a challenger

but on the actual delivery of benefits to the district. Given information levels in national elections (Fiorina, 1982a), this assumption, too,
appears reasonably accurate though it undoubtedly fails for some
highly salient issues. Third, (2) assumes that legislators maximize
issue-by-issue, which seems to imply a considerable degree of issue
independence or separability. While in many cases the latter does not
hold, in view of legislator uncertainty about the future shape of the
agenda (Fiorina, 1974, pp. 81–83), legislators proceed one issue at a
time anyway. Finally, (2) is an "objective" calculation; it summarizes
the actual benefits and costs of government activity (discounted, but
by constituents, not the legislator). In reality, benefits and costs are
rarely fully and/or symmetrically perceived. In the distributive
arena, from which the model arose, the assumption is reasonable
because of the tangible nature of government programs. When we
move to the regulatory arena, however, particularly the newer regulation, the costs and benefits of government programs are far more
difficult to identify, let alone attribute.

Two general classes of factors would produce less than perfect
perception and attribution of programmatic effects. The first is
characteristics of the effects themselves: what is their nature and to
whom do they accrue? The second is characteristics of the program:
the process by which effects are produced affects how they are ultimately attributed. The body of this paper takes one factor from each
class and analyzes its effects via further modifications of (2). From
the first class we take group concentration, and from the second we
take delegation of legislative power.

Group Concentration

The first modification of (2) involves recognition that the
benefits and costs of government programs are not perfectly perceived. Indeed, legislators spend considerable time and effort trying
to enhance perceptions of program benefits (Mayhew, 1974). Thus, the
legislator would begin with a net benefits function that takes account
of the probabilities (p_j, q_j) of changes in district welfare (i.e., political
benefits and costs) being associated with government programs:

$$N_j(x) = p_j b_j(x) - q_j c_j(x)$$
$$\text{where } 0 \le p_j, q_j \le 1 \tag{3}$$

Consider two classes of benefits, one of which comes in the form of
official U.S. Treasury checks, the second of which comes in the form
of cleaner air. Other things being equal, the first entails a much
higher p than the second. Similarly, consider two costs, one of which

comes in the form of a draft notice, the second of which comes in the form of a 0.01 percent increase in the inflation rate. Other things being equal (hard to imagine in this case), the first entails a much higher q than the second. The probabilities in question may reflect a variety of factors other than the form of the benefits and costs, but I assume that the legislator takes all relevant variables into account (including his own ability to affect p and q) and forms estimates that obey the laws of probability.[1]

The second necessary modification of (2) reflects the fact that a legislator knows that he generally will not be held solely accountable for the perceived net benefits. He can appropriate credit for a share a_j, less than the full perceived benefits, and will suffer blame for a share s_j, less than the full perceived costs. The magnitudes of these shares will reflect a variety of factors, including the legislator's party, committee positions, perceived reputation, and so forth, but generally speaking, the "bigger" the issue, the less responsible is an individual representative for the perceived benefits and costs.[2] When modified for anticipated success in claiming credit (a_j) and shifting blame (s_j), (3) becomes (4):

$$N_j(x) = a_j p_j b_j(x) - s_j q_j c_j(x)$$
$$\text{where } 0 \leq a_j, s_j \leq 1 \tag{4}$$

1. To elaborate: I assume that at the time of decision the legislator treats p and q as fixed. At least four major real-world factors would affect estimates of p and q. These are: (1) the forms that benefits and costs take, as noted in the text; (2) the characteristics of voters who feel the incidence of program consequences (e.g., education levels, organizational features); (3) the efforts of political opponents to enhance perceptions of program costs; and (4) the legislator's own efforts to heighten perceptions of program benefits. Considerations (3) and (4) make the point that recognition of program benefits and costs hinges on strategic behavior as well as on the characteristics of public policies and those they affect. Thus, prior to the decision stage in a legislature we would expect policy advocates and opponents to attempt to influence their colleagues' p and q estimates. By the decision stage, however—the focus of this analysis—I assume that legislators have incorporated (though not necessarily accurately) behavioral expectations into their calculations.

2. Again, at the time of decision I assume that a and s estimates are fixed. Also as before, I assume that they incorporate both objective factors and strategic expectations. Examples of objective factors that would magnify attributions of responsibility are: (1) membership in the legislative majority party; (2) membership on a legislative committee with jurisdiction over the policy at issue; and (3) high seniority, leadership position, or other indications of heavyweight status. Examples of strategic expectations include: (1) efforts of the political opposition to associate the legislator with program costs and discount his association with program benefits; and (2) the legislator's own efforts to be associated with benefits and costs in just the opposite manner. In addition, the independent efforts of legislative colleagues to claim credit and avoid blame might affect a legislator's perceived responsibility, i.e., such efforts impose external costs on other legislators.

Call (4) the politically relevant net benefits function. Initially, I will not treat x as variable. Instead, assume that x has been exogenously specified by the executive, party leaders, an interest group, or some other actor with agenda power. Then, in deciding whether or not to support x, the rank-and-file legislator will calculate the politically relevant net benefits and support x if (4) is positive. Equivalently, if

$$\frac{a_j p_j}{s_j q_j} > \frac{c_j(x)}{b_j(x)} \tag{4'}$$

the legislator will support the proposed policy.

Thus, (2) is a special case of (4) in which information is perfect ($p = q = 1$) or at least symmetric ($p = q$), and political responsibility is total ($a = s = 1$) or, again, symmetric ($a = s$). As mentioned, where benefits and costs are very tangible and where the individual legislator is the prime mover (as in the distributive arena) (Ferejohn, 1974), the special case may be approximated. But (4) is a more realistic formulation when we examine government programs more complicated than cement-pouring.

From the standpoint of government efficiency the implications of (4) are discouraging. Weingast, Shepsle, and Johnsen (1981) have demonstrated that an assembly of district representatives would be exceedingly unlikely to choose a policy efficient in the standard sense of equation of marginal social benefits and costs. Condition (4') above suggests how district representatives could favor programs not efficient even in the weak sense of benefits in excess of costs. If the legislator believes that the benefits of the program are more visible than the costs ($p > q$) and/or that he or she can claim credit for a program's benefits while evading responsibility for its costs ($a > s$), she will favor programs whose costs to her district exceed benefits. Consider the consequences of various p/q and a/s ratios shown below:

		p/q				
		1.00	1.50	2.00	2.50	3.00
	1.00	1.00	1.50	2.00	2.50	3.00
a/s	1.50	1.50	2.25	3.00	3.75	4.50
	2.00	2.00	3.00	4.00	5.00	6.00

The entries show the maximum cost-benefit ratios for which a legislator would support a policy under the specified conditions. Thus, if a legislator believes that program benefits are twice as likely to be noticed as program costs ($p/q = 2$) and that he could claim credit for a portion of the benefits twice as great as the costs for which he would bear responsibility ($a/s = 2$), then he would be willing to support a program whose costs to his district were four times as great as the benefits. Mayhew (1974) has discussed the congressional penchant for programs whose benefits are highlighted and costs hidden, and also congressional procedures for claiming credits and evading costs, so there is reason to believe that legislative "sins of commission" as described above occur with some frequency.

Of course, an even-handed treatment should note that opposing asymmetries produce inefficiences of the opposite nature. Consider the following examples:

		p/q			
		0.25	0.50	0.75	1.00
	0.25	0.06	0.13	0.19	0.25
a/s	0.50	0.13	0.25	0.38	0.50
	0.75	0.19	0.38	0.56	0.75
	1.00	0.25	0.50	0.75	1.00

These examples show how legislative "sins of omission" occur. If a legislator believes that the benefits of a program are only half as visible as the costs ($p/q = 0.5$) and that he is twice as likely to bear responsibility for the costs as receive credit for the benefits ($a/s = 0.5$), then he will decline to support a program whose benefits to his district are not at least four times greater than its costs.[3] Under those conditions the politically relevant net benefits of a program whose cost-benefit ratio was only one to three would be negative.

It seems likely that all the various social science disciplines have something to say about the variables and conditions that would produce the kinds of asymmetries illustrated above. I will focus on the relative concentration of those who receive the benefits and bear the costs of government programs. There is widespread agreement on the importance of group concentration for public-policy formation. Schattschneider (1935), Buchanan and Tullock (1962), and Lowi

3. The public-choice branch of political economy would probably discount the empirical significance of asymmetries of the second class in favor of the stylized fact that real-world legislatures traffic primarily in special-interest legislation. In contrast, the political science literature contains observations that suggest the importance of asymmetries of the second class. Consider, for example, Wilson's (1974, p. 139) contention that individuals are more sensitive to threatened deprivations than to promised gains ($p < q$?), and Fiorina's (1974, pp. 38–39) presumption of an ungrateful electorate—one that is more likely to remember who does what to them than who does what for them ($a < s$?). Actually, the political science wisdom and the public-choice stylized fact are mutually consistent. If the former were accurate, legislative sins of omission would be quite prevalent, but by their nature they tend to be unobserved. The situation is reminiscent of the decisions versus nondecisions argument, so I should probably say no more.

(1964) consider benefit concentration and cost diffusion to be the hallmarks of distributive politics, and in the regulatory realm Stigler (1971), Peltzman (1976), and Wilson (1974, 1980) all identify the distribution of regulatory benefits and burdens as a critical variable. A very heterogeneous lot, all agree on the importance of the concentration variable.

When analysts attribute a legislative action to the relative concentration of regulatory burdens and benefits, what precise mechanisms underlie their arguments? Taking the asymmetric cases, concentrated benefits/diffused costs (CB/DC) and diffused benefits/concentrated costs (DB/CC), one could interpret the effects of relative differences in concentration in terms of the asymmetries previously discussed.[4] A plausible interpretation of legislator support of "special interest" legislation would be that $p_j > q_j$, and $a_j > s_j$. The per capita stake of the losers is small. Thus, they are relatively less likely to realize their losses from the unfavorable legislation and to recognize any role their representative played in its passage. The members of the special-interest group, however, have a high per capita stake, a greater incentive to bear information costs—perhaps enough to invest in a trade association or other formal organization. They are likely both to realize the effects of government actions on their welfare and to keep tabs on the actions of individual legislators. The expected result? Legislative sins of commission.

In contrast, symmetrical arguments lead to an interpretation of the DB/CC case as $p_j < q_j$, and $a_j < s_j$. The concentrated and perhaps organized interests who bear the costs are aware of those costs and the legislators who imposed them, whereas the diffused and probably unorganized beneficiaries may not be cognizant of the benefits, let alone who provided them. The expected result is legislative sins of omission.

The discussion thus far has presupposed legislative consideration of a single policy option. Generally, of course, there are a variety of means to the same end. What is most important for our purposes is

4. The tentative language of the paragraph in the text reflects the fact that *concentration* and *diffusion* are terms that take on fairly rich meanings in the literature. Wilson (1974) adopts these terms, using *concentration* to refer to a cost or benefit "specific to a certain sector of society conscious of its special identity" (p. 140) and "high per capita" benefits or costs conferred "on a small, organizable sector of society" (p. 158). This is contrasted with *diffusion* as costs or benefits falling "on a large, diverse group with no sense of special identity and no established patterns of interaction" (p. 140) and "low per capita" benefits or costs imposed "on a large, hard-to-organize segment of society" (p. 158). Peltzman (1976) also refers to group size and per capita stakes. Based on my reading of the literature I think that the defining assumptions made in the text below are consistent with the manner in which various authors have used the terms *concentrated* and *diffused*, but the reader should bear in mind that these are my interpretations of the arguments of a heterogeneous group of writers.

that alternative means typically produce different, politically relevant net benefit functions. Some will involve clear differences in benefits or costs, as when public policy decrees that the path to clean water lies in a treatment plant for every community rather than effluent taxes. Or different alternatives may induce different politically relevant net benefits by producing different p, q, a, or s estimates. The costs of clean water, for example, might be smaller but more visible if each household and firm received a monthly effluent tax bill. Other alternatives might serve to lessen the legislator's perceived responsibility for the effects of a program. One such alternative is delegation of legislative authority to administrative agencies.

Delegation

Observers who complain about the supposed congressional penchant for bureaucratic command and control actually conflate two charges: that inefficient policy instruments are chosen, and that an inefficient or otherwise undesirable bureaucratic mode of implementation and enforcement is adopted. Both charges are important, but I will confine myself to the second, less obvious one.

To the contemporary observer, legislative reliance on the administrative process looks very natural. The suggestion that enforcement of public policies should depend on the initiative of the individual litigant seems unnatural, if not silly. It was not always so. Congress fought for more than a decade over proposals to regulate the railroads, and though the short-haul/long-haul controversy is better known, the most important issue concerned the method of administering the proposed law. According to Cushman (1941, p. 45):

> The first major problem and also the last which confronted those working for the federal regulation of railways was whether or not a commission should be set up to administer the law. It was generally agreed that federal control had become imperative, but those supporting such control were divided into two camps. The first, led by Judge Reagan of Texas, and chairman of the House Committee on Interstate and Foreign Commerce, demanded drastic regulation by statute to be enforced directly by the Department of Justice and the courts. Reagan was able to carry the House with him to the very last. The other group, headed by Senator Cullom, a former governor of Illinois, insisted that federal regulation of railways should be administered through a commission set up for that purpose. This vital difference of opinion persisted throughout the entire period of discussion and was only adjusted, as we have seen, in conference committee a few weeks before the actual passage of the Act of 1887.

Judge Reagan's "drastic regulation by statute" provided that violators

> shall forfeit and pay to the person or persons who may sustain damage
> thereby a sum equal to three times the amount of the damages so sus-
> tained, to be recovered by the person or persons so damaged by suit in
> any district or circuit court of the United States . . . and the person or
> persons so offending shall for each offence forfeit and pay a penalty of
> not less that one thousand dollars . . . one-half of such penalty or pen-
> alties . . . to be paid to the informer. (Haney, 1910, p. 296)

As the years passed, delegation to administrative agencies may have
come to seem more natural, but even if delegation had never again
created controversy (but it has), the political decision of 1887 would
call for explanation.[5]

Even in the absence of historical evidence of a political choice between administrative and legal-judicial forms of regulation, one
could still raise the question: why not attempt to regulate without
extensive reliance on bureaucratic entities? Some academic critics of
current safety and health regulation argue that careful design of liability law could provide firms with incentives to adopt safety and
health standards which in the long run would be as beneficial as and
far less costly than current regulatory approaches. Or to take a less
hypothetical example, in the debate over the Civil Rights Act of 1964
the individual versus federal role in enforcement was the subject of
much attention. Consider that incentive-based schemes for regulating environmental pollution would probably lessen legislative reliance on the administrative process. Constitutional limitations on
legislative delegation of the taxing power would virtually require that
Congress set emissions-tax levels (probably with the aid of specialized committee staff); the role of administrators would be down-
graded to one similar to that of the IRS. One can make cogent arguments against proposals such as the foregoing, to be sure, but the
existing administrative forms of regulation are equally arguable.
Why, then, do legislators delegate, or, to foreshadow later discussion,
under what conditions do they delegate?

The most common explanation of legislative delegation is *complexity*. This explanation views delegation as an inevitable feature of
modern society. Problems are complex, time and other resources
scarce; therefore, delegation. Certainly there is some merit in such
arguments, but a little thought suggests that other considerations
must be important as well.

---

5. In the past the court system was viewed as a more natural organ for the administration of public policy than it is today. For a fascinating history of judicial administration
of government programs in the old Northwest Territory, see Brisbin (1981).

In the first place, where is it shown that the complexity of public problems has increased faster than the capacities of elected officials to deal with them? The amateur legislators of the nineteenth century spent four to five months per year in Washington, accompanied only by a few clerks. Today's professional legislators spend full time on the job and are served by approximately 25,000 staff employees. Consider, too, that the justification (though not the explanation) for the transformation of Congress first into committee government and then into subcommittee government was the purported specialized expertise such a division of labor would foster. Perhaps increases in resources and expertise have not kept pace with the increasing complexity of social and economic problems, but the case is not *prima facie* obvious.

Furthermore, Congress has delegated selectively, not across the board. And complexity is not the key variable. As Jaffe (1973, pp. 1189–90) observes: "The monumental detail of the tax code suggests that Congress can and does legislate with great specificity when it regards a matter as sufficiently important." This is not to deny any role for the IRS, but Congress does not pass tax bills stating that the IRS should set tax rates for the "public interest, convenience, and necessity."[6] Congress has chosen to legislate any number of seemingly complex issues. Where the incentive exists, legislators find the time and resources to deal with complexity.

A second reason to doubt the complexity explanation of delegation arises from an honest look at the ability of the administrative system to deal with complexity. "How could we possibly expect Congress to draw up standards for literally thousands of dangerous substances? Delegation to an agency is obviously necessary." But has delegation solved the problem? TOSCA authorizes EPA to regulate more than 50,000 potentially hazardous substances. Thus far, EPA has managed to address an average of less than one chemical per year of effort.[7] Is it not conceivable that augmented congressional staffs could deal with complex issues as competently as and perhaps considerably faster than executive or independent agencies?[8]

6. There is good reason to believe that the courts would strike down any broad delegation of the power to tax (Aranson, Gellhorn, and Robinson, 1981). Nevertheless, Congress shows little tendency even to probe the limits of delegation in this area.

7. Mendelhoff (1981) discusses this and other failures of presently constituted administrative regulation in the health and safety area.

8. One of Wilson's (1980) reviewers, FTC official Robert Reich (1980, p. 37), regards such a proposal as practical, though he rejects what he believes to be its implications:

If there is no single, non-political truth called the public interest—or none that regulatory agencies are capable of discovering—why not rid ourselves of these

186 MORRIS P. FIORINA

Nor is it obvious that the traditional legal system is incapable of handling modern complex problems. Specialized courts already exist, and, speaking generally of delegation to administrative agencies, Posner (1977, p. 480) argues:

> The idea was that Congress could not deal efficiently with the technical, particularistic, rapidly changing problems of a complex modern industry such as railroading. . . . But this is an unconvincing explanation for the creation of the independent agencies. The regulation of railroads and of other industries that have been brought under the administrative process could just as well have been delegated to the courts, whose traditional province is precisely to formulate rules governing relatively technical economic activity, using (as we have seen) neutral, apolitical criteria such as efficiency. One can argue that the case method constrains the rulemaking effectiveness of the courts, but since the agencies have with rare exceptions relied exclusively on the case method as their legislative technique the argument provides little basis for preferring agencies to courts.

In short, the objective complexity of a public-policy matter is far from sufficient explanation for broad delegation of legislative authority.

A second explanation of delegation focuses not so much on legislative minimization of decisionmaking costs as on the quality of the resulting decisions. This is the old public-administration model of the nonpolitical administrative process. According to this venerable view the administrative process has certain inherent advantages over judicial enforcement of legislative enactments. First, administration is conducted by nonpolitical officials who carry out the policy as intended by Congress. In contrast, dependence on the legal system entails delays, prohibitive expenses, inconsistency of legal interpretation across jurisdictions, and so forth. Second, the administrative process is more flexible than the legal process. Rather than freeze public policy into law, Congress can state its general intent and allow the agency to fine-tune the law to fit changing economic, social, and technological conditions. Third is the complexity argument again: administration is conducted by experts who will do a job superior to that of nonexpert legislators and judges.

Whatever the original merits of such arguments, little in our overall historical experience justifies the benign view of administrative

---

old bureaucracies and reassign their responsibilities to Congress? Congressional staffs are already so large . . . that most agency staffs could be added on almost unnoticed. Their recommendations for regulations could be fed up to elected representatives following the same route as complicated pieces of proposed legislation. In short, if the line between politics and administration is a charade, why not obliterate it?

regulation presupposed by the good-government model. Such arguments still provide rhetorical ammunition on occasion, but it is doubtful whether many serious observers regard them as the principal explanation for legislative delegation.

In its essential respects the complexity argument holds that delegation to administrators minimizes legislative decision costs, where the costs in question—time, patience, staff, and other resources—are "politically neutral." A number of observers, however, see in delegation an opportunity for legislators to minimize political costs. Woll comments (1977, p. 173):

> A major reason for the power of the bureaucracy in policy formulation is the frequent lack of congressional incentives to adhere to the Schecter rule and establish explicit standards for administrative action. This is particularly true in the regulatory realm, an area involving political conflict that legislators often wish to avoid. Congress is always willing to deal *rhetorically* with problems requiring regulation and with the area of regulatory reform but real decisions on the part of the legislature will undoubtedly raise the ire of powerful pressure groups on one side or the other that are affected by government regulation.

By charging an agency with implementation of the regulatory mandate, legislators not only save themselves the time and trouble of making specific decisions, they also avoid or at least disguise their responsibility for the consequences of the decisions. In terms of the model developed earlier, delegation affects legislators' estimates of a and s. Delegation of legislative authority to administrators shifts the responsibility for the costs and benefits public policies produce.

The remainder of this paper applies the legislative calculus developed earlier to the "shift the responsibility" theory of delegation. In order to focus clearly on the factor of diminished responsibility a number of *ceteris paribus* assumptions will be made. Policy instruments will be held constant so that the simple fact of delegation does not alter the association of benefits and costs with government activities (estimates of p and q) or the actual benefits and costs themselves. I assume that delegation *only* places added political daylight between the legislators and those who feel the incidence of legislative actions. In other words, delegation does not change the actual policy, x, that is adopted; rather, legislators agree with Mayhew (1974, p. 135) that "there is every reason to believe that the regulatory agencies do what Congress wants them to do." Thus, for the present I am skirting the principal concern of Theodore Lowi: delegation without standards, which allows the law to be brokered, bargained, and otherwise continuously transformed by administrators. Shifting legislative responsibility to administrators may well have an effect on the ultimate benefits and costs of the program, but for now I ignore that complication.[9]

Group Concentration and Shifting the Responsibility

Whereas earlier the hypothetical legislator was deciding whether to support a particular policy, we now permit the legislator to choose between alternative means of implementing the policy. We define two conditional net-benefits functions, one conditioned on a broad delegation of policy to an administrative agency, $N_j(x|D)$, and one conditioned on a narrow delegation to a housekeeping agency or, as in the previously cited Reagan bill, no delegation to an agency at all, $N_j(x|L)$:

$$N_j(x|D) = a_j^d p_j b_j(x) - s_j^d q_j c_j(x) \tag{5a}$$

$$N_j(x|L) = a_j^l p_j b_j(x) - s_j^l q_j c_j(x) \tag{5b}$$

The shift-the-responsibility (SR) assumptions are as follows:

$$a_j^l > a_j^d, s_j^l > s_j^d$$

That is, the legislator believes that a broad delegation lessens his perceived responsibility for the ultimate costs of the program more than a narrow delegation (recall how quickly protest centered on Congress after the FDA acted to ban saccharin under the Delaney clause). The narrower the delegation, the less able is the legislator to claim that the agency (or court) acted in violation of his or her understanding of the law. On the other hand, a broad delegation will also lessen the legislator's ability to claim credit compared to a narrow delegation because the perception of the agency as an independent actor responsible for its own decisions will be stronger. Thus, there will be a trade-off between a legislator's loss in ability to claim credit and gain in ability to shift blame, and his attitude toward delegation will hinge on the trade-off. The legislator will prefer the broad delegation if (5a) is greater than (5b), which implies the following condition on the district benefit-cost ratio:

$$\frac{s_j^l - s_j^d}{a_j^l - a_j^d} \cdot \frac{q_j}{p_j} > \frac{b_j(x)}{c_j(x)} \tag{5'}$$

9. Elsewhere (Fiorina, 1982b) I have proposed that possible agency transformation of legislative enactments could be examined with the aid of an uncertainty model that views legislators as choosing among policy lotteries with specified characteristics.

The comparative statics of (5′) are intuitively plausible. *Ceteris paribus*, legislator preferences for delegation increase with the costs of the policy, the probability of associating those costs with government policy (q), the probability of being held accountable for the costs of a nondelegated policy (s_j^l), and the ability to claim credit for the benefits of a delegated policy (a_j^d). Conversely, legislator preferences for delegation decline with the benefits of the policy, the probability of associating the benefits with government policy (p), the ability to claim credit for the benefits of a nondelegated policy (a_j^l), and the probability of being held accountable for the costs of a delegated policy, (s_j^d).

Consider again our two cases, CB/DC and DB/CC. Their defining characteristics are now:

$$\text{CB/DC: } p > q, a_j^l > s_j^l, a_j^d > s_j^d$$
$$\text{DB/CC: } p < q, a_j^l < s_j^l, a_j^d < s_j^d$$

These defining characteristics and the SR assumptions imply:

$$\text{CB/DC: } a_j > \overset{s_j}{a_j^d} > s_j^d$$

$$\text{DB/CC: } s_j > \overset{a_j}{s_j^d} > a_j^d$$

While these incomplete rankings insure that the left-hand side of (5′) is positive, they do not contain enough information to determine whether the ratio of accountability differences is greater than, equal to, or less than one. In the absence of any information, assume that the slippages in ability to claim credit and ability to shift costs are equal, i.e., the ratio of differences equals one. Then in the CB/DC case a sufficient condition for the legislator to prefer narrow delegation is that $b_j(x) \geq c_j(x)$. In Figure 1 all (b,c) combinations below the 45° line through the origin would produce preferences for narrow delegation. Some (b,c) combinations above the line would result in narrow delegation preferences as well, with the area of preferences for narrow delegation getting larger as the disparity between p and q increases ($p > q$). An illustrative example ($p = 4q$) appears in the figure.

In contrast, the DB/CC case yields a sufficient condition for broad delegation preferences of $b_j(x) \leq c_j(x)$. In Figure 2 all (b,c) combinations above the 45° line are guaranteed to produce delegation preferences. Some below the line may do so as well, with the area of delegation preferences increasing with the disparity between p and q ($p < q$). An illustrative example ($p = q/4$) appears in the figure.

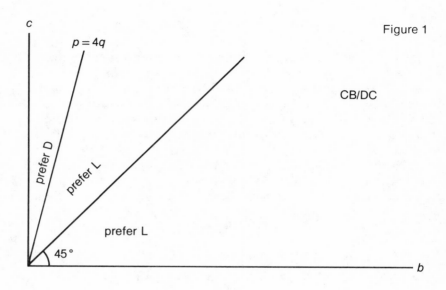

Figure 1

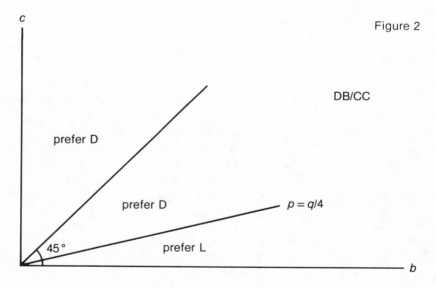

Figure 2

If the ratio of accountability differences is not unity, the preceding sufficient conditions would be correspondingly affected, but I think that probable departures from unity would only reinforce the pictures conveyed by the figures. In the CB/DC case s_j^l is already very low; given its lower bound of zero, the possible slippage $(s_j^l - s_j^d)$ is sharply limited. Thus, the ratio of slippage is more likely than not to be less than one. Because $p > q$, this implies that $b_j(x) \geq c_j(x)$ is a stronger sufficient condition than in the case just analyzed. Conversely, in the DB/CC case a_j^l is already low, so the possible slippage $(a_j^l - a_j^d)$ is limited. The ratio of slippage is more likely than not to be greater than one, which (because $q > p$) implies that $b_j(x) \leq c_j(x)$ is a stronger condition than in the case where the ratio is unity. Admittedly, this argument falls short of a rigorous demonstration, but I think it persuasive enough to conclude that Figures 1 and 2 portray the general qualitative implications of the model.

My mentor and discussant taught us that an important feature of worthwhile theory is that it suggests nonobvious hypotheses. (To the best of my recollection, however, he never taught us how to deal with the unfortunate fact that nonobvious hypotheses are more likely to be wrong than obvious ones.) Thus, I am pleased to point out that some of the implications of the preceding analysis are nonobvious. Moreover, I will make a good-faith argument that they are accurate as well.

Let us begin with the obvious implications. The general conclusion suggested by the analysis summarized in Figures 1 and 2 is that, *ceteris paribus*, legislators whose districts are the greatest objective beneficiaries of government policy are most likely to favor nondelegated policies. It is the representatives of loser districts and the more marginal winners who support delegation. The logic here is straightforward; winners have greater benefits for which to claim credit and/or smaller costs to evade than losers. Thus, delegation of policy implementation may be a compromise big winners make in order to gain support from less enthusiastic colleagues. If so, there is a general suggestion that greater use of delegation will coincide with (geographically) less universal net benefits. If more than a majority of districts were greatly benefited, delegation would be more likely to be rejected, to facilitate credit-claiming by the winners. This does not necessarily imply that delegation entails increased inefficiency, for a few districts might have huge benefit-cost ratios and the rest close to unitary ones. But delegation seems generally to accompany distributions of net benefits that are not uniform across legislative districts.

A second implication is somewhat less obvious. Figures 1 and 2 suggest that, other things being equal, preferences for delegation are less likely in the CB/DC case than in the opposite DB/CC case. This seems to fly in the face of the prevailing wisdom which holds that the older regulatory agencies, with their vague mandates, benefit specific industries at the expense of the general consumer, while the newer agencies, with their relatively more specific mandates, are attempts to benefit the average consumer, worker, citizen, etc., at the expense of specific industries. Thus, the fact seems to be that greater use of delegation occurs in the CB/DC case than in the DB/CC case. We could accept the fact and take the coward's way out by suggesting that other things were not equal, but let us instead take a closer look at the situation.

The preceding objection is based on an examination of regulatory programs, narrowly defined. It compares the extent of delegation within a narrow range of policies. When the range is expanded the objection loses force. The most extreme example of a CB/DC policy that I have been able to find is the Price Anderson Act, which limits private liability for nuclear accidents to 60 million dollars. This law benefits a particular industry at specific geographic sites and spreads the potential costs over a goodly number of generations of American, Mexican, and Canadian nationals. It is a clear law, written in black and white, not a regulation promulgated by the old AEC.

What is the quintessential example of special-interest legislation? Most political scientists would probably suggest either special tax provisions or industry-specific subsidies. The tax code contains thousands of the former, many of which benefit nothing so broad as a whole industry; rather, they provide relief for specific firms and even individuals. These provisions are matters of law, not simple IRS rulings. Similarly, subsidy programs confer quite specific benefits and impose extremely general costs, and Congress itself sets levels and eligibility requirements. Here, too, the administrative agencies play more of a housekeeping role.

Finally, consider many examples of state regulation—occupational licensure, liquor regulation, etc. These are widely recognized as examples of state-sponsored cartelization of industries. I hesitate to advance nationwide conclusions here, but in the states with which I am familiar the law was typically quite specific. Those who wish to alter the status quo lobby the legislature, not the relevant state agency or commission.

In sum, when we consider a broad range of CB/DC policies we find numerous policies based on clear legislative enactments rather than broad delegations. This perspective in turn throws a very different light on the broad delegations bestowed on the older economic regulatory agencies. Perhaps at origin they were DB/CC, as the traditional accounts suggest. Dismissing such accounts as Pollyanna-ish has been popular in recent years (e.g., Kolko, 1965; Stigler, 1971), but maybe the revisionists are too quick. I am not arguing that the enactment of diffused-benefit legislation should be equated with the public-interest model or denying that capture may occur sometime after the initial enactment of legislation. But if the legislator calculus developed in this paper seems plausible, the extensive delegations of authority to the older regulatory agencies suggest that, at least in the beginning, legislators were not obviously ripping off their constituents for the benefit of the capitalists but were instead seeking reelection by benefiting a broad range of constituents.

A third set of implications concerns trends in delegation over time. The literature suggests a gradual increase in legislative propensity to delegate, at least from 1887 to approximately 1970, with something of a reversal in the past decade. The legislator calculus we have developed could accommodate such facts (if they are facts) in several ways. First, if most of regulatory history were CB/DC, contrary to the discussion of the preceding paragraph, then delegation would become more likely if q increased. More and better information about the diffused costs of regulation, increased organization of diffused interests, more political entrepreneurship in behalf of diffused interests, and so forth would cause a general increase in q and expand the region of preferences for delegation in Figure 1. Alternatively, and consistent with the discussion of the preceding paragraph, the rise in delegation could reflect increased legislative efforts in behalf of diffused interests, that is, increased activity in the DB/CC arena.

If the latter suggestion were the case, narrower delegations by recent Congresses submit to a simple explanation. Increasing organization of diffused beneficiaries—as exemplified by the rise of public interest groups—would naturally result in an increase in p. This would contract the area of preferences for delegation in Figure 2.

The preceding empirical interpretations are meant as no more than suggestive. Multiple theoretical interpretations of the same purported facts bring home the point that research that would permit a clean meeting between theory and reality does not currently exist. For example, the distribution of benefits and costs is a critical indicator of what theoretical world to apply, but there are great disagreements surrounding attempts to measure even aggregate benefits and costs, let alone their distribution in states and congressional districts.[10] Moreover, given reasonable discount rates, the benefits and costs in question must be those accruing in the immediate aftermath of regulatory origin. Whom the ICC was benefiting in the 1950s has little relevance to legislative decisions in 1887.

10. See, for example, the continuing debate over measuring the welfare effects of transportation regulation: Spann and Erickson (1970), Zerbe (1980), and Braeutigam and Noll (1984).

Does Delegation Affect Policy Choice?

Thus far we have taken x, the policy in question, as given. This might correspond to the constrained-floor stage of a parliamentary regime, or Congress operating under a closed rule. Suppose x is a policy subject to amendment by legislators seeking to maximize their politically relevant net benefits. It will greatly simplify matters here to return to the original Shepsle-Weingast assumption of a scalar x. The legislator maximizes net benefits (Equation 4) by choosing x so that

$$a_j p_j b_j' - s_j q_j c_j' = 0$$

which implies that

$$\frac{a_j p_j}{s_j q_j} = \frac{c_j'}{b_j'} \tag{6}$$

In the CB/DC case, $p > q$ and $a > s$ imply that $c_j' > b_j'$. Given the properties of $b_j(x)$ (increasing at a decreasing rate) and $c_j(x)$ (increasing at an increasing rate), the politically relevant net-benefits function for a legislator is maximized by an x that is greater than that which would equate marginal benefits and costs. Conversely, in the DB/CC case, $p < q$ and $a < s$ imply that $c_j' < b_j'$, which implies that the optimal x is smaller than that which would equate marginal benefits and costs. Thus, allowing legislators to amend reinforces the earlier analysis of legislative sins of commission and omission.

How will delegation affect the legislator maximization process? Unpredictably, it turns out. Maximizing $N_j(x|D)$ and $N_j(x|L)$ (Equations 5a and 5b) results in (6a) and (6b) respectively:

$$D: \qquad \frac{a_j^d}{s_j^d} \cdot \frac{p_j}{q_j} = \frac{c_j'}{b_j} \tag{6a}$$

$$L: \qquad \frac{a_j^l}{s_j^l} \cdot \frac{p_j}{q_j} = \frac{c_j'}{b_j} \tag{6b}$$

If the left-hand side of (6a) is ($> = <$) that of (6b), the properties of $c_j(x)$ and $b_j(x)$ insure that the x^* that maximizes $N_j(x|D)$ is ($> = <$) the x^{**} that maximizes $N_j(x|L)$. The left-hand side of (6a) is greater than the left-hand side of (6b) if

$$a_j^d s_j^l > a_j^l s_j^d \tag{7}$$

Nothing in the shift-the-responsibility assumptions or the defining characteristics of the CB/DC and DB/CC cases determines whether (7) is true or false or provides any reasonable suggestion about the likelihood it holds or not. Thus, in this simple model the option to delegate has no systematic effect on a legislator's preference for the scope of the policy.[11]

And what of the ultimate question, the existence and description of a legislative equilibrium? Even with the assumption of a scalar x, if legislators are free to choose both the level of x and the extent of delegation, there is little prospect of equilibrium (McKelvey, 1979). If we place various restrictions on the amendment process (e.g., Fiorina, 1982b) an equilibrium will exist, though it is still difficult to describe that equilibrium without making specific assumptions about functional forms. And of course the equilibrium will vary with the process assumptions made in the analysis. This is an unfortunate situation, my only defense being that it plagues all theoretical efforts in political science, not just the preceding analysis.

Toward Social Relevance

To address once again the purpose of this book: the authors were asked to relate their research to pertinent questions of regulatory policy and to suggest examples of research projects that would be useful to undertake (for reasons related to possible applications). The temptation is to deal rather perfunctorily with such charges, irrelevance being almost a point of pride to some political scientists, but while what follows is brief, it has the merit of sincerity.

Our society is currently engaged in a widespread and multifaceted debate about the desirability of the existing regulatory order. Critics charge that present-day regulation results in unaccountable bureaucrats serving a variety of particularistic interests (including their own) by imposing major inefficiencies on the national economy. One need not accept such a wholesale condemnation of the existing order to recognize that there is much room for improvement. But to whom do we look for that improvement? Do we demand that our judges revitalize the delegation doctrine (Aranson, Gellhorn, and Robinson, 1981)? Even if they were so inclined, that would be to risk confrontation with powerful political interests in and out of government, as well as to leave citizens to deal with problems and dangers

---

11. In an earlier paper (Fiorina, 1982b) I analyzed a special case of the SR model in which a condition like (7) always held. Thus, in that special case the option to delegate increased each representative's preferred level of regulation.

that the nullified legislation was intended to address. Moreover, many of the critics of the existing order would include judges in their blanket indictment; unlimited delegation maximizes the discretionary power of judges, who in turn may use that power to further interests with which they sympathize—often, the critics charge, the interests of the regulators.

I suppose that power-hungry bureaucrats are not unheard-of and that more than a few judges allow personal preferences to color their judicial decisions, but I would not direct policy proposals toward reform of either the bureaucracy or the judiciary. We might as well put first things first. The simple fact is that regulatory programs are created and maintained by democratically elected legislators. Those who believe that the existing order is too bureaucratic, too coercive, too discretionary, or what-not must deal with the fact that the people's representatives allow that order to persist. Either the evaluations of the critics are not widely shared by the electorate (a possibility that probably deserves more consideration than it gets), or our understanding of the incentives facing legislators is not adequate, or both. These are the questions I think research proposals should address.

The point of view in this paper is that legislators do not delegate primarily in the good-intentioned hope that the experts will make better decisions, nor in the innocent and understandable attempt to minimize the costs of making decisions. Rather, delegation is principally a political decision. To be sure, there are a variety of political reasons to delegate, only one of which—shifting responsibility—has been examined here. Elsewhere (Fiorina, 1982b) I have surveyed some of these, each of which deserves a great deal more investigation. Moreover, others could undoubtedly produce numerous other political considerations after giving the question some thought. The analysis in this paper is an example, at best. It is intended to demonstrate possibilities rather than to produce firm conclusions. I am not certain, for example, that (4) is rich enough as a model of the legislator's calculus. Nor am I fully comfortable about examining the responsibility-shifting potential of delegation in complete separation from the policy-transforming potential. The latter may be more critical, or it may be that the interaction between the two provides a strong political basis for delegation. Finally, analyses based on the preferences of individual legislators rather than the predicted decision of the entire legislature are clearly second-best. But given the restricted ability of our formal models to specify legislative equilibria, it is uncertain how soon and how closely we can approach the best.

I am satisfied with the likelihood that reasonably simple models can produce relatively general statements about various patterns, trends, and other regularities in the politics of regulation. The reader may not agree with the statements made herein, but if not, I urge him to do better. If some political scientists are motivated to do so, this paper will have succeeded; but if political scientists continue to argue that it all depends on some critical incident or personality, others will continue to ask what political science has to say about regulatory policy.

COMMENT: *William H. Riker*

The agenda for this volume is commendable, and, in the case of political science, it is long overdue. Political scientists have for the most part ignored the subject of regulation during the last forty years, greatly to the disadvantage both of the subject and of political scientists. In the 1940s one main textbook on this subject (Fainsod and Gordon, 1941) was the joint product of a political scientist and an economist. I suspect it was used in courses in one department about as often as in the other. In the 1940s political scientists abandoned the field and the subsequent discussions of the subject have reflected the preoccupations of economists, which, while interesting, offer very little scientific explanation of the regulatory process.

Economists considering the subject of regulation have primarily described how the regulatory process, an intervention in the market, has distorted market efficiency (if they oppose regulation) or compensated for market failures (if they favor regulation). Economists, being believers in the efficiency of markets, are more prone to talk about market distortions created than about market failures remedied. Still, approaching from either angle, economists are necessarily talking about the effects of regulation, not about its origins.

It is of course important to understand the consequences of regulation, both as a matter of scientific description and in order to estimate the net effect on social welfare. But we also want to know something about the causes, again both for scientific description and in order to control the process of regulation as it is expanded and contracted. I think we have to call on political science for this. Of course, economists who are preoccupied with market failure have a cause all prepared: the existence of externalities justifies the intervention. My own limited investigation (mainly into neighborhood effects on real estate prices) convinces me that most externalities are either imaginary or run in the opposite direction from the folklore. Consequently, I am very skeptical about that facile attribution of cause.

If we ignore the heralds of market failure, the only attribution of cause that economists have offered is the so-called capture theory. I admire this theory. It is the only descriptive, non-normative economic theory about the origin and purpose of regulation and I think George Stigler ought to be greatly praised for it. But it is simply not adequately descriptive. The reason is that it is really a political theory in embryo, not an economic theory.

The problem with an economic description of regulation is that it focuses on the wrong people. To adapt a metaphor I have used elsewhere, the whole action of regulation is up on the acropolis, while the figures in economic theory are down in the agora. The one quasi-political economic theory, that is, the capture theory, tells a story about people from the agora going up to the acropolis and bribing venal politicians to send some soldiers down to regulate the agora for the advantage of the bribers. The problem with this theory is that it locates all the initiative in the agora, so that the outcome is bound to reflect only the concerns of the people below.

I think this story has the emphasis wrong. All decisions are made by the people on the acropolis and they are the ones who, as far as I can see, initiate all the action. As I would tell it, the people on the acropolis come down into the agora looking for clients. When these grand fellows from the acropolis find the clients, they undertake, within broad limits, to do something nice for the poor folks who have agreed to subject themselves to clientship. This is a reverse capture theory. The capturers are the people of the acropolis and the captured are the people in the agora. Now, I do not deny that the constraints their clients place on them limit what the people of the acropolis can do. I do insist that what comes out of the regulatory process must be understood mainly in terms of what the politicians think is to their advantage rather than in terms of the advantage of business.

The great merit of Fiorina's paper is that from the beginning he proceeds as if the main point of the description of regulation is to analyze what politicians want. This puts the emphasis in the right place.

Turning to the details of his theory, it seems to me that he does not go quite far enough. His fundamental equation is still in terms of economists' interests, namely, costs and benefits. While the politician must make such a calculation, of course, what is being maximized is not simply the net benefit to the district but the net effect on the politician's future. I think one can conceive of legislators as engaged constantly in trying to develop loyalty in the electorate. A legislator in a marginal seat obviously needs loyalty in the electorate. A legislator in a safe district still has to worry about opponents in primaries and, worse, opponents in catastrophic and unanticipated elections, such as that of 1974 for Republicans. What concerns a legislator most deeply, therefore, is building up a reservoir of loyalty large enough that it can be used to survive unknown future crises.

Given that view of the process, I can easily imagine a situation in which for alternative regulatory schemes x and y, where $N_j(y) > N_j(x)$, a representative from the jth district would nevertheless choose x because the loyalty to be engendered by x is likely to be more enduring, or likely to involve a few more people, or some such reason.

Fiorina assumes that the probability of reelection maximized by the legislator is a "monotonically increasing function of the district net-benefits function." This does not seem at all obvious to me, and I suspect that eventually the statement will be revised. In the meantime, I think Fiorina has done an elegant job of describing one fundamental part of the legislator's calculus. I am impressed by the nonobvious and enlightening inferences he has drawn from it.

7

Why the Regulators Chose to Deregulate

Martha Derthick and Paul J. Quirk

Between 1975 and 1980, three independent regulatory commissions—the Civil Aeronautics Board, the Interstate Commerce Commission, and the Federal Communications Commission—modified or abandoned some of their most important functions for the sake of achieving deregulation. Reformers who sought to end anticompetitive regulation in those years expected regulatory agencies to resist this change, both to preserve the organizations and to serve the interests of the regulated industries whose captives they were presumed to be—industries that, as the reformers correctly anticipated, would generally resist procompetitive deregulation.

That the three commissions undertook to change policy themselves, besides being profoundly puzzling, is worth analyzing because it had very important consequences for the politics of reform. It increased pressure on Congress to take action, because Congress felt its prerogatives were being challenged. It increased pressure on Congress to act in a strongly procompetitive way, because Congress could not easily endorse less reform than the regulatory commissions themselves chose to undertake. It compelled the protected industries to reexamine their opposition to reform by thoroughly destabilizing the regimes in which they had a stake.

This paper is the responsibility of the authors alone and not of the trustees, officers, or other staff of the Brookings Institution or of the Klingenstein Fund, which has contributed financial support. Miss Derthick, who worked on this paper while in residence at the Center for Advanced Study in the Behavioral Sciences, also wishes to thank the Center and the John Simon Guggenheim Memorial Foundation for fellowships. Support for the Center fellowship came from the National Institute of Mental Health (Grant # 5T32MH14581–06) and the Exxon Educational Foundation.

This essay is adapted from part of a book on the politics of pro-competitive deregulation that is in preparation at the Brookings Institution. The book focuses on airlines, trucking, and telecommunications. These three are not the only recent examples of successful procompetitive deregulation. We chose to concentrate on them because they appear most puzzling. The airline case is interesting because Congress carried reform to the extreme length of providing for the abolition by stages of the CAB. In the other two, procompetitive deregulation was achieved over the opposition of interests as powerful as the trucking industry, the Teamsters' Union, and AT&T. The central question addressed by the longer study is why diffuse, broadly encompassing, but poorly organized interests—namely, consumers and the general public, who stood to benefit from improved efficiency—triumphed over the tangible, particularistic, well-organized interests that benefited from regulatory protection. The analysis attempts to account for the unexpected strength of such intangible influences on policymaking as the reasoned arguments of policy analysts, the symbols evoked by the rhetoric of political leaders, and the susceptibility of the Washington community to fashions in policy. In the book, analysis of why the commissions chose to deregulate is preceded by an extended account of how deregulation developed into a fashionable idea, having its origins in academic criticism of regulation and owing its political appeal largely to the need of officeholders to address such diverse phenomena as the bankruptcy of the Penn Central railroad, the problem of severe inflation, the disaffection of the general public with an increasingly intrusive government, and the rise of consumerism as (at least) a widespread and influential state of mind, if not actually a mass movement. Here we have room only to allude to these crucial elements of the political context in which the commissions acted.

For the commissions to undertake procompetitive deregulation required fundamental reorientation, especially for the CAB and ICC, both of which had followed highly protectionist courses in the early 1970s. Immediately prior to its reform, the CAB was refusing to make new route awards, enforcing capacity limitation agreements and a rigid fare structure, and severely limiting low-cost charter flights. So extreme was CAB protectionism that it constituted a very important stimulus to reform. Nothing so enlivens reform as egregious examples of what is believed to need reforming. It is often said in Washington, not altogether facetiously, that the CAB chairman who should be credited with bringing about deregulation was neither John Robson (1975–1976), who instituted competitive pricing practices, nor Alfred E. Kahn (1977–1978), who moved to end controls over entry, but Robert D. Timm, who instituted the unprecedentedly protectionist policies of 1973–1974. The *New York Times* reported in the spring of 1973 that airline executives considered Timm's appointment as CAB chairman one of the best things that had happened to their industry since the invention of the jet engine.[1] Timm's counterpart at the ICC, George Stafford—who was chairman from 1969 to 1977—told a congressional committee in the spring of 1975 that less regulation would cost consumers more in the long run, and the ICC's annual report for that year opened with a stiff and righteous statement that refused even to discuss regulatory reform.[2]

The FCC is a more complicated case because it abandoned protectionism and began admitting competition to AT&T in long-distance communications and in terminal equipment in the 1960s, several years before anything like a movement for procompetitive deregulation developed within the Washington community.[3] This early anomaly is to be explained, we believe, mainly by the search of the Common Carrier Bureau, a fledgling organization in the 1950s with a new chief in 1964, for a more satisfying conception of self and purpose. (Before 1952, when industry-oriented bureaus—broadcasting and common carrier—were formed, the FCC had been organized along functional lines, with accounting, legal, and engineering divisions.) Initially, the Common Carrier Bureau was uncertain how to behave toward a giant monopolist that provided good service at prices that tended to fall even without pressure from regulation, thanks both to technological progress and to the rapid growth of its market. But in the 1960s the Common Carrier Bureau began to be more aggressive and more self-consciously independent of the regulated industry, after having been criticized in congressional hearings for being too lax with AT&T.[4] In response to issues raised by entrepreneurs with new technologies and, we believe, to the gigantism of

1. *New York Times*, 8 April 1973.

2. *National Journal*, 5 July 1975, p. 996. Interstate Commerce Commission (1975), p. 1: "The rhetoric that surrounded the continuing debate over the benefits and obligations of transportation regulation this year is not to be found in this report, nor should it be. This is a report of the manner in which the Interstate Commerce Commission carried out its responsibilities, with an analysis of the condition of the industries regulated. As such, it is hoped that the report illuminates the need for regulation."

3. The procompetitive evolution of common carrier regulation is documented and analyzed, among other places, in U.S. House of Representatives (1976) and Brock (1981), chapters 8 and 9. This evolution can be traced at least as far back as the *Above 890* decision of 1959 which authorized private long-distance microwave systems. In retrospect, the decision in *Above 890* was very important, but in contrast to decisions of the late 1960s it appears not to have expressed a consciously procompetitive policy. See Hinchman (1981).

4. Interview with Bernard Strassburg, former chief of the Common Carrier Bureau, 4 October 1979, and Strassburg (1977).

AT&T, which belied any need for protection and instead fostered feelings of frustration and hostility among official regulators, it undertook as a conscious regulatory tactic to admit competition to AT&T within limited spheres. However, the procompetitive trend of Common Carrier Bureau action in this period, in contrast to later decisions, was not deregulatory. On the contrary, because AT&T was in a position to use predatory pricing against the new competitors the FCC increased its efforts to supervise AT&T's rates. Not until 1979 or 1980 could the FCC be said to have undertaken to deregulate the common carrier industry.

Despite differences in the timing of their retreat from protectionism and differences as well in the political explanations for that retreat, it is reasonable for our purposes to discuss all three commissions together. Between 1975 and 1980, in advance of any legislation prescribing procompetitive deregulation (legislation was forthcoming for airlines in 1978 and for trucking in 1980 but is still pending for telecommunications), they substantially and more or less simultaneously retreated from the traditional practice of public utility regulation, which entailed controls over entry and prices. The CAB steadily liberalized rules governing charter flights; introduced flexibility in fares by approving discounts, ending the mandatory application of a mileage formula that resulted in equal fares for flights of equal distances and creating a zone of permissiveness with a range from 70 percent below to 10 percent above the standard coach fare previously prescribed; and, most importantly, abandoned the traditional practice of limiting entry through competitive selection of carriers and began to institute instead a policy of multiple permissive entry whereby operating rights were granted to all fit applicants on the basis of brief proceedings to determine fitness. The ICC substantially expanded unregulated areas—commercial zones—around cities and airports, a measure that virtually deregulated the New York City–New Jersey–Philadelphia area; eased entry by adopting an explicitly procompetitive test for deciding entry cases and granting over 95 percent of all applications for entry; introduced low rates as a criterion in the award of operating rights and proposed to introduce flexibility in rate-setting; proposed the adoption of master certification, a procedure that would have exempted whole industry segments from regulation; and voted to eliminate antitrust immunity for collective rate-making on single-line rates. The FCC decided to withdraw from regulating all kinds of terminal equipment, from the basic telephone to far smarter and more complex alternatives, and to confine its regulation of service offerings to basic services—that is, providing capacity for unenhanced transmission of information, of which long-distance voice telephone service is the most familiar example. It chose to stop regulating enhanced services, which entail computer-processing applications that restructure or verify information. It permitted AT&T to enter the deregulated markets, but only through a separate subsidiary.

This shared exercise in organizational self-denial is puzzling indeed, and the purpose of this paper is to account for it.[5] We attempt to show that an array of external forces together pushed the commissions in the direction of procompetitive deregulation, but because the chairmen were the foci of these external influences and the agents that converted these forces into commission action, our analysis will concentrate on them—their role, their power, and how they defined policy goals.

The Chairman

Although each commission was collegial in form, the chairman had emerged as the chief executive and dominant figure.[6] The President had been given the power to name chairmen, and the chairmen in turn had been given executive functions such as ap-

---

5. *Self-denial* may overstate or distort the position of the FCC, for it did not simply retreat from regulation. More precisely, it sought to substitute a market-oriented (or structural) approach to controlling the conduct of firms—above all, AT&T, of course—for the supervision of pricing and entry (the behavioral approach of traditional public utility regulation). This entailed retreat by the FCC from habitual functions, but it entailed assertion of the right to perform new ones, including the imposition of a separate subsidiary requirement on AT&T and supervision of relations between the parent and the subsidiary. The ambiguity of the FCC's retreat derived from the special complexity of procompetitive deregulation in the telecommunications industry. Because AT&T enjoyed various degrees of dominance in various segments of the telecommunications market, action that was both procompetitive and deregulatory was incomparably harder to conceive of than in the airline and trucking industries, which were potentially highly competitive. For the competitive potential of the latter to be realized, it was necessary only for government restraints to be removed. But as government restraints were removed from telecommunications markets, new dilemmas promptly arose, as the FCC had discovered in the course of pursuing the procompetitive initiatives of the late sixties and early seventies. The essential issues were to prevent AT&T from subsidizing competitive services with profits from the remaining monopoly portion of its services and to assure competitors nondiscriminatory access to AT&T transmission facilities. In the short run, the FCC responded by trying harder to regulate in the traditional way, with heightened pressure on AT&T to provide reliable data on costs. In 1979–1980, in a sharp departure from past practices, it chose maximum reliance on market forces. It is this choice that makes the FCC's behavior parallel to that of the CAB and ICC and enables us to discuss the three together, albeit with due acknowledgment of the special ambiguities and complexities of the telecommunications case. As policymakers were plagued by that complexity, so are we.

6. For detailed, inclusive evidence see Welborn (1977).

pointment and supervision of personnel (typically with the appointments subject to commission approval), distribution of business among personnel and among administrative units, and supervision of the use and expenditure of funds. These changes grew out of a tradition of administrative reform, classically exemplified by the Brownlow Report of 1937, that favored hierarchy, unity, and coordination within the federal executive branch.[7] At the extreme this view argued for abolishing independent commissions as a regulatory form. In its milder version it argued for improving presidential supervision and broadening the internal powers of the chairmen. The latter had considerable effect. The CAB was reformed according to these principles in 1950 and the FCC in 1952, although it was not until 1969 that Congress acceded to a presidential request to restructure the ICC similarly.[8] Until then, executive power in the ICC was lodged in three division chairmen, commission members who attained their positions through seniority. The chairmanship rotated among the remaining members, with the result that the commission chairman, rather than having exceptional power, had an exceptional lack of it. But once the anomalous case of the ICC was dealt with at the outset of the Nixon Administration, all the commission chairmen were chief executives, owing their appointments as such to the chief executive in the White House.

As chief executives, the commission chairmen generally expected and were expected by others to conform to type: to be active, to have an agenda or program, and to measure their success by the amount of their agenda accomplished. As of 1975–1976, it was very hard to conceive of an agenda that would not somehow respond to the gathering support for procompetitive deregulation—an effort at policy change that originated with experts in academic settings and eventually was embraced by the Council of Economic Advisers, the Antitrust Division of the Department of Justice, every President of the United States after Gerald Ford took office in 1974, key members of Congress—including, notably, Senator Edward M. Kennedy—and the federal courts, specifically the Circuit Court of Appeals for the

7. Commission on Law and the Economy (1979), p. 14. Chapter 2 of this report contains an excellent summary of studies of the regulatory agencies.

8. Reorganization Plan No. 13 of 1950, 64 Stat. 1266; 66 Stat. 712; *Public Papers of the Presidents: Richard Nixon, 1969*, item 274, pp. 534–36. The formal grant of authority to the FCC chairman is relatively weak and is, moreover, hedged by an administrative order of the commission dating from 1956 that, according to Welborn (1977), grew out of the members' belief that chairmen had become overbearing (p. 23). FCC chairmen have been only slightly hampered by these restrictions, however. The difference between their dominance and that of other commission chairmen who are formally more powerful is minor. See Welborn, p. 133. See also Ritchie (1980), chapter 13.

District of Columbia. Commission chairmen were uniformly influenced to accept procompetitive deregulation as a policy goal and
in varying degrees to promote it no matter what their prior policy
convictions may have been.

Nominally independent, the regulatory commissions are in truth
derivative organizations, heavily dependent in various ways on the
three major branches of government. The members and chairmen
owe their appointments to the President, although, in contrast to his
appointees to line departments, he cannot remove members at will.
The commissions owe their existence to Congress and need from it
not just tangible support in the form of appropriations but continuing approbation of what they do. Federal courts can overturn their
decisions. When all three branches or important elements of all three
adopt a shared approach to regulatory policy, chairmen are likely to
respond. To some extent, this is what happened with respect to procompetitive deregulation.

President Ford and after him President Carter signaled support
for procompetitive deregulation in two ways: by endorsing reform
legislation and by appointing to the regulatory commissions several
persons who were advocates of such reform or at least were expected
to be open-minded about it. Even though the use of presidential appointments was insufficient in the short run to create procompetitive, deregulatory majorities in the commissions (and hence does not
by itself account for the policy changes we seek to explain), along
with other presidential actions it constituted a cue to chairmen and
other members that these presidents favored procompetitive deregulation and thus might be expected to reward with reappointment
chairmen and members who supported that policy position. For procompetitive deregulation to occur within the commissions when it
did, some members had to switch policy position—and presidential
cue-giving undoubtedly contributed to these switches (of which we
will have more to say below when we discuss how chairmen influenced the votes of commission members).[9]

9. Despite their advocacy of procompetitive deregulation, presidents Ford and
Carter did not give explicit instructions on regulatory policy to their appointees, perhaps because their own positions were not clearly enough defined or deeply enough
held to make instructions possible, perhaps because they thought instructions inappropriate for appointees to independent agencies. John Robson, who instituted important procompetitive, deregulatory changes as chairman of the CAB in 1975–1976,
told an interviewer that he never talked to anyone in the Ford Administration about
his views on airline regulatory policy. "Now, I can't tell you that somebody in the Ford
Administration didn't think that [deregulation] was what I *would* do," Robson said.
"But they never talked to me about it." (Interview with Richard Smithey of the Yale
School of Organization and Management, xerox ms. 24 July 1981. All subsequent quo-
tations from Robson are from this interview, a condensed version of which appeared

In Congress, it was leading subcommittee units, or, more precisely, their chairmen, who became advocates of procompetitive deregulation. Oversight hearings and committee reports were powerful weapons with which to embarrass and ridicule the regulatory commissions for anticompetitive conduct. Senator Kennedy, as chairman of the Subcommittee on Administrative Practice and Procedure of the Senate Judiciary Committee, applied these weapons to the CAB in 1974–1975. Three years later, as chairman of the Subcommittee on Antitrust and Monopoly, Kennedy held hearings on trucking regulation as well, though these were less dramatic, less publicized, and less well staffed than the hearings on the CAB. That Kennedy's subcommittees did not have jurisdiction over regulatory legislation may have tended to limit the effect of his activities on them. But this limitation was amply offset by the glamour of his person, which attracted the attention of the press, and the pressure that his activity exerted on the Senate subcommittees that did have jurisdiction. With Kennedy showing so much interest in procompetitive regulatory reform and developing bills for that purpose, it became very hard for Howard W. Cannon, the chairman in 1974–1975 of the Subcommittee on Aviation of the Senate Commerce Committee, and later chairman of the full committee, to show no interest. Cannon, too, held hearings, though his began with an impartial tone rather than as critiques of the commissions.

In telecommunications affairs, in contrast to trucking and airline regulation, congressional interest in procompetitive deregulation originated within a subcommittee that did possess legislative jurisdiction: the Subcommittee on Communications of the House Interstate and Foreign Commerce Committee, which was created as a distinct entity in 1975. (Communications had previously been combined with energy in the subcommittee structure.) With the

---

in *The Bureaucrat* 11, no. 2 [Summer 1982]: 32–38.) Similarly, A. Daniel O'Neal, who instituted procompetitive deregulation while chairman of the ICC in 1977–1979, told us that he had talked to President Carter only once before his appointment and that the President had asked him only one very vague question about deregulation. As O'Neal recalled it, the President asked him what he thought of the Ford Administration's proposals for trucking deregulation, and he replied that he agreed with some but not others, an answer that the President did not further examine (interview, 10 December 1979). Before Alfred Kahn was appointed chairman of the CAB he paid a visit to the White House in which President Carter and his staff provided not instructions but assurances of the depth of their own commitment to deregulation and their desire that he accept the office (interview, Mary McInnes, 6 January 1981). White House staff members in the Ford and Carter administrations who strongly favored procompetitive deregulation and who were deeply involved in developing deregulation bills did not attempt to guide the policy choices of regulatory agency chairmen, restrained apparently by the belief that such intervention was both impractical and improper.

blessing first of subcommittee chairman Torbert H. MacDonald and then of his successor, Lionel Van Deerlin, the staff plunged promptly into regulatory reform, then burgeoning as a field of political and policy action. It prepared hearings and issued a staff report that roundly attacked the FCC for anticompetitive restrictions on cable TV, and held oversight hearings on domestic common carrier regulation that stressed the inability of the FCC to regulate effectively. In 1976 it undertook hearings on competition in the telecommunications industry.

Among the federal courts, the Circuit Court of Appeals for the District of Columbia Circuit became the leading critic of anticompetitive regulation. Because this court was much the most important single reviewer of regulatory agency action (it is sometimes called the supreme court for regulation) its attitude was especially influential. Judge J. Skelly Wright quite clearly, and the rest of the court to some extent, had come to expound the reigning academic and populist critique of the regulatory agencies. Thus, in *Moss* v. *CAB*, a 1970 case that involved the board's procedures for determining air fares, Wright wrote that the essential question was "whether the regulatory agency is unduly oriented toward the interest of the industry it is designed to regulate, rather than the public interest it is designed to protect." In devastating language that came as a shock to the CAB, he concluded that it was indeed wrongly oriented.[10] Subsequently this court began to take an explicitly procompetitive position. Thus, in *Continental Airlines* v. *CAB* in 1975, the court speaking through Judge Leventhal found that the Federal Aviation Act required the board to "foster competition as a means of enhancing the development and improvement of air transportation service on routes generating sufficient traffic to support competing carriers."[11] In *P. C. White Truck Line, Inc.* v. *ICC* in 1977, the court in a *per curiam* opinion ruled that the ICC could not deny an application for operating rights solely on the ground that the applicant had failed to prove the inadequacy of existing service, but was required to weigh the possible benefit to the public from increased competiton.[12]

The most significant action of this court was its decision against the FCC in the *Execunet* case in 1977. In 1975 the FCC had found that the offering of Execunet, a long-distance service of MCI, one of AT&T's new competitors, was unlawful. The FCC argued that MCI had been authorized to offer only private-line services, whereas Execunet was

10. *Moss* v. *C.A.B.*, 430 F. 2d 891 (1970).
11. *Continental Air Lines, Inc.*, v. *C.A.B.*, 519 F. 2d 944 (1975).
12. *P. C. White Truck Line, Inc.*, v. *I.C.C.*, 551 F. 2d 1326 (1977).

essentially a public telephone service because it allowed a subscriber to call anywhere MCI had facilities. The Circuit Court found that the FCC had erred in rejecting MCI's Execunet tariff because it had failed to determine that the public interest would be served by creating an AT&T monopoly in public interstate long-distance telephone service. In its closing sentences the court said: "the Commission must be ever mindful that, just as it is not free to create competition for competition's sake [a reference to a landmark decision of the Supreme Court, *FCC* v. *RCA Communications, Inc.,* in 1953] it is not free to propagate monopoly for monopoly's sake. The ultimate test of industry structure in the communications common carrier field must be the public interest, not the private financial interests of those who have until now enjoyed the fruits of *de facto* monopoly."[13]

The institutional influences that we have described thus far were mainly in the nature of sanctions: punishments or threats of punishment for carrying out anticompetitive regulation. While they might explain the moderating of anticompetitive positions, they do not suffice to explain why regulatory commission chairmen began promoting procompetitive deregulation. To understand that, it is necessary to understand that for the chairmen above all, these external influences also created opportunities and promised rewards.

Persons who wanted to achieve procompetitive deregulation detected an opportunity in the developments we have described and were therefore more attracted to office in the commissions at this time than they would otherwise have been. The best illustration is Alfred Kahn, a distinguished academician who had been serving as chairman of the New York Public Services Commission and who very nearly preferred staying in New York to heading the CAB. But he found it hard to say no to a personal plea from President Carter and to resist service in the place where legislative action seemed imminent.[14]

Less predictably, chairmen with no independent commitment to procompetitive deregulation also responded to the opportunity for action that the gathering momentum for reform created, and they proved quite willing to embrace the increasingly prevalent definition of what ought to be done. Perhaps they became persuaded that the prevailing view was correct on its merits, or perhaps they perceived that to be guided by prevalent views increased both their chances of achieving something and of being widely applauded for it. The atti-

13. *MCI Telecommunications Corp.* v. *F.C.C.,* 561 F. 2d 365 (1977). More generally on the aggressiveness of this particular court of appeals, see Polsby (1979).

14. U.S. Senate (1977), pp. 55–56; McInnes interview; interview, Alfred E. Kahn, 23 June 1981.

tude of John Robson to service as CAB chairman illustrates this prototypical will-to-act of the chief executive:

> The fact is I didn't have very many views on [airline regulatory policy].
>   I had talked to the Ford administration about some other posts in government. Then I said to myself, "You are in a time when government isn't going to have any money; no agency is going to have money. You aren't going to be able to do much from the standpoint of new domestic programs. It is not clear how well the Ford administration is going to do. But you know you have the airline deregulation issue on the table because it has already surfaced." It was a topic I believed had gained some momentum and attracted some attention. The intellectual underpinnings were available. There were studies that had been done by academic economists such as Jim Miller, Jordan, Eads and others. This work had gone on for probably a decade. Then Ted Kennedy had surfaced the issue in hearings he held late in 1974 and 1975 so that deregulation became politically more visible. It seemed to me that the CAB provided a unique opportunity to do something—to be at a place at a time when something was happening. It was clear there was going to be action on the CAB frontier. . . .
>   In terms of personal reward you don't get a chance to change things significantly very often in your life.

Though action tends to bring its own rewards (in fun, excitement, and a sense of accomplishment), audience approval adds to the satisfaction, and by 1975 the regulatory commissions had a growing audience. For some decades they had been one of the backwaters of American government, attended to mainly by client groups, the lawyers of the client groups, and a small number of professors of law and political science who were intermittently assigned by presidents or Congress to study them, invariably with highly critical results. Except when scandals broke out, they received little or no attention from the national press, which for official Washington is an overwhelmingly important audience in its own right as well as the medium through which other audiences are reached. This changed when the movement for regulatory reform got under way with some seriousness. What the consumer movement, Senator Kennedy, and two presidents thought was important the press was inclined to cover and, what's more, was newly helped to cover by passage of the Government in the Sunshine Act in 1976, which for the first time opened meetings of the regulatory commissions to the press. Regulatory commission chairmen became the subjects of news. Partly this was because as leaders of reform they were causing action to occur, but it is equally the case that a heightened exposure to press coverage heightened their will to act and gave them additional incentives to act in pursuit of procompetitive deregulation, of which the press uniformly approved. Editorials throughout the country overwhelmingly supported procompetitive deregulation, and a few members of the Washington press corps followed the story closely and sympathetically.

Finally, among the external influences bearing on the chairman one must take account of other chairmen, at least after Kahn achieved his well-publicized successes in administrative deregulation at the CAB. He became a model for other chairmen to emulate and the standard by which the press, congressmen, and other audiences judged their performance. Thus, for example, a fellow commission-member intimated that the FCC under Charles Ferris was trying to "out-Kahn Alfred."[15] A story about the FCC in the *New York Times* that compared Ferris to Kahn elicited from a member of the Senate Commerce Committee the unflattering observation, to Ferris's face, that his performance did not merit the comparison.[16]

Largely in response to this varied combination of external influences, all chairmen of the CAB, ICC, and FCC between 1975 and 1980 moved toward procompetitive deregulation no matter what their seeming preferences. Whether as a grudging necessity (presumably the case for chairmen who began from a protectionist position) or as a prized opportunity (for those who entered office as ardent deregulators), all acted as the rising critique of regulation prescribed that they should.

In George Stafford's last years as chairman, the ICC backed away from its stiff, unyielding defense of regulation and began to acknowledge some need for reform. The decision to expand unregulated commercial zones was taken in 1976. Because President Ford replaced him as chairman of the CAB at the end of 1974, Robert Timm did not have much chance to show what kind of chairman he would be in a changed environment, but there is persuasive evidence of his adaptability. Under prodding from the Office of Management and Budget the CAB began a self-study early in 1975, soon after he left office as chairman, and in a memorandum to his successor, Timm, the arch-protectionist, all but urged that this study endorse deregulation: "this reappraisal committee . . . must go far beyond administrative or housekeeping concerns . . . they should question the continuing viability of the Federal Aviation Act and specifically whether the mandate to promote an infant industry is necessary or advisable

15. Remarks by Commissioner Joseph R. Fogarty before the New England Conference on Public Utilities Commissioners, 30 May 1979.

16. *Amendments to the Communications Act of 1934*, in U.S. Senate (1979a), pt. 3, pp. 2070–71, 2082–84.

212   MARTHA DERTHICK AND PAUL J. QUIRK

in the changed circumstances of the present day. . . . If deregulation
by function (rates, routes, etc.) seems indicated, they should further
examine how and in what time span the phasing out should occur.
The group should examine the wisdom of regulation per se and
should set standards and prerequisites for the imposition of regulatory controls."[17]

John Robson, Timm's successor at the CAB, entered office "objective and agnostic" but soon became a deregulator and in the spring of
1976 testified before the Senate Commerce Committee that "economic regulation should be redirected so domestic air transport is, in
time, essentially governed by competitive market forces."[18] Stafford's
successor at the ICC, A. Daniel O'Neal, had a record as an ICC member that showed him to be consumer-oriented and "interested in protecting the little guy" but uninterested in, if not downright hostile to,
deregulation. He told the Senate Commerce Committee in his confirmation hearings in 1973 that "vigorous enforcement of regulatory
laws . . . probably is the best course to follow."[19] As late as 1975 he remarked to a conference: "There is . . . something cavalier about the
attitudes of those who appear willing for others to sustain serious
losses so that we can test some economic theories."[20] To yet another
conference he remarked that although regulation did not work well
enough, "for what most citizens expect from transportation, it will
work better than the marketplace."[21] Yet soon after his elevation to the
chairmanship, he began arguing for easier entry into the trucking
business and instituted a wide array of procompetitive policy changes.
Under O'Neal, deregulation became the goal of the ICC.

Charles Ferris, who presided over deregulation at the FCC, arrived in office as a self-professed generalist or, alternatively, a specialist in figuring out how to make action occur in Washington. He
had served for some years as a staff member to the Democratic majority in the Senate and, more briefly, to the Democratic Speaker of
the House. Initially agnostic on the issues before the FCC, especially
common carrier issues, he began before long to promise deregulation in both broadcasting and common carrier affairs.

In the absence of prior conviction, the influences of organizational role and political context combined to make deregulators of

17. Memo, Timm to O'Melia, "Committee on Regulation," 15 January 1975, CAB
files.
18. U.S. Senate (1976a), p. 346.
19. U.S. Senate (1973), p. 174. The characterizations of O'Neal's record at the ICC
are his own, taken from our interview with him.
20. Moore and Moore (1976), p. 35.
21. Public Interest Economics Foundation (n.d.), p. 150.

Robson, O'Neal, and Ferris. Even Kahn, whose independent commitment to increased competition is beyond doubt, seems to have sensed that pressures of role and context dictated immediate action when his academician's instinct was to pause for inquiry. He told an early audience (Kahn, 1977) that "very much like the Red Queen in *Through the Looking Glass,* I am in the interesting position of being responsible for executing the sentence first, with the verdict already in, and the trial postponed until some indefinite date in the future, when I may be able to return to more leisurely academic study. I regard it as my job to preside over an effort to restore this industry as much as proves feasible to the rule of competition, cautiously, thoughtfully, and sensitively, even though my own preference would have been to study it for several years first." So qualified were the CAB's initial comments on the Kennedy-Cannon reform bill in the summer of 1977 that Kahn "'at some considerable embarrassment to myself'" had to send a second letter to the Hill to make clear that the original document did endorse reform.[22] Eventually Kahn (1978) abandoned a commitment to gradualism in favor of "something as close to total deregulation as the law will permit, to be achieved as quickly as possible." Kahn himself seems to have been unsure to what extent his initial restraint was merely tactical and to what extent it expressed uncertainty of belief. At one point he wrote to a staff member: "I do not myself know to what extent I declare a commitment to gradualism insincerely, merely to reassure Congress and the industry that I am not a madman, and that I am solicitous of the financial fortunes of the industry, and anxious not to impair them. I am sure I do so also because I don't believe in *any* economic prediction with more than, say, 65 percent conviction. Undoubtedly an additional reason is my lack of opportunity to have absorbed the work of others who have studied this industry."[23] At any rate, it seems clear that even Kahn carried deregulation farther and faster than he at first thought prudent. Much as the agnostics became believers, this believer became more deeply committed to action on his beliefs. The experience of office tended to move all the chairmen toward more deregulation than they initially advocated.

The one exception to this generalization was Darius Gaskins, an economist appointed by Carter in 1980 to head the ICC. Strongly committed to procompetitive deregulation, Gaskins was constrained by congressional sources. One was Senator Cannon, who admonished the ICC in a speech in October 1979 not to make major moves

22. Washington *Star,* 13 and 15 July 1977.

23. Memo, Alfred E. Kahn to Roy Pulsifer, "Your Comments on My January 20 Talk to the Security Analysts," 24 January 1978, CAB files.

in trucking deregulation that could preempt congressional action. Another was the Senate Appropriations Committee, which in a more or less simultaneous report instructed the ICC not to implement any policy changes while new legislation was pending.[24] Commission action under O'Neal had attained enough momentum to elicit this counteraction from Congress, which sought time to make the decisions about trucking deregulation itself. In a letter responding to Cannon's speech, O'Neal as chairman and Gaskins as his impending successor pledged to take no final action in major deregulatory proceedings before 1 June 1980, the date by which Cannon had promised to produce passage of a bill. Thus, Gaskins was forced to defer to the legislature, yet he continued the ICC's independent pursuit of procompetitive deregulation with actions that he judged to be within the terms of his agreement with Cannon.

The Staffs

The preceding section shows how the commission chairmen were powerfully encouraged by the gathering support for procompetitive deregulation to act in that particular way. But if external forces moved them in that direction, why did not internal forces hold them back? How were they able to overcome the opposition of staffs to a fundamental revision of agency missions?

In none of the three cases was internal opposition insurmountable or even a serious obstacle. In all three, staffs eventually either acquiesced in procompetitive deregulation or themselves became influential advocates of it. We now will attempt to explain why. Again we approach the analysis from the perspective of the chairmen. We will argue that they found support for procompetitive deregulation from four classes of staff members: dissidents, newcomers, deferrers, and converts. Before very long, these categories embraced virtually everyone who mattered.

Dissidents

Within the regulatory commissions were a few staff members who from personal experience or exposure to external criticism had ceased to believe in what they were doing even before reform-oriented chairmen arrived. When the drive for reform developed under President Ford they were available to fill a variety of influential roles.

One outstanding example was Betty Jo Christian, for some years a

24. U.S. Senate (1979b), p. 50. The conference committee repeated this instruction: U.S. House of Representatives (1979a), p. 15. A copy of Senator Cannon's speech is in our files.

litigation attorney in the ICC general counsel's office and then chief of the litigation division. During her years as a litigator Christian had become convinced of the need to reexamine policies and practices of the ICC that she found hard to defend in court because they violated reason and common sense.[25] President Ford appointed her to the commission in 1976, and she proceeded consistently to vote for granting entry and liberalizing entry policies.

Another example of a dissident was J. Michael Roach, a lawyer who held various staff positions in the CAB between 1967 and 1974 and who, he told us, came to a dissenting view on airline deregulation through "one of those Paul-on-the-road-to-Damascus experiences." Late in 1969, he had been assigned to write the board's decision in a route case with no instructions whatever except the name of the winning airline. The "revelation" was "sitting down with a blank legal tablet" and realizing that it was up to him to contrive the board's reasons for the decision. And after he was done, the board did not change a word of what he had written.[26] It came to him as vivid proof of what many in the CAB knew or sensed: the board's alleged rationales for route awards were not the real rationales, but were artifices designed to give the gloss of legal reasoning to awards made privately by the board on other grounds. Not that there was anything corrupt about these other grounds as staff members understood them. Roughly, the board acted in a commonsensical way to make sure that every carrier got a reasonable share of new route authority and that none was exposed to financial hazard.[27] Not everyone was disillusioned by the need to rationalize these decisions in ways that would make them seem the work of experts and enable them to survive tests in court. Some very intelligent people found the exercise to be fun "much in the way that doing crossword puzzles is fun."[28] But persons with a strong moral sense could be outraged or guilt-stricken, as was Roach. "I realized that I was spending my time constructing lies," he recalled. "It was an evil thing I was participating in." It was not "the worst of evils—not like dropping napalm in Viet Nam," but still wrong. And it was not even very sensible or practical, Roach thought, because in "passing out cookies" the board "often passed out the wrong cookie." Roach left the CAB at the end of 1974 and for several months worked on an airline deregulation bill as a

25. Interview, 12 February 1980.

26. Interview, J. Michael Roach, 26 November 1980.

27. There is a remarkably candid acknowledgment of this approach in U.S. Civil Aeronautics Board (1969), section 21,872.03, page 14,776.

28. The source of this quotation, a career civil servant, asked to remain anonymous.

staff member of the Council on Wage and Price Stability, one of the agencies represented in the Ford Administration's task force on regulatory reform. He left the government in the fall of 1975 but returned two years later to work as special assistant to the new chairman of the CAB, Alfred Kahn.

Dissidents such as these, having become expert in regulation through the practice of it, brought special skills and credibility to the reform effort, but such persons were likely in one way or another to leave the jobs that they no longer fully believed in performing, and hence to cease being dissidents. In the period we are analyzing, Christian was no longer on the staff of the ICC, having been elevated to the commission, and Roach was no longer on the staff of the CAB, although he was on the chairman's personal staff.

Nonetheless, dissidence had a significant influence in the CAB, at least. For several years, staff members of the Bureau of Operating Rights had been showing a disposition to doubt the board's anticompetitive policies. Some of this questioning may have arisen from personal experience, such as Roach related to us, but another important source of it was the bureau's assistant director, Roy Pulsifer, who was an avid reader of the economics literature that criticized airline regulation and who encouraged other staff members to study it too, challenging them to disbelieve in what they were doing. If there was intellectual inquiry in this, there was also a measure of iconoclasm. "The government was dull," Roach remarked to us in an effort to explain Pulsifer's behavior, "and he found fun, challenge, and excitement in educating young people and stirring things up. . . . Roy likes to beat up on you and force you to think." He liked telling well-intentioned people that they were practicing "witchcraft." And there was outrage and moralism in Pulsifer too. He came to see first the protected industry and later the whole government establishment in Washington as parasitic and, in a profound sense, corrupt. When we interviewed him in his office at the CAB in 1980, he had become a radical libertarian and had a picture of the famous free-market economist, Milton Friedman, displayed on his desk.

It may seem inexplicable that early in 1975, when the CAB undertook a self-study, it turned to Roy Pulsifer to do this job. Pulsifer's attraction (in addition to a dozen years of highly competent service at the CAB) was that he would be credible because he was known to be critical. Members of the Office of Management and Budget, in urging on Chairman Timm an appraisal of the CAB's functions, had urged also the use of an independent outside consultant, in the belief that the CAB's staff could not be disinterested. The choice of Pulsifer was apparently designed to demonstrate that OMB was wrong. Promised independence, Pulsifer formed a study group consisting of three CAB staff members and an independent economist, Lucile S. Keyes, who was one of the earliest critics of airline regulation and still a very active one. In July 1975, this group recommended flatly that federal law be amended to eliminate protective entry, exit, and price control in the domestic airline industry in three to five years (U.S. Civil Aeronautics Board, 1975). Incredibly, the CAB's own inquiry had ended in a radical recommendation for deregulation, an event that impressed attentive congressmen and their staffs. If the CAB's own study concluded that regulation was harmful, surely the case for it must be very weak. Within the CAB, the report helped enable John Robson and a staff task force that he assembled to take a surprisingly strong stand in favor of deregulation.

Pulsifer's radical dissent and his opportunity to express it in an official document were unique. Outside the CAB, dissenters did not become an important asset to reform-oriented chairmen. Ironically, not even Pulsifer was personally consulted or relied on. Robson, judging Pulsifer to be idiosyncratic and moreover not wishing to be upstaged by a staff member, refrained from embracing his report. Instead Robson created his own staff task force to study the need for changes, within which were several doubters whose doubts owed much to Pulsifer's personal influence. Under Kahn, Pulsifer felt ill-used by the newly arrived advocates of deregulation with whom the chairman staffed the top levels of the CAB, and deprived of credit for a reform that he had advocated two or three years before, at some risk to his career, when the new arrivals were still in their university chairs (or wherever).

Newcomers

The administrative powers of chairmen proved very important in securing staff support for procompetitive deregulation. In all the commissions the chairman could appoint personnel, reorganize administrative units, and reassign functions, although in the ICC these powers were so recently established and had been so little used by their first holder, George Stafford, that both O'Neal and Gaskins faced a very different sort of challenge from that of their counterparts at the CAB and FCC. As of 1977, the ICC chairman still had to secure his right to executive leadership, whereas at the CAB and, to a lesser extent, the FCC that right was taken for granted. It is not surprising, therefore, that at both the CAB and FCC chairmen used new appointments and reorganizations as major techniques for securing staff support for their policy goals. At both places but especially at the FCC, new appointees to the staff in turn became an important source of influence on the chairman, strongly urging deregulation on him and boldly inventing the means to achieve it, rather than merely helping him to attain what he had independently defined.

At the CAB, Kahn at first sought to work with the incumbent staff, but he soon grew frustrated. As his goals became clearer with experience of airline regulation, he realized that incumbents at the top of the staff were not likely to help him attain those goals. They were inclined to emphasize what law and precedent said could *not* be done rather than look for enlarged definitions of what *could* be done. With the aid of an intensely loyal managing director whom he had brought from New York, Kahn began to make changes, and after six months people he had chosen had been installed at the top of the organization.

The bureaus in charge of routes and rates were consolidated into a single Bureau of Pricing and Domestic Aviation with a director from outside the organization. A new Office of Economic Analysis was created. A new general counsel was brought in, and a new personal assistant to Kahn. All were associated—through professional training, personal experience, or academic publication—with the rise of procompetitive deregulation. The new general counsel, Philip J. Bakes, Jr., had been assistant chief counsel to Kennedy's investigation of the CAB. The new special assistant to Kahn was the former member of the routes staff whom we quoted a few paragraphs ago as having had the "Paul-on-the-road-to-Damascus" experience that revealed to him the evils of CAB route-setting. The head of economic analysis was Darius Gaskins, an economist with strongly procompetitive views who would later be named chairman of the ICC by President Carter. The head of the new consolidated bureau (the consolidation was the price of his coming after Kahn decided he had to have him) was Michael E. Levine, a law professor with training in economics who had made his professional debut in 1965 with a seminal article in the *Yale Law Journal* criticizing airline regulation. They were all young and very bright. Several were brash, especially Levine, and rode roughshod over industry and staff alike. They were eager to push the Federal Aviation Act to the limits of permissible discretion, and equally eager to take on arguments in court over where those limits might lie.

Veteran careerists of high rank, genuinely respected by this group yet rejected, left the organization, were bypassed, or withdrew into passive dissent. Arthur Simms, who had headed the rates bureau and had run the domestic-passenger-fare investigation, a massive and meticulous effort of the early 1970s to establish rules for rate-setting, left when it became clear that there was simply no longer a tolerable place for him. Pulsifer stayed but grew hostile to the newcomers. Both felt, in Simms's words, that what the new arrivals were doing "was just goddamned illegal and wouldn't stick. I felt that they were twisting the statute beyond all legal recognition and the government ought not to do that."[29]

At the FCC, Ferris did not install prominent advocates of procompetitive deregulation as deliberately as did Kahn at the CAB, but what he did was tantamount to that. He enlarged the role of economists in policymaking by enlarging the functions of the FCC's Office of Plans and Policy and naming an economist to head it. Both this economist, Nina W. Cornell, and Ferris's general counsel, Robert R. Bruce, from a leading Washington law firm, were strongly critical of traditional public utility regulation. As such, they exemplified the latest and best thinking, and Ferris, as an action-oriented generalist, sought precisely such persons for his staff. Walter Hinchman, who was chief of the Common Carrier Bureau when Ferris took office and who favored procompetitive policy changes without favoring a retreat from regulation, left in 1978 out of sheer fatigue and was replaced briefly by an economist from within the FCC and then, in 1979, by a lawyer, Philip L. Verveer, who had been lead counsel for the Department of Justice in the preparation of its antitrust suit against AT&T. When Cornell and Bruce, as generalists in favor of procompetitive deregulation, were joined by a Common Carrier Bureau chief who shared that objective, the way was prepared for the outcome of the *Computer II* inquiry in the spring of 1980. *Computer II* represented a sweeping retreat from traditional public utility regulation, with its focus on rate-setting. Instead, it embraced a structural approach to preventing predatory conduct that relied heavily on requiring AT&T to form a separate subsidiary and on authorizing resale of its services. This result incorporated the beliefs of leading staff members, which in the course of internal discussion became the beliefs of the chairman, too.[30]

29. Interview with Arthur Simms, 25 November 1980.

30. Interviews with Nina W. Cornell, 24 April 1981, and with Charles D. Ferris, 28 July 1981. The regulatory philosophies of influential staff members are set forth in speeches: Remarks by Robert R. Bruce before the Federal Communications Bar Association, 21 June 1979; remarks by Philip L. Verveer before the Federal Communications Bar Association, 25 January 1980; and, most pointedly, "Telecommunications Regulation and Competition in a Post-Industrial Society," presented by Nina W. Cornell before the Armed Forces Communications and Electronics Associations, 11 January 1979. Dr. Cornell told her audience: "The Federal Communications Commission has entered a period of self-examination in which its policies toward competition and regulation are being extensively reevaluated. One basic goal of this reevaluation process is to allow the competitive marketplace, wherever possible, to determine the cost, price, quantity, quality, and diversity of communications services available to the public. With this objective, the Commission is examining all of the communications markets it regulates to determine those policies and rules that tend to restrict competition

Veteran careerists in the Common Carrier Bureau posed no obstacle to the *Computer II* decision because none existed. Much of the career staff left in the late 1970s, often in order to avoid the effects of newly harsh conflict-of-interest laws that threatened to limit their employment opportunities upon departure from the civil service. So weakened was the bureau that in 1979 the Senate Appropriations Committee took note in a report of its "apparent disarray" and expressed disappointment with "the high turnover of key personnel and the lack of progress in key areas."[31] Rather than a bastion of veteran careerists, the bureau was badly in need of rebuilding. Under Verveer it was rebuilt with persons who had no experience with or commitment to traditional public-utility regulation.[32]

Deferrers

By *deferrers* we mean staff members who did the work in support of procompetitive deregulation because it was what incumbent authorities—the chairmen or commission majorities—instructed them to do. Some measure of deference is always to be found in hierarchical organizations; they cannot function without it. In pursuit of the goals of procompetitive reform, the normal authority of office-

---

and delay technological change that might be eliminated. Ultimately, I hope the Commission will decide to have regulation only where competition is not possible." Much of this uncompromising speech was devoted to identifying "inherent defects" in the regulatory process.

31. U.S. Senate (1979c), pp. 65–66.

32. Even if veteran careerists had been present, they might have had a hard time mounting a strong defense of regulatory practices that were widely acknowledged to be hapless and ineffective. The FCC's regulation of common carrier affairs was uniquely vulnerable to criticism that was pragmatic as well as, or rather than, principled. Whether critics thought regulation of AT&T ill-conceived (and there was much more room for dispute on this point than in the airline and trucking industries, which had none of the characteristics of a natural monopoly), all agreed that the FCC had achieved very little control over AT&T's rate-setting—a point that was not merely conceded but given particularly convincing expression by various FCC commissioners, administrative law judges, and Walter Hinchman, who was for more than four years chief of the Common Carrier Bureau. Hinchman's public statements argued with equal vehemence both the necessity of regulating AT&T and the futility of doing so. This confession of helplessness made it easier for the committed deregulators of the Ferris administration to argue for their alternative structural approach. For an analysis of the obstacles faced by the FCC, see Crandall (1979). For Hinchman's views, see "The Future of AT&T: For Whom *Does* (the) Bell Toll??" remarks before the Communications Networks Town Meeting, Houston, 13 January 1981, in which he asserts that "the FCC has never been able to hold Bell accountable to the just, reasonable, and nondiscriminatory standards of the Communications Act"; that its effort to do so reached a high-water mark in 1970–1978, with consequences for Bell's pricing behavior that were "virtually nil"; and that after 1978 the commission "retreated in disarray from this admittedly difficult task" and largely dismantled the few regulatory mechanisms that offered any hope of constraining Bell.

holders was reinforced by the authority of expert opinion generally and by other sources of external criticism. Though commission staffs were not under the same compulsion as chairmen to define agendas for action, they were hardly immune to the currents of critical opinion swirling around them. Intangible sanctions—embarrassment, ridicule, the opprobrium of informed opinion—were falling heavily on these agencies, which therefore were suffering a loss of pride and self-esteem. Belief in the correctness of their mission was undermined, and they were under much pressure to demonstrate that they were capable of renewal and improvement.

Deference to leadership was especially important in the ICC. For one thing, it was traditional there. Whereas the CAB staff not infrequently talked back to the board, according to one consultant's study (Barber and Associates, 1977) it was unusual in the ICC for the commission and staff to talk to each other at all. The ICC staff traditionally was preoccupied with, indeed overwhelmed by, the agency's routine tasks. The ICC staff processed over 5,000 applications for operating rights per year. Perhaps because its routines were far less burdensome, the CAB staff appears to have had more time to think critically about them, and when it was invited to think critically, through creation of the special staff study, it did not hesitate to make an utterly radical and heretical response, one that, according to John Robson, other board members than he "treated . . . like a new father with a dirty diaper, sort of holding it out in front of them with two fingers." In the ICC when O'Neal as chairman created a staff task force in 1977 and invited the members to think critically, they responded with moderate procompetitive proposals of the sort they supposed the commission wanted. In an interview the head of the task force attributed its generally procompetitive tone more to the commission than to the staff. "It was a reaction to changes that were in the wind," he told us. "There was probably a majority on the commission for reform by that time," though the task force "didn't realize how quickly things were changing on entry in the commission" or "it might have gone farther than it did."[33] Nor did Darius Gaskins, O'Neal's successor, find the ICC staff in general to be resistant to the policy changes he sought.[34]

Staff deference was relatively important to reform at the ICC also because the ICC chairman had more difficulty than chairmen at the CAB and FCC in bringing newcomers to the staff. The chairman's authority was so much less well established at the ICC that O'Neal and Gaskins could not count on the commission to acquiesce in their

33. Interview with George Chandler, 19 February 1980.
34. Interview with Darius Gaskins, 28 January 1981.

choices of personnel. In contrast to Kahn, O'Neal made relatively few staff changes, though he too resorted to reorganization. Besides securing his own authority by abolishing the specialized, highly autonomous units characteristic of the old subdivided commission, he created an Office of Policy and Analysis, put an economist in charge, and began to draw on it for analytic advice on the progress of procompetitive reform. When Gaskins succeeded O'Neal, he made a few personnel changes, including the appointment of persons who had participated in deregulation at the CAB, but he continued to rely heavily on incumbent staff members and to find them in general responsive. "We have been able to persuade the staff that we're moving in the right direction," he told us.[35]

How much use a chairman could make of deference depended in large part on how far he wished to carry policy change. Up to a point, deference could be elicited even in the CAB, with its deeper tradition of staff independence. Their pride wounded by the Kennedy hearings and the faint scandal associated with the Timm chairmanship, veteran careerists at the CAB cooperated with Robson in the spring of 1976 in preparing the CAB's own procompetitive reform bill. This legislative proposal was far milder than Robson's oral presentation of it seemed to promise. Even under him there was a visible gap between the goals the chairman was professing and what the highest-ranking, most prestigious members of the incumbent staff were willing to advocate. And when Kahn after Robson persisted in pursuing radical goals through commission action rather than awaiting statutory changes, veteran careerists did not defer but were replaced or pushed aside. That this sort of contretemps did not develop at the ICC is to be explained not just by the greater propensity of that staff to defer but also by the fact that as administrative deregulation at the ICC became radical, Congress intervened to stop it and to take legislative action instead.

Converts

Some incumbent careerists, though not dissidents prior to the development of procompetitive reform, became believers in it, "converts" who enthusiastically cooperated with the new leadership. They may have been convinced of its merits, they may have been acting opportunistically to obtain higher ranks and salaries, or they may have been caught up in the excitement that typically accompanies significant policy change.

Converts appear to have been especially important at the CAB. "There were a lot of lawyers willing to do what we wanted—young

35. Ibid.

ones receptive to opportunity," according to Elizabeth E. Bailey, an economist appointed to the CAB by Carter and, if anything, a more zealous deregulator than Kahn. According to Bailey, the new unit heads whom Kahn found in turn "found people—sub-groups of young lawyers—there (at the CAB) between four and nine years, 15's but not 17's, 14's but not 18's, who became upwardly mobile."[36] The sense of excitement through which converts could be made was especially keen at the CAB because of the personality of Kahn, whose extraordinary combination of dynamism, magnetism, expertise, and wit made at least some people believe that there was no one else in the world like him and that working for him was more fun than they would ever have again.

The bright, young, ambitious staff members who were potential converts may have been more numerous proportionately at the CAB than elsewhere because the CAB was an elite organization, with a staff generally believed to be of superior competence and élan. "The selectivity at the CAB was a notch above that at the ICC," according to an administrator who had held high-ranking positions in both. "We hired fewer lawyers, with the result that they tended to be more inquisitive, more receptive. . . . The whole ethos was different."[37] The CAB housed converts for some of the same reasons it housed dissidents. While the contrast with the FCC was less clear and direct than with the ICC, if only because the functions were much less similar, a civil servant in the CAB who had come from the FCC told us he had found the CAB a much better place to work. Particularly during the period of reform under Kahn, a time in which he had achieved rapid promotion, it had been "incredibly exciting, a wonderful challenge." He couldn't "conceive of a better time."[38]

Drawing on some combination of these four categories of supporting staff members, pro-reform chairmen could secure reasonably prompt staff support for what they sought to do and congenial advice on what they ought to do. Staff members who did not cooperate could be bypassed. "The pricing group two years after deregulation still comes up to us with the same old boiler plate," Elizabeth Bailey remarked. "You tend to build around a group like that."[39] All the

36. Interview with Elizabeth E. Bailey, 6 May 1980.

37. Interview with Gary Edles, 22 April 1981.

38. Interview with Paul Gretsch, 11 July 1979.

39. Bailey interview. There was no cluster of dissidents in the rates staff comparable to that in the routes staff, perhaps because the rates staff had had a more satisfying relation with the board in its protectionist years. At least after the Domestic Passenger Fare Investigation of the early 1970s, which produced an elaborate, refined scheme for regulating rates, the board had deferred to the rates bureau. Rates had come to seem an arcane, technical subject on which it was necessary to solicit staff advice, in

pro-reform chairmen built around old groups by enhancing the size and functions of policy analysis units, staffed mainly with economists, though none could rely exclusively on generalist staff units.

In addition to the powers and authority of the chairman as chief executive, one other very important factor common to the commissions helps to account for the surprising ease with which staff support was induced. Not much behavior needed to be changed. "It was all done by twenty people," Michael Roach remarked of the CAB, probably without much exaggeration. These were small agencies. The CAB had only 780 employees; the ICC, 2,200; the FCC, 2,100, of whom 240 were in the Common Carrier Bureau. More to the point, the major operational subunits were not numerous. Regulation of transportation entailed controls over entry (routes or operating rights) and supervision of prices (rates or fares). In the CAB a Bureau of Economics was in charge of fares and a Bureau of Operating Rights was in charge of routes (before Kahn consolidated them into a single bureau). In the ICC the main organizational unit was the Office of Proceedings, with sections for finance, operating rights, and rates. In the FCC the crucial unit was the Common Carrier Bureau. To achieve rule and policy changes, pro-reform chairmen needed either to control these components or to circumvent them with the aid of personal assistants and generalist staffs, such as offices of policy analysis or general counsels. This was not a task of vast scope. Moreover, it was in the nature of procompetitive deregulation that once new policies and rules were promulgated by regulatory agencies they were largely enforced by the private actions of firms in the newly competitive markets. Deregulation, after all, granted permission for at least some firms—the would-be price-cutters and entrants into hitherto restricted markets—to do what they wished to do, and it thereby forced others—the hitherto protected firms—to follow suit and to compete whether they wanted to or not. That was the logic underlying deregulation. It meant that the compliance of private actors was not generally problematic and that the success of policy change did not depend on changing the attitudes or administrative behavior of far-flung field staffs, which in these cases did not even exist.

Commission Members

Chairmen needed the support of other commission members as well as staffs. Including the chairman, the CAB contained five

---

contrast to route awards that were made by the board on commonsensical or political grounds and left to the staff to justify.

members; the ICC, eleven; and the FCC, seven. To achieve reform the chairman had to command a majority of the votes. In none of the commissions did new appointments under Ford and Carter occur to a sufficient extent, with sufficient swiftness, or with a sufficient policy bias to provide reform majorities by themselves. The CAB did not have a majority of Ford-Carter appointees until September 1978, and the ICC did not have such a majority until April 1980. The critical burst of initiatives on behalf of procompetitive deregulation in both agencies occurred too soon to be accounted for solely by these changes. In making appointments to the FCC in the years crucial to deregulation, the Carter Administration paid at least as much attention to sex and ethnic identity as to policy orientations. Nonetheless, reformist chairmen were not seriously hampered by the opposition of commission members. When the chairman and staff collaborated, commission members generally deferred. With some qualifications, this was the pattern in both the CAB and the FCC. Given the lack of a tradition of executive leadership, the ICC was a rather different case.

Commission members generally tended to defer to chairmen. The formal executive powers that all chairmen possessed gave them a great advantage over commission members, who theoretically were confined to consideration of policy and who in practice found it difficult to participate effectively even in policy without having command of the staff. In truth, commission members had very little to do and few resources with which to do it. "I don't know why anyone would want to be a member of a multi-member agency," Robson told an interviewer. "I think it would be devastatingly boring." Tenney Johnson, who was a member of the agency of which Robson was chairman, thoroughly agreed with this view. "You don't think you're doing anything," he said. "It's enervating to anyone with a mind. The chairman is the focal point, constantly embroiled, but as a member you have to play a lot of golf."[40]

That the chairman was the President's choice besides being in charge in his own right was important. The CAB chairman is appointed by the President for a one-year term, while the chairmen of the ICC and FCC serve at the pleasure of the President for unspecified terms. This creates some presumption that the chairman is pursuing the President's policies and therefore is entitled to support from commission members who are of the same political party as the President. In short, the chairman is entitled to a working majority. To the extent that the White House shared this presumption, it was disposed to appoint commission members who were known to be acceptable to the chairman. To the extent that commission members

40. Interview with R. Tenney Johnson, 20 November 1980.

of the dominant party shared this presumption, they would routinely vote with the chairman to give him his working majority and to enhance their own chances of reappointment.[41] Neither for the White House nor for commission members were these considerations always controlling, but enough appointments were designed to support the chairman and enough members were willing to support him to make the creation of majorities ordinarily manageable rather than problematic.

In the CAB and FCC it was a rare chairman who could not achieve dominance—perhaps with the resentment of the members, but dominance nonetheless. A disgruntled member of the FCC, wishing to expose the dominance of Ferris in his first six months in office, calculated that in 502 votes from 25 October 1977 to 31 May 1978 there were splits on only nineteen occasions. Otherwise, the commission unanimously supported the chairman. This was no different from the pattern under Ferris's predecessor. "The chairman is dominant for reasons of law and procedure," this member told a state broadcasters' association. "He selects the general counsel and other key staff. He and his personal staff meet regularly with bureau and office chiefs to plan and discuss upcoming agenda items. Some draft policy recommendations are submitted to him alone; while the staff is hard put to decline sharing them with commissioners on request, commissioners are not informed that they exist."[42] When this member's term expired, Ferris let the White House know confidentially, via his administrative assistant, that he did not want her to be reappointed and suggested someone to consider in her place. The President appointed the person whom Ferris suggested.

John Robson secured the unanimous support of CAB members for his controversial presentation to Congress in the spring of 1976, and thereby assured its effect, despite the fact that none of the members had shown any interest in procompetitive deregulation and one of them, Lee R. West, had developed a very strong personal antipathy to Robson and resentment of his highly assertive style of leadership. Robson's explanation for this unanimity was that it "came from

41. By law a vacancy occurs each year in each agency, and resignations are common. Because the partisan advantage of the majority is restricted by law to a margin of one vote, a President can promptly secure a partisan majority and can ordinarily expect also to install a majority of appointees within a relatively short time, depending on the size of the commission. (A President could more quickly place a majority of appointees on the five-member CAB than the eleven-member ICC.) For a discussion of the appointment power and other techniques of presidential influence over the commissions, see Brigman (1981).

42. "The FCC—An Inside View," delivered by Margita E. White before the Georgia Association of Broadcasters, 1 February 1979.

an amalgam of persuasion, loyalty, fear of political retribution, institutional pride, and tactic." It was not based on "true conviction."

Kahn as chairman had all the advantages normally attaching to his office, plus one fellow Carter appointee (Bailey) who was ideologically committed to procompetitive deregulation, plus quite exceptional personal powers of charm, persuasion, expertise, and ability to exploit the opportunities for publicity freshly made available by the Sunshine Act and the press's interest in deregulation. Kahn made sessions of the CAB more than the public meetings that by law they now must be. He consciously made them public performances, a form of theater at which the audience—the general press, the trade press, the industry, the CAB staff—watched him pursue with his pedagogue's passion for reasoned inquiry the questions of why airline regulation was as it was and why it could not be done differently. Within the board he needed only one more vote to add to his own and Bailey's, and he was able to get it from one or both of the other Democrats on the board, West or G. Joseph Minetti, even though his procompetitive goals far surpassed what they had previously endorsed under Robson, let alone what was presumably congenial to them.

The ICC, by contrast, posed a challenge to its chairman because of its large size and its legacy of independent, decentralized functioning. Under President Carter the ICC was allowed to shrink for the sake of making it more manageable. As members left they were not replaced. Because these departing persons had been protectionist, by default the commission grew more reformist. Thus, the President's willful abstention from his appointment power, rather than a conscious exercise of it, initially contributed to creating a procompetitive majority at the ICC. In 1979, procompetitive members were added, and in the meantime one member had switched to the procompetitive side on questions of entry. Even so, Chairman Gaskins told us that for him securing cooperation of the commission was more difficult than securing cooperation of the staff. This was in sharp contrast to the other commissions, where the chairman, with the acquiescence of the commission, secured control of the staff and then, with the support of the staffs, pursued procompetitive, deregulatory goals to which the members generally agreed because when the chairmen and staffs were allied they had little choice.

As in relations with the staff, how much deference the chairman could expect to elicit depended very much on how far he wished to go. At the FCC both Ferris as chairman and Verveer as Common Carrier Bureau chief had suggested publicly that divestiture of AT&T ought to be a condition of allowing AT&T to compete in deregulated markets, and they apparently were prepared to claim that the FCC had the

228 MARTHA DERTHICK AND PAUL J. QUIRK

authority to impose divestiture.[43] But they drew back, because divestiture was too much for most FCC members, just as it was obviously far too much for most members of Congress (though under threat of adverse judicial action, divestiture of local operating affiliates turned out not to be too much for AT&T). Two members of the FCC dissented in *Computer II* on the ground that the structural requirements imposed on AT&T were too drastic, but there was no disposition within the commission to resist the sweeping withdrawal from regulation embodied in the *Computer II* decision.

At the CAB Kahn had a majority but not unanimity for his radical changes. Richard J. O'Melia, a Republican who had been appointed to the board by President Nixon after many years on the staff, persistently dissented in strong terms. Robson believed that O'Melia supported him out of political loyalty, despite being intellectually opposed to deregulation. "I think Dick had a very strong sense that when his people were in he had an obligation to follow the chairman's lead," Robson told an interviewer. But it was also the case that Robson's actions, mainly involving reductions in fares and liberalization of charter rules, were much easier to reconcile with the board's historic practices than was Kahn's pursuit of multiple permissive entry, which involved abandoning traditional tests of fitness and the competitive award of routes. It was possible for veteran staff members to concur in what Robson did or concretely proposed to do, and this in turn encouraged Democrats West and Minetti to go along with the Republican Robson, whereas the dissents of the Republican O'Melia under Kahn coincided with the estrangement of high-ranking veterans within the staff. In this situation O'Melia, as a staff veteran as well as a Republican, had no cause to do anything other than follow his convictions rather than defer.

In relations with other members, as in relations with the staff, each chairman benefited intangibly and immeasurably from the backing of prevailing opinion—both elite, expert opinion and the opinion that prevailed in the White House, where decisions were made on the appointment and reappointment of commission members. The White House, even in these years, did not make appointments to any of the regulatory commissions solely on substantive grounds, but substance played a larger part than usual, because of the interest of presidents Ford and Carter and their staffs in procompetitive deregulation. In both the CAB and ICC crucial votes for procompetitive deregulation

43. *Telecommunications Reports* vol. 45, no. 45, 12 November 1979, p. 5; *Amendments to the Communications Act of 1934*, U.S. Senate (1979a), pt. 4, p. 3106; F.C.C. 80–189, Final Decision in Docket No. 20828 (Second Computer Inquiry), p. 110.

were forthcoming from at least one member whose term was nearing expiration and who was believed by the chairman's office to be disposed to cooperation in part on that account. Nor were members immune to the sanctions imposed by critics in Congress and the courts. For CAB members as well as that agency's staff, the Kennedy hearings came as a particularly nasty blow to pride. Joseph Minetti, who had been on the CAB since 1956, liked to call it the Tiffany of regulatory agencies; restoring the shine became important.

No member of any of these agencies became an outspoken or well publicized defender of traditional regulation. Ironically, Daniel O'Neal before becoming chairman came as close to that role as anyone. Members usually do not have sufficient stature to command general attention in any event. None argued that the public interest or the well-being of the transportation and communications industries depended to any significant extent on continuing to regulate. With the exception of one member of the FCC whom a high-ranking staff source referred to caustically as the member from AT&T, none seems to have been thought of by procompetitive activists as a consistent spokesman for, let alone a captive of, the regulated firms. In 1975–1980 capture was nowhere in sight.

Conclusion

What we have been describing is plainly a dynamic process in which influence is reciprocal. External pressures caused the commissions to act—members and staffs, as well as the chairmen. Or at least, external forces largely created the opportunities for and set the limits of feasible action. But then the commissions' own actions gave further encouragement to outsiders (a point that would be clearer if we had more opportunity here to describe the actions of Congress). Within each commission the chairman influenced members and staff, but to a lesser extent they also influenced the chairman and one another. If diagrammed, this process would show arrows pointing in all directions, with some variations in emphasis among different agencies. In the FCC the staff probably had more influence on the chairman than vice versa, whereas in the ICC it was the other way around. The CAB is an intermediate case. Everyone involved tended to move toward a more procompetitive, deregulatory position as these interactions occurred. Those within the commissions who would not move fast enough tended to be left behind, deprived of influence and even sometimes of office. Kahn moved beyond what Robson had done and faster than he initially expected to move. In the ICC "the rate of change was more than anybody dreamed possible," a veteran administrative-law judge told us. "O'Neal as chairman got the momentum for change really accelerating," and then O'Neal "became passé" as new procompetitive members were added, including Gaskins as chairman.[44] In the FCC the final decision in *Computer II* in the spring of 1980 was far more deregulatory than the tentative decision taken only a year before under a different Common Carrier Bureau chief.

It was the convergence of external influences on the commissions—the tendency of the President, congressional critics, courts, and elite opinion simultaneously to push them in the direction of procompetitive deregulation—that largely accounts for the commissions' choosing that course of action. Ideas advanced by economic analysts and then disseminated by a Washington-based movement for procompetitive reform were the underlying source of the convergence. They were a coordinating force in a governmental universe that is normally chaotic. Whether the commissions were influenced mainly by the ideas themselves—because they were in the air—or by the sanctions and rewards disposed of by influential institutions (the President, who makes appointments to the commissions; members of Congress, who could call them to account and embarrass them in public; the courts, who could reverse their decisions and chastise them in whatever language the judges chose) is impossible to tell, but surely the institutional sanctions were important enough to cause all the commissions substantially to moderate anticompetitive behavior. Yet the commissions would not have carried reform so far had not prevalent ideas directly influenced the chairmen. Individuals may have been attracted to the office of chairman because they already believed in procompetitive deregulation and saw a chance to achieve it or because they held the chairman's office at a time when that was the only new, exciting, and important goal the office could be used to achieve, but our point is valid either way: prevalent ideas had much of their effect by serving as cues for activists and entrepreneurs, among whom commission chairmen were perforce included by reason of the expectations attaching to their role.

The alacrity with which the commissions espoused the prevailing definition of the public interest, contrary to the interests of the regulated industries, does not prove that earlier analysts were wrong in arguing that commissions had become very protective of the regulated industries. It proves only that such a bias was not inherent in them or in American political institutions. Even if typical, that bias was not inevitable but depended on political circumstances. However

44. Interview, Robert Glennon, 9 December 1980.

their prior behavior may be characterized, the commissions proved in the period we are analyzing to be highly responsive to prescriptions for action that violated industry preferences as thoroughly as they violated the commissions' own precedents.[45]

Broadly speaking, the commissions behaved in 1975–1980 much as the original theory of them stipulated that they would. They served as vehicles for converting the disinterested views of experts into public policy, although the expert views had originated, ironically, largely as criticisms of their own conduct and came to prevail inside the commissions not because the commissions were independent but because they were highly vulnerable to the appointive, monitoring, and review powers of the President, congressional critics, and judges. Once converted, the commissions proved in general to be effective vehicles for advancing the goals of procompetitive deregulation. The vague, encompassing delegations of power that Congress had made to them gave them broad discretion to act, while the later success of administrative reformers in securing the primacy of the chairmen had endowed them with a suitable internal mechanism for concerting action. In all three cases the commissions took major, formal actions on behalf of procompetitive deregulation before Congress did, and thereby helped spur Congress to act.

COMMENT: *Kenneth A. Shepsle*

This book is devoted to social science and regulation, and we political scientists have been given much of the contents. The papers by Lowi, Fiorina, and Derthick and Quirk confirm my own suspicions, arrived at from perusing the economics literature on regulation, that within-discipline variance is perhaps even greater than between-discipline variance.

Lowi argues that the inherent characteristics of policy affect politics and political institutions. It is an enchanting, nonobvious view that sits uncomfortably with the recent neo-institutionalism in both political science and economics. Fiorina's focus is on legislative delegation, but his broader concern is with the way self-interest manifests itself in particular institutional settings. He argues that in representative legislatures pecuniary and nonpecuniary incidences on

45. The most careful of the scholarly critiques of the independent regulatory commissions (Bernstein, 1955) did not assert that they were inherently biased in favor of the regulated interests, but stressed the default of congressional and presidential supervision.

geographic constituencies are the motive forces informing the preferences and animating the behavior of self-interested legislative agents. Unlike Lowi, Fiorina argues that the policy characteristics that drive politics are not exogenous but, rather, are matters of choice. These, in turn, are driven by constituency incidences, and the technology of credit-claiming and blame-ducking. Derthick and Quirk, focusing on the politics of deregulation, seek explanations for regulatory phenomena in the convergence of forces stimulated by prevalent ideas, in their instance the ideology of deregulation.

Taking some slight liberties, I assume that all three papers are interested in explaining political activity. Whereas Lowi attaches significance to policy characteristics as an independent variable and Fiorina focuses on constituency incidence, Derthick and Quirk find the fundamental explanation in the realm of ideas. I am most comfortable with Fiorina's approach. Perhaps this is because he draws on some of the modeling by Barry Weingast and me of legislator preferences induced by geographic incidence. Nevertheless, I remain, at least for the moment, agnostic. On the one hand, there is in Fiorina's work an emphasis on the demand side of policymaking with a concomitant slighting of the institutional supply side. On the other hand, there are attractive elements in the other two approaches.

No grand synthesis will be unveiled in these brief comments; my assignment is to discuss the arguments of Derthick and Quirk, to which I now turn. In doing so, I shall first criticize their undiluted argument and then attempt to graft it, if only tentatively and superficially, to Fiorina's approach.

The Central Puzzle of Internal Deregulation

Derthick and Quirk seek to resolve a puzzle in bureaucratic behavior. At least one variant of the standard wisdom asserts that bureau heads are motivated chiefly, if not exclusively, by the objectives of protecting and expanding their turf. Yet Derthick and Quirk suggest that major deregulatory movement has taken place in the last five years with the cooperation and occasionally the initiative of regulatory agencies. In some instances, Derthick and Quirk maintain, regulatory commission chiefs and entrepreneurial commission staff comprised the leading edge of reform by deregulation. They note, however, that pro-deregulation appointments did not occur in sufficient numbers or in a sufficiently timely manner to transform majorities on commissions to the deregulatory cause through personnel replacement. What occurred was that the appointment of new commission chairmen, actively promoting deregulation or at least not avowedly hostile to it, combined with a convergence of institutional forces in the environment of the commissions—the President, Congress, federal courts, academic and journalistic studies—to stimulate commissioners and staff activists to consider deregulatory alternatives. In most cases deregulatory momentum was a reality before Congress had taken formal action.

The deregulatory thrust of the last five years is a fascinating story. However, Derthick and Quirk's account, relying on the force of ideas, the convergence of external influences, and the prominent role played by highly motivated individuals, leaves as many puzzles as it solves. The central question remains unanswered: why was the doctrine of deregulation so compelling that it motivated key individuals to effect a major redirection of policy? Indeed, why was the deregulation doctrine compelling in some policy areas but not in others? Federal regulatory activity did not exactly dry up in the late 1970s. Derthick and Quirk offer an answer of sorts to the first (but not the second) at the end of their essay, suggesting that "prevalent ideas had much of their effect by serving as cues for activists and entrepreneurs." But this response posits no mechanisms by which policy alternatives such as procompetitive deregulation get onto the public agenda, nor does it hint at how prevalent ideas are transformed into decisive political actions.

Let me attempt to supplement their arguments in two distinct ways. I suggest, first, why "prevalent ideas" might have some bearing on policymaking, and second, on whom the force of ideas might make a difference for policy outcomes.

Ideas and the Politician

My own view on the force of ideas is to see them as one of the hooks on which politicians hang their objectives and by which they further their interests. Let me give two examples, one drawn from nineteenth-century American pork-barrel history and one of recent vintage.

1. Andrew Jackson vetoed the Maysville Road bill in 1830. The bill sought to extend the National Road from Maysville, Kentucky, on the Ohio River, to Lexington, Kentucky. The ideological hooks on which he hung his veto, and the explanations to which historians give a good deal of credence, were (a) the unconstitutionality of national government activity in internal improvements wholly contained within the boundaries of a single state, and (b) the state of the Treasury and the fiscal ideology of retiring, not increasing, national debt. Remini offers as an aside, to which he devotes a single sentence in six pages of discussion, "the fact that the road

was located in Henry Clay's state did not sit well with some Jackso-
nians, and several of them spoke against the bill when it was introduced into the House" (Remini, 1981, pp. 251–52). This sounds to
me like a shrewd politician not about to give his major opponent
the stuff of which credit-claiming is made. Obviously constrained
politically from justifying the veto on those grounds, Jackson
sought out ideas, wholly apart from the motive force that pro-
voked the behavior. The ideas proved to be popular, but were they
in fact the motivation for the veto or were they just cosmetic?
Hard to say, and this is precisely the problem with offering the
force of ideas as an explanation.

2. More recently, and more directly germane to the subject matter of
   this book, is the story of Senator Kennedy's conversion to free-
   market ideology and deregulation. Thinking about the presidency in 1974 and seeking ways to make himself more attractive
   to the moderate and conservative factions of the Democratic
   Party, he contacted his old friend Steven Breyer, then a professor
   of law at Harvard, on the subject of deregulation. Breyer presented some economic and legal arguments for natural gas deregulation. Shocked, politician Teddy rejected the idea of undertaking deregulation of natural gas because it would not sit well with
   his Massachusetts constituents. Breyer and Kennedy ultimately
   discovered that airline deregulation combined the ideology of deregulation with the rhetoric of consumerism in such a way that a
   broad panoply of interests could be made happy.

The force of ideas? No, I think it better to suggest the convenience
of ideas. And, in a sense, for both President Jackson and Senator
Kennedy, one could argue that it was the perversion of an idea, since
one could imagine circumstances (and the Kennedy story as it applies to natural gas deregulation actually provides one) in which precisely the opposite idea served that same politician on some other
occasion.

My point, then, is that ideas are vehicles or instruments that politicians use to further their own objectives. Fenno (1978) suggests
that politicians see part of their task as that of justifying their Washington behavior to their constituents. One prominent form of this
justificatory behavior has little to do with ideas. Rather, it involves
telling constituents how their agent has showered the district with
goodies or done battle with a rigid Washington bureaucracy. From
time to time, however, justifications take an ideological form: it's
good for the little guy; it serves the public interest, necessity, or convenience; it protects the federal treasury from raids; etc. Like the

pork-barrel and constituency-service rationales, this is simply another kind of hook on which to hang explanations of Washington behavior. In sum, political entrepreneurs seek for their actions rationales—pecuniary or intellectual—that solidify and extend their political support.

Politicians clearly feel that justifying their behavior is necessary. They are held accountable for their political actions by constituents, opinion leaders, and opposition politicians, and thus must provide an accounting to them. If politicians cannot appeal directly to the pecuniary consequences of their actions or, given the uncertainty, fear hanging their justifications on that hook (Fiorina's argument), then prevalent ideas may be of instrumental value to them as a marketing strategy. This is not to deny that politicians believe their own justifications; most politicians are not cynical about the ideas and ideologies they employ. But we are talking here, for the most part, about neither scholars nor true believers. Rather, we are talking about practical men who are devoted to assembling and retaining political support, winning elections, and building institutional power bases. Prevalent ideas, from the cruder forms of patriotism to subtle principles of economics, are enlisted in these endeavors.

Deregulation and Congress

The idea of deregulation caught the fancy of a number of institutional politicians. Derthick and Quirk convincingly report on the commitment to a procompetitive redirection of the regulatory agencies by the Ford and Carter administrations, new commission chairmen and their staffs, and prominent legislators. I would like to suggest that two legal principles or practices, the erosion of the nondelegation doctrine and the limited use of the criterion of substantive due process, focus attention on legislative committees as key principals in this story. As a consequence, Derthick and Quirk's passing references to Congress, and their emphasis on the momentum for regulatory reform preceding formal acts by Congress, miss a very important point. While they are quite right that Congress, the collective institution, did not engage in lawmaking early on, they have not given sufficient attention to the other mechanisms by which (parts of) Congress can cue, signal, suggest, extort, and bully nominally independent agencies.

This is not the place to develop these points at any great length. Briefly, the argument consists of the following points. First, over the last two centuries the Supreme Court has systematically relaxed the doctrine of nondelegation, thereby permitting Congress to delegate substantial amounts of legislative discretion to executive and independent agencies. Moreover, these delegations have been increasingly accompanied by no or, at best, ambiguous guidance as to legislative intent, a point amply documented in the work of Lowi. Intent must be inferred by agency heads; mistaken inferences run the risk of stimulating legislative sanctions—investigations, hearings, legislative veto, reduction in appropriations, limitations on statutory authority. *Ex post* sanctions become *ex ante* incentives, and agencies are consequently attentive to the preferences of those in a position to impose them or initiate the process. Typically, this is not Congress per se but, rather, a congressional committee or subcommittee.

Second, the reticence of the courts to employ substantive criteria to evaluate agency behavior means that there is a good deal of constitutional freedom to engage in major policy shifts without statutory changes.

Putting these two points together, we have an arrangement in which ambiguous delegations of legislative power to agencies are accompanied by the possibility of sanctions monitored by specific legislative agents: committees and subcommittees. Agency heads and bureau chiefs are likely to be sensitive to, if not completely accommodating of, committee preferences. And they are likely to be so even if it entails major shifts in direction, because the courts have been relatively permissive in this regard.

Admittedly this argument has been greatly oversimplified. Nevertheless, it does identify an important source of congressional influence on agency behavior short of lawmaking. It also identifies important actors in this process. Thus, even if Congress did not legislate in the areas of trucking, airlines, and telecommunications, the preferences of well-situated legislators—Ted Kennedy, Howard Cannon, Lionel van Deerlin—would surely attract the attention of agencies.

This argument also suggests some limits on the power of prevalent ideas. Because well-situated legislators can veto or block (through threat of sanctions), it appears necessary that they be persuaded (for whatever reason, instrumental or otherwise) by such ideas if the latter are to have some effect on policy direction. It is, then, not the fact of a prevalent idea per se, but the fact that key institutional actors find it compelling, which affects policymakers.

Conclusion

My basic point is that to appreciate why regulators choose to deregulate, it is important to understand the institutional regime in which they and their agencies are embedded. An institutional re-

gime is a structure of incentives against which practical politicians—
legislators, bureau chiefs, executives, etc.—adjust their actions. It is
the system of channels through which forces converge and prevalent
ideas flow. At the center of this institutional regime is Congress and
its committees, as lawmakers, delegators of statutory authority, and
monitors of agency discretionary behavior. To answer the question of
why the regulators chose to deregulate, one must examine what
changed in the structure of Congress or in the preferences of key
legislators. I cannot imagine a completely satisfactory answer to the
question put by Derthick and Quirk in which Congress does not
figure prominently.

PART IV

Applications of Social Scientific Methods: Case Studies

8

Regulation of Risk
A Psychological Perspective

Paul Slovic,
Baruch Fischhoff, and
Sarah Lichtenstein

Technology has enhanced society's ability to utilize the environment, eradicate dread diseases, and fashion a life of comfort and leisure. But it has become increasingly apparent that these benefits are accompanied by a variety of hazardous side effects. Hardly a day passes that does not reveal some new danger in our foods, our homes, our workplaces, our leisure activities, or our natural environments.

In a world in which more and more Americans are coming to see themselves as the victims rather than the beneficiaries of technology, it is not surprising that the control of hazards has become a major concern of society and a growing responsibility of government. During the past decade, an unprecedented assemblage of powerful regulatory bureaucracies has been created and charged with answering myriad forms of the question: "How safe is safe enough?" The cost of these efforts to manage risk has been estimated at $1.4-$4.2 billion per year (Fischhoff, Hohenemser, Kasperson, and Kates, 1978). Yet despite this massive effort (some would say because of it), the public feels increasingly vulnerable to the risks from technology and believes that the worst is yet to come (Harris, 1980). Regulatory agencies have been embroiled in rancorous conflicts, caught between a

This work was supported by the National Science Foundation under Grants PRA 79-11934 and PRA 81-16925. Any opinions, findings, and conclusions or recommendations expressed in this chapter are those of the authors and do not necessarily reflect the views of the National Science Foundation.

241

fearful and unsatisfied public on one side and frustrated technologists and industrialists on the other. The latter see the pursuit of a "zero-risk society" as trampling individual rights, thwarting innovation, and jeopardizing the nation's economic and political stability. How these conflicts are resolved will affect not just the fate of particular technologies but the fate of our society and its social organization as well.

The urgent need to reduce conflict and improve the management of risk poses a challenge to scholars and scientists from many disciplines. Technical issues, such as the identification of hazards and the assessment of the probability and magnitude of their consequences, require the efforts of physical scientists, biological scientists, and engineers. Social issues, pertaining to the evaluation of these identified hazards and the decisionmaking invoked in their management, require the knowledge and skills of lawyers, political scientists, geographers, sociologists, and economists.

Psychology, too, can contribute to the management and regulation of risk. In recent years, empirical and theoretical research on the psychology of decisionmaking under risk has produced a body of knowledge that should be of value to those who seek to understand and improve societal decisions. This chapter aims to describe some components of this research. Rather than being comprehensive, we focus on investigations grounded in cognitive psychology, psychometrics, and decision theory, with emphasis on our own research program and the related work of a few colleagues. Our efforts are guided by the assumption that those who promote and regulate high-risk technologies need to understand the ways people think about risk, the outcomes of technology people deem to be important, and the values they attach to these outcomes. Without such understanding, well-intended policies may be ineffective, perhaps even counterproductive.

Overview of This Chapter

This chapter is divided into four sections. In the first section we describe research on human intellectual limitations, with particular focus on the problems that occur when people seek to make sense out of a probabilistic environment and attempt to resolve the value conflicts arising from decisions about beneficial but potentially hazardous activities. We point out the difficulties people have in thinking intuitively about risk and uncertainty. We argue that people's perceptions of the world are sometimes distorted and that their preferences can be unstable, vague, or inconsistent. The results of this research run counter to the traditional presumptions of knowledge and rationality that underlie economic approaches to decisionmaking under risk. In doing so, these results challenge the viability of market mechanisms for managing risk and thereby suggest that institutional regulation of risk is needed. A common reaction of industry and government officials to evidence of ignorance, misinformation, or faulty thinking has been to call for educational programs to correct these shortcomings. Although we applaud such efforts and do believe that people are educable, our emphasis is on the obstacles educational programs must overcome in order to be effective.

The second section of this chapter shows how some of the findings of the first section can be applied to two specific policy problems. Both the problems described here concern the extent to which people engage in actions that protect them from risk: purchasing flood insurance and wearing seat belts. We argue that, to be effective, policies need to be based on knowledge regarding the determinants of people's protective behavior. Empirical research can play an important role in providing such knowledge.

The third section describes research on the perception of risk. This research explores what people mean when they say that a technology or activity is "risky." We find that many attributes other than death rates determine judgments of riskiness. Such attributes include catastrophic potential, risk to future generations, and dread. In contrast with the first section, the tone of this section is optimistic. We find that laypeople have strong, consistent, and reasonable views about risk. In fact, their model of what constitutes risk appears to be much richer than that held by most technical experts.

The final section is a discussion of the problems encountered in trying to answer the question: "How safe is safe enough?" We first discuss the general nature of acceptable-risk problems and the approaches one could take to solve them. We then discuss the issue of establishing safety standards or goals for hazardous technologies. Our analysis points to social issues that have been neglected in past proposals for safety goals and shows how risk-perception research can provide guidance on these issues.

Confronting Human Limitations

The traditional view of human mental processes assumes that we are intellectually gifted creatures. Shakespeare referred to man as "noble in reason, infinite in faculties . . . the beauty of the world, the paragon of animals." Economic theory, with its presumption of well-informed, rational (utility-maximizing) decisionmakers, has echoed this theme. As economist Frank Knight (1921, p. 227) put it, "We are so built that what seems reasonable to us is likely to be confirmed by experience or we could not live in the world at all." Given freedom of choice and adequate information, people's capacity for rational decisionmaking should allow the marketplace to manage risk quite adequately. In such a world, there would be little need for regulatory interventions.

Over the years, economists and others have come to recognize that the idealized views on which the free market approach is based do not hold. The real issue is not whether to regulate, but how much to regulate and how to do it. Provision of information to consumers, standards, restrictions, and bans compete as alternative modes of intervention (Joskow and Noll, 1981; Lave, 1981). To make effective choices among these options, it is necessary to know something of the nature and extent of human intellectual limitations. Although we are far from having complete understanding, much has been learned in recent years that may have implications for regulatory policy.

Bounded Rationality

An important early critic of the rational model's descriptive adequacy was Herbert Simon, who drew on psychological research to challenge traditional assumptions about the motivation, omniscience, and computational capacities of decisionmakers. As an alternative to utility maximization, Simon (1957) introduced the notion of "bounded rationality," which asserts that cognitive limitations force people to construct simplified models of the world in order to cope with it. To predict behavior "we must understand the way in which this simplified model is constructed, and its construction will certainly be related to 'man's' psychological properties as a perceiving, thinking, and learning animal" (p. 198).

During the past twenty years, the skeleton theory of bounded rationality has been fleshed out. We have learned much about human cognitive limitations and their implications for behavior, particularly with regard to decisions made in the face of uncertainty and risk. Numerous studies show that people (including experts) have great difficulty judging probabilities, making predictions, and otherwise attempting to cope with uncertainty. Frequently these difficulties can be traced to the use of judgmental heuristics, which serve as general strategies for simplifying complex tasks. These heuristics are valid in many circumstances, but in others they lead to large and persistent biases with serious implications for decisionmaking. Much of this work has been summarized by Kahneman, Slovic, and Tversky (1982), Nisbett and Ross (1980), Slovic, Fischhoff, and Lichtenstein

(1977), and Tversky and Kahneman (1974). In the remainder of this section we shall discuss two general manifestations of bounded rationality that are particularly relevant to regulation of risk. These topics are *judgmental biases* and *uncertain preferences*.

Judgmental Biases in Risk Perception

If people are to respond optimally to the risks they face, they must have reasonably accurate perceptions of the magnitude of those risks. Yet the formal education of most laypeople rarely includes any serious instruction in how to assess risks. Their subsequent learning is typically restricted to unsystematic personal experience and news media reports. Perhaps it should not be surprising that people often are misinformed, rely on suboptimal risk-assessment heuristics, and fail to understand the limits of their own knowledge.

Availability. One inferential strategy that has special relevance for risk perception is the availability heuristic (Tversky and Kahneman, 1973). People using this heuristic judge an event as likely or frequent if instances of it are easy to imagine or recall. Because frequently occurring events are generally easier to imagine or recall than are rare events, availability is often an appropriate cue. However, availability is also affected by factors unrelated to frequency of occurrence. For example, a recent disaster or a vivid film could seriously bias risk judgments.

Availability bias is illustrated by several studies in which people judged the frequency of forty-one causes of death (Lichtenstein et al., 1978). In one study, these people were first told the annual death toll in the United States for one cause (50,000 deaths from motor vehicle accidents) and then asked to estimate the frequency of the other forty causes. Figure 1 compares the judged number of deaths per year with the number reported in public health statistics. If the frequency judgments equaled the statistical rates, all data points would fall on the identity line. Although more likely hazards generally evoked higher estimates, the points were scattered about a curved line that lay sometimes above and sometimes below the line representing accurate judgment. In general, rare causes of death were overestimated and common causes of death were underestimated. In addition to this general bias, sizable specific biases are evident in Figure 1. For example, accidents were judged to cause as many deaths as diseases, whereas diseases actually take about fifteen times as many lives. Homicides were incorrectly judged as more frequent than diabetes and stomach cancer deaths. Pregnancies, births, and abortions were judged to take about as many lives as diabetes, though diabetes actually causes about eighty times more deaths. In keeping with availability considerations, causes of death that were overestimated (relative to the curved line) tended to be dramatic and sensational (accidents, natural disasters, homicides), whereas underestimated causes tended to be unspectacular events that claim one victim at a time and are common in nonfatal form (e.g., smallpox vaccinations, stroke, diabetes).

The availability heuristic highlights the vital role of experience as a determinant of perceived risk. If one's experiences are misleading, one's perceptions are likely to be inaccurate. Unfortunately, much of the information to which people are exposed provides a distorted picture of the world of hazards. One result of this is that people tend to view themselves as personally immune to certain kinds of hazards. Research shows that the great majority of individuals believe themselves to be better-than-average drivers (Svenson, 1981), more likely than average to live past 80 years old (Weinstein, 1980), less likely than average to be harmed by products that they use (Rethans,

Figure 1. *Relation between judged and statistical frequencies for forty-one causes of death.*

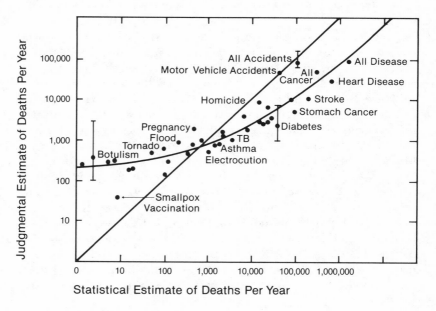

SOURCE: Lichtenstein et al., 1978.

1979), and so on. Although such perceptions are obviously unrealistic, the risks may look very small from the perspective of each individual's experience. Consider automobile driving: despite driving too fast, following too closely, etc., poor drivers make trip after trip without mishap. This personal experience demonstrates to them their exceptional skill and safety. Moreover, their indirect experience via the news media shows that when accidents happen, they happen to others. Given such misleading experiences, people may feel quite justified in refusing to take protective actions such as wearing seat belts (Slovic, Fischhoff, and Lichtenstein, 1978).

In some situations, failure to appreciate the limits of available data may lull people into complacency. For example, we asked both laypeople and experienced mechanics to evaluate the completeness of a fault tree showing the problems that could cause a car not to start when the ignition key was turned (Fischhoff, Slovic, and Lichtenstein, 1978). Respondents' judgments of completeness were about the same when looking at the full tree as when looking at a tree in which half of the causes of starting failure were deleted. In keeping with the availability heuristic, what was out of sight was also out of mind. The only antidote to availability-induced biases is to recognize the limitations in the samples of information received from the world and produced by one's own mind. Doing so requires a knowledge of the world and of mental processes that few people can be expected to have. Even scientists often have difficulty identifying systematic biases in their data.

Overconfidence. A particularly pernicious aspect of heuristics is that people typically have too much confidence in the judgments based upon them. In another follow-up to the study on causes of death, people were asked to indicate the odds that they were correct in choosing the more frequent of two lethal events (Fischhoff, Slovic, and Lichtenstein, 1977). Odds of 100 to 1 or greater were given 25 percent of the time. However, about one out of every eight answers associated with such extreme confidence was wrong (fewer than 1 in 100 would have been wrong had the odds been appropriate). At odds of 10,000 to 1, people were wrong about 10 percent of the time. The psychological basis for this unwarranted certainty seems to be insensitivity to the tenuousness of the assumptions upon which one's judgments are based. For example, extreme confidence in the incorrect assertion that homicides are more frequent than suicides may occur because people fail to appreciate that the greater ease of recalling instances of homicides is an imperfect basis for inference.

Overconfidence manifests itself in other ways as well. A typical task in estimating uncertain quantities such as failure rates is to set upper and lower bounds so that there is a certain fixed probability that the true value lies between them. Experiments with diverse groups of people making many different kinds of judgments have found that true values tend to lie outside the confidence boundaries much too often. Results with 98 percent bounds are typical. Rather than 2 percent of the true values falling outside such bounds, 20–50 percent usually do so (Lichtenstein, Fischhoff, and Phillips, 1982). That is, people think that they can estimate uncertain quantities with much greater precision than they actually can.

Unfortunately, once experts are forced to go beyond their data and rely on judgment, they may be as prone to overconfidence as laypeople. Fischhoff, Slovic, and Lichtenstein (1978) repeated their fault-tree study with professional automobile mechanics (averaging about fifteen years of experience) and found them to be about as insensitive as laypersons to deletions from the tree. Hynes and Vanmarcke (1976) asked seven "internationally known" geotechnical engineers to predict the height of an embankment that would cause a clay foundation to fail and to specify confidence bounds around this estimate that were wide enough to have a 50 percent chance of enclosing the true failure height. None of the bounds specified by those individuals enclosed the true failure height.

Further evidence of expert overconfidence may be found in many technical risk assessments. For example, an official review of the Reactor Safety Study (U.S. Nuclear Regulatory Commission, 1978, p. vi) concluded that despite the study's careful attempt to calculate the probability of a core meltdown in a nuclear reactor, "we are certain that the error bands are understated. We cannot say by how much. Reasons for this include an inadequate data base, a poor statistical treatment [and] an inconsistent propagation of uncertainties throughout the calculation." The 1976 collapse of the Teton Dam provides another case in point. The Committee on Government Operations attributed this disaster to the unwarranted confidence of engineers who were absolutely certain that they had solved the many serious problems that arose during construction (U.S. Government, 1976).

Uncertain Preferences: Difficulties in Evaluating Risk

The process of evaluation is the heart of decisionmaking for the individual and the policymaker. Evaluating the (good and bad) outcomes associated with hazardous activities might seem to be relatively straightforward. Certainly people know what they like and dislike. Research has, however, shown the assessment of values to be as troublesome as the assessment of facts. Simon (1956) is well known for his assertion that boundedly rational individuals are motivated to obtain only some satisfactory, and not necessarily maximal, level of achievement, a tendency he labeled *satisficing*. In recent years, criticism of the traditional utility maximization theory has taken a somewhat different turn. With regard to the consequences of hazardous activities, many investigators now question whether people have stable, precise values or utilities that can be measured and integrated with probabilistic considerations by means of the expected utility principle (see, e.g., Arrow, 1982; Fischhoff, Goitein, and Shapira, 1982; Fischhoff, Slovic, and Lichtenstein, 1980a, b; Kahneman and Tversky, 1979; March, 1978; Schoemaker, 1982; Slovic, Fischhoff, and Lichtenstein, 1982; Tversky and Kahneman, 1981). Evidence is mounting in support of the view that our values are often not clearly apparent, even to ourselves; that methods for measuring values are intrusive and biased; that the structure of any decision problem is psychologically unstable; and that the processes whereby elusive values are integrated into decisions within such unstable structures lead to actions that differ in dramatic ways from the predictions of utility theory.

Labile Values.   Along with contemplating the probabilities of various decision consequences, we must assess how desirable they are. What do we want to happen? What do we want to avoid? How badly? Such questions seem to be the last redoubt of unaided intuition. Who knows better than the individual what he or she prefers? When one is considering simple, familiar events with which people have direct experience, it may be reasonable to assume that they have well-articulated preferences. But that may not be so in the case of novel, unfamiliar consequences potentially associated with outcomes of events such as surgery, carbon dioxide–induced climatic change, nuclear meltdowns, or genetic engineering. In these and other circumstances, our values may be incoherent, not sufficiently thought out (Fischhoff, Slovic, and Lichtenstein, 1980a, b). When we think about risk management policies, for example, we may be unfamiliar with the terms involved (e.g., social discount rates, minuscule probabilities, megadeaths). We may have contradictory values (e.g., a strong aversion to catastrophic losses of life but an awareness that we are no more moved by a plane crash causing 500 fatalities than one causing 300). We may occupy different roles in life (parent, worker, child), each of which produces clear-cut but inconsistent values. We may vacillate between incompatible but strongly held positions (e.g., freedom of speech is inviolate, but it should be denied to authoritarian movements). We may not even know how to begin thinking about some issues (e.g., the appropriate tradeoffs between the outcomes of surgery for cancer vs. the very different outcomes from radiation therapy). Our views may change so much over time (say, as we near the hour of decision or of experiencing the consequences) that we are disoriented about what we really think.

At least one regulator has appreciated the difficulties posed by uncertain and labile values. Former FDA Commissioner Donald Kennedy wrote (1981, p. 60):

> There is genuine public ambivalence about risk in this country—not about how much risk there is, but about how much risk we want. Our citizens are uncertain about how much government intervention in the interest of their health they will tolerate, and they are also uncertain about how many other things—new inventions, creature comforts, old habits, progress—they are prepared to sacrifice to become safer. One does not resolve such doubts merely by stating the risks more precisely.

Competent technical analyses may tell us what primary, secondary, and tertiary consequences to expect, but not what these consequences really entail. To some extent we are all prisoners of our past experiences, unable to imagine drastic changes in our world, our health, or our relationships.

Unstable Decision Frames.   In addition to the uncertainties that sometimes surround our values, perceptions of the basic structure of a decision problem are also unstable. The acts or options available, the possible outcomes or consequences of those acts, and the contingencies or conditional probabilities relating outcomes to acts make up what Tversky and Kahneman (1981) have called the decision frame. Much as changes in vantage point induce alternative perspectives on a visual scene, the same decision problem can be subject to many alternative frames (see Figure 2). The frame that a decisionmaker adopts is determined in part by the external formulation of the problem and in part by the structure spontaneously imposed by the decisionmaker. Tversky and Kahneman have demonstrated that normatively inconsequential changes in the framing of decision problems significantly affect preferences. These effects are noteworthy because they are sizable (often complete reversals of preference), because they violate important consistency and coherence requirements of economic theories of choice, and because they influence not only behavior but how the consequences of behavior are experienced.

Tversky and Kahneman (1981) have presented numerous illustrations of framing effects, one of which involves the following pair of problems, given to separate groups of respondents.

1. Problem 1. Imagine that the United States is preparing for the outbreak of an unusual disease, which is expected to kill 600 people. Two alternative programs to combat the disease have been proposed. As-

sume that the consequences of the programs are as follows: If Program A is adopted, 200 people will be saved. If Program B is adopted, there is 1/3 probability that 600 people will be saved, and 2/3 probability that no people will be saved. Which of the two programs would you favor?

2. Problem 2. (Same cover story as Problem 1.) If Program C is adopted, 400 people will die. If Program D is adopted, there is 1/3 probability that nobody will die, and 2/3 probability that 600 people will die. Which of the two programs would you favor?

The preference patterns tend to be quite different in the two problems. In a study of college students, 72 percent of the respon-

Figure 2.   *Decision framing: Three perspectives on a civil-defense problem.*

A civil defense committee in a large metropolitan area met recently to discuss contingency plans in the event of various emergencies. One emergency threat under discussion posed two options, both involving some loss of life.

Option A: Carries with it a .5 probability of containing the threat with a loss of 40 lives and a .5 probability of losing 60 lives. It is like taking the gamble:

.5 lose 40 lives
.5 lose 60 lives

Option B: Would result in the loss of 50 lives:

lose 50 lives

The options can be presented under three different frames:

I. This is a choice between a 50–50 gamble (lose 40 or lose 60 lives) and a sure thing (the loss of 50 lives).

II. Whatever is done at least 40 lives will be lost. This is a choice between a gamble with a 50–50 chance of either losing no additional lives or losing 20 additional lives (A) and the sure loss of 10 additional lives (B).

III. Option B produces a loss of 50 lives. Taking Option A would mean accepting a gamble with a .5 chance to *save* 10 lives and a .5 chance to *lose* 10 additional lives.

SOURCE: Fischhoff, 1983a.

dents chose Program A over Program B and 78 percent chose Program D over Program C. Another study, surveying physicians, obtained very similar results. On closer examination, we can see that the two problems are essentially identical. The only difference between them is that the outcomes are described by the number of lives saved in Problem 1 and the number of lives lost in Problem 2.

To explain these and many other violations of utility theory, Kahneman and Tversky (1979; see also Tversky and Kahneman, 1981) have developed a descriptive model called *prospect theory*. The primitives of this theory are a value function, $v(x)$, which attaches a subjective worth to each possible outcome of a gamble or prospect, and a probability-weighting function, $\pi(p)$, which expresses the subjective importance attached to the probability of obtaining a particular outcome. The attractiveness of a gamble that offers a chance of p to gain x and a chance of q to lose y would be equal to $\pi(p)v(x) + \pi(q)v(y)$. The value function is defined on gains and losses relative to some psychologically meaningful (neutral) reference point. A second feature of the value function is that it is steeper for losses than for gains, meaning that a given change in one's status hurts more as a loss than it pleases as a gain. A third feature is that it is concave above that reference point and convex below it, meaning, for example, that the subjective difference between gaining (or losing) $10 and $20 is greater than the difference between gaining (or losing) $110 and $120.

Perhaps the most notable feature of the probability-weighting function is the great importance attached to outcomes that will be received with certainty. Thus, for example, the prospect of losing $50 with probability 1.0 is more than twice as aversive as the prospect of losing the same amount with probability .5. For intermediate probabilities, the weighting function is somewhat insensitive to changes in probability. For example, a .5 chance of winning $50 would not be 25 percent more attractive than a .4 chance of winning $50.

The way a problem is framed determines both the reference point (the zero point) of the value function and the probabilities that are evaluated. If π and v were linear functions, preferences among options would be independent of the framing of acts, outcomes, or contingencies. Because of the characteristic nonlinearities of π and v, however, different frames often lead to different decisions.

One important class of framing effects deals with a phenomenon that Tversky and Kahneman (1981) have called *pseudocertainty*. It involves altering the representations of protective actions so as to vary the apparent certainty with which they prevent harm. For example, an insurance policy that covers fire but not flood could be presented either as full protection against the specific risk of fire or as a reduction in the overall probability of property loss. Because outcomes that are merely probable are undervalued in comparison with outcomes that are obtained with certainty, Tversky and Kahneman hypothesized that the above insurance policy should appear more attractive in the first context (pseudocertainty), which offers unconditional protection against a restricted set of problems. We have tested this conjecture in the context of one particular kind of protection, vaccination. Two forms of a "vaccination questionnaire" were created. Form I (probabilistic protection) described a disease expected to afflict 20 percent of the population and asked people whether they would volunteer to receive a vaccine that protects half the people receiving it. According to Form II (pseudocertainty), there were two mutually exclusive and equiprobable strains of the disease, each likely to afflict 10 percent of the population; the vaccination was said to give complete protection against one strain and no protection against the other.

The participants in this study were college students, half of whom received each form. After reading the description, they rated the likelihood that they would get vaccinated in such a situation. Although both forms indicated that vaccination reduced one's overall risk from 20 percent to 10 percent, we expected that vaccination would appear more attractive to those who received Form II (pseudocertainty) than to those who received Form I (probabilistic protection). The results confirmed this prediction: 57 percent of those who received Form II indicated they would get vaccinated, compared with 40 percent of those who received Form I.

The pseudocertainty effect highlights the contrast between reduction and elimination of risk. As Tversky and Kahneman have indicated, this distinction is difficult to justify on any normative grounds. Moreover, manipulations of certainty seem to have important implications for the design and description of other forms of protection (e.g., medical treatments, insurance, flood- and earthquake-proofing activities).

Another category of framing effects comes from the way one is to respond to a decision problem. Although people are sometimes free to choose their response mode, typically some external source defines the problem as involving either judgment (of individual options) or choice (selecting one from two or more options). Many theories of decisionmaking postulate an equivalence between judgment and choice, assuming that each option x has a value $v(x)$ that determines its attractiveness in both contexts (see, e.g., Luce, 1977). However, recent research has demonstrated that the information-processing strategies involved in making choices are often quite different from the strategies employed in judging single options. In particular, much of the thinking prior to choice appears to be aimed at constructing a concise, coherent set of reasons that justify the selection of one option over the others (Slovic, 1975; Tversky, 1972). Judgments of single options are based either on different justifications or on a variety of non-justificatory processes. As a result, choices and evaluative judgments of the same options often differ, sometimes dramatically.

An example of the differences that can occur between evaluation and choice comes from two experiments (Lichtenstein and Slovic, 1971, 1973), one of which was conducted on the floor of the Four Queens Casino in Las Vegas. Consider the following pair of gambles studied in the Las Vegas experiment:

Bet A: 11/12 chance to win 12 chips
            1/12 chance to lose 24 chips
Bet B: 2/12 chance to win 79 chips
            10/12 chance to lose 5 chips

where the value of each chip has been fixed at 25 cents. Notice that Bet A has a much better chance of winning, but Bet B offers a higher payoff. Subjects indicated, in two ways, the attractiveness of each bet in many such pairs. First they made a simple choice, A or B. Later, they were asked to assume that they owned a ticket to play each bet, and they were to state the lowest price for which they would sell this ticket.

Presumably, these selling prices and choices are both governed by the attractiveness of each gamble. Therefore, subjects should have stated higher selling prices for the gambles that they preferred in the choice situation. In fact, subjects often chose one gamble, yet stated a higher selling price for the other. For the pair of gambles shown above, A and B were chosen about equally often. However, Bet B received a higher selling price about 88 percent of the time. Of the subjects who chose Bet A, 87 percent gave a higher selling price to Bet B, thus exhibiting an inconsistent preference pattern. Grether and Plott (1979), two skeptical economists, replicated this study with numerous variations designed to show that the observed inconsistencies were artifactual. They obtained essentially the same results as Lichtenstein and Slovic and numerous other investigators (Slovic and Lichtenstein, 1983).

What accounts for this inconsistent pattern of preferences for gambles? Lichtenstein and Slovic concluded that subjects used different cognitive strategies when setting prices than when making choices. Subjects often justified the choice of Bet A in terms of its good odds, but they set a higher price for B because they were greatly influenced by its large payoff. For example, people who found a gamble basically attractive used the amount to win as a starting point. They then adjusted the amount to win downward to accommodate the less-than-perfect chance of winning and the fact that there was some amount to lose as well. Typically, this adjustment was small and, as a result, large payoffs caused people to set prices that were inconsistent with their choices.

Another example of the interaction among framing, response mode, and justificatory processes comes from a study in which we presented college students and members of the League of Women Voters with two different but logically related tasks. Task 1 was a variation of the civil-defense problem shown in Figure 2. The cover story was the same but the options read as follows:

Option A carries with it a .5 probability of containing the threat with a loss of 5 lives and a .5 probability of losing 95 lives. It is like taking the gamble:

.5 lose 5 lives
.5 lose 95 lives

Option B carries with it a .5 probability of containing the threat with a loss of 40 lives and a .5 probability of losing 60 lives. It is like taking the gamble:

.5 lose 40 lives
.5 lose 60 lives

Subjects were asked to select one of these two options. In the second task, they were asked to rate their agreement with each of three functions representing the way that society should evaluate lives in multi-fatality situations (see Figure 3) after reading elaborate rationales for adopting each of the functional forms. Briefly, the linear form (curve 1) represents the view that every life lost is equally costly to society. The exponentially increasing function (curve 2) represents the view that large losses of life are disproportionately serious (e.g., loss of 20 lives is more than twice as bad as loss of 10 lives). Curve 3 represents a reduced sensitivity to large losses of life (e.g., loss of 20 lives is less than twice as bad as loss of 10 lives).

More than half of all subjects chose option A in Task 1 and agreed most with curve 2 in the second task (Figure 3). However, option A indicates a risk-seeking attitude toward loss of life, whereas curve 2 represents risk aversion. Choice of option A would be consistent with curve 3, which was the least favored. These inconsistent results were not altered appreciably by changing the degree of elaboration in the rationales given for the three curves.

Figure 3.   *Task 2: The impact of catastrophic events. Subjects were asked to rate their agreement with the principles embodied in each of the above three proposals. (Two pages of instructions explaining the meaning of the curves preceded the task.)*

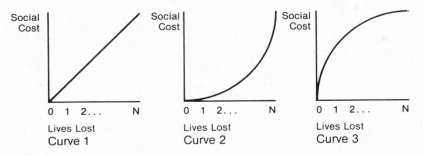

SOURCE: Fischhoff, Slovic, and Lichtenstein, 1980a.

Subjects who were confronted with the inconsistency in their responses refused to change. They claimed to see no connection between the two tasks. Most appeared to be relying on some variant of the following justification for choosing option A: "It would be immoral to allow the loss of 40 or more lives when option A presents a good chance of coming out of the situation with only a few lives lost." This perspective was evoked by the structure of the choice problem but not by the task of evaluating the three functional relationships.

Implications for Regulatory Policy

Bounded rationality, in the form of difficulties in probabilistic thinking and risk perception, ill-defined and labile preferences, information-processing limitations, and the presence of potent and easily manipulated decision frames, provides a rather striking contrast to the presumption of rationality embodied in much economic and regulatory theory. Cases in which bounded rationality provides the more accurate description of people's behavior point to the need for regulatory policies different from those implied by economic rationality. When judgmental limitations restrict people's ability to fend for themselves in the marketplace, some regulators have argued that "public intervention [is] necessary for the protection of working men and women in this country" (Bingham, 1979). That is, one cannot assume that market mechanisms will lead to an optimal solution. On the contrary, those who are better informed may exploit that status to strategic advantage. When laypeople are poorly informed about a

technological hazard, special educational efforts may be a necessary
condition for meaningful public participation in policy setting. When
education is not practical, the public may have to be represented by
elected or appointed officials or by public interest groups. When technical experts are also prone to judgmental difficulties, then corresponding corrections in their role are also necessary.

It would be premature, however, to make any blanket recommendation. In any particular situation one needs to know how serious
judgmental limitations are and how readily market mechanisms can
overcome them. In some cases, trial-and-error experience will enable people to learn about the issues that most concern them and to
develop adaptive strategies (Hogarth, 1981). In others, though, crucial information may be unavailable or feedback may be so ambiguous and delayed as to prevent learning (Einhorn and Hogarth, 1978).
In some cases, competitive forces and the need to appeal to the more
"rational" actors may promote the availability of more attractive options. In other cases, markets appear to maintain or even compound
the biases of individual investors (Arrow, 1982; Dreman, 1977, 1980;
MacKay, 1970; Russell and Thaler, 1983).[1] Clearly, research to clarify
this issue should be given high priority.

Our knowledge of human intellectual abilities and limitations is
incomplete. Nevertheless, enough is known, we believe, to argue that
approaches to risk management should start with the presumption
of bounded rationality and should investigate the extent to which
various market and regulatory mechanisms can overcome the limitations of individual minds.

Implications for Assessing Values

Decision problems with high stakes tend to be unique and
unfamiliar. They draw us into situations in which we have not adequately evaluated the implications of values and beliefs acquired in
simpler, more familiar settings. Yet, at the same time, many have argued that values must be made explicit and incorporated into regulatory decisionmaking (see, e.g., Kennedy, 1981). But how should this
be done? Some analytic methods call for direct elicitation of values
through surveys, hearings, and the like, whereas others infer values
from the preferences revealed in ongoing decisions. Both approaches assume that people know their own values and that elicita-

1. In his foreword to MacKay's remarkable book, Bernard Baruch observed: "Yet
I never see a brilliant economic thesis expanding, as though they were geometrical
theorems, the mathematics of price movements, that I do not recall Schiller's dictum:
'Anyone taken as an individual is totally sensible and reasonable—as a member of a
crowd, he at once becomes a blockhead'" (p. iii).

tion methods are unbiased channels that translate subjective feelings into analytically usable expressions.

These assumptions may not always be valid. The strong effects of framing and information-processing considerations, acting upon inchoate preferences, can make elicitation procedures major forces in shaping the expression of values (Fischhoff, Slovic, and Lichtenstein, 1980a, b). Where this is the case, we believe that elicitors of values may have to become active partners in their respondents' response processes. That is, they must help respondents to evoke and reconcile the incoherent positions they might adopt on an issue. Ordinarily, elicitors are loath to assume such a role, for fear of influencing their respondents. However, when the method shapes the message, some influence is inevitable: better, then, that it should be made explicit and balanced.

In sum, subtle aspects of how problems are posed, questions are phrased, and responses are elicited can have substantial impacts on judgments that supposedly express the precise nature of people's preferences. Nevertheless, we are not wholly pessimistic on this score. Research to be described later in this chapter indicates that psychometric survey methods can identify the general categories of issues and outcomes that people deem important in the evaluation and management of risk. The macrostructure of preference may be better defined, more stable, and more readily measurable than the microstructure.

Implications for Informing People about Risk

Many theorists have argued that the most important function of a regulatory agency is to insure that workers, patients, and citizens are properly informed about the risks they face (see, e.g., Joskow and Noll, 1981). Such information can presumably help people make better decisions in the marketplace and thus obviate the need for severe regulatory interventions. However, despite good intentions, creating effective informational programs may be quite difficult (Slovic, Fischhoff, and Lichtenstein, 1980b, 1981a). Doing an adequate job means finding cogent ways of presenting complex technical material that is clouded by uncertainty and may be distorted by the listener's preconceptions (and perhaps misconceptions) about the hazard and its consequences. Moreover, as we have seen, people are often at the mercy of the way problems are formulated. Those responsible for determining the content and format of information programs thus have considerable ability to manipulate perceptions and behavior.

The stakes in risk problems are high: industrial profits, jobs, energy costs, willingness of patients to accept treatments, public safety and health. Potential conflicts of interest abound. When subtle aspects of how (or what) information is presented can change people's behavior, someone needs to determine which formulation should be used. Making that decision takes one out of the domain of psychology and into law, ethics, and politics. The possibilities for manipulation suggest that informational programs cannot be left to any one group (e.g., employers, unions, physicians, toxicologists). Indeed, the way to get the most balanced message may be to subject it to diverse critiques, with each group challenging features that it considers to be confusing or misleading.

We have here been emphasizing the difficulties people have in comprehending and estimating risks. Some observers, cognizant of these difficulties, have concluded that the problems are insurmountable. We disagree. Although the broad outlines of the psychological research just described suggest a pessimistic view, the details of that research give some cause for optimism. Upon close examination, it appears that people understand some things quite well, although their path to knowledge may be quite different from that of the technical experts. In situations where misunderstanding appears to be rampant, people's errors can often be traced to inadequate information and biased experiences, which education may be able to counter.

Studies of Protective Behavior

In this section we shall describe studies of two kinds of protective behavior: insurance, and the use of seat belts. This research was designed to provide basic knowledge relevant for regulatory decisions.

National Flood Insurance Program

Although few residents of flood and earthquake areas voluntarily insure themselves against the consequences of such disasters, many turn to the federal government for aid after suffering losses. Policymakers have argued that both the government and the property owners at risk would be better off financially under a federal insurance program. Such a program would shift the burden of disasters from the general taxpayer to individuals living in hazardous areas and would thus promote wiser decisions regarding the use of flood plains (Kunreuther et al., 1978).

Without a firm understanding of how people perceive and react to risks, however, there is no way of knowing what sort of disaster insurance program would be most effective. For example, the National Flood Insurance Program took the seemingly reasonable step of lowering the cost of insurance in order to stimulate purchases. However, despite heavy subsidization of the rates, relatively few policies were bought.

An integrated program of laboratory experiments and field surveys by Kunreuther et al. (1978) and Slovic, Fischhoff, Lichtenstein, Corrigan, and Combs (1977) was designed to determine the critical factors influencing the voluntary purchase of insurance against the consequences of low-probability events such as floods or earthquakes. Analysis of the survey data revealed widespread ignorance and misinformation regarding the availability and terms of insurance and the probabilities of damage from a future disaster. The laboratory experiments showed that people preferred to insure against relatively high-probability, low-loss hazards and tended to reject insurance in situations where the probability of loss was low and the potential losses were high. These results suggest that people's natural predispositions run counter to economic theory (e.g., Friedman and Savage, 1948), which assumes that risk-averse individuals should desire a mechanism that protects them from rare catastrophic losses.

When asked about their insurance decisions, subjects in both the laboratory and survey studies indicated a disinclination to worry about low-probability hazards. Such a strategy is understandable. Given the limitations on their time, energy, and capacity for attention, people have a finite reservoir of concern. Unless they ignored many low-probability threats they would become so burdened that productive life would become impossible. Another insight gleaned from the experiments and the survey is that people think of insurance as an investment. Receiving payments for claims seems to be viewed as a return on the premium—one that is received more often with more probable losses. The popularity of low-deductible insurance plans (Fuchs, 1976; Pashigian, Schkade, and Menefee, 1966) provides confirmation from outside the laboratory that people prefer to insure against relatively probable events with small consequences.

One surprising survey result was that homeowners' lack of interest in disaster insurance did not seem to be due to expectations that the federal government would bail them out in an emergency. The majority of individuals interviewed said they anticipated no aid at all from the government in the event of a disaster. Most appeared not to have considered how they would recover from flood or earthquake damage.

If insurance is to be marketed on a voluntary basis, consumers' attitudes and information-processing limitations must be taken into account. Policymakers and insurance providers must find ways to communicate the risks and arouse concern for the hazards. One method found to work in the laboratory experiments is to increase the perceived probability of disaster by lengthening the individual's time horizon. For example, considering the risk of experiencing a hundred-year flood at least once during a twenty-five-year period, instead of considering the risk in a single year, raises the probability from .01 to .22 and may thus cast flood insurance in a more favorable light. Another step would have insurance agents play an active role in educating homeowners about the proper use of insurance as a protective mechanism and providing information about the availability of insurance, rate schedules, deductible values, etc. If such actions are not effective, then it may be necessary to institute some form of mandatory coverage. Recognizing the difficulty of inducing voluntary coverage, the National Flood Insurance Program now requires insurance as a condition for obtaining federal funds for building in flood-prone areas.

Seat Belts

Another form of protection that people do not often use is the automobile seat belt. Promotional efforts to get motorists to wear seat belts have failed dismally (Robertson, 1976). Despite expensive advertising campaigns and buzzer systems, fewer than 15 percent of motorists "buckle up for safety." Policymakers have criticized the public for failing to appreciate the risks of driving and the benefits of seat belts. However, results from risk perception research provide an alternative perspective that seems at once more respectful of drivers' reasoning and more likely to increase seat-belt use.

As noted above, people often disregard very small probabilities. Reluctance to wear seat belts might, therefore, be due to the extremely small probability of incurring a fatal accident on a single automobile trip. Because a fatal accident occurs only about once in every 3.5 million person-trips and a disabling injury only once in about every 100,000 person-trips, refusing to buckle one's seat belt may seem quite reasonable. It may look less reasonable, however, if one frames the problem within a multiple-trip perspective. This is, of course, the perspective of traffic safety planners, who see the thousands of lives that might be saved annually if belts were used regularly. For the individual, during fifty years of auto travel (about 40,000 trips), the probability of being killed is .01 and the probability of experiencing at least one disabling injury is .33. In laboratory experiments, we found that people induced to consider this lifetime perspective responded more favorably concerning the use of seat belts (and air bags) than did people asked to consider a trip-by-trip perspective (Slovic, Fischhoff, and Lichtenstein, 1978). More recent studies suggest that television and radio messages based on this lifetime-cumulative-risk theme can increase actual seat-belt use somewhat (Schwalm and Slovic, 1982).

Characterizing Perceived Risk

If it is to aid hazard management, a theory of perceived risk must explain people's extreme aversion to some hazards and their indifference to others, and the discrepancies between these reactions and experts' recommendations. Why, for example, do some communities react vigorously against the location of a liquid-natural-gas terminal in their vicinity, despite the assurances of experts that it is safe? Why, on the other hand, do communities situated below great dams generally show little concern for experts' warnings? Over the past few years researchers have been attempting to answer such questions as these by examining the opinions that people express when they are asked, in a variety of ways, to characterize and evaluate hazardous activities and technologies. The goals of this descriptive research are (a) to develop a taxonomy of risk characteristics that can be used to understand and predict societal responses to hazards, and (b) to develop methods for assessing public opinions about risk in a way that could be useful for policy decisions.

The Psychometric Paradigm

Psychometric scaling methods and multivariate analysis techniques have been used to produce quantitative representations of risk attitudes and perceptions (Brown and Green, 1980; Fischhoff, Slovic, Lichtenstein, Read, and Combs, 1978; Gardner et al., 1982; Green, 1980a, b; Green and Brown, 1980; Johnson and Tversky, in press; Renn, 1981; Slovic, Fischhoff, and Lichtenstein, 1979, 1980a, b; Vlek and Stallen, 1981; von Winterfeldt, John, and Borcherding, 1981). Although each new study adds complexity to the picture, some broad generalizations have emerged.

Researchers employing the psychometric paradigm have typically asked people to judge the current and desired level of risk (or safety) of diverse sets of hazardous activities, substances, and technologies, and to indicate their desire for risk reduction and regulation of these hazards. These global judgments have then been related to judgments about other properties of each hazard, including:

Characteristics that have been hypothesized to account for risk perceptions and attitudes—for example, voluntariness, dread, knowledge, controllability.

Benefits to society.

Number of deaths in an average year.

Number of deaths in a disastrous year.

Among the generalizations that have been drawn from the results of psychometric studies are the following:

1. Perceived risk is quantifiable and predictable. Psychometric techniques seem well suited for identifying similarities and differences among groups with regard to risk perceptions and attitudes (see, for example, Table 1).

2. "Risk" means different things to different people. When experts judge risk, their responses correlate highly with technical estimates of annual fatalities (Figure 4, top). Laypeople can assess annual fatalities when asked (and produce estimates somewhat similar to the technical estimates). However, their judgments of risk are sensitive to other factors as well (e.g., catastrophic potential, threat to future generations) and, as a result, are not closely related to their own (or experts') estimates of annual fatalities (see Figure 4, bottom).

3. Even when groups disagree about the overall riskiness of specific hazards, they show remarkable agreement when rating those hazards on characteristics of risk such as knowledge, controllability, dread, or catastrophic potential.

4. Many of these risk characteristics are highly correlated with each other, across a wide domain of hazards. For example, voluntary hazards tend also to be controllable and well known, and hazards that threaten future generations tend also to be seen as having catastrophic potential. Analysis of these interrelationships shows that the broader domain of characteristics can be condensed to three higher-order characteristics or factors. These factors reflect the degree to which a risk is understood, the degree to which it evokes a feeling of dread, and the number of people exposed to the risk (see Figure 5). This factor structure has been found to be similar across groups of laypersons and experts judging large and diverse sets of hazards. Making the set of hazards more specific (e.g., partitioning nuclear power into radioactive waste transport, uranium mining, and nuclear reactor accidents) appears to have

Table 1   *Ordering of Perceived Risk for 30 Activities and Technologies*

	Experts	League of Women Voters	College Students	Active Club Members
motor vehicles	1	2	5	3
smoking	2	4	3	4
alcoholic beverages	3	6	7	5
handguns	4	3	2	1
surgery	5	10	11	9
motorcycles	6	5	6	2
X-rays	7	22	17	24
pesticides	8	9	4	15
electric power (non-nuclear)	9	18	19	19
swimming	10	19	30	17
contraceptives	11	20	9	22
general (private) aviation	12	7	15	11
large construction	13	12	14	13
food preservatives	14	25	12	28
bicycles	15	16	24	14
commercial aviation	16	17	16	18
police work	17	8	8	7
fire fighting	18	11	10	6
railroads	19	24	23	20
nuclear power	20	1	1	8
food coloring	21	26	20	30
home appliances	22	29	27	27
hunting	23	13	18	10
prescription antibiotics	24	28	21	26
vaccinations	25	30	29	29
spray cans	26	14	13	23
high school & college football	27	23	26	21
power mowers	28	27	28	25
mountain climbing	29	15	22	12
skiing	30	21	25	16

NOTE: The ordering is based on the geometric mean risk ratings within each group. Rank 1 represents the most risky activity or technology.

little effect on the factor structure or its relationship to risk perceptions (Slovic, Fischhoff, and Lichtenstein, in press).[2]

5. Many of the various characteristics, particularly those associated with the factor "dread risk," correlate highly with laypersons' perceptions of risk. The higher an activity's score on the dread factor, the higher its perceived risk, the more people want its risks reduced, and the more they want to see strict regulation employed to achieve the desired reductions in risk (see Figure 6). The factor labeled "unknown risk" tends not to correlate highly with risk perception. Factor 3, "exposure," is moderately related to lay perceptions of risk. In contrast, experts' perceptions of risk are *not* related to any of the various risk characteristics or factors derived from these characteristics.

6. The informativeness or "signal potential" of an accident, which appears to determine its social impact, is systematically related to both "dread risk" and "unknown risk" factors (Figure 7).

7. In agreement with hypotheses originally put forth by Starr (1969), people's tolerance for risk appears related to their perception of benefit. All other things being equal, greater perceived benefit is associated with a greater tolerance for risk. Moreover, tolerance depends on various qualitative aspects of risk, including its voluntariness, familiarity, catastrophic potential, and perceived uncertainty. In sharp contrast to Starr's views, however, our respondents did not believe that society has managed hazards so well that optimal tradeoffs among these characteristics have already been achieved.

Implications of Risk Perception Research

In the results of the psychometric studies, we have the beginnings of a perceptual/psychological classification system for hazards. Ultimately, we need not only a better psychological taxonomy but one that also reflects physical, biological, and social/managerial elements of hazards. Such a taxonomy would be a potent device for understanding and guiding social regulation of risk. We are far from this goal.

---

2. The invariance obtained thus far with factor-analytic studies does not imply, however, that approaches based on different methods and assumptions would produce similar results. In fact, Tversky and Johnson (1981) have shown that a very different hazard structure results from representations based on judgments about how similar one hazard is to another with respect to risk. The implications of such differences remain to be determined.

Figure 4.   *Judgments of perceived risk for experts (top) and laypeople (bottom) plotted against the best technical estimates of annual fatalities for twenty-five technologies and activities. Each point represents the average responses of the participants. The dashed lines are the straight lines that best fit the points. The experts' risk judgments are seen to be more closely associated with annual fatality rates than are the lay judgments.*

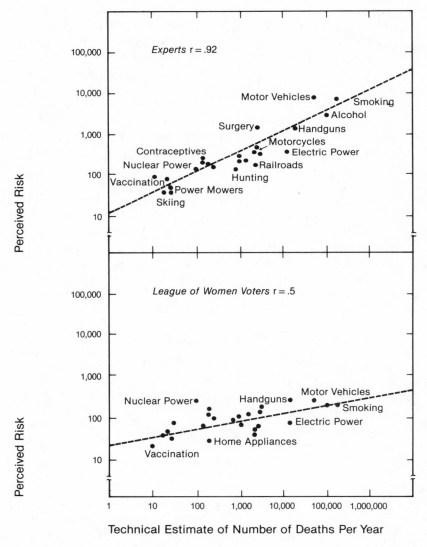

SOURCE: Slovic, Fischhoff, and Lichtenstein, 1979.

Figure 5. *Hazard locations on Factors 1 and 2 of the three-dimensional struc-ture derived from the interrelationships among eighteen risk characteristics. Fac-tor 3 (not shown) reflects the number of people exposed to the hazard and the degree of one's personal exposure. The diagram beneath the figure illustrates the characteristics that comprise the two factors.*

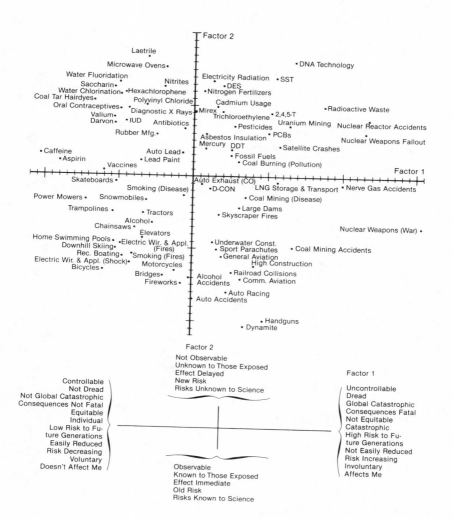

Figure 6. *Attitudes toward regulation of the hazards in Figure 5. The larger the point, the greater the desire for strict regulation to reduce risk.*

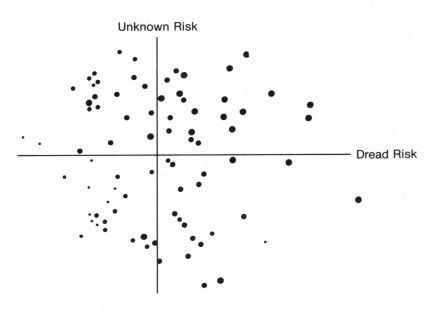

SOURCE: Slovic, Fischhoff, and Lichtenstein, in press.

Forecasting public response. Despite an incomplete understanding of public attitudes and perceptions, we have attempted to use the results from risk perception studies to explain and forecast reactions to specific technologies. Nuclear power has been the principal object of such analysis because of the obvious role of social factors governing this important technology. As Alvin Weinberg (1976, p. 19) observed, reflecting on the future of nuclear power, "the public perception and acceptance of nuclear energy . . . [have] emerged as the most critical question." The reasonableness of the public's perceptions has been the topic of an extensive public debate, filled with charges and countercharges. One industry source (*EPRI Journal,* 1980, p. 30) has argued that public reaction to Three Mile Island has cost "as much as $500 billion . . . and is one measure of the price being paid as a consequence of fear arising out of an accident that according to the most thorough estimates may not have physiologically hurt even one member of the public."

Risk perception research offers some promise of clarifying the concerns of opponents of nuclear power (Fischhoff, Slovic, and Lichtenstein, 1983; Slovic, Fischhoff, and Lichtenstein, 1981b; Slovic,

Figure 7. *Relation between signal potential and risk characterization for thirty hazards in Figure 5. The larger the point, the greater the degree to which an accident involving that hazard was judged to "serve as a warning signal for society, providing new information about the probability that similar or even more destructive mishaps might occur within this type of activity."*

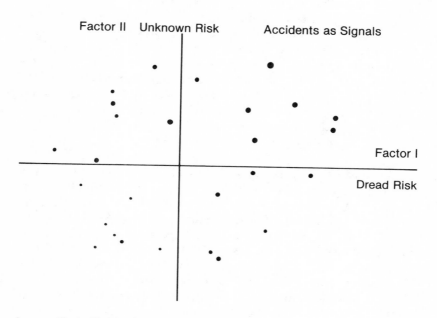

SOURCE: Slovic, Fischhoff, and Lichtenstein, 1984.

Lichtenstein, and Fischhoff, 1979). In particular, psychometric studies show that these people judge its benefits as quite low and its risks as unacceptably great. On the benefit side, most opponents do not see nuclear power as a vital link in meeting basic energy needs; rather, they view it as a supplement to other sources of energy which are themselves adequate. On the risk side, nuclear power occupies a unique position in the factor space, reflecting people's views that its risks are unknown, dread, uncontrollable, inequitable, catastrophic, and likely to affect future generations (see Figure 5). Opponents recognize that few people have died to date as a result of nuclear power. However, they do have great concern over the potential for catastrophic accidents. Furthermore, much of the opposition to nuclear power can be understood in terms of basic psychological principles of perception and cognition or deep-seated differences in values, which are not likely to be changed by information campaigns that focus on safety. What might improve the industry's status is convincing information about its benefits, perhaps in conjunction with energy shortages. A superb safety record might, over time, reduce opposition, but because nuclear risks are perceived to be unknown and potentially catastrophic, even small accidents will be highly publicized and will have immense social costs (see Figure 7). This fact, we shall see later, has direct implications for the setting of safety standards (Slovic, Fischhoff, and Lichtenstein, 1980c).

This type of research may also forecast the response to technologies that have yet to catch the public's eye. For example, our studies indicate that recombinant DNA technology shares several of the characteristics that make nuclear power so hard to manage (Slovic, Fischhoff, and Lichtenstein, in press). If it becomes the object of public attention, this new technology could face some of the same problems and opposition now confronting the nuclear industry.

Comparing risks. One frequently advocated approach to broadening people's perspectives is to present quantified risk estimates for a variety of hazards, expressed in some unidimensional index of death or disability, such as risk per hour of exposure (Sowby, 1965), annual probability of death (R. Wilson, 1979), or reduction in life expectancy (Cohen and Lee, 1979; Reissland and Harries, 1979). Even though such comparisons have no logically necessary implications for decisionmaking (Fischhoff, Lichtenstein, Slovic, Derby, and Keeney, 1981), one might still hope that they would help improve people's intuitions about the magnitude of risks. Risk perception research suggests, however, that these comparisons will not be very satisfactory for this purpose. People's perceptions and attitudes are determined not only by the sort of unidimensional statistics used in such tables but also by the variety of quantitative and qualitative characteristics described above. To many people, statements such as "the annual risk from living near a nuclear power plant is equivalent to the risk of riding an extra three miles in an automobile" give inadequate consideration to the important differences in the nature of the risks from these two technologies.

In short, "riskiness" means more to people than "expected number of fatalities." Attempts to characterize, compare, and regulate risks must be sensitive to this broader conception of risk. Fischhoff, Watson, and Hope (1983) have made a start in this direction by demonstrating how one might construct a more adequate measure of risk. They show that variations in the scope of one's definition of risk can greatly change the assessment of risk from various energy technologies.

Deciding How Safe Is Safe Enough

The bottom line in risk regulation is usually presented as an answer to some variant of the question: "How safe is safe enough?" The question takes such forms as: "Do we need additional containment shells around our nuclear power plants?" "Is the carcinogenicity of saccharin sufficiently low to allow its use?" "Should schools with asbestos ceilings be closed?"

Frustration over the difficulty of answering such questions has led to a search for clear, implementable rules that will determine whether the risks from a given technology are acceptable. Among the many seeking to solve the mystery of acceptable risk have been Bazelon (1979), Comar (1979), Council for Science and Society (1977), Crouch and Wilson (1982), Griesemeyer and Okrent (1980), Howard, Matheson, and Owen (1978), Lave (1981), Lowrance (1976), Okrent and Whipple (1977), Rowe (1977), Salem, Solomon, and Yesley (1980), Schwing and Albers (1980), Starr (1969), and ourselves (Fischhoff et al., 1981). Despite these efforts, no magic formula has been discovered. Nevertheless, some progress has been made, not the least of which includes a heightened respect for the complexities of the task.

Approaches to Acceptable Risk: A Critique

Our own efforts in this area were instigated and supported by the Nuclear Regulatory Commission (NRC). It has always been known that nuclear reactors could be made safer—at increased cost. However, as long as it was difficult to quantify safety, the question of how much safety at what price was rarely addressed explicitly. Beginning with the Reactor Safety Study (U.S. Nuclear Regulatory Commission, 1975), the technology of measuring risk has advanced rapidly. Now that quantitative estimates of safety are thought to be feasible for many aspects of the nuclear fuel cycle, the need to determine how safe reactors *should* be has taken on greater significance.

At the urging of Congress and the nuclear industry, the NRC has been working intensively to develop an explicit safety goal or philosophy. This goal would clarify the commission's vague mandate to "avoid undue risk to public health and safety" and, by doing so, would guide specific regulatory decisions.

The NRC asked us to take a comprehensive, critical look at the philosophical, sociopolitical, institutional, and methodological issues crucial to determining how best to answer the question, "How safe is safe enough?" We approached this task in a general way, not restricted to nuclear power or any other specific technology (Fischhoff et al., 1981). Guided by our own psychological perspective and aided by decision theorists Stephen Derby and Ralph Keeney, we attempted to:

- Clarify the nature of acceptable-risk problems and examine some frequently proposed, but not entirely adequate, solutions.
- Characterize the essential features of acceptable-risk problems that make their resolution so difficult. These features include uncertainty about how to define acceptable-risk problems, difficulties in obtaining crucial facts, difficulties in assessing social values, unpredictable human responses to hazards, and problems of assessing the adequacy of decisionmaking processes.
- Create a taxonomy of decisionmaking methods, described according to how they attempt to address the essential features of acceptable-risk problems. The major approaches we discussed were: *professional judgment*—allowing technical experts to devise solutions; *bootstrapping*—searching for historical precedents to guide future decisions; and *formal analysis*—theory-based procedures for modeling problems and calculating the best decision, such as risk/benefit, cost/benefit, and decision analysis.
- Specify the objectives that an approach should satisfy in order to guide social policy. These include comprehensiveness, logical soundness, practicality, openness to evaluation, political acceptability, institutional compatibility, and conduciveness to learning.
- Evaluate the success of each approach in meeting these objectives.
- Derive recommendations for policymakers and citizens interested in improving the quality of acceptable risk decisions.

Conclusions.   The following conclusions emerged from our analysis:

- Acceptable-risk problems are decision problems, that is, they require a choice among alternatives. That choice depends on the set of options, consequences, values, and facts invoked in the decision process. Therefore, there can be no single, all-purpose number that expresses the acceptable risk for a society. At best, one can hope to find the most acceptable alternative in a specific problem.
- None of the approaches we considered is either comprehensive or infallible. Each considers some features of acceptable-risk problems but ignores others. As a result, not only does each approach fail to give a definitive answer, but it is biased toward particular interests and particular solutions. Hence choosing an approach is a political

act that caries a distinct message about who should rule and what should matter. The search for an *objective* method is doomed to failure and may obscure the value-laden assumptions that will inevitably be made.

- Acceptable-risk debates are greatly clarified when the participants are committed to separating issues of fact from issues of value. Nonetheless, a clear-cut separation is often impossible. Beliefs about the facts of the matter shape our values; those values in turn shape the facts we search for and how we interpret what we find.

- The determining factor in many acceptable-risk decisions is how the problem is defined (i.e., which options and consequences are considered, what kinds of uncertainty are acknowledged, and how key terms are operationalized). Until definitional disputes are settled, it may be impossible to agree on a course of action.

- Values, like beliefs, are acquired through experience and contemplation. Acceptable-risk problems raise many complex, novel, and vague issues of value for which individuals may not have well-articulated preferences. In such situations, the values expressed may be greatly influenced by transient factors, including subtle variations in how value questions are posed by interviewers, politicians, or the marketplace. These conflicts within each individual's values are distinct from the conflicts between different individuals' values. Both types of conflict require careful attention.

- Although a distinction is often made between perceived and objective risks, for most new and intricate hazards even so-called objective risks have a large judgmental component. At best, they represent the perceptions of the most knowledgeable technical experts. Even experts' understanding may be incomplete; indeed, their professional training may have limited them to certain traditional ways of looking at problems. In such cases, nonexperts may have important supplementary information on hazards and their consequences.

Recommendations.   We concluded that no one solution to acceptable-risk problems is now available, nor is it likely that a single solution will ever be found. Nonetheless, the following recommendations, designed to enhance society's ability to make decisions, were made to regulators, citizens, legislators, and professionals:

- Explicitly recognize the complexities of acceptable-risk problems. The value judgments and uncertainties encountered in specific decision problems should be acknowledged. More generally, we should realize that there are no easy solutions.

- Acknowledge the limits of currently available approaches and expertise. Although no approach is infallible, we should at least avoid the more common mistakes. Our aim should be a diverse and flexible approach to decisionmaking that emphasizes comprehensiveness.

• Improve the use of available approaches. Develop guidelines for their conduct and review. Make the approaches sensitive to all aspects of the problem and to the desires of as many stakeholders as possible. Analysis should proceed interactively in order to sustain its insights and absorb its criticisms.

• Make the decisionmaking process compatible with existing democratic institutions. The public and its representatives should be involved constructively in the process, both to make it more effective and to increase the public's understanding of hazard issues.

• Strengthen nongovernmental mechanisms that regulate hazards. Decisions reaches in the marketplace and in the political arena provide important guidelines for most approaches. Those mechanisms can be improved by various measures, including reform of the product-liability system and increased communication of risk information to workers and consumers.

• Clarify government involvement. Legislation should offer clear, feasible, and predictable mandates for regulatory agencies. The management of different hazards should be coordinated so as to build a legacy of dependable precedents and encourage consistent decisions.

Toward a Safety Goal

Justification. Our analysis of decisionmaking approaches was used by the NRC in the planning stages of its program to develop a safety goal (U.S. Nuclear Regulatory Commission, 1981). Upon completion of this analysis, we were asked to participate in the development of the goal itself. Before doing so, we felt it necessary to critique the effort in light of our earlier conclusion that, because the risk level associated with a technology is the outcome of specific decisions, there can be no single, all-purpose number (standard or goal) that does the job. In a decisionmaking process, the option chosen is one that emerges as best according to some criterion of attractiveness. By contrast, goals and standards essentially categorize options in terms of pass/no pass; all might be acceptable, or none. Beyond the obvious efficiency of setting a generally applicable decision rule, are there any other justifications for goals and standards? Fischoff (1983b, 1984) wrestled with the question of when one would want to rely on standards as a regulatory tool and concluded that there were, indeed, circumstances in which standards were warranted. Table 2

Table 2   *Conditions Justifying the Development of Safety Standards*

1. When predictability is important.

2. When one need not choose a single best option.

3. When a single (standardizable) feature captures the most important aspect of a category.

4. When the general standard accurately postdicts specific past decisions and predicts future ones.

5. When one wants to make a statement to reflect the goals of policymakers (who assume the symbolic standard will be compromised reasonably by those who apply it).

6. When one hopes to shape the set of future options.

7. When the decision process leading to the standard is of higher quality than could be maintained in numerous specific decisions.

SOURCE: Fischhoff, 1984.

gives a list of conditions that might justify the development of a pass/ no pass safety standard.

In addition to providing a theoretical rationale for goals and standards, these analyses have explored the many subtle and complex problems involved in transforming a goal from a political statement to a useful tool, one that can be unambiguously applied by regulators and understood by the regulated. Here one faces issues such as (a) defining the category governed by the standard (e.g., is a cosmetic a drug?); (b) determining the point and time of regulation (e.g., plant by plant or company by company? at which stage of production and use?); (c) tailoring standards to mesh with engineering and design capabilities; (d) deciding whether to regulate technical matters (nuts and bolts) or performance ("as long as you meet this goal, we don't care how you do it"). Once one has decided where to place the standard, the critical question involves how to measure risks in order to determine whether they are in compliance with the standard.

Social and behavioral issues.   Having satisfied ourselves that general goals and standards had a place in the regulator's armamentarium (the NRC had presumed this), we proceeded to consider the detailed process of establishing a safety goal. Our objective was to critique, from our perspective as behavioral scientists and decision theorists, what tended to be seen as primarily a technical problem, dealing with the design, construction, and licensing of reactors and the ability of probabilistic techniques to assess and verify reactor risks.

There has been no shortage of proposed safety goals over the years. Solomon, Nelson, and Salem (1981) counted 103 criteria pertaining to reactor accidents, which they categorized as follows:

1. Criteria for the safety of reactor systems: e.g., an upper limit for the acceptable probability of a core-melt accident.
2. Criteria for allowable risks to individuals in the vicinity of the plant site.
3. Criteria for the maximum allowable expenditures to avert a person-rem of radiation exposure.

The criteria proposed by the NRC fell within these generic categories. A detailed discussion of these various criteria is beyond the scope of this paper (see Fischhoff, 1983b). Suffice it to say that (a) they tended to rely on comparisons with current risks from other sources, particularly other means of generating electricity; (b) they were concerned with a rather narrow view of the reactor risks of nuclear power, focusing on immediate and latent fatalities from accidents, physical damage to the reactor and adjoining property, and costs of cleanup and replacement electricity; and (c) their implementation was unclear—they could have only symbolic value or could constitute an additional burden on an already complex regulatory process.

We believe that these features will lead the goals to be quite controversial. As mentioned earlier, risk perception research indicates that comparisons with other risks of life or risks from competing energy sources do not constitute meaningful benchmarks and should not be a primary factor in determining safety goals. Many different aspects must be considered when evaluating a technology's risk, including perceived uncertainty regarding the probabilities and consequences of mishaps, potential for catastrophe, threat to future generations, and potential for triggering social disruption. Nuclear power is unique in many of these respects. Although the safety goals are sensitive to many of these features, they lack an explicit logic for integrating qualitatively different risks. Without this link, it is difficult to apply the standards to a specific case.

A recurrent question during the safety-goal design process was whether to place special emphasis on avoiding large accidents. One important proposal, the alpha model, assumed that the seriousness or social impact of losing N lives in a single accident should be represented by the function N^α, where α is greater than 1.0. By attributing greater social disruption to large accidents, this model implies that extra money and effort should be expended to prevent or mitigate large accidents. Because the relationship is exponential, the spectre of low-probability, catastrophic accidents can come to overwhelm all other considerations.

Although psychometric studies and other surveys have pinpointed perceived catastrophic potential as a major public concern, further investigation has indicated that the alpha model is incorrect (Slovic, Lichtenstein, and Fischhoff, 1984); the societal costs of an accident cannot be modeled by any simple function of N. Accidents are interpreted as signals containing information about the nature and controllability of the risks involved. As a result, the perceived seriousness of an accident depends on the message it conveys as well as on its actual toll of death and destruction. An accident will have relatively little societal impact beyond that of its direct casualties if it occurs as a result of a familiar, well-understood process with little potential for recurrence or catastrophe. In contrast, an accident that causes little direct harm may have immense consequences if it increases the judged probability or seriousness of future accidents. The relationship between signal potential, accident seriousness, and the characteristics of a hazard (Figure 7) may help predict the seriousness of various mishaps.

As a case in point, the concept of accidents as signals helps explain society's strong response to some nuclear power mishaps. Because reactor risks are perceived as poorly understood and potentially catastrophic, accidents with few direct casualties may be seen as omens of disaster, producing indirect or "ripple" effects resulting in immense economic costs to the industry or society. One implication of signal value is that safety goals should consider these indirect costs. A second implication is that great effort and expense might be warranted to minimize the possibility of small but frightening reactor accidents.

Conclusion

A final general question, which occurs in relation to the safety goals and which may be the fundamental question motivating risk perception research, is: should policy respond to public fears that experts see as unjustified? This question was recently argued before the U.S. Supreme Court in the form of a (disputed) ruling that the undamaged reactor at Three Mile Island (there are two reactors there) could not be restarted until the NRC considered the effects of restart on the psychological health and well-being of neighboring residents. Most experts from the nuclear industry believe that public fears of restart are groundless.

There are, however, many reasons for laypeople and experts to disagree. These include misunderstanding, miscommunication, mistrust, and misinformation (Fischhoff, Slovic, and Lichtenstein, 1983). Thus, public concern need not reflect public ignorance. Discerning the causes underlying a particular disagreement requires careful thought to clarify just what is being disputed and whether agreement is possible given the disputants' differing frames of reference. Also needed is careful research, to clarify just what it is that the various parties know and believe. Once the situation has been clarified, the underlying problem can be diagnosed as calling for a scientific, educational, semantic, or political solution.

The most difficult situations will be those in which the participants cannot agree on what the problem is and have no recourse to an institution that will resolve the question by arbitration or by fiat, and those in which education is called for, yet fails (after some reasonably diligent effort). Policymakers then face the hard choice between going against their own better judgment by using the public's assessment of risk (in which they do not believe) or going against the public's feeling by imposing policies that will be disliked. However, fears that are ignored can result in stress or psychosomatic illness, which can be as real in their impact as they are illusory in their source. When strong public opinions are ignored, hostility, mistrust, and alienation can result. Because a society does more than manage risks, the policymaker must consider whether the social benefits to be gained by optimizing the allocation of resources in a particular decision are greater than the social costs of overriding a concerned public.

In sum, risk questions are going to be with us for a long time. For a society to deal with them wisely, it must understand their subtleties. We believe that psychological research is essential to achieving this understanding.

COMMENT: *Richard A. Winett*

Slovic, Fischhoff, and Lichtenstein argue not only that a cognitive, psychological perspective is important in the development of regulations, but also that the formulation of specific regulations always needs an empirical basis and justification. Thus, their focus is on psychological, particularly cognitive, aspects of risk and regulation. As a psychologist, I will primarily discuss what I see as some of the conceptual and methodological strengths and weaknesses of their approach.

At the outset, let me state that I was extremely impressed with the breadth of the work they presented. Their attempts to apply basic cognitive theory and data to the major concerns of our times are highly commendable. Their work is in vivid contrast to what a lot of psychological research has become—highly sophisticated methodology used to explore trivial questions.

I do have a number of comments and suggestions for future research in this field, particularly on the first part of the paper, which is then used partly as a basis for the development of standards and policies for deciding how safe is safe enough. I might add that while I feel knowledgeable enough to comment on the first part of the paper, I am much less expert of the issues and methodology raised in the remainder.

Readers should be aware that psychological theory, perspectives, and methodology are not monolithic. Psychologists disagree among themselves on the most important determinants of behavior and how to address research and policy questions.

Slovic, Fischhoff, and Lichtenstein reviewed a number of well-known studies on choice behavior that showed how personal characteristics, recent events, limits on available information and information processing, and the way choices are framed markedly contribute to the choices that are made. They note that this work "provides a rather startling contrast to the presumption of rationality upon which much economic and regulatory theory is based."

I both agree and disagree with this point. Behavioral in contrast to cognitive psychology is based on the assumption that the major determinants of behavior are external, i.e., that environmental contingencies such as social and material rewards, feedback, and punishments are the primary determinants of behavioral outcomes. This extreme (Skinnerian) position was modified during the 1970s, and we now have a combined cognitive-behavioral position (Bandura, 1977).

What is particularly interesting about the behavioral perspective is its great similarity to the traditional economic conception of utility maximization (Kagel and Winkler, 1972). While a complete understanding of choice and response in any situation requires assessment of cognitive, behavioral, and environmental factors, one can ask which factors are more powerful or better predictors. My own field research, particularly in the area of residential energy conservation, suggests three conclusions. First, environmental factors such as energy cost and family income allocated to energy have the dominant effect on consumer responsiveness (Winkler and Winett, 1982). Second, modification of real-life consumer behavior by cognitive strategies is not nearly as effective, and certainly not as easy, as is suggested by laboratory research on choice behavior (Geller, Winett, and Everett, 1982). Third, there are ways to influence choices through information strategies, but they are not as subtle as work suggested by laboratory studies. That is, there is an effective information technology based on behavioral psychology and communications theory that can improve efficiency of economic or market forces and, at times, override these forces in terms of consumer choice behaviors (Winett and Kagel, 1984). This technology is based on a particular theory and procedures and does not involve simple (or subtle) information-giving (Ester and Winett, 1982).

Let me add that a major issue that has frequently been ignored in economic models of utility maximization and, not surprisingly, in regulation requiring consumer information is that certain information media are not effective in creating informed consumers, let alone in modifying behavior. Small labels on bottles of pills, for example, are ineffective, while frequently repeated T.V. ads are more effective. Theory and regulation must address this issue (Winett and Kagel, 1984).

I have some other concerns about the work by Slovic, Fischhoff, and Lichtenstein. I am distressed that most of their work on choice behavior has involved what psychologists like to call verbal reports, with these reports made in time-limited laboratory settings. Social scientists are wary of two things. First, verbal reports may not, and often do not, match behavior. A subject may say that he or she will do A but under real-life conditions, where experience and consequences are more vital, may quite often choose B. Second, the results of laboratory studies may not hold up well in real life. Let me provide an example from my own longitudinal experiments in the field, not survey research.

Some of my work has involved the development of thermal/comfort standards and energy conservation strategies in buildings. One seemingly simple question in this research has been in what temperatures people can actually comfortably work and reside on the job and at home in the winter and summer, and how much energy can be saved if energy use is aimed at these levels. Prior to our work, this question for the most part had been addressed by verbal reports in laboratory settings. That is, groups of six to eight people were placed in environmental chambers for a few hours. The experimenter, without telling study participants the readings, varied the temperature and humidity. Clothing with standard insulation values was also worn. Periodically, using standard scales, participants voted anonymously on their level of comfort (Rohles, 1981). Notice that the procedure is very short-term and involves only writing, rating, and verbalizing behavior, i.e., marking the scales. Participants in the studies are not changing thermostat settings, let alone paying for heating or cooling.

In these studies (ASHRAE), used to set heating and cooling standards world-wide, it was found that when wearing moderate amounts of clothing, 75°F was the mean temperature voted as comfortable. This means that at less than 75°F most people were reporting they were uncomfortable.

The results of our field research with hundreds of consumers studied over many months are quite discrepant with the laboratory studies. In these studies, temperature and humidity in participants' homes were measured continuously, using special instruments. Energy use was calculated daily, and frequent measures were made of clothing worn and perceived comfort. Various strategies based on an information technology were used to inform consumers about simple energy-conservation techniques and to motivate related behavior changes. While consumers easily saved significant amounts of energy and money, the comfort, clothing, and temperature data are most important for the point at hand. Wearing similar amounts of clothing to those of participants in the laboratory studies, the consumers in the study lived throughout the winter at a mean temperature of about 63°F (with much lower temperatures at night when asleep) while reportedly maintaining comfort. The difference in energy use between a home or building heated to 75°F and one heated to 63°F is about 50 percent. These data also suggested that prior thermostat regulations for buildings (since rescinded) were justified; we have comparable data supporting higher summer temperature regulations, and the winter data have been replicated in subsequent field research.

The point here is that whenever and wherever possible, standards and regulations, and procedures to assure compliance to standards, should be developed using experimental field research methods. This will usually involve trying out, with citizens' consent, various policies or regulations and assessing citizens' responses. At other times, this may involve testing the limits of some regulation, e.g., to what home temperatures can people adapt fairly readily? It can and should also mean (as is indicated in Slovic, Fischhoff, and Lichtenstein, in press) testing various compliance procedures in the field, e.g., what types of media messages (if any) affect vehicular restraint use.

Having lauded the field experiment and criticized the approach taken by Slovic, Fischhoff, and Lichtenstein, let me indicate a number of very important aspects of their approach. First, field studies can be very expensive. Laboratory studies can be very inexpensive and can easily be repeated. Second, when situations are dangerous and entirely unknown, field experiments are simply not appropriate. For example, exposing citizens purposefully and systematically to different carcinogen levels is obviously unethical. Likewise, when we are trying to predict response to an extremely infrequent and relatively unknown set of circumstances, field experiments are not appropriate. We cannot create several types of nuclear accidents and see how people respond (although we can and should be prepared to collect data systematically after these events occur).

This is where and why the work of Slovic, Fischhoff, and Lichtenstein is of such vital importance. They are truly pioneers, for both the field of psychology and that of regulation of risk. They are trying to incorporate into this field reasonably well-substantiated findings about human behavior and cognition and to make clear the importance of adding social values to technological, legal, and economic considerations.

Though their work on risks in nuclear accidents is in the preliminary stages, they have already made important contributions to the regulation of nuclear power plants. By adding what appears to be known about public response to seemingly catastrophic events (e.g., Three Mile Island) and how the public evaluates risk, their analyses serve as a warning to both government and industry. Safety criteria and regulations must be extremely strict, even if this entails much larger costs, because a single incident can have a devastating effect on the industry.

Nevertheless, a basic inconsistency in their approach must be resolved if their work and that of other psychologists and decision theorists is to be taken more seriously. In the first half of the paper they emphasize the instability of choice behaviors, citizens' risk assessments, and so on, given the availability of information, the nature of previous experience, and how questions are framed. While I have argued that their approach probably overestimates this instability, clearly, and at the very least, they demonstrate that the method of approach and questioning can influence both opinions and actual behavioral decisions. If this is the case, the task of incorporating public opinion and values into policy decisions on risk seems quite difficult.

Can I arrive at a different assessment of regulation of safety at nuclear power plants simply by phrasing a question differently or by waiting until the media have presented a particular side of an issue or incident? Slovic, Fischhoff, and Lichtenstein would have to answer this question in the affirmative. If they agree, their efforts in the future should focus more on tapping enduring values or positions or perhaps even on determining a summated mean of values and positions based on asking different questions and at different times. Thus, one main future task is to develop a methodology for dealing with this problem.

As an outsider to their field, it has been relatively easy to poke holes in some of the work they have presented. This is probably possible only because they have attempted to tackle an enormous and, as they conclude, highly complex and emotion-laden problem. I hope some of these comments will contribute in a small way to their highly commendable work.

9

Conflicting Regulations
Six Small Studies and an Interpretation

Theodore Caplow

The topic of this chapter is *regulatory conflict,* that is, contradictory or incompatible directives issued to a regulated organization by two or more public regulatory agencies. The regulated organization may be a private enterprise such as a manufacturing company, or a public enterprise such as a local school district. The regulatory agencies may be federal, state, or local. The conflict may arise in diverse ways: in the attempt to enforce statutes with divergent purposes, out of jurisdictional conflict between agencies at different levels, by inadvertence, or because of defective communication among the parties to the regulatory process. Regardless of how regulatory conflicts originate, they invariably present operational problems for the regulated organizations they affect and political problems for the regulated agencies involved. Included under this topic are perceptions of regulatory conflict that may develop in a regulatory domain in the absence of any substantive conflict, either as a challenge to the legitimacy of a type of regulation or as a response to programmatic differences among regulatory agencies.

Although regulatory conflict often receives mention in the discussion of regulatory issues, it has not attracted much serious interest until recently and, so far as I have been able to discover, no empirical studies of regulatory conflict as a distinct problem were undertaken in the United States prior to the six small studies conducted in 1980 and 1981 and reported here. Five of these exploratory investigations were carried out at the Institute for the Study of Social and Legal

Change, University of Virginia. The sixth was done by the General Accounting Office for submission to Congress. For all practical purposes, the study of regulatory conflict is still in its infancy and the summary of it that follows will necessarily raise many more questions than it can begin to answer. Nevertheless, the existence of regulatory conflict is hardly debatable and the desirability of understanding it better is self-evident.

An Organization Theory of Regulatory Conflict

I conceive the regulatory process as a type of interorganizational behavior involving several sets of organizational actors connected by an intricate web of vertical relationships (goal setting, performance control, mandatory reporting, adjudication, sanctions), horizontal relationships (cooperation, competition, conflict, accommodation), oblique relationships that have both horizontal and vertical elements, and multi-step relationships whereby, for example, A's mandates are enforced by B upon C.

From the standpoint of any particular organization in the web, organizations vertically below are resources to meet the demands imposed by organizations vertically above. An increase in the number of organizations above it will usually be interpreted as a deterioration in an organization's position. An increase in the number of organizations below will ordinarily be interpreted as an improvement. An increase or decrease of organizations on the same horizontal level is not so readily interpreted: such organizations compete among themselves for scarce resources but may also provide mutual support in resisting the demands of organizations above or in enforcing demands upon organizations below.

Perhaps the most useful way of understanding a web of organizational relationships is to examine the formation and dissolution of coalitions throughout the web (Bacharach and Lawler, 1980). Some years ago I proposed (Caplow, 1968) that the relationships formed by collective actors in an interorganizational web can usefully be visualized as coalitions of two partners against a mutual antagonist in a chain of linked triads, and I suggested that the following two axioms seem to govern the formation of coalitions in such sets:

1. A coalition partner in one triad may not be an opponent in another.

2. A collective actor who is offered a choice between incompatible winning coalitions may be expected to choose the winning coalition in the superior triad.

Axiom 2 may be said to account for the ability of most organizations to maintain their authority structures most of the time despite continuously available opportunities to form mutinous coalitions.

Among the crucial triads in a web of organizational relationships are the familiar triads: legislature–regulatory agency–regulated organization; legislature–regulatory agency–court; regulatory agency–regulated organization–potential competitors; and the particularly important configuration of regulatory agency–regulatory agency–regulated organization.

What Noll in Chapter 2 of this book calls capture-cartel theories of regulatory behavior gave major attention to the tendency for improper coalitions to develop between regulatory agencies and regulated organizations against the legislative bodies that mandated the regulatory process and against potential competitors of the regulated organizations. This coalition is, of course, not unique to regulation (Ferejohn, 1974), but it has been observed very frequently in the public regulation of common carriers and other monopolies, in the regulation of independent professions, insurance companies, and building contractors, and in some forms of health and safety regulation. It implies an adversary relationship between the coalition and potential or actual competitors of the regulated entities. Although this has been a common pattern in the public regulation of private corporations, there have been numerous exceptions—notably, the FDA, which has had an adversary relationship with the regulated industries from the beginning. In addition, in numerous state regulatory situations adversary relationships have prevailed intermittently.

With the expansion of the regulatory process to cover nonbusiness institutions and many aspects of corporate activity besides pricing and competitive practices, two other types of coalitions have become increasingly salient: coalitions of regulatory agencies and organized interest groups, and coalitions of regulated organizations against a regulatory agency. Political parties have increasingly been drawn into these configurations as partners or antagonists of existing coalitions.

While identification of coalitions is a convenient way of tracing the lines of force that run through the web of organizational relationships involved in the regulation of any particular type of activity, it cannot give anything like a complete picture. The admirable collection of case studies assembled by Wilson (1980) illustrates how each regulatory domain develops a distinctive culture and a special perspective on regulation so that it cannot be understood by references to general principles alone. For example, the distinctive features of public education as a regulatory domain have been described at length by Brandt (1981) and are summarized succinctly by Scott in his comments on this paper. Drawing on the work of Meyer (1979), Kirp (1976), and Bankston (1981), and his own work on the regulation of institutional sectors, Scott makes two important observations: first, in education, increasing centralization of financial responsibility has not been accompanied by centralization of programmatic authority, and second, this separation permits the imposition of reporting and accounting rules by the central authority in an attempt to gain substantive authority. Scott's succinct description of the distinctive features of public education as a regulatory domain goes far to explain why it is such a rich field for the study of regulatory conflict. Officials at the school level are in the maelstrom of a battle for authority among local, state, and federal agencies, and the fundamental conflict over policy authority is manifest in conflicting orders from these adversaries. Of course, the idiosyncratic features of education are not the whole story. When they are set against the background of certain familiar principles of organizational analysis, a deeper understanding of regulatory conflict in education emerges. The following general principles are useful in illuminating special cases:

1. *The equilibrium condition in rule enforcement transactions is not compliance but an acceptable and, often, negotiated degree of partial compliance.* This principle, first enunciated in general terms by Homans (1950), has recently been documented with respect to judicial and regulatory processes by Stone (1975), Johnson (1979), and Sproull (1981), among others. Even within the tight hierarchical structure of a single organization, when we examine any sector of rule enforcement empirically we expect to discover the four types of normative evasion that Merton (1949) identified long ago: innovation, retreatism, ritualism, and rebellion. The probability of compliance is much lower when rules imposed by an organization seek to attain goals that are not a high priority of the regulated organization. One mode of resistance in that situation is to challenge the legitimacy of the enforcing authority by showing, if possible, that its rules are irrational, lack statutory authority, or conflict with the rules of other agencies. To put the matter bluntly, when there are no conflicting regulations, regulated organizations may find it necessary to invent them in order to justify noncompliance.

2. *In a web of horizontal and vertical interorganizational relationships, horizontal coalitions between regulatory agencies may be expected to lower the cost of enforcement and to raise the expected degree of compliance, while vertical coalitions between regulating and regulated organizations should have the effect of increasing the cost of enforcement for regulatory agencies*

outside the coalition. The effects of horizontal coalitions among regulated organizations are less predictable. Conceivably, such a coalition may lower the cost of enforcement but also lower the expected degree of compliance. The breakdown of consensus among regulatory agencies may involve inconvenience and some short-term costs for regulated organizations, but it will also increase their ability to resist regulation either directly, by playing off one agency against the other, or through political channels, by advancing the inconsistency of regulatory purposes as a grievance.

3. *The age of an interorganizational relationship has significant implications for the character and outcome of interorganizational transactions.* Stinchcombe (1965) contends that organizational forms are permanently marked by the characteristics developed in their formative period. Kaufman (1975) and Kimberley, Miles, et al. (1980) characterize the nature of organizational life cycles. Weaver (1978) demonstrates that the regulatory agencies established in the United States prior to World War II differ in nearly every respect from agencies developed since World War II. The older agencies tend to form vertical coalitions with the organizations they regulate and the legislative committees that oversee them. The newer agencies are more likely to seek horizontal coalitions with courts and organized interest groups and to develop adversary relationships with both the organizations they regulate and the legislative bodies from whom their mandates are derived.

4. *Modern organizational theory emphasizes the internal diversity of organizations and the presence in every sizable organization of conflicting factions and inconsistent purposes.* This diversity has two important consequences for the regulatory process, as March and his collaborators have pointed out (March and Simon, 1958; Cyert and March, 1963; March, 1981). Organizational decisions—including *pari passu* the decisions that regulatory agencies make when they issue, interpret, or enforce regulations and the decisions that regulated organizations make when they obey, partially obey, resist, or evade regulations—are the result of political processes within each organization whereby shifting coalitions struggle for ascendancy and arrive at various compromises and bargains. The classic demonstration of this point is Allison's (1971) demonstration that neither the United States nor the Soviet Union was able to achieve effective coordination of its bureaucratic components during the Cuban missile crisis and that those agencies in turn were unable to suppress conflict among their internal factions in order to carry out coherent policies. Even in the confrontation of two great powers at the brink of nuclear war, many of the actions taken on each side had an acciden-

tal and unintended character. Under less extreme conditions, there is apt to be even less coordination of parts and pieces in the organizational machinery; it is not at all uncommon for one set of agents in a regulatory agency to pursue goals different from their colleagues' (Alfred, 1975; DiLeonardi, 1980) or for an agency to promulgate regulations inconsistent with its own policies in order to appease internal or external opponents of those policies (Attewell and Gerstein, 1979).

5. *The boundary coalition between representatives of potentially hostile organizations may provide the means of resolving conflicting regulations or may be an additional source of conflict.* A boundary coalition (Caplow, 1968) typically develops at the point of contact between two potentially hostile organizations that are in permanent contact with each other. The coalition of their respective representatives becomes a kind of shock-absorber managing and controlling the tension between the two organizations. From the standpoint of each representative the other organization appears to be divided into a faction of friends headed by the coalition partner and a faction of antagonists that includes most of the organization's top management. As most of each representative's contacts with the opposing organization are mediated through the partner, each tends over time to become increasingly dependent on the other, and both become increasingly isolated from their own organizations. When a boundary coalition occurs at the point of contact between a regulatory agency and a regulated organization, an idiosyncratic regulatory relationship can easily develop without any formal shift in regulatory policy (Weaver, 1980).

To summarize: problems of regulatory conflict have a common character derivable from the web of inter- and intra-organizational relationships in which the regulatory process occurs. These problems can best be understood by analyzing the shifting pattern of coalitions out of which regulatory conflict develops.

Six Small Studies

The first small study of regulatory conflict at the Institute for the Study of Social and Legal Change was undertaken by Steven Nock and the author in central Virginia in March and April 1980. Thirty-four knowledgeable persons in banking, human services, educational administration, and industrial management were interviewed. The interview consisted of two set questions, followed by extended conversation. The questions were:

1. Do you often run into conflicting government regulations?

2. Can you give me some specific examples of pairs of regulations
   that impose contradictory requirements on you such that you cannot conform to one without violating the other?

Of the thirty-four respondents, twenty-nine gave enthusiastic affirmative responses to question 1 and then, faced with question 2, were
unable to specify a currently active pair of conflicting regulations.

The criteria for a pair of conflicting regulations were fairly stringent. We rejected instances of conflicts between statutes, conflicts between the intent and the effect of a regulation, conflicts between the
regulatory purposes of one agency and another, and conflicts about
regulatory jurisdiction, as well as conflicting regulatory customs and
unwritten rules, limiting the scope of question 2 to written official
regulations that were unequivocally incompatible. The interviews
brought out a number of points about the respondents' perceptions
of conflicting regulations in situations in which they had not been
able to specify a pair of regulations that satisfied the criteria:

1. Regulations were often perceived to be in conflict when the policies and goals of two or more agencies regulating the same activity
   were divergent, despite adaptive steps taken by either the regulators or the regulated to make the regulations compatible.
2. Conflict was often perceived when the same activity was regulated
   by federal, state, and local agencies, even when an actual regulatory conflict had been avoided by an explicit rule about which
   jurisdiction prevailed in given circumstances.
3. Conflict between regulations was commonly perceived when the
   purposes of the underlying statutes seemed incompatible, as, for
   example, freedom of information and privacy statutes.

This primitive inquiry suggested a number of new questions. It
directed attention to the illusion of conflicting regulations, to the
conditions that favor its development, and to the organizational
functions—as yet unspecified—that the illusion may serve. It suggested a look at the mechanisms that avoid conflicting regulations in
the weak situation where agencies have divergent mandates and in
the strong situation where the empowering statutes are contradictory. It reminded us that the reaction of regulated institutions to the
regulatory process is not a simple matter of compliance or noncompliance but a complex, patterned activity that cannot be understood
without extensive description and analysis, and it suggested a further search for pairs of conflicting regulations, adaptive mechanisms
that prevent their occurrence, and reactions to them when they occur. Accordingly, we designed a second little study in which two in-

vestigators, using a standardized interview form, interviewed casual samples of persons responsible for regulatory compliance in several types of profit-making establishments subject to federal, state, and local regulations: banks, nursing homes, oil companies, commercial dairies, and trucking firms.

The second little study, perhaps because it utilized less stringent criteria, did discover some unmistakable pairs of conflicting regulations and provided additional insights about how the cross-purposes and divergent goals of multiple regulatory agencies are perceived as conflicting even when they have been reconciled procedurally.

Some respondents in the second little study named more than a dozen regulatory agencies by whom they were concurrently controlled. With respect to most of these agencies, the desirability of compliance with regulations is taken for granted and, in many instances, the regulatory process is welcomed. In each field, however, nearly every respondent identified one or two regulatory agencies whose requirements created difficulties for one of the following reasons:

1. New regulations have been issued that run counter to an established and recognized body of regulations: for example, in the banking industry, regulations based on the Community Reinvestment Act of 1978 seem to require banks to make real estate loans on questionable collateral in designated urban areas, and in old-age institutions a recent revision of state fire regulations made certain buildings unsuitable for the type of occupant for whom they were specifically designed under other recent regulations.

2. Some changes that are not based on new legislation, judicial decisions, or public policy occur in regulatory practice: bankers in the sample reported that the interest of state bank examiners had shifted from financial soundness to management quality, leaving them uncertain as to how to prepare for audits.

3. Established regulations have contradictory purposes: in the trucking industry a firm seeking a new route had to obtain a formal qualification by demonstrating its technical and financial ability to service the route appropriately, but the qualification, once awarded, was not subject to further review, did not require the maintenance of capability, and could be transferred or sold.

4. Regulations seem to invite cheating: certain state regulations require interstate truck drivers to report a nearly perfect match between the amount of fuel purchased in a state and the amount consumed on the highways of that state, a feat that can only be accomplished by falsifying records.

5. Compliance with some regulations is too costly to be feasible: a custodial institution with a total staff of three persons insisted that two additional full-time persons would be required for proper performance of the paperwork required of them by various regulatory agencies.

6. Regulations are sometimes misunderstood by regulatory agents. In one reported incident a commercial dairy was fined for not having fly screens installed in mid-winter by an inspector who misread a printed rule.

7. Regulations sometimes seem to be self-defeating: two of the bankers we interviewed maintained that the regulations promulgated under the Community Reinvestment Act have had the perverse effect of discouraging real estate loans to the poor.

Although each of the fields that we lightly probed seemed to offer abundant material, it began to seem too abundant. It therefore seemed preferable to proceed with the study of conflicting regulations in one field at a time. We elected to start with public elementary education because of the salience in that field of the several types of problems enumerated above, the social importance of the function performed by the public schools, the rapid growth of regulatory activity in recent years, and the sheer weight of current regulation there.

A third little study was accordingly designed and carried out. Two doctoral candidates, in sociology and education respectively, interviewed the superintendent of every school division within seventy-five miles of Charlottesville, together with as many of their aides as were conveniently available, using a standardized interview form that encouraged extensive response. The previous little studies having given us a general picture of how conflicts in regulatory processes are structured, this third study was able to focus directly on identification of areas of regulation that are perceived by school administrators to involve regulatory conflict. In response to the question, "Do you sometimes find that two regulatory agencies are at cross-purposes with each other?" all but one of the twenty-three superintendents interviewed answered affirmatively and most of them cited multiple examples. Over twenty-five examples of conflicting regulations were mentioned by two or more superintendents. They claimed to be subject to conflicting regulations about pupil attendance, compulsory immunization, tuition for nonresident students, health examinations for employees, bilingual education, individual education plans, the placement of handicapped pupils, paying for pupils in special schools, grievance procedures, termination of teacher contracts, competency testing, OSHA safety codes, fire regulations, supervision of CETA personnel, the content of employee applications, mandated vocational education, special education, free and reduced-price lunches, free textbooks for children of welfare families, budget cycles, pupil-teacher ratios, and appeals from dismissal, among other matters.

In some instances the conflict of regulations may have been illusory but in other instances it was explicit and unmistakable. Although the sample was small, it furnished us with clear examples of each of six types of conflict in the regulatory process:

1. Conflict between inconsistent regulations from a single agency:

I can give you one instance that came through just recently. It's with HEW in terms of statistical data on employees and prospective employees. Now, as far as I'm concerned it's not that difficult to get the data—how many blacks versus whites; how many females, males; as far as sex discrimination or racial discrimination of employees—persons who are already employed. But when you're trying to get this data on prospective employees, that's difficult because we have one regulation that says on your application you cannot ask race, national origin, sex, etc., to prevent race or sex discrimination, etc. Then, you're turned around by the same organization saying, "We want this information so that you can prove to us that you're not discriminating."

2. Conflict between the regulations of different agencies:

If you want to get into special categories, you run into problems with grant funds from various and sundry sources that come into conflict with local or state regulations whatever they happen to be. The type of thing I'm talking about there would be such as a CETA grant.

3. Conflict between the regulations of different levels of government:

Pursuant to § 22–274.26 of the Code of Virginia, which deals with privacy of student records, a school system can give student records to law enforcement officials. However, the regulations to the federal law dealing with student privacy, the Family Educational Rights and Privacy Act (Buckley Act), prohibits release to law enforcement officers. This puts the school system in a direct conflict. The Virginia Attorney General has ruled that records cannot be given in light of the two statutes, but the conflict in regulations still exists. In addition, the regulations to 94–142 speak to access to student records, further confusing the issue.

4. Conflict between inconsistent statutes:

Well, one thing that we're dealing with right now is this Chapter 10. It's a revision of the old code, Chapter 22. Chapter 22 has been revised and one point that is giving us a lot of concern right now is 22.1–4, "Appointment of Tie-breaker." The first way they confused this thing is that they changed the title of the old Trustee Electoral Board to the School Board Selection Commission. Now they left the question in everybody's mind, "Does that mean that we just change the title or does it mean that we have to change the title and have a whole new school board appointed?" They didn't clarify it. Then, we talk about this tie-breaker, and it reads in such broad terms that we don't know what it is and we're trying now to get an opinion from the Attorney General because the law says that it must be done before we have a School Board meeting.

5. Conflict between regulations and judicial rulings:

The Virginia Code 22–275.1 through 12 assigns the school superintendent the responsibility of enforcing compulsory attendance on students. Under the regulations, offenders are to be taken to court if necessary. However, the state criminal code has decriminalized this offense, and the Commonwealth of Virginia vs. Theo Giesy and Daniel Giesy. Now, as superintendent I am required to initiate court proceedings against violators of the Virginia Code, but the courts will not enforce this code now.

6. Conflict between regulations and the ideological premises of the regulated institution:

Well, for example, you're supposed to have the least restricted environment and yet the state will turn around and accredit all these proprietary schools for LD or emotionally disturbed or some such thing. Well, hell, that's the very antithesis of mainstreaming. . . . So you talk about conflict in regulations, I have about eight students outside the school system in LD, so I hired a LD teacher for a self-contained classroom. Now someone says you can't do it, I say, "We will do it. And then you people find the logic in sanctioning my sending the student out of the school division all the way to Richmond to the *most* restricted environment. At least here he can go outside and play with other children."

Another type of regulation that arouses wide resentment among school administrators is marginally related to the problems enumerated above. It involves programs mandated by federal or state agencies that impose substantial costs on local school systems without providing sufficient funds to cover them. Bilingual education, individual educational planning for the handicapped, mandated special education, and the CETA program were repeatedly mentioned as imposing cost without providing the necessary funds. The following comment is typical in tone:

We've had federal money projects—CETA; all these others. To start off with, they came and wanted to know if we can use these people; can you give these people a job; can you put them in your program? Well naturally, we are in a position where we will take any help we can get from whatever source it is; they'll go on for twelve months. Now this is federal money to start with but when they go off, the—School Board is liable for their unemployment compensation as long as they're eligible to draw it. We've come pretty close to losing more than we've gained on that one.

This thicket of regulations and regulatory intentions is, for the most part, of recent origin. Federal involvement in local public education was negligible prior to the mid-1960s. By 1980, every type of activity associated with local school systems, from the planning of cafeteria menus to the content of classroom teaching, was under active federal supervision. The speed of this movement and the super-imposition of a complete control structure on top of the existing structures of state and local control probably account for the extraordinary prevalence of conflicting regulations in the field of elementary education, but we do not yet have enough data to advance that explanation with confidence. About all that can safely be inferred from the findings of the third little study is that elementary education offers a rich field for the study of conflicting regulations.

When we saw the extent of the problem of conflicting regulations in elementary education, it seemed desirable to compare the position of the public elementary schools vis-à-vis regulatory agencies with the position of another type of organization for whom conflicting regulations are a much less serious problem. The second little study included a number of commercial bankers who reported conflicting regulations but were relatively unconcerned about them. Some had described the work of the regulatory agencies in their field with approbation. Accordingly, we undertook a fourth little study of regulation by multiple agencies as it affects commercial lenders. For convenience, the study was limited to retail automobile financing.

This investigation was carried out in central Virginia in January 1981. Two doctoral candidates interviewed one or more lending officers in each of eighteen lending institutions that make loans to consumers for the purchase of new automobiles and one or more of the people responsible for putting consumers in touch with credit sources in each of three automobile dealerships. The lending institutions included commercial banks, savings and loan associations, manufacturers' financial subsidiaries, independent loan companies, and credit unions.

Although all these firms are subject to multiple regulatory agencies and, in the case of the banks, to state and federal agencies with overlapping jurisdictions, there were very few complaints about conflicting regulations from these respondents and these few referred only to the complexity of the forms to be filled out in credit transactions. There appeared to be no substantive problems at all.

Each type of lender looks to a specialized agency on its own side of the regulatory fence for detailed instructions about how to comply with the whole body of regulations by which they are affected. They are given specific procedures to follow in their transactions in order to comply with all applicable regulations. The mediating organization is continuously available to resolve questions that arise in special cases and to provide supplementary procedures for them. The protection that lending institutions obtain from this arrangement is nearly perfect. Because all institutions of the same type follow the same detailed procedures, none has a problem of compliance with conflicting regulations unless all of them do, and then the responsibility for resolving the problem and satisfying the regulatory agencies remains with the mediating organization. Although lending institutions are individually audited and examined, the only questions ordinarily raised by examiners have to do with whether the standard procedures have been appropriately followed in particular transactions. Lending officers do not have to be familiar with the statutes that empower the regulatory agencies or even with the language of the regulations, so long as they are meticulous about procedures.

The device of a mediating organization as a way of protecting financial institutions from regulatory cross-pressures seems to have been invented independently for each type of lending firm, and the mediating organizations take quite different forms. For automobile dealers and the local offices of loan companies, the mediating organization is the legal department at corporate headquarters. For commercial banks in Virginia, it is a section of the state's banking department. For savings and loans associations and credit unions, the mediating function is performed by their respective trade associations.

It is tempting to ask why elementary schools, hospitals, trucking companies, and other public and private institutions subject to conflicting regulations have not imitated the example of the lending firms and developed buffer organizations of their own. The answer seems to be that they have repeatedly tried to do so but have not succeeded. For example, superintendents' associations in elementary education and trade associations in the trucking industry have tried to act as mediators. The problem appears to be that regulated activities in other areas cannot as readily be reduced to standard procedure as can the writing of automobile loans, a relatively simple activity in which every transaction closely resembles every other. What elementary schools and trucking firms do is much less readily standardized. Indeed, there are other operations in commercial banks, such as making capital loans to real estate developers, that are less readily standardized, and with respect to these activities banks do report conflicting regulations as a problem.

The fifth little study was carried out in New Zealand by the author in March 1981. The managing directors or partners of nineteen varied enterprises, assembled at the University of Waikato for a management seminar, were interrogated about their experience with conflicting regulations. Some interesting contrasts with American experience were apparent.

New Zealand differs from the United States in several ways. New Zealand has only two levels of government, national and local, that exercise regulatory power; it is much smaller; it has only one rather small ethnic minority (Maori); and the relationship between organized labor and management is more hostile in New Zealand. Regulation has a longer tradition in New Zealand than in the United States. Sometimes characterized as the world's first welfare state, New Zealand regulated factory safety, minimum wages, job discrimination, environmental pollution, and consumer credit decades before these were subject to federal regulation in the United States.

In some areas, such as import-export and currency controls, the sphere of regulation is much wider in New Zealand than in the United States. The budget of the national government accounts for about half of the GNP, and the tax on individual and corporate incomes is correspondingly high. The largest corporation in New Zealand has only about 16,000 employees, so public authority appears more formidable to private companies than it does in some other advanced industrial countries with mixed economies.

The New Zealand managers who were interviewed about conflicting regulations were puzzled by the concept but seemed to agree that if such a problem arose, the government agencies involved would work out a resolution as soon as the problem came to their attention. The managers took for granted that it would be done. Although their responses told very little about the resolution of conflicting regulations, they were revealing with respect to the relationship that prevails between regulatory agencies and regulated institutions in that country and the very different attitudes of the participants in the regulatory process from that of their American counterparts. None of the New Zealand managers, when describing the regulatory process, questioned the legitimacy of any regulation or the common sense and good will of any regulatory official. There are many policy differences between regulatory agencies and the entities they regulate, but the attitudes of the parties to the regulatory process in New Zealand are much more cooperative. In the United States the managers of regulated institutions, both private and public, frequently resent and despise regulatory officials, and the latter often reciprocate with open hostility toward the institutions they regulate. The New Zealand experience and related evidence from Japan, West Germany, and other highly industrialized countries (Badaracco, 1981) suggest that an adversarial relationship between regulators and regulated may not be an inevitable concomitant of the modern state, as we tend to assume. It may instead reflect some real and curable defects in the American regulatory structure.

The sixth little study of conflicting regulations was carried out by the Comptroller General and reported to the U.S. Congress in June 1981. Fifty of the nation's largest firms were asked to provide specific examples of regulatory conflict and overlap that had affected them adversely. The forty-two companies that responded to the inquiry provided seventy-eight examples of regulatory conflict and overlap, most frequently singling out the Equal Employment Opportunity Commission, the Environmental Protection Agency, the Food and Drug Administration, and the Occupational Safety and Health Administration. Fifty-two of the seventy-eight complaints involved one or more of these four agencies. For each of the fifty-two examples involving EEOC, EPA, FDA, or OSHA, the agencies were first invited to respond, justifying their actions, and the complaining companies were then given a further opportunity to comment. In a few instances this exchange clarified a misunderstanding, but more often than not it took the form of a self-justification by the agency on technical grounds and a rebuttal by the complaining company challenging the agency's facts.

Among the seventy-eight complaints of conflict and overlap were three cases of alleged inconsistent enforcement, with differing interpretations of the same rule made by different departments or inspectors of a single agency. The seventy-five other complaints fell into three categories: interacting requirements, overlapping jurisdictions, and duplicate enforcement.

In the twenty examples of interacting requirements, compliance with the regulations of one agency brought a company under the jurisdiction of, and usually into noncompliance with, the rules of another. The situation most commonly reported was that a company's effort to comply with the Department of Energy's requirement to switch large boilers from petroleum to alternative energy sources created a problem of compliance with the clean air standards of the Environmental Protection Agency.

Fourteen of the fifty-two examples reflected overlapping jurisdictions between two or more federal agencies or between federal and state agencies. For example, no fewer than four federal agencies seem to have authority for classifying and labeling flammable materials, and some state agencies have that authority as well. The complaints in this area have mostly to do with the difficulty or impossibility of meeting inconsistent requirements.

Eighteen of the fifty-two examples had to do with duplicate enforcement where two or more agencies have responsibilities for investigating complaints, issuing permits, making inspections, imposing penalties, and prescribing corrective measures. In a number of the examples given, the final disposition of a case by one regulatory agency did not prevent another agency from taking up the case again on the same facts and imposing a different requirement. This problem is often reported with respect to discrimination complaints, which can be addressed to several different agencies at each level of government.

The report of the study submitted to Congress recommended more effort by OMB and the regulatory agencies to assess the effects of interacting requirements, to identify conflicting regulations and overlapping jurisdiction, to recommend changes in regulatory legislation in order to remove sources of conflict and overlap, to review parallel rules concurrently, and to increase state and local participation in regulatory coordination. It is still too early to say whether these recommendations, the principal thrust of which is to assign the responsibility for removing conflicting regulations to the Director of the Office of Management and Budget, will have any significant effect on the problems discovered by the study.

The Direction of Further Research

What did we learn from the six little studies? Needless to say, all of them, including the GAO study, were preliminary explorations of a problem that deserves and will undoubtedly get further attention. Because the problem of conflicting regulations does not seem to have been systematically examined by anyone before 1980, the six little studies cast a fair amount of light on the terrain without, of course, providing a clear picture of it. The main conclusions to be derived from them are as follows:

1. The problem of conflicting regulations is relatively recent in the United States. Although isolated instances certainly occurred before 1964, the appearance of a pattern of regulatory conflict is associated with the expansion of federal regulatory activity that was initiated by the Johnson Administration in the mid-1960s

and continued through 1980. This expansion was checked by the Reagan Administration as a matter of policy. Some proposals for the curtailment of regulatory activities have been initiated—as, indeed, some were by the Carter Administration—but it is impossible to say at the present time whether federal regulation of business firms, educational institutions, health care institutions, transportation, and local public agencies can or will be undone. It seems unlikely. In any event, the federal regulatory expansion of the 1970s accounts directly for most of the regulatory conflicts discovered so far. These conflicts typically take the following forms: the encroachment of federal agencies upon fields that were already closely regulated by state and local authorities; the competition of new or newly enlarged federal agencies for jurisdictional territory; and the collision of regulatory agencies pursuing contradictory mandates, either on their own or to implement legislation enacted to achieve somewhat divergent goals.

2. Conflicting regulations are a serious problem in some fields of regulated activity and a trivial problem in others. We do not yet have anything like the complete picture, but elementary education and commercial banking seem to represent the two extremes. In elementary education many administrators spend nearly all their time and energy trying to cope with conflicting regulations, to the detriment of routine administration and the morale of their staffs. In commercial banking conflicting regulations constitute a minor procedural problem that is satisfactorily handled by designated specialists. Manufacturing establishments fall somewhere in between. For most of them conflicting regulations are intermittent annoyances that do not seriously interfere with normal operations, but in some industries they are a major grievance. We are not able to explain these variations or to say whether they are mainly attributable to differences in the regulated activities or in the purposes of the regulators.

3. We began this study with a view of regulatory conflict as a sociological phenomenon arising naturally out of the interaction of bureaucratic programs with different purposes and perspectives. What we initially wanted to find out was how regulated enterprises resolved the dilemmas created for them by conflicting regulations. This issue remains but now seems relatively unimportant compared to the political implications of regulatory conflict. In fields where regulatory agencies are politically compatible with each other and with the organizations they regulate, as in commercial banking, regulatory conflicts are relatively rare, gen-

erally take the form of overlapping jurisdictions, and can usually be resolved by a procedural rule worked out by the agencies in consultation with the regulated organizations. These easy solutions are impossible when the regulatory agencies have a standing antagonism, as in the case of the Environmental Protection Agency and the Department of Energy, or have an adversary relationship with the firms or institutions they regulate, as in the case of the Food and Drug Administration and the pharmaceutical industry. The American tradition of pluralism invites us to accept chronic feuds as normal. Foreign experience and the grievances expressed by school superintendents and manufacturers in two of our studies suggest that it ought to be regarded as pathological.

4. It is difficult to determine which set of antagonisms has the more deleterious consequences: between regulators with incompatible mandates, or between regulators and regulated. Both kinds of antagonisms are intertwined and mutually reinforcing. The perception, held today by many corporate managers and, with somewhat different nuances, by many educational administrators, of central government as irrational, clumsy, and malicious has been largely developed by exposure to the contradictory directives of various regulatory agencies and to the inconsistent priorities they reflect. Similarly, the open hostility of some regulatory officials toward the people whose activities they regulate reflects their own perception of themselves as fighting a crusade against social evils— discrimination, pollution, fraudulent advertising—without much public support and against the active resistance of organizations engaged in socially undesirable practices. This is not a wholesome condition. The incoherence of the total regulatory pattern and the adversary relationship between some regulatory agencies and their clients have undoubtedly played some part in the relative decline of per capita productivity in United States industry (from first in the world to ninth) from the mid-1960s to the early 1980s and in the questionable overall performance of the public schools during the same period. Faulty regulation is surely not the sole cause of these ills, but it must be admitted as a contributing factor.

5. Foreign experience suggests that it is possible for a national government to maintain very tight regulatory control over private firms and local institutions without an adversary relationship, provided that each side acknowledges the legitimacy and essential good will of the other side, that regulatory activity is backed by the majority of citizens, and that regulators are invested with an

aura of legality and fair play. The recent expansion of federal regulatory activity in the United States has not enjoyed any of these
advantages. As the several contributors to Wilson's (1980) admirable book show in detail for the major agencies involved in the new
regulation—FDA, OSHA, EPA, and OCR—the development of
their jurisdictions owes more to bureaucratic entrepreneurship
and legislative accident than to any substantial public support. No
public consensus has ever developed to sustain such dramatic new
policies as bilingual education, equal employment for the handicapped, pre-censorship of consumer advertising, or mandatory
installation of safety devices not yet developed. These measures,
which might be acceptable in other circumstances, are bound to
be interpreted as provocative when they do not express legislative
intent, when they do not enjoy much official backing outside the
agency that promulgates them, and when the promulgators are
perceived as ideological opponents by the people whose habits
they are trying to change. The situation is not helped by the tendency of Congress to enact new statutes empowering regulation
without examining possible consequences or by the inclination of
federal courts at all levels to rewrite regulations in the course of
reviewing regulatory disputes, without necessarily agreeing with
what other federal courts have decided in parallel cases.

6. While the six little studies enable us to speculate about the causes
and cures of regulatory conflict, their limited findings should not
be taken for a solid body of information, which we still lack. The
U.S. General Accounting Office (1981) study concluded that regulatory conflict was not a severe problem and did not impose a great
economic burden on manufacturers, although it did so in part by
excluding from its purview excessive regulation and failures in
the rule-making process. That finding is consistent with the
results of the first little Virginia study, which looked for and was
unable to find satisfactory examples of conflicting regulations. It
is not consistent with the findings of the study of school superintendents or with published research on regulation of certain industries, such as air transportation and pharmaceuticals, that are
particularly exposed to regulation (Olson and Trapani, 1981;
Schwartzman, 1976). Even if it were ultimately confirmed that
flatly conflicting regulations are rare in American regulatory
practice and that such conflicts are usually resolved by a procedural rule soon after they are detected, the widespread perception of regulatory conflict among competing agencies and levels
of government would still be correct. The adversary relationship
between regulators and regulated that has developed with the
expansion of federal jurisdiction and the climate of distrust that

envelops numerous regulatory processes are surely not acceptable as permanent conditions. Whether the solution should be sought in a general retrenchment of regulatory activity, improved rule-making procedures, or safeguards against the imposition of regulatory policies that have not achieved majority support is a question that deserves more consideration than it has so far received.

The following specific questions need particularly to be addressed in a broad range of regulatory situations:

1. What interorganizational configurations are conducive to the development of regulatory conflict? What configurations prevent such development?

2. By what processes are conflicting regulations or regulatory purposes resolved at the political level? At the administrative level? At the operating level of regulated institutions? How are these related in practice?

3. In what ways does regulatory conflict diminish the effectiveness of the regulatory process—for example, by providing formal justification for noncompliance, by decreasing the visibility of regulated activities, or by generating political pressure for deregulation?

4. In what ways does regulatory conflict contribute to the effectiveness of the regulatory process—for example, by providing alternate standards of institutional performance or by increasing administrative accountability? In what situations, if any, is it advantageous from the standpoint of public benefit to maintain ambiguity in regulatory standards?

5. Who takes the initiative in the resolution of regulatory conflict or in the development of accommodative strategies when conflicts are irresolvable? How do the initiatives taken by regulatory agencies to resolve conflict compare with those taken by regulated institutions? What is the role of outside organizations, especially courts and legislatures, in the resolution of regulatory conflict? What part is played by buffer organizations representing the regulated institutions?

6. To what extent do conflicting regulations impair the performance of regulated institutions? Can such effects be detected and measured at the administrative level of regulated institutions? At the operating level? Are they short-term or persistent?

7. To the extent that regulatory conflict is unintended and unwanted, what innovations in rule-making procedures or enforcement practices of regulatory agencies might reduce its incidence?

The widespread concern about conflicting regulations is a symptom of the same crisis in the relationship between the federal government and the people it represents that led to the election of the Reagan Administration on a platform of opposition to the continued expansion of federal services and federal powers. But bureaucratic contraction seems to be much more difficult to accomplish than bureaucratic expansion, and deregulation seems seldom to be as easy as regulatory expansion. If these perceptions are correct, and certainly verifying and explaining them is an important task for future research, the problems reviewed in this paper are likely to persist unless and until fundamental reforms are introduced in federal rule-making and enforcement practices. Such reforms seem to require a body of knowledge about regulatory conflict that we do not yet possess. Much further research is required to discover how regulatory conflicts, real and perceived, develop in complex regulatory situations and how such conflicts are resolved or accommodated at various organizational levels.

COMMENT: *W. Richard Scott*

The leitmotiv of this commentary is that in order to fully understand regulatory processes, their determinants and consequences, we need to recognize that the principal actors involved—both regulators and regulatees—are predominantly organizations. I believe that by attending to the organizational aspects of regulatory activity we will be better able to account for some of the complexity, conflict, and apparent failures of regulatory attempts.

I begin by commenting briefly on Caplow's chapter, attempting to note its strengths and limitations. The remainder of my comments are organized into three clusters. The first focuses attention on the regulatory agencies and stresses the value of viewing regulatory policies as organizational outputs. The second shifts attention to the subject of regulatory policy and argues the utility of viewing the reactions of regulatees in terms of organizational processes. The third set of comments again shifts focus, this time to concentrate on the interorganizational structure of connections linking the regulators and the regulated.

First, some comments are in order on Caplow's research style. In general, I believe that an approach that relies on a series of loosely related, small-scale studies has much to recommend it. It can permit a rapid sifting and sharpening of the research issues as we apply what we learn from one study in designing the next. All too often in scientific research we find ourselves trapped for too long in collecting and analyzing data generated by faulty designs or in addressing questions we have come to view as irrelevant or off the mark. Interrelated, small-scale, exploratory research ventures allow incremental learning and seem to be particularly well suited to the mapping of new research terrain—or old terrain with new conceptual equipment. Moreover, this approach may well become the research paradigm of the 1980s as we confront the prospect of reduced research support and the challenge of learning how to conduct useful research with meager resources.

While I like this research approach in principle, I have serious reservations about Caplow's use of it in his five studies. (I leave aside the GAO study.) There is too little consistency in definitions or interests across these studies, with the consequence that interesting ideas from study one—e.g., the effects on organizations of perceived regulatory conflict—are not pursued in succeeding studies. The result is a disappointing lack of developed ideas or cumulative findings. Indeed, I would argue that the principal findings from Caplow's five studies are:

1. The extent of regulatory conflict reported by respondents is a function of the strictness with which conflict is defined.

2. The level of regulatory conflict varies (a) across types of organizations and (b) across societies.

3. The level of perceived conflict is a function of the presence of mediating organizations.

These generalizations strike me as a meager return from five studies.

In the first, theoretical section of his paper Caplow introduces and pursues a large number of issues. The major concept introduced involves coalitions evolving among linked triads of organizations. This perspective seems to be stimulated primarily by Caplow's review of the regulatory and organizational literature rather than by his own exploratory studies. The concept of organizational coalitions is surely relevant to the regulatory arena, but the axioms presented are not very illuminating. Caplow correctly notes that many crucial triads have been identified in regulatory studies and observes that the patterns vary importantly among sectors, but he provides no help in explaining or predicting such differences. Indeed, it is not even clear why the triad is the relevant unit in attempting to account for or map regulatory linkages.

The first half of Caplow's paper is largely devoted to a discussion of selected organizational processes and problems relevant to regulatory conflicts. Because this is my own principal concern, the remainder of my commentary is devoted to explicating these ideas.

Regulation as Organizational Output

A central question raised by Caplow's paper is: Why do some regulations conflict? Although the question is not directly addressed by any of the studies, his paper implies that the problem is fundamentally one of inconsistent legislative goals and/or the movement of new federal agencies into arenas already occupied by state and local regulators. Both factors are no doubt important, but others of a more strictly organizational nature should not be overlooked.

Consider first the case of a single agency. As early as 1958 March and Simon proposed that organizational participants representing multiple interests are unlikely to share common objectives. Hence, decisions within organizations frequently emerge out of bargaining processes among shifting coalitions. (See also Cyert and March, 1963.) The recognition that organizations may exhibit internal conflict over preferences allows us to account for much conflict among decisions within a single agency without positing irrational actors or pernicious decision processes. This view merely assumes an organization of several rational actors, rather than one, as March (1981) has noted. Conflicts may also arise in the presence of common preferences but divergent perceptions or varying assumptions about cause/effect relations (Thompson, 1967).

Early views presumed that if conflicting goals could not be resolved by negotiation, they could be managed by sequential attention first to one, then another, objective (Cyert and March, 1963). More recent perspectives, however, allow for the possibility that conflicting goals or activities may be simultaneously pursued by actors within a single agency, due to the loose coupling of organizational units (Weick, 1976) and the presence of organizational slack (Cyert and March, 1963; March, 1981).

Such developments are especially likely to occur when the area is controversial and the regulatory agency is vulnerable. For example, Attewell and Gerstein (1979) describe how the Food and Drug Administration, the agency responsible for the administration of methadone maintenance programs, incorporated many of the objections of other agencies, such as the Bureau of Narcotics and Dangerous Drugs, into its own policies and protocols. Attewell and Gerstein

(1979, p. 326) adduce some reasons for such compromises:

> The FDA, attempting to appease or coopt both friends and foes of methadone maintenance, allayed the criticism of foes via a hedge of restrictive regulations. This attempt by government policy regulations to appease all interested parties is quite general, especially in contentious areas. It is frequently a prerequisite for obtaining the necessary broad political support required for the passage of enabling legislation, and also stems from the policy bureaucracy's desire to minimize conflict and opposition to its plans. In most cases this kind of policy-making behavior leads mainly to an excess of regulation and lack of flexibility. At its worst, it results in quite incompatible demands being included in policy and placed upon local implementating agencies.

It is only a small step from this situation, in which a single agency exercises jurisdiction over some policy domain but takes into account the often legitimate and always pressing concerns of other interested groups, to one in which multiple agencies share jurisdiction. Allison (1971, p. 67) has admirably explicated the multiple-agency condition in his organizational-process model of decision making. In Allison's Model II:

> A government consists of a conglomerate of semi-feudal, loosely allied organizations, each with a substantial life of its own. . . . [E]ach organization attends to a special set of problems and acts in quasi-independence on these problems. But few important issues fall exclusively within the domain of a single organization. Thus government behavior relevant to any important problem reflects the independent output of several organizations partially coordinated by government leaders.

Under such conditions—and they are expected to be widespread in a complex, federalist, democratic state emphasizing checks and balances—it does not seem difficult to account for the development of conflicting regulations.

Caplow's studies not only document the presence of conflicting regulations, they also call attention to the substantial variation across sectors or arenas in extent of regulatory activity. In my brief comments I can do no more than sketch some plausible organizational bases of such variation that merit more attention than they have received to date.

Several analysts, including Caplow, have noted variance in regulatory policies associated with time of founding. Weaver (1978), for example, argues that regulatory agencies established prior to the 1940s are quite different in structure, program, and supporting constituencies from agencies developed in the past three decades. The older agencies are more likely to be industry-specific, supportive in orientation toward client organizations, guided by general legislative mandates, and responsive to interests of business and congressional committees. The newer agencies are more likely to relate to multiple industries, to be adversarial in orientation, to have specific and detailed statutory guidelines, and to be responsive to public interest groups and the courts. Such contrasts may not be true in all particulars, but they suggest the value of an organizational-cohort view that assumes that organizations are profoundly shaped by the conditions present at the time of their founding. Indeed, Stinchcombe (1965) proposes that organizational forms are permanently imprinted, carrying through their life-span characteristics developed in their formative period.

Another possible explanation of variation is that agencies are in differing stages of an organizational lifecycle. Bernstein (1955) has already profitably applied the lifecycle concept to regulatory agencies. Such efforts will not only contribute to but should benefit from recent work on this topic by organization theorists (Kaufman, 1975; Kimberly, Miles, et al., 1980).

Regulatory agencies differ not only in the number and variety of types participating in the formulation of policy, as already noted, but also in the structures involved in policy implementation (McLanahan, 1980). Some agencies, for example, have their own inspection and enforcement machinery, while others must rely on the cooperation of separate, quasi-independent agencies (Downs, 1967).

Finally, as Caplow and others have pointed out, the nature of the structures and processes present in regulatory agencies may be expected to vary by policy sector (Wildavsky, 1979). In the final section I will have some general comments to make on this important source of variance.

Response to Regulation as Organization Process

Under what conditions will an organization comply with the requirements of a regulatory agency? In theory, a host of conditions must be met if an organization is to comply with a regulation demanding some change in its behavior, e.g.:

1. The organization must be aware of the demand.
2. The organization must interpret the demand correctly (that is, consistently with the intent of the regulator).
3. The organization must have control over the relevant actors and their behaviors.

4. The regulators must be in a position to observe compliance with their demands.

5. The regulators must be willing and able to sanction the organization for noncompliance and the sanctions involved must be sufficient to induce conformity.

Such a list might easily be extended (Pfeffer and Salancik, 1978).

Each of these conditions is problematic. Whether an organization is even aware of a regulation is as much a function of the organization's information-processing and attention structure as of the characteristics of the signals it receives from its environment (March and Olsen, 1976; Sproull, 1981). And awareness does not guarantee accurate interpretation of external demands. Johnson's (1979, p. 34) research on the response of administrative organizations to judicial decisions supports his expectation that such decisions "would be interpreted so as to require minimal change within the organization." Considered together, organization awareness and interpretation are aspects of a more general process labeled *enactment:* the view that organizations cognitively construe the environments to which they respond by selective attention and interpretation (Weick, 1979).

Whether the explanation given is one of authority leakage, loose-coupling, or the power of lower participants, students of organizations are increasingly recognizing that the capacity of organizations to control the behavior of their participants is severely limited (Downs, 1967; Weick, 1976; Prottas, 1978). Not surprisingly, the ability of external systems to exercise control or detect noncompliance is even more limited. Stone (1975) has compiled a convincing and sobering catalog of the limitations of legal actions and sanctions aimed at correcting corporate misbehavior. Summing all requirements—from attention to correction—there is little reason to be sanguine about the likelihood of organizational compliance with regulatory efforts.

Moreover, the dependent variables of interest must be organizational behaviors viewed as a plural, not a singular, noun. It is important to recognize the variety of perceptions and practices associated with varying locations in an organizational structure, as well as the likelihood that higher-level officers will perceive and respond to regulations differently from lower officials (Davis et al., 1977; Sproull, 1981). Loose-coupling is not only a horizontal but a vertical phenomenon in organizations. It means that the actual behavior of organizational performers exhibits decoupling from formal descriptions of behavior and even from structural changes intended to signal the presence of behavioral changes (Meyer and Rowan, 1977; M. Meyer, 1979; Weatherley and Lipsky, 1977).

Interorganizational Linkages among
Regulators and Regulated

Caplow observes that regulatory activity varies from one policy arena to another, not just in time of origin, extent of development, and degree of contradiction or conflict, but also in the development of mediating organizations. My colleague, John Meyer (Meyer, 1983; Scott and Meyer, 1983), and I argue that current theoretical models stressing relations among organizations—e.g., Evan's (1966) organization-set model or Warren's (1967) interorganizational-field model—place primary emphasis on horizontal relations among interdependent organizations. Such exchange and competitive relations are clearly important but have caused us to neglect vertical connections of super- and subordination among organizations: connections that increasingly stretch from the national to the local level. Organizations are increasingly linked into these vertical systems, and the vertical ties have become increasingly central to the functioning of organizations.

The vertical connections vary in many ways from one type of organizational system (or institutional sector) to another. John Meyer (1983) has suggested that one of the principal bases of divergence is the locus of authority: at what level in the system does legitimate decisionmaking occur, and what is the domain of this decisionmaking? To illustrate, Meyer argues that education within the United States is characterized by fragmented centralization. Although financing of education is increasingly centralized, federal officials lack programmatic authority over educational decisions. They lack authority to determine what is to be taught by what types of teachers to which students and what educational standards are to govern the process. The authority they do have is legitimated by reference to a set of special purposes—most commonly, the reduction of inequalities (Kirp, 1976). The upshot is that many limited special programs emerge, each with its own purposes, budgets, and control systems and with no basis for integration into a unified and consistent structure.

The specific combination of centralized appropriations and decentralized substantive authority gives rise to particular modes of interlevel control: the burgeoning of accounting or statistical controls, and the substitution of procedural, technical, and budgetary rules for substantive policies. Rather than a unified hierarchical system connecting central federal agencies through regional and state offices to local service units, we have multiple linkages among organizations at differing levels, some linking federal and state offices with the latter exercising discretion over the allocation of funds to local districts, others connecting federal and local units with state offices serving as intermediaries, and still others connecting federal and local agencies and bypassing intermediate units. Organization theory predicts that organizations will map the complexity of their task environments into their own structures. Thus, we would expect school districts that deal with these fragmented and varied programs to become highly differentiated and laden with comparable categories of participants: accountants, bookkeepers, filing clerks, and computer technicians. Empirical studies suggest that this is indeed the case (Bankston, 1982).

Caplow is correct in stressing the value of buffering units in this connection; however, in my opinion, his discussion of the situation in education is misleading. Schools do have units that mediate between them and their regulatory environments: these units are called school districts. Caplow's informants were superintendents. Since they directly confront the fragmented regulatory systems, we expect their reports of conflicts and confusion. We would expect a somewhat less chaotic description of the regulatory arena from principals, because of the buffering services performed by district officers.

A better example of a type of organization directly confronting an active regulatory environment in the absence of mediating structures is provided by the hospital (Scott, 1982). Although hospital administrators obtain some assistance from their state and national professional associations, their organizations must deal directly with an incredibly large assortment of uncoordinated federal, state, and local agencies (Somers, 1969; Kinzer, 1977). There seems little doubt that this fact is connected with the rapid growth in multi-hospital chains and systems (Brown and Lewis, 1976).

These few observations must suffice to suggest a much larger set that begins to take seriously the task of describing the manifold types of vertical connections linking organizations and of pursuing their implications for the structure and function of organizations. To my mind, this is one of the most challenging tasks confronting students of organizations, and it is the task that will most effectively link our efforts with the interests of those who seek to understand regulatory policy and its effects—both intended and unintended.

10

Self-Regulation as Market Maintenance

An Organization Perspective

Mitchel Y. Abolafia

American history and social thought reveal a fairly consistent skepticism concerning self-government in industry. With the exceptions of wartime expediency and the short-lived National Industrial Recovery Act (1933–1935), industry's efforts at cooperative self-regulation have been restricted by antitrust laws. These restrictions, however, are largely confined to explicit control of production and price. Recognizing the economic benefits of other forms of cooperation, the courts have established a rule of reason within which many aspects of self-regulation are considered legitimate. The organizational structure for this cooperation is found in the industrial councils, boards, and trade associations that are the focus of this chapter.[1]

I am indebted to Patricia Knadler for her research assistance. I also wish to thank Paul Griffin, Gary Hamilton, Roger Noll, Charles Perrow, John Sutton, and an anonymous reviewer for their helpful comments. This study was financed in part by a Faculty Research Grant, University of California, Davis.

1. This chapter is explicitly about industry and market self-regulation. It does not deal with self-regulation by individual firms in the sense of the self-control that advertisers or chemical firms might show in not producing potentially offensive or dangerous products. It also does not deal with self-regulation in the sense of industry dominance of federal departments (McConnell, 1966). Finally, I will only touch on the federations of trade associations known as peak associations, among which are the National Association Manufacturers (NAM) and the Chamber of Commerce, which coordinate networks of business organizations in pursuit of their political goals (Brady, 1943; Domhoff, 1970, 1978).

Much of the skepticism concerning self-regulation is based on the neoclassical belief that when collusion on price is precluded by law, self-regulation has little attraction for firms. Only the threat of government intervention could motivate firms to engage in the remaining legal forms of cooperative self-restraint. The underlying assumption is that regulation is the natural opponent of the market and that firms would not participate in any form of self-restraint if it were avoidable. But this assumption is at odds with the degree of voluntary organization in the market economy and with the history of self-regulation in particular. Although firms and their industry associations must often be coaxed, particularly in the area of consumer protection, self-regulatory structures predate much of government intervention and were often created as a response to market turbulence rather than threats from the state.

Self-regulation and market forces are not necessarily antithetical. In fact, actors in both competitive and oligopolistic markets have used self-regulation to reduce costs and to create more stable and predictable market relations. From this perspective self-regulation is an administrative system for reducing the uncertainty of competitive markets. Firms have organized associations since the early years of the industrial revolution, when increased competition and market volatility encouraged them to cooperate for their mutual benefit (Watkins, 1934; Chandler, 1977). For almost as long they have been organizing to obtain the benefits of regulation from the state (Kolko, 1965; Stigler, 1975). The aim of this chapter is to identify the market-maintaining function of self-regulation, some of the strategies enacted for this purpose, and the limitations of such strategic behavior from the perspective of public policy.

To understand the strategies and limits of self-regulation we must first clearly understand its traditional purposes. Firms participate in self-regulatory associations for the same basic reason that any organizations cooperate, i.e., to advance their own interests. Such cooperative arrangements require some degree of self-restraint (conformity) on the part of member firms. The incentive can be either anticompetitive collusion or the reduction of production and transaction costs. Through voluntary association, firms producing similar goods or services are able to share market information, set uniform standards, share the cost of product promotion, and pool resources for government lobbying. They may also develop norms and rules of commerce and establish arrangements for arbitration and conflict resolution (Bradley, 1965; Webster, 1971). Such cooperation to promote market stability may vary in formalization and degree of restraint from illegal cartels to informal local business groups, but it tends to derive from similar determinants.

314   MITCHEL Y. ABOLAFIA

The diversity of functions subsumed in the concept of self-regulation can be illustrated by two polar examples. One is the Association of Home Appliance Manufactures (AHAM). Founded in 1967 by firms making washers, dryers, refrigerators, and other large home appliances, AHAM pursues a wide range of self-regulatory activities (Hunt, 1975; Hemenway, 1975). Among these are the development of safety standards and product standards (performance dimensions), arbitration of consumer complaints, and certification of producers' claims for their products. These activities maintain and promote the appliance market by reducing the costs of production and the risks of competition, by increasing consumer confidence, and by making entry more difficult for new firms and foreign competitors with cheaper products. A complementary explanation for these activities is their value in deferring government intervention; although this was not the primary incentive for establishment, it has grown in importance in recent years (Hunt, 1975).

The second example is the cartel formed in the 1950s by the producers of heavy electrical equipment in the United States. For obvious reasons, this association had no name and performed only a limited range of functions, none of them public. As part of the cartel's regulatory function the members cooperated (conspired) to rig bids, fix prices, and divide markets in equipment valued at $1.75 billion in 1961 dollars. Among the largest of the cartel members were General Electric and Westinghouse, which together held 60 percent of the transformer market. The incentive to this cooperation was the chronic overcapacity of member firms, which had precipitated competitive pricing and produced low profits. Self-regulatory arrangements reduced competition and maintained an acceptable market share for all participants.

Both AHAM and the electric machinery cartel represent strategies of self-regulation. Of course, the cartel violated the Sherman Antitrust Act and its members were prosecuted. But the two industries shared a desire to enhance profits by organizing a mechanism of mutual restraint. In both cases firms wished to limit the areas in which they would compete. In the first case firms agreed not to compete over safety standards, product standards, and expenditures on information-gathering. In the second the restraint was over bids on contracts and prices that could be offered. The critical paradox of self-regulation is that a restraint of competition may be in the public interest if it reduces costs and maintains the competitive structure in the longer term. But it remains an empirical question whether the conflict between the public interest and the industry's interest can be resolved in the arena of self-regulation.

Commodity Futures: An Illustrative Case

At its extreme, self-regulation by industry takes the organizational form of a cartel. But whereas cartels are illegal and rare in the United States, the scope of *legal* self-regulation is extensive. Legal arrangements offering restraint in areas other than price and market share are best exemplified in the various professions, major league sports, and securities and commodity exchanges that have been given license by legislation and/or court decisions to regulate to a very large extent the relations of actors in the market. Self-regulation is also performed, but to a lesser extent, by the multitude of trade associations, which set standards and certify claims for nearly every product and service offered. In this study we will limit our attention to the strong form of self-regulation, in which rule-making and enforcement powers have the backing of the state.

One such case of strong self-regulation is offered by commodity futures exchanges. Exchange associations were first formed in the middle of the nineteenth century. Since that time a complex body of rules and regulations has been developed. Commodity exchanges regulate markets in which members buy and sell contracts. Members may trade for their own account or act as brokers for agents off the exchange who wish to make a transaction. Exchanges regulate the behavior of members by promulgating rules, monitoring behavior, and determining violations. At the exchanges, as in the other examples of strong self-regulation mentioned above, detection of a violation may result in fines, suspension, or expulsion.

Like most trade associations, the members of exchange associations elect a board of directors to supervise self-regulatory arrangements. The board is responsible for establishing the rules but often delegates other responsibilities to committees elected from among the members. Among these committees are Investigations and Audits, Business Conduct, Arbitration, and Market Reports. As the industry has increased in size, staff has been hired to gather statistics and market intelligence as well as information about possible rule violations. Applications for membership and sanctions for rule violations are still ultimately handled by the committees or the board. These organizational arrangements are similar to those in most self-regulatory associations and, in fact, have changed little since their creation.

Historical Context

The Chicago Board of Trade, the first and largest commodity futures exchange, was established in 1848 and inaugurated its self-regulatory structure in 1865. This was a period in which many industries established associations. The latter half of the nineteenth century in the United States saw the formation of the National Association of Cotton Manufacturers (1854), the predecessor to the American Iron and Steel Institute (1855), the U.S. Brewers Foundation (1862), the American Bankers Association (1876), and the American Paper and Pulp Association (1878), among others (Bradley, 1965; Lamb and Shields, 1971).

Most of the firms in these industries had been exposed to new and severe competition when the expansion of the railways removed the geographic barriers protecting their markets. As a result, they sought means to reduce the uncertainty of entry into new and distant markets. According to Watkins (1934) and Chandler (1977), it was the technological changes in transportation and communications that ended the unprecedented era of unrestrained commerce. "It was only after about a century and a half, from 1700 to 1850, of freebooting competition, of unrestrained and largely unregulated rivalry in trade that the common interests of enterprisers were again recognized and organization was achieved."[2] It was into this world of increasing competition and increasing cooperative arrangements that the Chicago Board of Trade was born.

The CBT was established with a heritage of rules of trade that had been developed by merchants at trade fairs since the eleventh century. The contracts and by-laws established in 1865 were extensions of regulations in the areas of contract terms, payment, inspection, and sampling developed at such fairs. What were really new were the formal hierarchical arrangements developed to maintain and enforce order in the market (Abolafia, 1981).

At its founding in 1848 the CBT was a loose association of local merchants for the general advancement of commerce. Among its first acts in that year were efforts to get the State of Illinois to improve the canal system and to pass legislation for a general system of banking (Taylor, 1917). Like most other forms of interorganizational cooperation, the CBT was founded for the purposes of information exchange and resource acquisition (Hirsch, 1972; Pfeffer and Salan-

2. Watkins (1934), p. 671. Polonyi (1944) makes the point that the market system did not endure unbridled competition for very long. His historic example is the British intervention in the labor market in the 1830s. The point is made again by Kolko (1965) in his discussion of the failure of the railroad cartel and the pressure brought by the railroads for government regulation. More recently, Hawley (1981) has shown how the absence of either public or private regulation in the Eurodollar market has led to precipitous overexpansion and increasing instability. The internationalization of various forms of currency and credit has left this market without state control and without any central (international) bank to regulate flows. The result is chaos and conflict between governments and transnational banks with competing interests. The self-regulation of the free market is proving too chaotic for anyone's interests.

cik, 1978). As the volume of trade increased in Chicago with the extension of the railroad, the association added the functions of standardization of contracts, establishment and enforcement of rules, and arbitration of disputes. By 1865 a structure of committees accompanied by a system of rules and by-laws was in place. This organizational rationalization complemented the rationalization of commodities trading accomplished by the formal adoption of the futures contract as the instrument of commerce on the CBT.

The futures contract evolved out of conditions developing in Chicago in the 1850s. As Chicago became a central Midwestern market, farmers and merchants began to arrange for delivery of a specified amount of grain at some future date. The first record of forward contracting in Chicago appeared on 31 March 1851 (Irwin, 1954). Such contracts were informal. Qualities were not standardized, terms of payment varied, and contracts were not interchangeable. By 1854 the CBT had standardized weights and in 1856 it had fixed grades (Hoffman, 1932). These new terms were quickly incorporated into forward contracts. It was not long before people with capital recognized the potential for profit in simply buying and selling these contracts for speculation. By the early 1860s standardized futures contracts were being bought and sold by farmers and merchants as well as by a growing pool of speculators at the Chicago Board of Trade. The unique character of these contracts is that they are contracts for later consummation, i.e., there is no exchange of title and only one or two percent of contracts ever result in delivery. Most are simply closed out before the consummation date by an equal and opposite transaction on the part of the trader. A trader who had bought 5,000 bushels of wheat would sell them rather than take delivery.

At almost the same time that the futures contract was developed, the CBT adopted its first rules to restrain behavior. In 1863 it adopted a rule providing for suspension of any member not complying with contract terms. By 1865 procedures for recovery from default, arbitration of disputes, and provision of a security deposit on all contracts (known as margin) had been developed. Since that time the Board of Trade and all the exchanges established thereafter have added to the mechanisms of restraint at their command. While use of these mechanisms has not been consistent, causing scandals and protests in the Populist and Progressive eras, it has always been sufficient to insure the survival of the institution.

The notion that some degree of restraint in the market may be desirable was tested in the Supreme Court, where it found support in the early part of this century. It was recognized that competition may

be enhanced by preventing unequal access to information or resources from distorting price determination. Trade associations
were found to provide such protection by their sharing of information.[3] One of the earliest and clearest statements of the principle was
given in *Chicago Board of Trade* v. *United States*. In this case the Supreme Court found that the CBT's call rule was a reasonable restraint of trade. The rule prohibited members from purchasing or
offering to purchase grain to arrive after the close of trading. The
rule was little different from a variety of others that restrained behavior in the markets. The Court found that the power of an association to restrain its members may be used for good or bad purposes.
Justice Brandeis, writing for the Court, made the point that all commercial actions contain some degree of constraint:

> Every agreement concerning trade, every regulation of trade, re-
> strains. To bind, to restrain, is of their very essence. The true test of
> legality is whether the restraint imposed is such as merely regulates
> and perhaps thereby promotes competition or whether it is such as
> may suppress or even destroy competition.[4]

In the next section we will examine how and when exchanges make
the strategic decision to restrain their members.

Strategies

Although much has been written about the antitrust implications (Stocking, 1954; Lamb and Shields, 1971; Webster, 1971) and
the economic bases (Hemenway, 1975; Hunt, 1975; Kudrle, 1975) of
self-regulation, little attention has been paid to the administration
and implementation of regulatory strategies. Yet it is in these strategies that we can best see the intentions of self-regulation. It is in the
action of the self-regulators, particularly in crisis, that we can discover the distribution of power in the associations and the limits of
cooperation. In the three cases presented below the limits of competition and cooperation are reached by members of three different
exchange associations. The organizational perspective developed
here examines how these limits get defined and the control mechanisms used to maintain the market.

As mentioned earlier, self-regulatory associations perform a
number of functions, e.g., public relations, government relations,
collection of statistics, development of uniform standards, and arbitration of conflicts. These functions reflect the strategic goals of the

3. *Maple Floor Manufacturers Association* v. *United States*, 268 U.S. 563 (1925).
4. *Chicago Board of Trade* v. *United States*, 246 U.S. 231 (1918).

associations. In the case of public and government relations, the objective may be legitimation or resource acquisition. In the case of statistics and standards it is likely to be cost reduction and avoidance of government intervention. By coordinating their efforts, firms are rewarded with the provision of expensive goods (lobbying, industry-wide statistics) and avoidance of some aspects of competition (standard sizes and design, knowledge of other firms' output and sales). Associations aim strategically to inhibit conflicts that might otherwise threaten general market stability. As Stocking and Watkins (1951, pp. 233–34) point out, all these activities may be considered innocent or even wholesome, but when taken together, they tend to constitute a restraint of trade:

> Standardization of products and of cost accounting methods, for example, may eliminate waste and lower costs, but it also helps insure uniform prices among trade rivals. Exchange of information on the credit of customers may help reduce bad debts, but it may also serve as a basis for boycotting "undesirable" customers. Statistical reporting on prices, output, sales, shipment, stocks, and the like, may aid producers in independently formulating sound price and production policies, but it may also afford a basis for a tacit understanding to stabilize prices and curtail output.

Commodity futures markets exhibit many of these goals. Among the formal functions of an exchange are:

Formalization of all contract terms.

Standardization of times and methods of trading.

Specification of required security deposit (margin).

Centralization of the release of price information.

Surveillance and restriction of market positions of traders.

Emergency power to limit or halt trading in any contract.

In the course of these activities, firms are controlled and coordinated in limited, specific areas of their behavior. It is a kind of voluntary mutual coercion by which firms agree to incur costs as long as their competitors do also. The motivation for this is the maintenance of conditions in the market that will help insure each firm's niche and the market's long-term integrity.

Students of regulation have shown strategies for the restraint of market-threatening competition to be often delegated to the economic regulatory agencies (Peltzman, 1965; Kolko, 1965; Stigler, 1975). The futures industry had no regulatory agencies to rely on back in 1865, so it created its own hierarchical arrangements based on the mutual dependency of its members. Like the Interstate Commerce Commission and the Civil Aeronautics Board, the boards of trade (exchanges) maintain the conditions that will support continued profits and the survival of firms already in the market.

For the majority of association members, the most desirable condition in the futures market is competition.[5] Ongoing competition attracts the commission-paying speculators from whom most members draw their income. Participants rarely want the market to be dominated by one or a few traders, for this creates an instability in which small traders are the most easily wiped out. Exchanges such as the CBT, therefore, act in the interests of the majority of their members when they prevent anticompetitive behavior.

Exchange members have chosen to self-regulate in order to keep trading competitive. The natural advantages of large traders must be restrained. Each actor uses the power at his or her command to get a favorable price. Large traders, with extensive market positions, can have a greater effect on price than can small traders. This is particularly true as the delivery date for contracts approaches and traders with large positions are able to withhold contracts from those seeking an offsetting trade. At this point the competition reaches its peak as aggressive traders push their advantage.

It is also at this point that market manipulations occur. Holders of contracts to buy may demand delivery on a short supply and exact an artificially high price. Holders of contracts to sell may aggressively flood the market with the commodity and bring the price down by

5. It is important to note that the terms *competition* and *conflict* are used here in the sociologist's rather than the economist's sense. *Competition* refers to mutually opposed efforts to secure some valued object. Thus, futures trading is competitive in the sense that two or more buyers (or sellers) seek the same limited number of bids (or offers). Futures trading is almost ideally competitive in that it occurs at open auctions on the floors of exchanges where all bids and offers are made. This behavioral definition of competition differs considerably from the formal economic definition. When the economist refers to a competitive market, he or she is likely to emphasize the large number of buyer and sellers, which insures that no single buyer or seller is able to influence the prices being established. Thus, the economist would emphasize the independent nature of each individual's actions. The sociologist looking at the same event is concerned with the behavioral rivalry involved in market relations and its implications for the distribution of economic rewards (Scherer, 1970). A second social process that will be central to this study is *conflict*, especially *market conflict*. Sociologists use the term to include situations in which two or more actors attempt to realize their opposed interests. Weber (1947) defines conflict as a relationship "insofar as action within it is oriented intentionally to carry out the actor's own will against the resistance of the other party or parties." This sort of situation arises in futures markets, particularly as the delivery date of a contract approaches, when a large portion of the contracts (bought or sold) is held by one or a few interests. Typically, these dominant interests will push their advantage by squeezing a more advantageous price out of those on the other side of the market who need an offsetting trade to close out their position. Conflict, then, is inherent when people use their bargaining power to establish price (Hieronymus, 1977).

delivering. In either case liquidation of outstanding contracts is not orderly, in that prices may rise or fall very sharply a few days before the contract closes. To a certain extent such competition occurs frequently as traders press their advantage based on the available supply of the underlying commodity. But, as the delivery date approaches and there are very few traders left, the competitors begin to address each other. The action shifts from competition over an object (price) to conflict between opponents over the limited number of contracts. On occasion the conflict results in the accusation that the market has been manipulated.

The implication is that at some point, to be determined retroactively in each situation by regulatory or self-regulatory authorities, aggressive trading becomes market-tampering. This involves a reaction to practices deemed unacceptable in terms of the interests of the members (or certain members). The free market is, then, really only free within the limits prescribed by members of the market. Parties to the competition are not free to reach their goal in *any* manner available. Although manipulations were fairly common in the early days of the exchanges, exchange rules and laws have since been established to inhibit them. But what are these restraints, when are they applied, and by whom are they initiated?

The answers to these questions are complex. Despite considerable effort by legal scholars no formal definition of *manipulation* has been established. Neither the Commodities Exchange Act, the Commodity Futures Trading Commission regulations, nor any exchange by-laws contain a definition. There are, however, several characteristics that the courts have associated with manipulation (Hieronymus, 1971). Manipulations are usually alleged to include: (1) a dominant or controlling position in either futures or deliverable supplies; (2) a distorted price; and (3) manipulative intent. Each of these characteristics is difficult to define. Their definitions are situation-specific, constructed by those who have been harmed or who feel threatened. Their application has been inconsistent and enforcement somewhat random.

In this section we will examine the self-regulation of manipulation. It is my position that manipulation is not an act per se but, rather, reflects a reactive decision about the degree of conflict that should be tolerated in the market. Whether manipulation has taken place cannot be predetermined: there is no fixed point for exchanges to identify beyond which all actions are manipulative.[6] Rather, the

6. Agricultural economists, notably Thomas Hieronymus and Roger Gray, generally argue that what is called *manipulation* is most often just extreme risk-taking. As Hieronymus (1977) has shown, deliverable supply, because of its expectational character, is not easily defined. If longs are squeezing shorts on the basis of a limited deliver-

definition is situationally determined according to whose interests are at stake and the amount of influence they can muster. It is for this reason that most accusations of manipulation are made after the fact, once the consequences of the struggle can be assessed by the interested parties.

Strategies for Conflict Resolution: A Typology

The line between competition and manipulation is clearly a matter of selective definition. Market members are reluctant to label any activity as manipulation. Exchange officials prefer the term *congestion*, which actually describes the situation when traders on one side of the market are unable to find traders on the other side to liquidate their contracts. This bypasses the critical issue of manipulative intent. It simply describes a conflict between the two sides of the market. In their role as regulators of the market, exchanges have an interest in resolving this conflict, because it may create short-term instability in trading. They have several strategies at hand for this purpose: containment, formal restraint, and cessation. In the following typology these strategies are classified from least to most severe, and examples of each are given.

Containment

By far the most common strategy of conflict resolution is containment. This refers to the situation in which an expiring contract, such as March wheat or December gold, is allowed to trade out under the watchful eye of exchange officials. Holders of dominant positions are cautioned to avoid any action that might be interpreted as manipulative, e.g., standing for delivery of more of a commodity than is available.

Under normal circumstances the market continuously resolves the question of how much will be bought and sold, by whom, and at what price. Under containment, the Board of Directors or a committee summons those holding dominant positions and tells them to maintain an orderly market. Traders will not be told exactly what they can and cannot do; rather, they will be encouraged to contain their activi-

---

able supply, they are taking the risk that more of the commodity can be certified or moved into position for delivery. Such risk-taking is part of competition, and it is not surprising that differences in expectations and attitudes toward risk often result in dominant positions at the end of a contract. Moreover, aggressive trading and manipulation have the same intent, i.e., profit. So where does one draw the line?

ties to their present position. The chairman of the Business Conduct Committee of the CBT recounted one such encouragement:

> The law allows you, and you have permission, to have 3 million bushels. This Exchange will not permit you to allow artificial prices to exist, in *our* best judgment. . . . I want your pledge that if people get *nervous* on one side of the market (being the opposite side), you are therefore, for orderly liquidation, to *make sure* these prices will never get out of control.[7]

In such a case the trader still has considerable discretion. He or she knows there are now limits. But the limits are loosely defined and it is up to the trader to estimate how much aggressive behavior will be tolerated. There is always the implied threat that more severe strategies of resolution can be invoked or that the individual's behavior might later be judged manipulative, resulting in the imposition of fines, suspension, or expulsion. Thus, containment is to some degree equivalent to the warnings given by regulatory agencies, but containment reveals the informal and clannish nature of self-regulation.

Case No. 1: March 1979 Wheat. The March 1979 wheat contract at the Chicago Board of Trade (CBT) presents a classic confrontation between buyers (longs) and sellers (shorts) in which the exchange made strategic use of its powers of containment. The basis of the conflict can be traced back to the small harvest of soft red winter wheat in the summer of 1978. This is the class of wheat that is most frequently and easily tendered for delivery though CBT contracts. Adding to the wheat shortage was a shortage of transportation facilities to move the wheat and of warehouse space in which to store it. Together, these factors represent the typical conditions for a squeeze, i.e., longs demand delivery on a large number of contracts when the deliverable supply is limited.

By September 1978, the CBT's Business Conduct Committee was aware of the shortage of deliverable wheat and ordered staff members in the Office of Investigations and Audits to watch the progress of the September contract. Table 1 shows the continuous surveillance that accompanies self-regulatory action at some futures markets. From this synopsis we can see that by 15 September the committee was already concerned enough about congestion in the expiring September contract to call in for discussion all traders with dominant

7. *Board of Trade v. Commodity Futures Trading Commission,* U.S.D.C. Northern Illinois, p. 81 (18 March 1979). Emphasis is my own. The subjectivity of the standard for artificial prices is signaled by the basis for evaluation: "if people get nervous."

long positions. By 18 September concern had centered on Leslie Rosenthal, who would be a major protagonist in the conflict over the next seven months.

Table 1   *Synopsis of Minutes of the Chicago Board of Trade's Business Conduct Committee Meetings (6 September 1978 – 15 March 1979)*

9/6/78	Committee reviewed September complex; requested Office of Investigations and Audits (OIA) to watch September wheat. Requested OIA to obtain cash and stock information on wheat and determined the makeup of plywood positions of houses discussed.
9/14/78	Committee directed that letters be sent to participants holding one million or more bushels in September wheat futures.
9/15/.78	Participants in September wheat appeared.
9/18/78	Donald Bidgood, Administrator of the OIA, advised committee of conversation with Leslie Rosenthal covering his futures position in September wheat. Committee requested OIA to monitor wheat.
10/2/78	Committe request OIA to obtain additional information and monitor December wheat.
10/16/78	Committee reviewed information concerning December wheat; requested OIA continue to monitor December wheat.
10/23/78	December wheat was discussed. Closer review of November contracts requested.
10/30/78	Reviewed December wheat situation; decision to continue to monitor.
11/20/78	Discussed December wheat contract; decision to continue to monitor.
11/27/78	Discussed December wheat; decision to monitor closely.
12/4/78	Requested letters be sent to participants holding one million contracts or more in December wheat. Also, decision to monitor closely. (Attached report detailing wheat supplies.)
12/7/78	Discussed December wheat; determined phone calls should be made to participants holding one million contracts or more in December wheat to inquire as to intentions.
12/11/78	Discussed December wheat; decision to continue to monitor. Meeting scheduled for 15 December 1978 to discuss the expiring contracts in wheat.
12/15/78	Leslie Rosenthal appeared and discussed the intentions of Rosenthal as it related to their December wheat house positions.

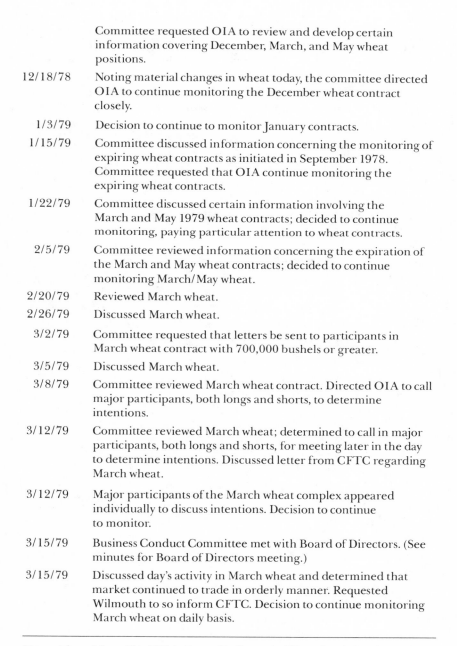

	Committee requested OIA to review and develop certain information covering December, March, and May wheat positions.
12/18/78	Noting material changes in wheat today, the committee directed OIA to continue monitoring the December wheat contract closely.
1/3/79	Decision to continue to monitor January contracts.
1/15/79	Committee discussed information concerning the monitoring of expiring wheat contracts as initiated in September 1978. Committee requested that OIA continue monitoring the expiring wheat contracts.
1/22/79	Committee discussed certain information involving the March and May 1979 wheat contracts; decided to continue monitoring, paying particular attention to wheat contracts.
2/5/79	Committee reviewed information concerning the expiration of the March and May wheat contracts; decided to continue monitoring March/May wheat.
2/20/79	Reviewed March wheat.
2/26/79	Discussed March wheat.
3/2/79	Committee requested that letters be sent to participants in March wheat contract with 700,000 bushels or greater.
3/5/79	Discussed March wheat.
3/8/79	Committee reviewed March wheat contract. Directed OIA to call major participants, both longs and shorts, to determine intentions.
3/12/79	Committee reviewed March wheat; determined to call in major participants, both longs and shorts, for meeting later in the day to determine intentions. Discussed letter from CFTC regarding March wheat.
3/12/79	Major participants of the March wheat complex appeared individually to discuss intentions. Decision to continue to monitor.
3/15/79	Business Conduct Committee met with Board of Directors. (See minutes for Board of Directors meeting.)
3/15/79	Discussed day's activity in March wheat and determined that market continued to trade in orderly manner. Requested Wilmouth to so inform CFTC. Decision to continue monitoring March wheat on daily basis.

NOTE: Adapted from *March Wheat Futures Trading on the Chicago Board of Trade,* Hearing before the Subcommittee on Conservation and Credit, 96th Congress, 28 March 1979, pp. 91–92.

In the December contract, the next expiring contract after September, the deliverable supply was even smaller. As the contract moved toward expiration the threat of manipulation increased. The committee again contacted the dominant longs. Rosenthal was once again summoned. After warnings from both the exchange and the Commodity Futures Trading Commission (CFTC), Rosenthal and a partner, Alan Freeman, continued to increase their position until they held 75 percent of the remaining long contracts with only two trading days left. One trader finally did liquidate his entire position on the last day. The other stood for delivery of 2.2 million bushels of wheat. During the last three days of trading the price of wheat rose more than 25 cents a bushel. The CFTC judged this to be uncommonly high in relation to wheat at other markets.

After the experience in December the March contract was watched closely. Letters of warning were sent to major participants early in the delivery month (March). Several days later these traders were phoned to ascertain their intentions in terms of liquidation or delivery. On 12 March, those holding major positions, both longs and shorts, were called before the Business Conduct Committee. At this point Rosenthal, Freeman, and two others held the vast majority of long positions. In later testimony the chairman of the committee described the meeting:

> These individuals gave me their verbal assurance that there would be an orderly liquidation. . . . They agree[d] to keep it an orderly situation, because of the basic cosmetics, that it looked bad, that three individuals or four individuals or a small number of individuals can create a lot of bad looking things, so that they must have utmost responsibility to the marketplace and to the people on the other side of the market. Those people cannot be allowed to pay outrageous prices.[8]

From this point until expiration, members of the Business Conduct Committee were in the pit monitoring the liquidation. The contract closed out on 21 March without any extreme fluctuation in price, but containment alone cannot be credited with the resolution. On 17 March Alan Freeman sued the CBT to prevent it from forcing him to offset instead of taking delivery. The CFTC saw this as a threat of manipulation and ordered a suspension of trading. The CBT fought the suspension in court and won. It was the CBT's containment action that resolved the conflict.

The application of group pressure, which characterizes containment, belies the reluctance of exchange members to interfere with

8. Ibid., p. 58.

market integrity. The president of the CBT expressed this reluctance in a letter to a CFTC official (U.S. House of Representatives, 1979b, p. 61):

> Free markets like the Chicago Board of Trade must perform the passive function of recording all prices honestly arrived at, no matter how rational or historically correct they may or may not be. All of our efforts to maintain vigorous, competitive trading would be for naught if we felt entitled to intervene whenever the collective judgment of the market place deviated from that of our Business Conduct Committee or our board of directors.

In specific circumstances this comes down to a reluctance to tell an aggressive trader to limit his or her profits. It goes back to the notion of drawing the line between aggressive trading and manipulation. How much profit is too much?

Most industry informants resented the CFTC and CBT intervention. One anonymous informant put it this way:

> Suppose they had let March wheat trade out and it went up a dollar. Even if the whole damn 8.8 million bushels had been liquidated at a whole dollar higher, that's 8.8 million dollars. Yeah, but how much is 8.8 million dollars? There's 160 million bushels of wheat in Chicago and more in Minneapolis and Kansas City. Now that's a lot of money. Well, 8.8 is a pittance to pay for the integrity of the market.

Despite this fanciful supposition, self-regulators are unlikely to let a conflict between the longs and the shorts go that far. There are too many powerful groups inside and outside the market, including farmers, several federal agencies, and Congress, demanding tighter control of speculative behavior. In the next section we will look at more severe strategies, instances in which exchange members overcome their reluctance to regulate.

Formal Restraint

Under the strategy of containment an exchange can apply pressure to see that those in a dominant position do not take full advantage of their market power. The strategy reduces the extent to which competitive forces may play themselves out, but it does not completely eliminate market power on either side. Contracts are still allowed to trade out and a certain amount of competitive advantage, based on supply and demand, may still be extracted.

Should containment fail, the exchanges have recourse to strategies that more specifically limit the behavior of traders. The strategy of *formal restraint* involves the board of directors invoking emergency powers to establish temporary trading rules. As with containment, the purpose is to induce orderly liquidation. This is to be accomplished by limiting activity in the market in several ways. These include: (1) limiting the size of permissible positions in a specific commodity; (2) reducing the number of available contracts; and (3) increasing margin requirements. Each method represents a different rule for restraining the conflict between buyers and sellers. In the following case study the dynamics of all three methods are examined.

Case No. 2: March 1980 Silver. To illustrate the several methods available within the strategy of formal restraint we will use the conflict over the March 1980 silver contract on the Commodities Exchange of New York (Comex).

In September 1979, when the price of silver was about $9 per ounce, the Board of Governors of Comex began an intensified surveillance of conditions in the silver market.[9] The twenty-four-member board was advised of several unusually large long positions (commitments to buy) in the December silver contract. The largest long positions were held by two brothers, Nelson Bunker Hunt and W. Herbert Hunt, oil billionaires from Dallas. They had held large positions in silver since 1974, and their buying had increased with inflation in 1979. The board was also alerted for the first time to the large long positions held by Naji Nahas, a Brazilian investor, and by Banque Populaire Suisse in an omnibus account for approximately forty-five anonymous foreign investors. From September through April the board met regularly to receive reports from the Comex Control Committee—a surveillance group privy to sensitive market information—the audit staff, and, after 4 October, the Special Silver Committee. The board also shared information with the Chicago Board of Trade (which also trades in silver contracts) and with the Commodity Futures Trading Commission (CFTC).

During the period from September to April the board met at least thirty-four times. The object was to avoid the possibility of manipulation in the silver market. To this end the board had at its discretion a number of methods of control. They began by applying the ordinary and standardized controls and graduated to the extraordinary. On 4 September 1979 the board, having learned of the positions of Nahas and the foreign investors, raised the original margin requirement from $2,000 per contract to $3,000 per contract and the maximum permissible daily price fluctuation, which had not been changed since 1974, from $0.20 to $0.40 per ounce. These moves were meant

9. The following account is drawn largely from Commodity Exchange, Inc. (1980).

to maintain market integrity while encouraging reduction in the number of outstanding contracts (open interest). Only two days later the board eliminated its limit-book procedure to facilitate trading, raised the margin to $5,000 per contract, and adopted a rule permitting limits to expand up to 200 percent of the assigned daily price fluctuation. In the following months original margin requirements were raised six times, peaking at $75,000 for contracts in the current month. The maximum permissible price fluctuation was increased three times.

Increasing margin is the simplest and most common restraining strategy. While making sure that obligations will be met on a rapidly rising or falling contract, it also discourages new people from entering the market and encourages others to leave rather than meet the new standards. This in effect restrains competition by limiting it to those who can meet the stakes. In this method a lot of people are pushed out and the dominants are left to play in an illiquid market. The creation of an illiquid market is antithetical to market maintenance. This self-destructiveness is a characteristic of restraining strategies. In order to address and contain the threat, the premise of competition is abandoned. Restraint may then be seen as part of the dynamic push and pull within a self-regulating market. What is significant is that this dynamic is not natural but is, rather, a matter of conscious administration in what remains a highly competitive arena.

At the same time that margins were being raised, efforts at containment had begun. The president of Comex instructed the control committee to request the holders of large positions to "monitor their situation." By 17 September the Comex staff was holding discussions with clearing members that led to assurances that no squeeze was intended and that positions in the market would be moved forward to more distant months. During the period from October through December the Special Silver Committee heard depositions from the Hunts, Nahas, and other large-volume traders. Despite these efforts, speculative interest in silver continued to grow, prices continued to climb, and the visible supply of silver that could be delivered against the contracts remained far too small.

Ultimately, extraordinary measures of control were decided upon. The containment of the autumn months had allowed the December contract to trade out in an orderly fashion. But by early January 1980 the board was concerned that the Hunts and the group of foreign investors controlled a large proportion of the deliverable silver in Comex depositories and that these same traders continued to evince a desire for delivery on their long contracts. These long contracts would enable them to request delivery on a very limited supply, most of which they already controlled. With the CFTC expressing concern and the Chicago Board of Trade having already imposed limits on the size of speculative positions, the Comex Board took action.

On 7 January 1980 the board adopted a temporary emergency rule establishing position limits in silver. This meant that no customer of a Comex member could hold more than a total of 2,000 contracts in the silver market by 31 January and no more than 500 contracts in the current delivery (spot) month and, by 18 February, 500 in the next calendar month. This would force those holding large positions to close out the majority of their positions rather than take delivery. At this point the Hunts collectively held about 12,000 contracts. Even if the brothers were not acting in concert, as they claimed, this would force them to reduce their positions considerably.

By 9 January it appeared that traders were increasing their positions in the nearby delivery month to the maximum, threatening congestion and delivery problems. It also appeared that some of the largest traders were transferring holdings to fictitious names and corporations. The price climbed to $35. The board reduced position limits from 500 contracts to 50 in January and February. It was at this point that margins were raised to their peak of $75,000 per contract.

Less than two weeks later, on 21 January, the board held an emergency meeting. According to the minutes of that meeting:

> Members of the Board noted that, as a result of the dearth of short sellers in the silver market, small numbers of buy orders were causing aberrational price increases in silver, and therefore, firms were unable to use the market as a dealer or refiner for hedging purposes. It was also noted that the position limits for the silver market, which were imposed by the Board on January 7, 1980, had not effected a significant change in the silver situation, total open interest had not materially reduced, the interest of the large market participants had not materially reduced, and the holders of long positions in the market continued to buy silver for the apparent purpose of taking delivery. It was recommended that the Board order liquidation trading only in the silver market with an exception for new short sales made solely for the purpose of effecting delivery.

With the price rising above $50, the order for only liquidation trading went out. On 21 January Comex had about 77 million ounces of silver available for delivery, while the number of outstanding contracts, many of them held by the Hunts and the foreign investors, was equal to 527 million ounces. Within six days the order resulted in a clear reduction in the number of outstanding contracts. The holders of long positions were being forced to close out rather than take de-

livery. Those buyers not forced out by high margins were now prohibited from new purchases. This distressed the large longs, who
were trying to meet the new position limits.[10] The bottom dropped
out of this illiquid market. On the first day of the liquidation-only
order the price fell $10. It continued to slide through February and
March, to a low of $10.80 per ounce on 27 March.

Thus the conflict was effectively restrained and reduced. The setting of position limits was a highly specific tactic aimed at the dominant longs. But by the time this action was taken a speculative bubble
had been created. Media coverage of the Hunts' involvement had attracted a host of smaller speculators hoping to ride on the Hunts'
coattails. Thus upward pressure continued. The liquidation-only order was used as a last resort.[11] It essentially broke the market and
reversed the fortunes of the large traders. The Hunts claim that the
strategic application of these methods was, in fact, a manipulation by
the exchange. (The timing and choice of strategy will be discussed in
the final section of this chapter.)

Cessation

The third and final type of conflict resolution involves the total *cessation* of competition. Participants in the market shut it down—
for their own good. Such action is extreme and rare. It usually sets off
a string of lawsuits by those who feel they could have done better by
playing it out, and it causes a major loss of income to members who
would have profited from commissions. Needless to say, an exchange
must feel extremely threatened before it will take such a move.

Case No. 3: March 1979 potatoes.   The New York Mercantile
Exchange (NYME), one of the smallest of America's commodity exchanges, is more than a hundred years old. Its most active contracts
are in potatoes, platinum, and petroleum products. Our interest is in
its March 1979 potato contract, which is based on the delivery of U.S.
No. 1 round white potatoes from Maine.

To understand the action taken in March 1979, we must go back to
May 1976. In that month the largest default in futures trading history occurred in the potato contract at NYME. Dominant longs had
pushed the price sky-high. Two Western potato growers decided
that the price was inflated, since the new crop was coming in. They

10. With no new buyers in the market they were forced to offset their positions
with the shorts, who now had the bargaining power.

11. Liquidation orders are infrequent: there were only thirty-five on the CBT in
the forty-four years from 1935 to 1979.

drove the price down in its closing months by high-volume selling and by moving large quantities of potatoes to market. As the contract expired the longs were unwilling to offset. They demanded delivery of 50 million pounds of potatoes. The CFTC prosecuted the traders involved but also publicly blamed NYME for its inadequate self-regulation.

When the NYME Board of Governors suspended trading in its spring contracts on 9 March 1979, it came as a total surprise to most traders. On Monday, 5 March, the administrative staff alerted the board that when shorts had begun delivery on the expired March 1979 contract it was found that 90 percent of the potatoes for delivery did not meet contract specifications. They had been damaged by bad weather during the growing season, but the pressure bruises did not show up until shipment. The board realized that if these early deliveries were bad, the whole crop might be undeliverable; the result could be a squeeze by the longs that would distort prices or, worse, precipitate another default.

On Thursday, 8 May, the board met. In their haste to offset their positions, shorts had already driven up the price. There was no corresponding rise in the cash market, and the board felt that the proper relationship between the futures and cash price, which underlies futures trading, was in jeopardy. Some believe that the price could have been pushed from approximately $6 per hundredweight to over $20 per hundredweight.

Based on this potential manipulation, NYME ordered a cessation of trading in the April and May contracts and their liquidation at respective settlement prices of $7.16 and $8.14, which were their closing prices on Thursday. No one was forced to make delivery for March. At the end of the month a settlement price would be set by a special committee for any remaining contracts.

The major issue here is the speed with which NYME acted. Industry analysts wondered why the board did not wait to see whether the whole crop was undeliverable (it was not). Several informants claimed that the shorts were protected while the longs were denied a chance for profit. Nevertheless, the CFTC heartily approved NYME's radical strategy. One commissioner even called it "in the best tradition of self-regulation."

Yet the strategy of cessation is hardly traditional.[12] It appears to be occasioned only by threatened or real defaults, which are the most serious conflict an exchange can face. A *default* is a refusal or inability

---

12. I was able to gather case studies of only two such actions in the last twenty years and only bits and pieces of several cases before that.

to fulfill the legal obligations of a contract. Since contract performance is the premise upon which the entire competition is played out, default would call into question the basic rules. By stopping the competition and setting a price the game is maintained, even if both sides are unhappy with the settlement. Of course, resolutions, especially such expensive ones, are hardly ever unbiased.

Factors Influencing Choice of Strategy

Exchanges are reluctant to stop competition. Most participants believe that the exchange is an instrument for assuring competition. Longs and shorts are competing to see whose convictions about the direction of price are correct. Price registers the state of the competition at any given moment. Considering traders' deep commitment to and engagement in the competition, it is not surprising that in most situations they prefer to "let 'em fight it out." Glick (1957, p. 127) quotes an egg trader on the Chicago Mercantile Exchange:

> As long as we're set up with the economic system we have, we either have to have free enterprise—which means you can have squeezes and corners—or we have to control the thing altogether and not even have a futures market. My own opinion about squeezes and corners is that I don't think women and children belong on the markets. The person who gets caught in a squeeze should be made to pay. They know what's going on and shouldn't get caught.

The law of supply and demand lies at the heart of the trader's belief system. For futures traders the law of supply and demand is more than economic theory. It is a social construction by which they attribute meaning and significance to their own behavior as well as to the behavior of commodity prices. It is the link between behavior in the pits and supply and demand in the world market that is critical. As long as traders believe that what happens in the pit is a reasonable facsimile of reality in the cash market, they are able to attribute their fortunes to economic forces rather than to the behavior of their aggressive peers. Thus, when traders express reluctance to allow intervention in the market, it is often accompanied by the statement that the market (supply and demand) will assert itself.

Reluctance to intervene is also a matter of costs. Any containment or cessation of trading will deny members possible commissions. Also it is likely to hurt at least one side of the market more than the other; usually, traders who are winning the competition will be denied further winnings. Finally, the reputation of the market will be damaged and its liquidity reduced for some time. With all these costs it is reasonable to ask what factors can overcome this rational reluctance and why one strategy is chosen over another. Four such factors follow.

Degree of Government Involvement

Although the self-regulatory structure preceded the era of regulatory agencies, in each of the cases above government agencies were involved. These agencies are part of the larger market control network. In recent years their involvement in these situations has become a major factor in the adoption of a self-regulatory strategy. In the wheat case at the Chicago Board of Trade, the CFTC sent warnings to the traders and the exchange starting in December. In the silver case at Comex, the Federal Reserve Board voiced concern seven months before the emergency, and the CFTC held meetings with the traders and exchange officials. In the potato case at NYME, rapid and dramatic action was taken with an eye to the regulatory consequences if another default occurred. But this does not mean that conflict resolution is only a response to federal prodding. In fact, several congressional hearings were held to examine the slowness of federal response in the wheat and silver cases. In these cases the CFTC was a late entrant to the proceedings.

The influence of government involvement is also affected by the size and strength of the exchange. The CBT, by far the largest of the exchanges, resisted government intervention when it came and managed to limit its activity to containment, which it had begun before the government was even aware of the situation. When the CFTC ordered a cessation of trading the CBT took them to court and won the right to trade out the contract.[13] Comex was clearly aware of government pressure and kept the CFTC informed of its actions. Its strong but perhaps somewhat belated actions always received CFTC approval. Expressions of concern from Congress and the Federal Reserve Board were indirect and seem to have had little effect on the independent and deliberate action at Comex, which was actively protecting its members from the Hunts.

It is at NYME, one of the nation's smallest exchanges, that the hand of government is most evident. NYME had been blamed and fined for the 1976 default. Its audit and surveillance systems had been heavily criticized by the CFTC in a 1978 review. By 1979 NYME was extremely sensitive, if not vulnerable. The CFTC was not even aware of the delivery problem, but its potential response influenced what appears to have been hasty action.

---

13. Many months later this decision was reversed, and its reversal was upheld by the U.S. Supreme Court in April 1980.

Not only are larger exchanges more capable of resisting federal pressure, they are better prepared to resolve conflicts. At both the Chicago Board of Trade and the Chicago Mercantile Exchange the directors have a reputation for informal shows of strength. Committee and board members appear to act as elder statesmen. Several informants told stories of board members acting against their own interests on important regulatory matters. Whether these stories are true is not the issue: what is critical is the attitude they indicate about the efficacy of self-regulation—the attitude that enables the CBT to control its members through containment and the threat of restraints.

Status of Dominant Competitors

The strategy chosen by an exchange to resolve a conflict is very much influenced by the identity of the dominant competitors. Status on an exchange varies on a continuum from elite insiders to unknown outsiders. Members of the board of directors, who are elected to that position because of their prominence, are the insider elite. Less prominent members of the exchange are simply insiders. There are also prominent outsiders, who are essentially the well-known, high-roller speculators. The vast mass of small-stake, unknown outsiders have the lowest status. Dominant positions in the market require large investments, so they are held only by elite insiders and prominent outsiders.

This sort of status differentiation seems to undermine the formal equality required for perfectly competitive markets. But as sociologists have found in most other situations, the formal equality of an institution is often undermined when it comes to a conflict between insiders and outsiders (Michels, 1962). The market is no different. The human beings who administer it can and do make these distinctions. Harold Demsetz (1969, pp. 4–5) made a similar observation about the stock market:

> There is little doubt that self-regulators are motivated by a concern for society that extends beyond a narrowly conceived notion of self interest. But there is even less doubt that their own interests and the interests of those with whom they associate most closely, their peers, will have an impact on their regulatory decisions.

The insider/outsider distinction has two major implications. The first is that treatment is not even-handed: insiders fare better at the hands of their peers. The second is that it is easier to get peers to put limits on their acquisitive tendencies than it is to control outsiders. The two implications operate together in the cases reviewed.

In the case of the Hunt brothers' dominant position in the silver market, the resolution reflects the strategic use of restraint by insiders against a prominent but troublesome outsider. While some in the industry claimed that the dramatic reversal of the silver market in January 1980 was a case of the market reasserting itself, other observers—among them the Hunts—identified a culprit more tangible than market forces.

In this view the purposive restraining action taken by the Comex Board was a disguise for manipulative action intended to bring down the price of silver. The Hunts maintained and Senator Proxmire, Chairman of the Committee on Banking, later confirmed that nine silver traders represented on the Comex Board held a total of 75 million ounces in short positions. These traders stood to lose millions for themselves or their firms as the price rose through autumn. Thus, the Comex Board members can be viewed as having simply switched hats from traders to rule-makers in furtherance of their self-interest. While the Special Silver Committee, formed in October, had purposely not included anyone with silver interests, skeptics point out that the Comex Board acts much like a private club, where personal and collective interests easily mingle. Insider interests required that the speculative bubble be broken. It was fortunate for Comex that government and public interests agreed.

In the wheat case at the Chicago Board of Trade the dominant positions were held by insiders. The two largest positions were held by Leslie Rosenthal and his partner Alan Freeman. At the time Rosenthal was vice-chairman of the CBT. The board did not have to go far to find Rosenthal, one of the most prominent traders on the exchange. They therefore seemed justified in accepting Rosenthal's assurance that he would liquidate in an orderly fashion. If Rosenthal had been in the wheat market since the supply shortage first appeared, he had already made a very tidy profit on his 2.5 million bushels. Containment, then, is the strategy of preference when dealing with cooperative insiders. Not only can the board rely on the traders' continuing cooperation, those in a winning position need not be denied some degree of profit.

In the potato case at NYME the shorts stood to take a beating if the price continued to rise. The longs who would have benefited appear to have been scattered unknowns. The shorts were hedgers from the potato-growing states as well as major brokerage and trade firms. It is not surprising that NYME's decision to set a settlement price at the current market price largely favored the shorts. In general, the maintenance of the market requires that hedgers and trade firms, who are the basis of and justification for the market, be protected.

Extent of the Conflict and Destructiveness of the Strategy

These two factors are treated together because of their strong interactive effects on choice of strategy. Whether an exchange chooses to invoke containment, formal restraint, or cessation is influenced by the severity of the conflict and by the effect conflict resolution will have on the integrity of the market. To use a cliché, one does not use a hammer to kill an ant. In the market, overkill can be very costly.

If an insider, such as Rosenthal in the wheat case, is pushing a bit too hard, containment should be sufficient. In such a case the trader is simply behaving in a manner that is likely to have negative consequences for other members. When Rosenthal and his colleagues' actions raised the threat of manipulation, the CBT sent out a message to the traders which one anonymous informant characterized as: "Get the hell out of here—quietly." The CBT fought to avoid stronger action because of the destructive impact it would have on the profitable and widely used wheat market.

In the Hunts' silver case the conflict was at fever-pitch when the exchange began its formal restraint. Silver prices had soared from $9 per ounce to $50 per ounce in six months. Such volatility is profitable in terms of commissions but it was clearly a distortion. The Hunts, with their hoard of silver and desire for delivery on expiring futures contracts, were firmly in position to squeeze the silver market. The jump in price had affected worldwide spot silver prices, as well as the value of the dollar and government securities. While Rosenthal's activities had barely affected the spot market, the Hunts' activities were damaging to the silver industry represented at Comex, silver-using industries, and other financial markets. The effects of the conflict were thus widespread. The restraining action taken was deemed necessary despite the destructive consequence it eventually had on trading volume at Comex. In this situation the industry was willing to take severe action.

In the potato case the relationship among the variables is clear. The board believed that if it did not take extreme action the situation might result in a default. The consequence of a default may well have been the banning of futures trading in potatoes, which had already been proposed in Congress several times; any self-regulatory action was preferable. NYME had to demonstrate its willingness and ability to control the market. While the action was initially very destructive for potato-trading at NYME, it led to a revised contract in which traders had greater confidence and, eventually, to an increase in trading volume.

All the factors influencing choice of strategy are closely related. But there is no single influence pattern, except that the most severe conflicts appear to result in the harshest remedies. Rather, the four factors described above combine in complex contingencies. For example, while the extent of the conflict might be expected to condition all other factors, it turns out that it is not always the major determinant of strategy. An exchange may take strong action before a conflict has reached major dimensions, because it is aware that outside pressure on the CFTC might force it to intervene at an early stage. On the other hand, the exchange may resist a destructive strategy even in a severe conflict, because of the profits being made on high-volume trading. In general, strategic choice in self-regulation is complex. Further research in this and other industries is needed to increase our understanding of self-regulatory strategy.

Discussion

In the three cases discussed above we have seen the operation of institutional arrangements for self-regulation in the futures markets. These arrangements restore efficiency and competition to the markets through a purposive restraint of trade. Not all self-regulatory actions involve such dramatic opposition of actors' interests; actors are often restrained by rules, procedures, or persuasion before competition turns into conflict. Most regulatory actions are routine and have a negative impact only on a small group of traders or an individual. In general, market members have agreed to occasional temporary restrictions of their freedom so that market integrity may be maintained and their businesses may prosper in the long run. Firms come to accept controls as an occasional annoyance, sometimes favoring them and sometimes not.

In examining the restraint of competition by self-regulation we have looked at markets that are among the most free and competitive in the modern economy; indeed, economists often study these markets for their competitive nature and price-determining functions. In theory, futures markets ought to operate as the free-market economists say: responding effectively to the laws of supply and demand. And if one charts futures prices, they do look like a textbook reflection of price theory. However, though price is a marvelously useful indicator, it obscures behavior. For instance, there are those, including commissioners of the CFTC, who thought that the rise and fall of silver prices at Comex reflected the automatic self-regulation of a free market. Though market forces certainly exist, the behavioral realities of power, trust, and legitimacy are also present. A complex system of formal and informal normative constraints is invoked to inhibit the use of power, to maintain trust, and to restore legitimacy, when necessary, to exchange relations. These sorts of interorganizational arrangements appear not just in oligopolies but even, and perhaps especially, under conditions of competition. Various competitive industries have found self-regulation a practical mechanism for the pursuit of common interests.

While classical and neoclassical models of the market do not seem helpful here, recent institutional models help us to understand why firms in a competitive market would submit to self-regulation. In economic terms, bureaucratized controls such as standardization of grades, formalization of contract terms, centralization of the release of information, and surveillance of market positions all serve to reduce transaction costs, that is, the costs of being in an exchange relationship with persons you cannot completely control. It is not surprising that economic actors rely on such controls. These arrangements reduce negotiation and the threat of dishonest exchange partners' opportunism.

Futures markets are more than arenas of free and open trade. They are markets surrounded by, or perhaps buffered by, hierarchy. This hierarchy is the membership association, which writes contracts, promulgates rules, and enforces both. Expanding on Coase (1937), Oliver Williamson (1975) has classified the conditions under which markets are replaced by hierarchies. He has identified basic factors that can be applied to the analysis of hierarchy in the commodity futures markets.

Williamson's organizational failures framework works quite well here. He has combined organizational and economic variables. These variables are said to interact to create advantages to internal organization and reduce the threat of market failure. The problem of small numbers (i.e., a few traders apply pressure since there are few trading partners) is reduced by the centralization of trading at exchanges. The problem of bounded rationality (i.e., comprehensive contingent-claims contracts are constrained by the contractor's limited predictive ability) is reduced by the formalization of contracts. The standardization of these contracts reduces the problem of complexity by fixing all provisions except price. Finally, the problem of opportunism (i.e., traders are involved in seeking self-interest using guile) has been reduced by the market surveillance and enforcement structures observed in the cases above.

But all this conflicts with Williamson's intention. The model is designed to predict when internal organizations will be created to replace the market. In self-regulation we see the creation of external organizations (i.e., external to the firms involved) to sustain the market. Thus, self-regulation is in its etiology similar to vertical integration: it is a means of reducing transaction costs. But instead of integrating forward or backward to remove the need for transactions in the market, self-regulation reduces the risk inherent in market transactions by circumscribing the possible behavior of one's competitors. Products and services must meet standards, claims for skill or performance must be licensed, and members must be willing to submit to arbitration of disputes or suspension of privileges.

Not all markets and industries can be expected to self-regulate. Since self-regulation is predicated on self-interest, the threats of opportunism by competitors and uncertainty in the environment must be high enough to provide selective incentives to cooperative relations. Such conditions are often found in professions in which practitioners cannot afford to have the profession lose its credibility and legitimacy or in industries producing goods with wide price fluctuations or elastic demand. It was not until tractors began to explode in fields across America that tractor companies formed an association to self-regulate. In baseball, the major leagues did not develop a true regulatory structure until 1920, after the 1919 World Series was discovered to have been fixed. But in other industries, such as home appliances, egg marketing, the television receiver industry, the grocery industry, and the drug industry, firms have cooperated to set standards that would limit competition where necessary in order to maintain a stable market for their products. Trade associations with these functions have been repeatedly brought before the courts, accused of antitrust violations. In general, the courts have treated the organizations case-by-case, deciding which arrangements were reasonable or unreasonable restraints of trade. Generally, trade associations may not restrict prices but may gather and disseminate information as to cost, volume, and price at last sale. Firms may meet and discuss these statistics as long as no concerted action is agreed on with respect to prices or restricting competition.

While Williamson's model can help to explain the advantages to firms of participation in self-regulatory associations in terms of transaction costs, it cannot speak to the limitations of such associations in terms of the firms' power, self-interest, and unequal resources. As our three cases showed, market conditions maintained by self-regulation create opportunities for monopoly abuses and even external costs to the general public. Self-regulation is pursued out of self-interest on the part of the individual firms and that self-interest is not forgotten as members participate in association activities. Most members adhere to rules on a day-to-day basis and even accept social pressure and containment actions with equanimity (when they are caught). But occasionally a member will test the boundaries, as did Rosenthal and Freeman at the CBT, and their power and status may be sufficient to inhibit strong enforcement. Or, as in the conflict at Comex, large commercial silver traders may influence the board to take action in their favor. The view of dominant economic actors is always better represented, due to their economic dominance and elite status. Congressman John Dingell (1966, p. 28309) has noted a similar phenomenon in trade associations:

> The trade association is not entirely free to thwart the determined will of its largest contributors. It may be that the smaller business members of a trade association contribute more in aggregate than the larger units. But the smaller units are typically not coalesced.... Two or three very large units in an industry trade association may contribute such a substantial portion of the total annual revenue that indication on their part that they might resign will quickly bring the trade association to heel.

This is probably an ineluctable limitation of self-regulation. Associations will never be made up of members of equal power. Interests will always be aggressively pursued despite collective agreement, and the method of market maintenance chosen may not always be in the public interest. For these reasons the futures markets are monitored by a federal regulatory agency, the CFTC. The government, for many reasons, cannot tolerate manipulation or price distortion in the futures markets. When such manipulation threatens to have an unfavorable impact on the balance of trade, the national debt, or the inflation rate, Congress and the executive departments feel compelled to exert control. The rapid growth of futures markets in the 1970s, fraud in the commodity options market, and, in particular, the inflationary effects of the Russian wheat deal led to the establishment of the CFTC in 1975.

While the futures industry is only one case, its experience suggests the hypothesis that when a market or industry becomes economically or politically significant, self-regulation will no longer be tolerated. One example of this is the number of industries in which federal agencies have turned the voluntary standards of associations into law (Hemenway, 1975; Harter, 1979). Among the purposes given for this were to ease information problems, to limit adulteration, and to improve product quality. The result, according to one association executive, is an unnecessarily adversary relationship between the industry and the government.

The limitations of self-regulation need not mean that it is totally useless or corrupt. There is a growing tendency for government to legislate a kind of modified self-regulation under which the industry assumes responsibilities delegated to it by a regulatory agency or Congress, which retains a supervisory role. Among the factors supporting this mode of regulation are the reduction in cost to the government, the expertise that industry personnel bring to complex and changing regulatory problems, and the avoidance of possible transaction costs if the government stepped in. As one might expect, industry leaders see this as a favorable alternative to direct regulation. Industry associations can find or develop considerable latitude in the interpretation of the mandate. The viability of such arrangements has recently been debated in the securities, accounting, and futures industries. Research on the effectiveness and possible modification of these arrangements would be an important contribution to the literature on regulatory policy.

Conclusion

One aim of this essay has been to put forth a market-maintenance perspective on self-regulation, as a corrective to the view that self-regulation is performed only to achieve anticompetitive purposes or to avert government intervention. While sharing the view of skeptics who would say that industries are not likely to regulate themselves out of altruistic concern for the consumer, this study develops the idea that self-regulation is part of a larger set of activities engaged in by industries for the reduction of market uncertainty. The cases discussed above include the threat of government intervention as a central and sometimes dominant factor in the strategic decisionmaking of self-regulators. The fact that the data cannot completely separate these competing hypotheses is in itself an important finding. In a market economy that is integrated and turbulent we find that both private industry and the state are averse to uncertainty. The result is a variety of arrangements for both private and public regulation throughout the economy.[14]

A second aim of this essay has been to elaborate the behavioral dynamics of strategic action by self-regulators. Although the transaction-costs model indicates why the market participants choose to establish organizational arrangements to reduce the uncertainties and risks of doing business, it cannot account for the differential enforcement observed in the cases cited here. Even if rationality dictates some form of self-regulation, it does not explain the highly stylized versions of competition and conflict resolution

14. From this perspective, deregulation is a reactionary anomaly caused by the costs of regulation. Once the costs of competition have asserted themselves, self-regulation or re-regulation may soon be considered.

exhibited. Rather, behavior, as discussed in the cases, is structured by institutional norms that define the boundaries of acceptable conduct and the labeling of violators, by the distribution of power among members, and by the distribution of power between the association and its environment. These observations suggest that economic models, such as Williamson's, of the process of organizing may be usefully elaborated by studying the social and political components of cooperative behavior.

This essay is a preliminary attempt to examine some of the behavioral issues in self-regulation. As a single case study it has raised more questions than it could possibly answer. Among them are: (1) the role of the government in supervising self-regulation; (2) the potential for reduction of elite-firm dominance in self-regulatory associations; and (3) the generalizability of strong self-regulatory arrangements to other industries. These questions demand a comparative study of a range of self-regulatory associations to explore these largely ignored aspects of economic regulation.

COMMENT: *Roger G. Noll*

Mitchel Abolafia's essay on self-regulation contains a very interesting description of three instances in which the normal trading processes of a free, competitive market were altered by a select group of participants in the market who also had the responsibility of supervising its orderly operation. The key questions raised by these examples, and addressed to some degree in the essay, are as follows. First, why do self-regulatory institutions such as commodity exchanges behave as they do? Second, is there more to a comprehensive theoretical explanation than a simple economic model of an exchange as a cartel? And in particular, does the sociological approach to organization theory provide unique insights into the general phenomenon of self-regulation or the specific issue of commodity exchange operations? Abolafia's thesis is that self-regulatory bodies should not be regarded solely, or even primarily, as cartels and that organization theory provides insights into their behavior that are not explained adequately by cartel theory.

The three cases examined by Abolafia have one common feature. It is that a relatively small group of traders developed a dominant position in a market such that they would have been able to extract very large profits had the market run to conclusion without intervention.

The three cases differ with respect to the size of the exchange in which the event took place, the identity of the traders (members of the governing body, other insiders, large-scale outsiders, and the small-scale, widows-and-orphans variety of outsiders), the role of the federal regulators, and the type of action taken by the exchange.

The simple economic explanation for the existence of an exchange and the behavior of its governors—a theory discussed in brief form by Abolafia—would be something like the following. Exchanges as market institutions succeed because they can reduce the transactions costs of trading. They do so in several ways, but the two most obvious are by providing a time and place for potential traders to congregate and a prenegotiated set of rules of transactions so that contracts do not need to be written for each trade yet buyers and sellers are provided with a security of transaction like that of an enforceable individual contract. Abolafia correctly points out that these are reasons for members to form exchanges even if the exchange provides no cartel benefits. Members derive income in two ways: as agents arranging trades for others, and as traders themselves. In both cases they benefit from low transactions costs, because a reduction in the costs of trading increases trading volume and reduces the minimum gain from trading that is necessary to produce a net profit.

Continuing the economic analysis of exchange behavior to its logical end produces a major problem. Members of an exchange set up their trading rules out of economic self-interest, and surely a dollar earned from a competitive market is as valuable as (and indistinguishable from) a dollar earned from two fairly routine market imperfections: a cartel arrangement among the traders operating the exchange, and the strategic use of insider information. The key question is what, if anything, would act naturally to inhibit an exchange from the latter two sources of income.

One can imagine several such natural limits. First, the gains from running an exchange must be limited by the advantages in transactions costs of an exchange arrangement. Otherwise traders who are not members of the cartel and not privy to inside information would do better trading off the exchange. Second, exchanges may compete with each other and thereby further limit the extent to which profits in excess of competitive earnings can be captured. Third, if exchange markets periodically collapse with enormous profits for exchange insiders at the expense of others, traders will be inclined to enter other investment markets. In this case, exchange insiders would face a trade-off between short-term gains accruing from manipulation of their special position against long-term losses arising from a general decline in the demand for their services as traders. Of course, to take full account of such an effect requires collective action—a single insider in a position to capture enormous gains will impose an external cost on other exchange members if the full profits are actually realized and as a result the market disappears in the future. Consequently, a rational cartel, in the straightforward economic sense, will be likely to limit the extent to which individual members can develop a dominant position in a market.

The main threat to an exchange that extracts supercompetitive profits for its members is competitive entry. Assuming that there are scale economies to an exchange over some relevant range (and there are good reasons to expect that this is so, because the market institution is a public good for its members), small defections from an exchange are not much of a threat. A greater source of worry is whether a coalition of the major insiders, the biggest trader/members, will defect. Consequently, standard cartel theory would predict that the major insiders would fare better—that is, would face less binding limits on the extent to which they can manipulate their way into a profitable position—than the other insiders.

The final factor operating on exchanges is government regulation. The political science cousin to cartel theory is the interest-group aggregation theory of what regulators are trying to do. This would predict that well-organized special interests would have a greater effect than others on the constraints imposed by regulators, and that these effects would be positively related to the size of the group as measured by numbers and wealth. In the case of commodity exchange regulation, the major organized groups are the exchanges themselves, the firms that are members, and the industries that use exchanges to hedge against unanticipated changes in commodity prices (e.g., to avert risk and to gain long-term stability in volatile markets). The major difference between the governance of the exchange and the behavior of the regulators is that only dollars count, all other things being equal, in exchange management, whereas votes also count to government officials. For example, regulators might be expected to be more sensitive than the exchange to the interests of the agricultural sector because they would give some attention to the number as well as the wealth of farmers. Thus, to the extent that the natural limits to cartel operations do not force the excess profits of exchanges to zero, regulators could be expected to bind the actions of the exchange—especially toward its major insiders—more than the exchange itself would freely choose to do.

At the same time, regulators would be more courageous in dealing with small exchanges than with large ones, because the latter have greater wealth and numbers.

The preceding rather simple theoretical framework seems to explain pretty well what happened in the three cases. Government regulators seriously threatened only the smallest exchange. Only in the wheat case did major insiders suffer damage from intervention by the exchange, and this was only after they had already made substantial profits. In the silver case a major outsider (the Hunts) and in the potato case minor outsiders were the ones to develop the dominant position, and in both cases actions were taken that strongly favored the insiders. In the potato case, it also favored hedging potato-industry interests. Thus, there do not appear to be any major surprises. Of course, there are also only three cases to explain, and plenty of independent variables to explain them. It is always conceivable that noneconomic explanations would be necessary to account for some aspects of a larger number of cases, but that does not appear to be the case here.

In the concluding parts of his paper, Abolafia discusses the application of Williamson's work to the problem of explaining why exchanges come into existence. An interesting point that deserves some further attention is why exchanges take the form of trade associations of a sort rather than commercial enterprises that are distinct from the traders, or even nationalized market institutions. All the reasons Abolafia develops provide a basis for explaining why a market institution would arise that looks like an exchange, with formal trading rules that avoid complicated contracting and that provide rich information flows for participants in the market. The central issue is what economic gains are provided from a collective organization of the traders, as opposed to a vertically segmented industry in which a firm engaged in providing a market institution sells its services to separate traders and brokers. This is, incidentally, the kind of issue that Williamson (1975) addresses in his theory of markets versus hierarchies, as opposed to the issue of why a particular service industry (e.g., exchanges) would arise in the first place.

The most obvious rationale for a collective exchange, rather than vertical segmentation, is the opportunity in the former for establishing a cartel. A vertically segmented exchange appears to have less reason to ration trading rights and to intervene to protect certain categories of traders than a collective association of trading agents would have. Once again, the straightforward explanation for this kind of institution appears not to be to preserve competitive markets but to undermine them.

Thus, I remain unconvinced by a main theme of Abolafia's analysis: that self-regulation in general and commodity exchanges in particular are not primarily vehicles for cartelization. To identify efficiency rationales for collective action is not to show that these are the primary benefits of collective action. Nevertheless, there is a very important feature of this type of study. Casual observation provides adequate evidence about the rich variety of market institutions that exist: retail trade with posted prices, free-flowing bids and offers in exchanges, structured auctions of various forms, and bilateral negotiations. Moreover, each can take place in any of three settings: a buyer and/or seller organizes the market, a collectivity of buyers and/or sellers organizes the market, or a third party undertakes to make the market. There is certainly no well-developed, systematic theory that identifies the conditions that lead to the development of a particular market institution, nor are there more than piecemeal explanations of how alternative institutional arrangements are likely to perform.

Much of the literature about exchanges is guilty of overstating the extent to which they represent the competitive, unfettered market in all its glory. To the contrary, exchange rules are elaborate and exchanges often intervene to alter the trend of market outcomes. Perhaps the nature of these markets is such that supercompetitive profits are all but unattainable (other than as random windfalls) and that Abolafia's view of self-regulation as benign from the point of view of income distribution and economic efficiency is largely correct; however, one is then struck by the difficulty, in terms of trading rules and regulations, of making a competitive market exist. Alternatively, exchanges may be more accurately viewed as in some important measure a means for cartelizing participation in a market and for conferring certain trading advantages on some of its participants. In either case, substantial theoretical and empirical work remains to be done to provide a solid explanation of how these institutions work, and why they exist.

PART V

The Research and Policy Agenda

11

Integrating Themes
and Ideas

At the CalTech/NSF Conference that was the genesis of this book, three distinguished scholars were asked to close the gathering by giving summary, integrative views about the papers and discussion at the conference. Each was asked to focus on one or a few regulatory policy issues of great importance and to suggest how research in social science might contribute to their resolution.

The three scholars represent different disciplines: Bruce Ackerman is a lawyer, James Wilson is a political scientist, and Philip Selznick is a sociologist. Yet the three summary statements, albeit differing in detail and emphasis, stressed common themes. Each sees the central question as organizational: constructing regulatory agencies that perform their functions better (e.g., contributing to efficiency and social justice). Each sees the American political system's particularism and sensitivity to special interests as a fundamental barrier to solving the problem.

Cost Benefit and the Constitution
Bruce A. Ackerman

Imagine a second Constitutional Convention. Not one convened to consider one or another patent remedy for a particular social disease—be it budget deficits or easy abortions. Imagine instead that we had the strength to emulate the first Convention—which sought to establish a framework of government equal to the foreseeable challenges of then-contemporary life. Two centuries onward, some of these challenges remain very similar to those confronting

351

the eighteenth century. But others are obviously different—notably, those involved in running an activist regulatory state. While our original system has, of course, adapted to these realities, surely a bit of constitutional self-consciousness might improve our rather creaky performance.

The thought required for a serious convention has hardly begun. Constitutional lawyers primarily concern themselves with individual rights rather than with the organization of governmental power;[1] social scientists primarily deal with the positive analysis of existing institutions rather than with the possibility of designing better ones.[2] The questions of constitutional reform raised by the activist regulatory state fall within the central focus of neither discipline. Intellectually speaking, we are at a very great distance from the *Federalist Papers*—the very idea of integrating constitutional law and political science into a single coherent whole seems, but for the Philadelphia example, an impossible dream.

A short comment is hardly the place to make a serious step toward reintegration. Rather than attempting a mock-comprehensive analysis, I shall concentrate on a single modern practice that deserves serious constitutional analysis and will suggest how social science might be of substantial use in a mature assessment. My focus will be the pervasive use of cost-benefit analysis in modern American government. I want to suggest that modern policy analysis[3] is not only something to be encouraged, but that it may in time come to serve as an institutional focus for a new system of constitutional checks and balances.

1. Thus, none of the leading casebooks in constitutional law makes any real effort to integrate contemporary political science into their appraisal of constitutional doctrine. Similarly, Laurence Tribe's treatise on constitutional law—justly viewed as the preeminent doctrinal exposition of the modern era—is written as if modern political science had nothing significant to contribute to an understanding of the organization of governmental power. See Tribe (1978). Indeed, a recent book by a leading constitutional lawyer goes so far as to call for a general retreat from any form of Supreme Court intervention in matters dealing with the organization of government power: see Choper (1980).

2. A signal exception is provided by the work of James Buchanan and a series of co-authors, most notably Buchanan and Tullock (1962). Unfortunately, Buchanan and his school seek to use constitutional law to destroy the activist welfare state rather than to redeem its promise of greater justice and enhanced welfare. For a comprehensive critique of Buchanan's most recent effort, see Rose-Ackerman (1982).

3. *Modern policy analysis* is a label that, transparently, embraces a multitude of (mal)practices, a myriad of value-laden decisions on the best way of proceeding in a particular case. For present purposes, I am interested in elaborating, not the innumerable issues that divide policy analysis, but those few fundamental analytic principles that unite them.

To make my point, I enumerate six features of good cost-benefit analysis and compare them with the kinds of decisionmaking we have learned to associate with Congress. In doing so, my point is *not* that cost-benefit is good and congressional politics is bad, but that both forms of institutional intelligence are essential in the ongoing process of modern government. The challenge, in short, is the one posed by the original *Federalist*: how we may use constitutional law to structure the varieties of available institutional intelligence in ways that will permit us to achieve that most illusive of polities—a genuinely enlightened democracy.

Let us begin, then, with the *comprehensive* ambitions of cost-benefit analysis. Any good policy analyst strives to appraise any particular proposal in terms of its opportunity cost—comparing it to the full range of competing initiatives that might replace the program under discussion. Obviously, this effort never totally succeeds; moreover, the attempt to be comprehensive introduces a multitude of oversimplifications of its own. Nonetheless, when viewed as a part of the policymaking process, it is obviously desirable to have an institution constantly forcing each special regulatory bureaucracy to justify its programs by comparing it to competitors that might be proposed in other sectors of our mixed economy.

This is especially true when another part of the process is dominated by a very different logic. As the present generation of political scientists has taught us, there are deep structural reasons why members of Congress tend to be concerned with particular benefits rather than abstract opportunity costs (Fiorina, 1977; Mayhew, 1974). Indeed, there is a pronounced congressional tendency to deny the existence of tradeoffs. Is it not wise, then, for the Constitution to create and protect an institution that will emphasize the hard truth—there is no such thing as a free lunch—that Congress might otherwise evade or suppress?

Second, cost-benefit analysis emphasizes *universalistic* criteria. It does not ask where you live, or whether you are Polish, but how much you are willing to pay for the proposed project. Not, mind you, that cost-benefit is committed to the existing distribution of income. Policy analysts need not give equal weight to everybody's willingness to pay; the fact that a poor person is willing to sacrifice a dollar may be given the same policy significance as a rich person's ten-dollar sacrifice. When technocrats engage in such distributive assessments, however, they typically design their weights in the light of one or another universalistic theory of distributive justice—utilitarian, contractarian, liberal, what-have-you. The policy analyst's first instinct is to reject the notion that a poor person is specially worthy of concern if he or she happens to live in the nth congressional district.

In contrast, congressional debate tends to be ostentatiously parochial: time and again decisions emphasize a program's effect on politically mobilized and geographically concentrated groups—what's good for the steel worker, for the South, and so forth. Once again, this is not some unfortunate accident but a systematic consequence of electoral politics in a decentralized political system like our own (Fiorina, 1977; Mayhew, 1974).

A third feature of cost-benefit is its *technical* character. Computer modeling can only occur on the basis of a sound use of highly esoteric concepts. In contrast, congressional discussion is characterized, and properly so, by generally accessible discourse. Each form of discourse, moreover, has the vices of its virtues. While congressional talk is essential in informing the general citizenry about basic value choices, technical work is necessary to grasp the relevant regulatory realities.

A fourth feature of cost-benefit is its *outcome orientation.* Policy analysts are constantly asking whether a program is actually delivering the goods. In contrast, members of Congress love to confuse symbolic satisfaction with the achievement of real-world gains (Edelman, 1964). They often try to claim credit for the provision of some short-term favor to some favorite group of constituents; whether the short-term gain will redound to the group's long-term advantage is typically assumed rather than proved.

This brings us to a fifth distinctive feature: the *conception of time* characteristically deployed in cost-benefit work. Competent analysts are trained to take a long view of their problem. For example, any well-prepared report will try to take into account costs and benefits that will accrue far into the future—often twenty or more years from now. In contrast, members of Congress take a short view. For obvious reasons, they are centrally concerned with the situation likely to obtain at the next election, and they discount the long-range consequences of their actions (Rose-Ackerman, 1980).

The sixth feature also has something to do with time, but not with the contrast between long- and short-term horizons. Here I want to focus on the place of *probabilistic reasoning* in the decisionmaking calculus. Policy analysts take probabilistic reasoning for granted and are expected to deploy the powerful vocabulary of expected utility, mean, and variance to explain the risks we are running. In contrast, the politician loves concrete events, not abstract probabilities. Three Mile Island attracts their attention in a way that the Rasmussen Report will never achieve (Mayhew, forthcoming).

In short, we have displayed before us two very different varieties of institutional intelligence: one strives to be comprehensive, universalistic, technical, outcome-oriented, and focused on the long view in a way that emphasizes risk and uncertainty. The other is parochial, interest-specific, generally accessible, symbolic, takes the short view, and emphasizes the concrete event. It is silly to think that we have to choose between these two forms of institutional intelligence. The challenge is to bring them together in satisfying ways.[4]

I believe we are failing to meet this challenge. Our present regulatory system is evolving in ways that give Congress the wrong role in the policymaking process. Rather than serving as a central forum for the democratic articulation of our basic political objectives, Congress is increasingly a place in which politicians try to influence particular bureaucratic decisions in ways that redound to the symbolic advantage of locally powerful constituencies. As a consequence, we are getting the worst, rather than the best, of both worlds. The system does not generate statutes that establish incisive and popularly supported goals for collective achievement, nor does it support a relatively impartial and systematic effort to translate statutory goals into real-world outcomes.[5]

If this is so, it follows that social scientists can make two kinds of contributions to the constitutional law of the regulatory state. The first involves help in defining credible institutional mechanisms by which we might successfully insulate particularized bureaucratic decisions from ad hoc congressional intervention. Rather than facilitating particularistic congressional credit-claiming, we must design constitutional mechanisms that foster technically competent bureaucratic decisions taking a relatively universalistic, long-run, outcome-oriented, and comprehensive point of view. The second task involves the redesign of congressional incentives to encourage legislators to invest more of their time and energy in legislative activities that do not yield highly visible rewards to well-organized local constituencies. We want to redirect their energies to a serious collective dialogue defining the nature of the ultimate objectives of regulatory activity.

4. This has been one of the organizing themes of modern political economy. See Schelling (1978), Allison (1971), and, most notably, Lindblom (1965, 1977), Lindblom and Braybrooke (1963), and Lindblom and Cohen (1979). These writers tend to strike a balance between forms of institutional intelligence in ways that I do not think do justice to the claims of the kind of policy analysis I am describing.

5. This is, of course, one of Lowi's (1979) abiding concerns, though I am not sure that he would accept my proposal as part of his solution. For some further reflections of mine on this problem, see Ackerman and Hassler (1981).

If we are to make progress on either of these objectives, lawyers will need a great deal of help from social scientists. For the hard fact is that our existing fund of legal ideas is more than usually shopworn. On the level of explicit constitutional doctrine, I very much hope that the Supreme Court will strike a blow against congressional particularism by declaring unconstitutional the modern practice by which a single House (or a single committee) can veto the decision of an administrative agency. Given the present poverty of analysis, however, we can only await the Court's decision of the cases now raising this issue—which should be easy ones—with fear and trembling. Similarly, the principal mechanism by which courts seek to force Congress to indulge in principled legislation—the nondelegation doctrine—has lapsed into disuse. Moreover, given the primitive state of present doctrine, no sane person can hope for its early revival.

On the humbler yet more significant level of administrative law, the outlook is not appreciably brighter. The past decade has witnessed a widespread reappraisal of the legal doctrines by which the New Deal sought to build a legal foundation for a fruitful interchange among an enlightened bureaucracy, a public-spirited Congress, and an impartial judiciary. This New Deal synthesis now seems hopelessly naive—not only to a few legal academics but to the legion of legislators, judges, and lawyers who find it increasingly difficult to play the roles assigned to them by the New Deal vision of the legal process. If we are to reestablish a credible foundation for administrative law, it will only be on the basis of models of bureaucracy and legislation that take account of the many valid points in the now-conventional critique of the New Deal ideal of expert public administration.

This does not only mean that lawyers must confront the disturbing implications of contemporary theories of public choice, legislation, and bureaucracy (Downs, 1957; Niskanen, 1971; Rose-Ackerman, 1978; Sen, 1970; Gibbard, 1973; Mueller, 1979; McKelvey, 1976; Satterthwaite, 1975). It also suggests that social scientists should consider seriously the normative implications of their positive analysis. Rather than endlessly explaining how it is that our legislators have become parochialized and our bureaucrats politicized, it would be nice if they also seriously analyzed the hypothetical performance of one or another reformed system. It is only by rigorously modeling behavior within a broad range of hypothetical institutional structures that we may gain a sense of the ways in which our constitutional predicaments may be ameliorated, if not eradicated.

Return to the image with which we began: if a second Constitutional Convention were held tomorrow, it is painfully apparent that constitutional lawyers and social scientists would have very little to say about a constitutional cure for the ills of the activist regulatory state. And yet we know that this present condition is not inevitable. There was a first Constitutional Convention, and it is hard to read *The Federalist* even today without glimpsing the possibility of a healthier intellectual condition, one in which lawyers and social scientists would contribute to a common dialogue defining the ways in which the Constitution may prevent congressional government from degenerating into a parody of the democratic ideal. It is not naive, Madison and Hamilton assure us, to hope for a form of government that is popularly responsive yet capable of formulating coherent and enduring public policy. We can, the Federalists tell us, hope for a government that is both democratic and enlightened.

If we are to redeem these hopes, we will have to do more than recapture the Federalist spirit. For the fact is that the first Convention confronted a task far easier than would a second one. The Founders merely sought to discipline the power of an American Republic whose aims were very limited. In contrast, we must make constitutional sense of the promise of the liberal activist state. We must try to create a system in which the pursuit of social justice is not trivialized by the proliferation of a host of particularistic handouts to politically powerful interest groups and in which the effort to improve the general welfare does not lead to the extinction of individual liberty.

Given these formidable challenges, we must be grateful that the moment for a second Constitutional Convention has not yet arrived. But if we are to be worthy of our ancestors, we must prepare for a time in which events will oblige us to answer questions the Founders saw no need to ask.

Neglected Areas of Research on Regulation
James Q. Wilson

There are at least four research strategies that might be encouraged in order to fill in what I think are some of the lacunae in our understanding of the nature of government regulation of the private sector. The first has to do with when and why government intervenes in the market. A second seeks to estimate the effects of regulation. A third examines alternate ways of intervening, trying to explain why one alternative rather than another is chosen and to estimate the relative effects of alternatives. The fourth attempts to understand alternative organizational structures and procedures and asks why we choose a particular structure or procedure and what difference the choice makes. Most research is on the second topic, namely, trying to estimate the effect of some government intervention in the market. Here the economists have been the primary contributors. A considerable amount of research has also focused on the first issue, explaining why the government intervenes in the market. Here a debate rages between those who believe regulation has something to do with interests capturing government in order to use its resources, produce cartels, and maximize wealth, and those who argue that there are more complex, diffuse—perhaps ideological—explanations for government intervention, possibly including a desire to serve the public interest.

By contrast, the third and fourth areas have been neglected. We do not ordinarily try to explain why government chooses command and control regulation rather than a subsidy, a tax break, or a modification of the legal code in order to achieve its ends. Nor do we much consider the effects of choosing one strategy or another, and even more rarely do we ask whether it makes any difference that we do these things through a commission or an agency, or how the agency is organized and proceeds.

The empirical foundation for useful research on these questions is rich. At all levels of government, numerous approaches to regulation have been tried. Depending on the year you begin, somewhere between twenty and fifty entities—i.e., states—have generated data. We also have an opportunity, thus far quite neglected, for international comparisons.

One reason these resources have not been extensively mined is that few of us have assumed that these questions were worth asking. It was always thought to be more important to explain why the government should intervene at all and to estimate the consequences of specific, existing regulations than to ask why government picks a particular form of control. Furthermore, we neglect the latter because gathering data about it is much more difficult than gathering data about the former. In trying to explain why the government intervenes, a scholar might look at roll-call votes, public opinion polls, or the number of marginal congressional districts. In trying to estimate the effects of a regulatory policy, a scholar is primarily concerned with economic efficiency, modified in some cases and to some degree by concerns for distribution and equity.

To examine alternative ways of intervening and alternative structures for such intervention poses much more difficult problems in finding data. Such research might involve travel, and whereas many people are willing to travel to Washington, far fewer are willing to spend much time in Harrisburg, Pennsylvania, or other places where the facts are to be found.

Are there good reasons for thinking it is worth investigating these matters of method and structure? I must confess I am not entirely sure. Let me focus on the fourth point, namely, the role of alternative organizational structures and procedures in both government and industry. Does it matter whether government operates in one way or another? And does it make a difference whether the entity on which it is operating is organized in one way rather than another?

Like others represented in this book, I have been guilty of practicing organization theory. Perhaps not like them, I am willing to confess my belief that its accomplishments so far have been extremely modest. There is a tendency in the practice of organization theory to believe earnestly that such a theory exists and that surely it must tell us something important, but in the last analysis one is not sure that one has learned anything. The reason is twofold. First, organizational analysis tends not to be outcome-oriented—that is, it tends not to explain why X rather than Y occurred. It usually explains why nothing occurs. Second, when the theory does explain why something occurs, it tends to overexplain. Every variable in the list generated by the organization theorists seems to conspire to the same result. We have a highly overdetermined system, and therefore we are not sure which one or few variables might make the difference. One source of these problems is that much of the best writing about organizations takes the form of a single case study.

Despite the absence of many strong results, I think we have some grounds for believing that the way government organizes itself may make a difference. Let me offer some reasons for that supposition. As I read the work of Robert Katzmann, I am persuaded that the Federal Trade Commission is different from the Antitrust Division. One reason is that the Federal Trade Commission gives organizational protection to both economists and lawyers in the form of the Bureau of Economics and the Bureau of Competition, whereas the Antitrust Division is a governmental law firm. At the Antitrust Division, efforts such as those of Donald Turner and others to smuggle a few economists into positions of influence have met with little or no success, while the struggle in the FTC between economic and legal perspectives has, I think, had some effect on the kinds of actions it brings, or at least has made its behavior somewhat different from the behavior of the Antitrust Division.

There are other examples. Like Roger Noll (see Chapter 2), I think that the change in the FCC with respect to cable television must surely have something to do with separation of the Cable Bureau from the Broadcast Bureau. With respect to the Environmental Protection Agency and the Department of Energy, I think it has made a difference that there was an effort, at least initially, to organize both those agencies along analytical lines. That is to say, organizational subunits were created to protect professional specialties. The lawyers were put in one place, scientists in another, and the economists in still another, and each of these organizationally protected professional specialties was then asked to apply its talents to such things as defining water and air standards or evaluating technologies. In the Department of Energy, problems were divided along the lines of research and development exploitation. This type of organization quickly changed under political pressures into a more substance-oriented organization. EPA was transformed so that its organization was concerned with water, air, and toxic substances, and the Department of Energy began to monitor energy resources such as coal, oil, and solar energy.

The reason for this structure can be understood from Bruce Ackerman's contribution to this volume: Congress prefers dealing with commodities it can recognize and that have geographical locations. They know where coal mines are found and where the sun shines. The farmers are concerned about toxic substances and not about clean air, and they prefer to deal with a unit that worries about toxic substances. Organizing agencies according to commodities or functions must (I think) make a difference, probably a greater difference than whether it is a commission, an administrative agency, or a set of rules on how the government proceeds.

Another working hypothesis is that how the private sector is organized makes a difference in how it responds. Here I do not even have any plausible examples, but it has been suggested by some that large bureaucratic corporations will respond in different ways than will small, nonbureaucratic firms. Holding size and bureaucratization constant, certain regulations may change the distribution of power within a firm so that certain professional specialties gain an advantage. OSHA, I think, has in many firms given greater professional clout to people with industrial hygiene and public health backgrounds. Similarly, the Internal Revenue Code has given a great boost to accountants and lawyers within firms, which in turn probably affects how the firm behaves. Although this is pure speculation, it seems worth investigating.

Now, how do we carry out these investigations? Much has been said about the differences between economic and noneconomic perspectives. I want to reopen that subject just a bit. I have worked from both perspectives (though certainly more often from the noneconomic) and I want to give you my estimate of the strengths and weaknesses of each. I do not want to put the issue as one of economists versus political scientists or sociologists, but as between two modes of thought that are represented in a number of disciplines. One is the black-box approach. According to this view the object of research is to estimate the effects on outputs of changes in inputs. In order to simplify the analysis, some assumptions are made about inputs, processes, and outputs. The usefulness of this approach derives from the fact that the simplifying assumptions often lead to interesting and testable hypotheses.

One assumption is that of self-interest. Most of us have a certain degree of self-interest and rationality, and it should not be surprising to learn that politicians, business executives, and bureaucrats probably have at least a comparable level. Another assumption is that many potentially important variables—especially process variables— can be ignored. Hence one can direct attention to getting as much evidence as possible about the range of variation in a few selected variables, rather than trying to canvass a long list. Much of the time these assumptions are not so bad that they inhibit good analysis, but sometimes they lead to weak and misleading results. The advantage of this approach is that it directs attention to outcomes and that most of the time it accords with our commonsense understanding of rational human behavior.

The other procedure is to try to explain apparently deviant cases or inherently interesting cases by a detailed examination of them. Single case studies are occasionally useful, because they focus our attention on a neglected feature of the situation. Far superior are comparative case studies such as the chapter by Martha Derthick and Paul Quirk in this book, in which several examples are systematically chosen, either to exhaust the possible cases or to show the full range of variation among a larger number of cases, and are worked through in considerable detail. The advantage of this approach is that it greatly enhances sensitivity to the factors that cause change. The black-box method tends to lead to static results and to inaccurate predictions. Though the inaccuracy can often be dealt with by modifying the structure of the model, often the model does not predict that change. Finally, case studies make students who practice them alert to the constraints imposed by institutions, laws, and procedures.

Each approach has its corresponding disadvantages. The black-box strategy rarely gives serious attention to the role of ideas and values. The problem is partly in the self-interest assumption, which in its extreme form denies the role of ideas. (In the less extreme version, ideas are nothing but coat hooks on which politicians and interest groups hang their self-interest in order to make it socially presentable.) I often wonder: if scholars, many of them economists, attach so little value to ideas, why do they write so many treatises that try to persuade us of the validity of their ideas? If they are prepared to say honestly that they do this only in order to advance in their profession and get tenure, I would regard that, at best, as refreshing honesty and, at worst, as flatly untrue. I have the feeling they are trying to persuade us. If we can be persuaded by an idea, I have enough belief in the continuity of human nature to suspect that others, not so fortunate as to be professors, can also probably be persuaded by an idea.

One reason ideas do not normally enter into black-box studies is that getting direct measures of ideas and values is very difficult. It ideas do enter, it is through proxies such as ratings by a pressure group or voting behavior. Once a proxy is used, the alternative interpretations of it immediately give encouragement to those who believe that it is not, in fact, ideas that are being proxied at all but some aspect of self-interest, broadly defined.

The comparative-case-study approach also has a disadvantage. It often tends to overlook the effect of incentives that operate at the margin on a large number of actors, voters, politicians, or the like. Moreover, the case study tends to provide an overdetermined explanation. Everything seems to lead to the result; by the time one finishes reading, the conclusion appears obvious and therefore possibly trivial. The black-box exercise often leads to nonobvious results and even when the predictions are confounded by reality, the utility-maximizing assumptions lead us to ask why behavior was *not* in accord with commonsense understandings.

These two strategies probably can be combined, but it is extremely expensive and difficult, and therefore rarely done. I tried to do it once in estimating production functions for police departments in relation to variations in crime rates. The project involved a comparative case study of a large number of police departments as well as the estimation of an econometric model. It took somewhere between two and a half and three years to write the article. I can understand why people facing a tenure decision in a few years might not want to rest their scholarly careers on one article that might take three years to produce. Nevertheless, it seems to me important that such projects be undertaken, because each side has something to contribute to the other.

My bias, of course, is very much to favor the strategy that Derthick and Quirk have embraced. I am aware, as I am sure they are, of the possible blind spots of that strategy: the tendency not to look for incentives that operate on large numbers of persons and to focus on the verbal behavior of a small number of actors. In any case, combining the two strategies holds out the prospect for obtaining both the virtues of outcome-oriented, systematic data (what I call the black-box approach) and the broader, deeper possibilities inherent in carefully worked out comparative case studies. This approach can open the questions that have been neglected in the area of regulatory behavior, namely: what difference does it make how we regulate, and what difference, if any, does it make whether we regulate by one organizational structure or another?

Focusing Organizational Research on Regulation   *Philip Selznick*

If social science is to be brought to bear effectively on the study of regulation, we need first to clarify what we mean by that elusive term. There is a strong temptation to identify regulation with the whole realm of law, governance, and social control. That is understandable, because the word itself, taken out of context, does have very broad connotations. Within the framework of public policy and administration, however, regulation has a more specific meaning but one that is not always made explicit or kept in mind.

In its central meaning *regulation* refers to sustained and focused control exercised by a public agency over activities that are valued by a community. The emphasis on valued activities is important because it is the effort to uphold public standards or purposes without undue damage to activities we care about that generates the persistent dilemmas of regulation. This conception excludes most of what goes on in the criminal justice system except that the community may adopt a regulatory approach to certain activities, such as gambling, that are illegal but tolerated. The mere fact that controls are ineffective, as in the evasion of taxes, does not, however, constitute regulation. Nor does restraint of law enforcement in the light of costs, resistance, or other values such as privacy amount to regulation. There should be public recognition that the regulated activity is worthwhile in itself and therefore needs protection as well as control.

Because the activity is valued, there is an inherent strain toward cooperation between the regulators and the regulated. In contrast to control that is indifferent (or hostile) to the activity in question, regulation entails respect for and deference to the system of private ordering. That ordering is, after all, the source of whatever it is we value, whether it be health care or economic productivity. To be sure, cooperation, respect, and deference are variable vectors of the need for control on the one hand and commitment to the enterprise on the other. But regulation is an inherently derivative phenomenon, parasitic upon a substantive activity. Therefore the problem of cooperation cannot be avoided.

I have some qualms about my reference above to private ordering. In our system most regulated enterprise is private, but nominally public agencies, such as colleges, hospitals, or utility companies, are also subject to regulation. The regulation of a public enterprise, however, should not be conflated with the routine exercise of authority within a government hierarchy. We have no good generic term for semi-autonomous units engaged in substantive activities, public or private, but perhaps *enterprise* will do.

The paradigmatic examples of regulators—FTC, FCC, FDA, etc.—suggest that the process is, ideally, sustained and focused. Regulation is not achieved by passing a law. There must be monitoring of relevant activities, continuing assessment of public values at stake, and rule-making sensitive to changing needs and circumstances. In other words, the process of control is intimately involved with the regulated activity. That is why we need quasi-permanent agencies capable of detailed assessment and rule-making. But the form of the agency is not crucial. It could even be a committee of Congress or of a state legislature, but in that case the committee would need an appropriate staff, including field offices, and would in time look very much like an autonomous regulatory agency.

Regulation is focused when it systematically attends to selected activities, values, or industries. This permits the development of expertise so that the regulatory staff is able to hold its own in dealing with a well-informed clientele; at the same time, it becomes competent to assess the capacity of an enterprise to cooperate and conform. The sharper the focus of control, the more readily can we develop legislative guidelines to check the discretion of the regulators.

These and other attributes of ideal regulation are worth noting because they point to conditions under which the effort to regulate is likely to be effective (including cost-effective) and when it is likely to fail. In other words, we need the same attention to the regulatory process as we give, say, to the judicial process. As Lon Fuller (1978) emphasized, adjudication is better suited to some forms of decision-making than to others.

It does not follow, of course, that as a practical matter we can avoid using regulatory agencies or courts for ends to which they are ill adapted. Sometimes we have to use blunt instruments. But a developed theory of the institutional form can alert us to inefficiency or overreaching and can suggest measures of control.

A corollary is that the study of regulation is not well served by a stark contrast between regulation and nonregulation. We need more complex models to specify the dimensions along which systematic variation may be expected—variation in objectives, strategies, and contexts. Some settings are more receptive to regulation than others; some activities are highly vulnerable to intrusive control yet may be conducive to self-regulation; some regulatory doctrines and methods are more legalistic and rule-bound than others. If the scientific study of regulation is to be advanced, more effort must be made to develop coherent models encompassing a range of variables and based on codification of available research and experience.

Bureaucracy and Regulation

The debate about regulation—and the quest for a social science handle—have brought renewed attention to the costs and benefits of bureaucratic organization. I want to comment briefly on some aspects of both public and private bureaucracy as they bear on regulation.

It was for a time fashionable to emphasize the limits of Weber's model of bureaucratic rationality and to stress the emergence of more flexible, purposive post-bureaucratic forms. That remains a relevant perspective. The experience of Watergate, however, reminded us that federal bureaucrats are not properly perceived as the President's soldiers, to be deployed and monitored from a command post in the White House. Officials in charge of agencies and programs are responsible to congressional mandates as well as to presidential direction. Their duties run to objectively defined purposes and values, and it is dereliction of duty to be supinely responsive to pressure, whether from self-interested clienteles or from a President's staff. The operative phrase is "supinely responsive." Clearly, officials should be open to direction from above and sensitive to claims from without. But genuinely responsive administration blends a posture of openness with a commitment to institutional integrity (Nonet and Selznick, 1978). It should not be equated with opportunistic adaptation to vagrant pressures or unprincipled demands.

At its best, public bureaucracy is a locus of value and a vehicle for transforming abstract purposes and policies into operative missions, rules, and procedures. The worth of bureaucracy, thus understood, lies in its capacity to define the public interest in a contextual way by implementing mandates while taking account of constraining conditions, special opportunities, and multiple values. Achievement of that competence is or should be the main objective of public administration. Therefore the most important procedures are those that enhance the cognitive competence of a regulatory agency.

Michel Crozier (1964, p. 187) once described bureaucracy as "an organization that cannot correct its behavior by learning from its errors." Crozier's insight, though overly restrictive as a definition, is important because it identifies what is both a central need and a characteristic pathology in administrative systems. Of course, cognitive competence is a variable achievement that is not equally important in all administrative systems. But it is especially important in those agencies, including regulatory agencies, that are governed by statutes that mandate a quest for the public interest.

Private Bureaucracy

An important variable affecting regulatory strategy and effectiveness is the character of private bureaucracy. In a study of industrial justice (Selznick, 1969) I argued that the protection of employee rights and the acceptance of collective bargaining are made significantly easier by the development of bureaucracy in industrial management. Professional management has its own imperatives, manifested in commitment to explicit policy, systematic procedure, and the maintenance of organizational equilibrium. In other words, the logic of management strains against arbitrary authority. As a result, private bureaucracy finds congenial at least a measure of managerial self-restraint. By itself this affinity cannot be relied on for protection of employee interests. Coercion and collaboration by unions and government have been essential. But the logic of bureaucracy makes its own contribution to the social foundations of industrial justice.

This approach looks to bureaucracy as a receptive institutional setting for social control. We expect that bureaucratic organizations, which are usually but not necessarily quite large, will have the disposition, competence, and resources to institutionalize regulatory policies once a decision has been made to accept them. So far as I know, this matter has not been closely studied over a range of policies. Obviously, it would be important to know what patterned variation occurs. Nevertheless, the history of many hard-fought issues, such as collective bargaining, affirmative action, and environmental protection, seems to confirm the broad hypothesis.

A corollary is the strategy of institutional design. This is not new, of course, and industrial relations remains an instructive example, but the idea has been receiving increasing attention among students of regulation (see Bardach and Kagan, 1982, chapter 8; Stone, 1975, chapters 17–19, and 1980, pp. 36ff.). I have in mind the implementation of regulatory policy by requiring the establishment of administrative or technical procedures and/or organizational units that will, in effect, commit the enterprise to sustained and effective concern for the values at stake. The strategy of institutional design is a way of mandating self-regulation. The enterprise is held to standards of rational and concerned decisionmaking but details are left to autonomous judgment. The implicit model is enterprise professionalism.

This strategy offers a special challenge to students of organization. As Christopher Stone (1980, p. 38) points out:

> These bureaucratic constraints . . . are particularly germane to a theory of controlling large organizations. . . . [A] ban on cyclamates in soft drinks is as intelligibly applied to a sole proprietor, who bottles soft drinks commercially in his garage, as to a 10,000 employee conglomerate. By contrast, bureaucratic standards, such as those that mandate reporting obligations between vice-president and president, are, as control devices, inherently corporate.

As I see it, the fundamental objective is to create responsible organizations, that is, to build into the operative structure of the enterprise the conditions that make for self-restraint. My impression is that sustained attention to this problem can be a promising focus for organization theory as well as for the study of regulation.

Bibliography

ABERNATHY, WILLIAM J. 1978. *The Productivity Dilemma.* Baltimore: Johns Hopkins University Press.

ABERNATHY, WILLIAM J., KIM B. CLARK, and ALAN M. KANTROW. 1983. *Industrial Renaissance.* New York: Basic Books.

ABOLAFIA, MITCHEL Y. 1981. "Taming the Market: Self-Regulation in the Commodity Futures Industry." Ph.D. dissertation, State University of New York at Stony Brook.

ACKERMAN, BRUCE A., and WILLIAM T. HASSLER. 1980. "Beyond the New Deal: Coal and the Clean Air Act." *Yale Law Journal* 89:1466–1571.

———. 1981. *Clean Air/Dirty Coal.* New Haven: Yale University Press.

AIKEN, MICHAEL, and JERALD HAGE. 1968. "Organizational Interdependence and Intra-Organizational Structure." *American Sociological Review* 33:912–930.

ALFRED, R. 1975. *Health Care Politics.* Chicago: University of Chicago Press.

ALLISON, GRAHAM T. 1971. *Essence of Decision: Explaining the Cuban Missile Crisis.* Boston: Little, Brown.

ARANSON, PETER, ERNEST T. GELLHORN, and GLEN O. ROBINSON. 1981. "The Legislative Creation of Legislators: The Delegation Doctrine in a Public Choice Perspective." Prepared for Liberty Fund, Inc., Seminar on Constitutional Limits to the Delegation of Regulatory Authority. Atlanta: Emory University.

ARNOLD, DOUGLAS R. 1980. *Congress and the Bureaucracy: A Theory of Influence.* New Haven: Yale University Press.

ARROW, KENNETH J. 1951. *Social Choice and Individual Values.* New York: John Wiley and Sons.

———. 1962. "The Economic Implications of Learning by Doing." *Review of Economic Studies* 29:155–173.

———. 1964. "Control in Large Organizations." *Management Science* 10: 397–408.

———. 1970. "Political and Economic Evaluation of Social Effects and Externalities." Pp. 1–23 in *The Analysis of Public Output,* ed. Julius Margolis. New York: National Bureau of Economic Research.

———. 1982. "Risk Perception in Psychology and Economics." *Economic Inquiry* 20:1–9.

369

ASCH, SOLOMON E. November 1955. "Opinions and Social Pressure." *Scientific American* 193:31–35.

ATTEWELL, PAUL, and DEAN R. GERSTEIN. 1979. "Government Policy and Local Practice." *American Sociological Review* 44:311–327.

AVERCH, HARVEY, and LELAND L. JOHNSON. 1962. "Behavior of the Firm under Regulatory Constraint." *American Economic Review* 52: 1052–1069.

BACHARACH, SAMUEL B., and EDWARD J. LAWLER. 1980. *Power and Politics in Organizations.* San Francisco: Jossey-Bass.

BADARACCO, JOSEPH L., JR. 1981. "A Study of Adversarial and Cooperative Relationships between Business and Government in Four Countries." Ph.D. dissertation, Harvard Business School.

BANDURA, A. 1977. *Social Learning Theory.* New York: Prentice-Hall.

BANKSTON, MARY. 1982. "Organizational Reporting in a School District: State and Federal Programs." Stanford, Calif.: Institute for Research on Educational Finance and Governance, Stanford University.

BARDACH, EUGENE, and ROBERT A. KAGAN. 1982. *Going by the Book: The Problem of Regulatory Unreasonableness.* Philadelphia: Temple University Press.

BARRINGER, FELICITY. 10 November 1981. "Over-Regulation? Public Finds Agencies Not Guilty." *Washington Post,* p. A-17.

BASLOW, MORRIS. 1984. "Whistleblowing vs. Proprietary Rights." Pp. 57–70 in *Science as Intellectual Property,* ed. Dorothy Nelkin. New York: Macmillan.

BAUMOL, W. J. 1967. *Business Behavior, Value and Growth.* New York: Harcourt, Brace and World.

BAUMOL, W. J., and D. F. BRADFORD. 1970. "Optimal Departures from Marginal Cost Pricing." *American Economic Review* 60:265–283.

BAUMOL, W. J., and A. KLEVORICK. 1970. "Input Choices and Rate-of-Return Regulation: An Overview of the Discussion." *Bell Journal of Economics* 1:162–190.

BAZELON, D. L. 1979. "Risk and Responsibility." *Science* 205:277–280.

BECKER, GARY S. 1983. "A Theory of Competition among Pressure Groups for Political Influence." *Quarterly Journal of Economics* 98: 371–400.

BENDIX, REINHARD. 1949. *Higher Civil Servants in American Society.* Boulder: University of Colorado Press.

———. 1968. "Bureaucracy." *International Encyclopedia of the Social Sciences* 2:206–219. New York: Macmillan.

BERNSTEIN, MARVER H. 1955. *Regulating Business by Independent Commission.* Princeton: Princeton University Press.

BESEN, S. M., B. M. MITCHELL, R. G. NOLL, B. M. OWEN, R. E. PARK, and J. N. ROSSE. 1977. "Economic Policy Research on Cable Television: Assessing the Costs and Benefits of Cable Deregulation." In *Deregulation of Cable Television,* ed. Paul W. MacAvoy. Washington, D.C.: American Enterprise Institute.

BINGHAM, EULA. 1979. Address. Pp. 56–61 in *Risk/Benefit Analysis in the Legislative Process*. Hearing before the U.S. House Committee on Science and Technology and the U.S. Senate Commerce, Science, and Transportation Committee, 24 and 25 July, 1979. Washington, D.C.: U.S. Government Printing Office.

BLACK, DONALD. 1976. *The Behavior of Law*. New York: Academic Press.

BLAU, PETER M. 1970. "A Formal Theory of Differentiation in Organizations." *American Sociological Review* 35:201–218.

BLAU, PETER M., and RICHARD A. SCHOENHEN. 1971. *The Structure of Organizations*. New York: Basic Books.

BLAU, PETER M., and W. RICHARD SCOTT. 1962. *Formal Organizations*. San Francisco: Chandler.

BRADLEY, JOSEPH F. 1965. *The Role of Trade Associations and Professional Business Societies in America*. University Park, Penn.: Pennsylvania State University Press.

BRADY, ROBERT A. 1943. *Business as a System of Power*. New York: Columbia University Press.

BRAEUTIGAM, RONALD R., and ROGER G. NOLL. 1984. "The Regulation of Surface Freight Transportation: The Welfare Effects Revisited." *Review of Economics and Statistics* 66: 80–87.

BRANDT, RICHARD M. 1981. *Public Education under Scrutiny*. Washington, D.C.: University Press of America.

BREYER, STEPHEN G. 1981. *Regulation and Its Reform*. Cambridge, Mass.: Harvard University Press.

BREYER, STEPHEN G., and PAUL W. MACAVOY. 1974. *Energy Regulation by the Federal Power Commission*. Washington, D.C.: Brookings Institution.

BRIGMAN, WILLIAM E. 1981. "The Executive Branch and the Independent Regulatory Agencies." *Presidential Studies Quarterly* 11:244–261.

BRISBIN, RICHARD A., JR. 1981. "Before Bureaucracy: State Courts and the Administration of Public Services in the Old Northwest, 1787–1850." Presented at the 1981 Annual Meeting of the American Political Science Association, New York.

BROCK, GERALD W. 1981. *The Telecommunications Industry: The Dynamics of Market Structure*. Cambridge, Mass.: Harvard University Press.

BROWN, MONTAGUE, and HOWARD LEWIS. 1976. *Hospital Management Systems: Multi-Unit Organization and Delivery of Health Care*. Germantown, Md.: Aspen Systems Corp.

BROWN, R. A., and C. H. GREEN. 1980. "Precepts of Safety Assessments." *Journal of the Operational Research Society* 11:563–571.

BRUNER, JEROME S., and CECILE C. GOODMAN. 1947. "Value and Need as Organizing Factors in Perception." *Journal of Abnormal and Social Psychology* 42:33–44.

BUCHANAN, JAMES M. 1965. "An Economic Theory of Clubs." *Economica* 32:1–14.

BUCHANAN, JAMES M., and GORDON TULLOCK. 1962. *The Calculus of Consent*. Ann Arbor: University of Michigan Press.

BURMAN, SANDRA, and BARBARA E. HARRELL-BOND. 1979. *The Imposition of Law.* New York: Academic Press.

BURNESS, H. STUART, W. DAVID MONTGOMERY, and JAMES P. QUIRK. 1980a. "Capital Contracting and the Regulated Firm." *American Economic Review* 70:342–354.

———. 1980b. "The Turnkey Era in Nuclear Power." *Land Economics* 56:188–202.

BURNS, T., and G. STALKER. 1966. *The Management of Innovation.* London: Tavistock Publications.

CANTER, RICHARD S. 1978. "Dispute Settlement and Dispute Processing in Zambia: Individual Choice versus Societal Constraints." Pp. 247–280 in *The Disputing Process—Law in Ten Societies,* ed. Laura Nader and Harry F. Todd, Jr. New York: Columbia University Press.

CAPLOW, THEODORE. 1968. *Two against One: Coalitions in Triads.* Englewood Cliffs, N.J.: Prentice-Hall.

———. 1975. *Toward Social Hope.* New York: Basic Books.

CAPRON, WILLIAM M., ed. 1971. *Technological Change in Regulated Industries.* Washington, D.C.: Brookings Institution.

CARY, WILLIAM L. 1967. *Politics and the Regulatory Agencies.* New York: McGraw-Hill.

CENTER FOR POLICY ALTERNATIVES, MASSACHUSETTS INSTITUTE OF TECHNOLOGY. 1980. "Benefits of Environmental Health and Safety Regulation." Prepared for the Senate Committee on Governmental Affairs, 25 March, 1980. Washington, D.C.: Government Printing Office.

———. 1982. "Analyzing the Benefits of Health, Safety, and Environmental Regulations." CPA Report # CPA-82-16. Cambridge, Mass.: Center for Policy Alternatives.

CHANDLER, ALFRED D. 1977. *The Visible Hand.* Cambridge, Mass.: Harvard University Press.

CHOPER, JESSE H. 1980. *Judicial Review and the National Political Process: A Functional Reconsideration of the Role of the Supreme Court.* Chicago: University of Chicago Press.

CLARK UNIVERSITY and DECISION RESEARCH. 1982. *The Nature of Hazard.* Report 82-8. Eugene, Ore.: Decision Research.

COASE, R. H. 1937. "The Nature of the Firm." *Economica* n.s. 4:386–405.

———. 1960. "The Problem of Social Cost." *Journal of Law and Economics* 3:1–44.

COHEN, B., and I. LEE. 1979. "A Catalog of Risks." *Health Physics* 36:707–722.

COHEN, HARRY. 1965. *The Demonics of Bureaucracy.* Ames: Iowa State University Press.

COHEN, LINDA. 1979. "Innovation and Atomic Energy: Nuclear Power Regulation, 1966–Present." *Law and Contemporary Problems* 43:67–97.

COHEN, MICHAEL, JAMES MARCH, and JOHAN OLSEN. 1972. "A Garbage Can Model of Organizational Choice." *Administrative Science Quarterly* 17:1–25.

COLSON, E. 1974. *Tradition and Contract: The Problem of Order.* Chicago: Aldine.

COMANOR, WILLIAM S., and BRIDGER M. MITCHELL. 1972. "The Costs of Planning: The FCC and Cable Television." *Journal of Law and Economics* 15:177–206.

COMAR, CYRIL L. 1979. "Risk: A Pragmatic De Minimus Approach." *Science* 203:319.

COMMISSION ON LAW AND THE ECONOMY. 1979. *Federal Regulation: Roads to Reform.* New York: American Bar Association.

COMMODITY EXCHANGE, INC. 1980. "Chronology of Activities relating to the Silver Market from September 1979 through March 1980." Press release. New York: Commodity Exchange.

CORNELL, NINA W., ROGER G. NOLL, and BARRY WEINGAST. 1976. "Safety Regulation." Pp. 457–504 in *Setting National Priorities: The Next Ten Years,* ed. Henry Owen and Charles Schultze. Washington, D.C.: Brookings Institution.

CORSON, JOHN, and R. S. PAUL. 1966. *Men near the Top.* Baltimore: Johns Hopkins University Press.

CORWIN, RONALD G. 1972. "Strategies for Organizational Innovation: An Empirical Comparison." *American Sociological Review* 37:441–454.

COUNCIL FOR SCIENCE AND SOCIETY. 1977. *The Acceptability of Risks: The Logic and Social Dynamics of Fair Decisions and Effective Controls.* Chichester, Eng.: Barry Rose.

CRANDALL, ROBERT W. 1979. "The Impossibility of Regulating Competition in Interstate Telecommunications Markets." Unpublished manuscript. Washington, D.C.: Brookings Institution.

CROUCH, E. A. C., and R. WILSON. 1982. *Risk Analysis.* Cambridge, Mass.: Ballinger.

CROZIER, MICHEL. 1964. *The Bureaucratic Phenomenon.* Chicago: University of Chicago Press.

CUSHMAN, ROBERT E. 1941. *The Independent Regulatory Commissions.* New York: Oxford University Press.

CYERT, RICHARD M., and JAMES G. MARCH. 1963. *A Behavioral Theory of the Firm.* Englewood Cliffs, N.J.: Prentice-Hall.

DAHL, ROBERT A. 1961. *Who Governs.* New Haven: Yale University Press.

DALES, J. H. 1968. *Pollution, Property and Prices.* Toronto: University of Toronto Press.

DANZIGER, JAMES N. 1975. "Comparing Approaches to the Study of Financial Resource Allocation." Pp. 55–85 in *Comparative Public Policy: Issues, Theories and Methods,* ed. by Craig Liske, William Loehr, and John McCamant. Beverly Hills, Calif.: Sage Publications.

DARBEL, A., and D. SCHNAPPER. 1969. *Les agents du système politique.* Paris: Mouton.

——. 1972. *Le système administratif.* Paris: Ecole Pratique des Hautes Etudes.

DAVIS, LANCE. 1974. "Self-Regulation in Baseball 1909–71." Pp. 349–386 in *Government and the Sports Business,* ed. Roger G. Noll. Washington, D.C.: Brookings Institution.

DAVIS, LANCE, and DOUGLASS NORTH. 1970. "Institutional Change and American Economic Growth: A First Step towards a Theory of Institutional Innovation." *Journal of Economic History* 30:131–149.

Davis, Margaret R., Terrence E. Deal, John W. Meyer, Brian Rowan, W. Richard Scott, and E. Anne Stackhouse. 1977. *The Structure of Educational Systems: Explorations in the Theory of Loosely-Coupled Organizations.* Palo Alto, Calif.: Stanford Center for Research and Development in Teaching, Stanford University.

Demsetz, Harold. 1969. "Perfect Competition, Regulation, and the Stock Market." Pp. 1–22 in *Economic Policy and the Regulation of Corporate Securities,* ed. H. G. Manne. Washington, D.C.: American Enterprise Institute for Public Policy Research.

Dickson, David. 1981. "Limiting Democracy, Technocrats and the Liberal State." *Democracy* 1:61–79.

DiLeonardi, J. W. 1980. "Decisionmaking and Protective Services." *Child Welfare* 59:356–364.

Dill, William. 1962. "The Impact of Environment on Organizational Development." Pp. 94–109 in *Concepts and Issues in Administrative Behavior,* ed. S. Mailick and E. H. Van Ness. Englewood Cliffs, N.J.: Prentice-Hall.

Dingell, John D. 20 October 1966. "Industrial Standards: A Two-Edged Sword." *Congressional Record* 112:28303–28315.

Dixit, Avinash K. 1970. "On the Optimum Structure of Commodity Taxes." *American Economic Review* 60:295–301.

Domhoff, G. William. 1970. *The Higher Circles.* New York: Vintage.

———. 1978. *The Powers that Be.* New York: Vintage.

Dorfman, Robert, and Henry D. Jacoby. 1970. "A Model of Public Decisions Illustrated by a Water Pollution Policy Problem." Pp. 173–231 in *Public Expenditures and Policy Analysis,* 1st ed., ed. Robert H. Haveman and Julius Margolis. Chicago: Markham Publishing.

Downs, Anthony. 1957. *An Economic Theory of Democracy.* New York: Harper and Row.

———. 1967. *Inside Bureaucracy.* Boston: Little, Brown.

Dreman, David N. 1977. *Psychology and the Stock Market.* New York: AMACOM.

———. 1979. *Contrarian Investment Strategy.* New York: Random House.

Eads, George. 1981. "Harnessing Regulation: The Evolving Role of White House Oversight." *Regulation* 5:19–26.

Eaton, Marian. 1980. "The Better Business Bureau: The Voice of the People in the Marketplace." Pp. 233–281 in *No Access to Law,* ed. Laura Nader. New York: Academic Press.

Eckert, Ross D. 1972. "Spectrum Allocation and Regulatory Incentives." In *Conference on Communications Policy Research: Papers and Proceedings.* Washington, D.C.: Office of Telecommunications Policy.

Edelman, Murray. 1964. *The Symbolic Uses of Politics.* Urbana: University of Illinois Press.

Edsall, T. 1981. "Two Aspects of Scientific Responsibility." *Science* 212:11–14.

Einhorn, H. J., and R. M. Hogarth. 1978. "Confidence in Judgment: Persistence of the Illusion of Validity." *Psychological Review* 85:395–416.

EISENSTADT, S. N. 1958. "Bureaucracy and Bureaucratization." *Current Sociology* 7:99–164.

ELECTRIC POWER RESEARCH INSTITUTE. June 1980. "Assessment: The Impact and Influence of TMI." *EPRI Journal* 5:24–33.

ELLING, RAY H. 1963. "The Hospital-Support Game in Urban Center." Pp. 73–111 in *The Hospital in Modern Society,* ed. Eliot Freidson. New York: Free Press.

EPSTEIN, R. A. N.d. *Cognitive Biases: The Institutional Framework.* Unpublished manuscript.

ERICKSON, KAI T. 1966. *Wayward Puritans.* New York: John Wiley and Sons.

ERLICH, EUGENE. 1913. *Grundlegung der Soziologie des Rechts.* Munich: Duncker and Humblot.

ESTER, P., and R. A. WINETT. 1982. "Toward the Development of Effective Antecedent Strategies for Resource Management Programs." *Journal of Environmental Systems* 10:201–222.

ETZIONI, AMITAI. 1959. "Authority Structure and Organizational Effectiveness." *Administrative Science Quarterly* 4:43–67.

―――. 1960. "Two Approaches to Organizational Analysis: A Critique and a Suggestion." *Administrative Science Quarterly* 5:257–278.

EVAN, WILLIAM M. 1966. "The Organization Set: Toward a Theory of Interorganizational Relations." Pp. 173–188 in *Approaches to Organization Design,* ed. James D. Thompson. Pittsburgh: University of Pittsburgh Press.

FAINSOD, MERLE, and LINCOLN GORDON. 1941. *Government and the American Economy.* New York: W. W. Norton.

FENNO, RICHARD. 1978. *Home Style.* Boston: Little, Brown.

FEREJOHN, JOHN A. 1974. *Pork Barrel Politics: Rivers and Harbors Legislation, 1947–1968.* Palo Alto, Calif.: Stanford University Press.

FERGUSON, ALLEN R., and LEONARD LEE LANE, eds. N.d. "Transportation Policy Options: The Political Economy of Regulatory Reform." Washington, D.C.: Public Interest Economics Foundation.

FEYERABEND, PAUL. 1978. *Science in a Free Society.* New York: Schocken.

FIORINA, MORRIS P. 1974. *Representatives, Roll Calls, and Constituencies.* Lexington, Mass.: D. C. Heath.

―――. 1977. *Congress: Keystone of the Washington Establishment.* New Haven: Yale University Press.

―――. 1981. "Universalism, Reciprocity, and Distributive Policymaking in Majority Rule Institutions." Pp. 197–221 in *Research in Public Analysis and Management,* vol. 1, ed. John P. Crecine. Greenwich, Conn.: JAI Press.

―――. 1982a. "Congressmen and Their Constituencies: 1958 and 1978." Pp. 33–64 in *Proceedings of the Thomas P. O'Neill, Jr. Symposium on the U.S. Congress,* ed. Dennis Hale. Boston: Eusey Press.

―――. 1982b. "Legislative Choice of Regulatory Forms: Legal Process or Administrative Process?" *Public Choice* 39:33–66.

FIORINA, MORRIS P., and ROGER G. NOLL. 1978. "Voters, Bureaucrats and Legislators." *Journal of Public Economics* 9:239–254.

FISCHHOFF, BARUCH. 1977. "Cost Benefit Analysis and the Art of Motorcycle Maintenance." *Policy Sciences* 8:177–202.

———. 1982. *Standard Setting Standards*. Report 82-9. Eugene, Ore: Decision Research.

———. 1983a. "Predicting Frames." *Journal of Experimental Psychology: Learning, Memory and Cognition* 9:113–116.

———. 1983b. "Acceptable Risk: The Case of Nuclear Power." *Journal of Policy Analysis and Management* 2:559–575.

———. 1984. "Setting Standards: A Systematic Approach to Managing Public Health and Safety Risks." *Management Science* 30:823–43.

FISCHHOFF, BARUCH, B. GOITEIN, and Z. SHAPIRA. 1982. "The Experienced Utility of Expected Utility Approaches." Pp. 315–339 in *Expectations and Actions: Expectancy-Value Models in Psychology,* ed. Norman T. Feather. Hillsdale, N.J.: Lawrence Associates.

FISCHHOFF, BARUCH, C. HOHENEMSER, R.E. KASPERSON, and R.W. KATES. 1978. "Handling Hazards: Can Hazard Management Be Improved?" *Environment* 20:16–20, 32–37.

FISCHHOFF, BARUCH, S. LICHTENSTEIN, P. SLOVIC, S. DERBY, and R.L. KEENEY. 1981. *Acceptable Risk*. New York: Cambridge University Press.

FISCHHOFF, BARUCH, P. SLOVIC, and S. LICHTENSTEIN. 1977. "Knowing with Certainty: The Appropriateness of Extreme Confidence." *Journal of Experimental Psychology: Human Perception and Performance* 3:552–564.

———. 1978. "Fault Trees: Sensitivity of Estimated Failure Probabilities to Problem Representation." *Journal of Experimental Psychology: Human Perception and Performance* 4:330–344.

———. 1980a. "Knowing What You Want: Measuring Labile Values." Pp. 117–141 in *Cognitive Processes in Choice and Decision Behavior,* ed. T. Wallsten. Hillsdale, N.J.: L. Erlbaum Associates.

———. 1980b. "Labile Values: A Challenge for Risk Assessment." Pp. 57–66 in *Society, Technology, and Risk Assessment,* ed. Jobst Conrad. London: Academic Press.

———. 1983. "'The Public' vs. 'The Experts': Perceived vs. Actual Disagreements about the Risks of Nuclear Power." Pp. 235–249 in *Analysis of Actual vs. Perceived Risks,* ed. V. Covello, G. Flamm, J. Rodericks, and R. Tardiff. New York: Plenum.

FISCHHOFF, BARUCH, P. SLOVIC, S. LICHTENSTEIN, S. READ, and B. COMBS. 1978. "How Safe Is Safe Enough? A Psychometric Study of Attitudes towards Technological Risks and Benefits." *Policy Sciences* 8:127–152.

FISCHHOFF, BARUCH, S. WATSON, and C. HOPE. 1983. "Defining Risk." Report 82-15. Eugene, Ore.: Decision Research.

FRIEDLAENDER, ANN F. 1969. *The Dilemma of Freight Transport Regulation.* Washington, D.C.: Brookings Institution.

FRIEDMAN, LAWRENCE M. 1968. *Government and Slum Housing: A Century of Frustration.* Chicago: Rand McNally.

———. 1975. *The Legal System: A Social Science Perspective.* New York: Russell Sage.

FRIEDMAN, LAWRENCE M., and JACK LADINSKY. 1967. "Social Change and the Law of Industrial Accidents." *Columbia Law Review* 67:50–82.

FRIEDMAN, LAWRENCE M., and STEWART MACAULAY. 1977. *Law and the Behavioral Sciences,* 2nd edition. Indianapolis: Bobbs-Merrill.

FRIEDMAN, MILTON, and L. J. SAVAGE. 1948. "The Utility Analysis of Choices involving Risk." *Journal of Political Economy* 56:279–304.

FRIENDLY, HENRY J. 1962. *The Federal Administrative Agencies: The Need for Better Definition of Standards.* Cambridge, Mass.: Harvard University Press.

FUCHS, V. R. 1976. "From Bismarck to Woodcock: The Irrational Pursuit of National Health Insurance." *Journal of Law and Public Policy* 19:347–359.

FULLER, LON L. 1978. "The Forms and Limits of Adjudication." *Harvard Law Review* 92:353–409.

FURNER, MARY O. 1975. *Advocacy and Objectivity: A Crisis in the Professionalization of American Social Science, 1865–1905.* Lexington: University Press of Kentucky.

GARDNER, G. T. et al. 1982. "Risk and Benefit Perceptions, Acceptability Judgments, and Self-Reported Actions Toward Nuclear Power." *Journal of Social Psychology* 116:179–197.

GARWIN, RICHARD L. 1983. "Who Proposes, Who Disposes, Who Pays?" *Bulletin of the Atomic Scientists* 39b:9–11.

GELLER, E. S., R. A. WINETT, and P. B. EVERETT. 1982. *Preserving the Environment: New Strategies for Behavior Change.* Elmsford, N.Y.: Pergamon Press.

GELLHORN, WALTER. 1941. *Federal Administrative Proceedings.* Westport, Conn.: Greenwood Press.

GELLMAN, AARON J. 1971. "Surface Freight Transportation." Pp. 166–196 in *Technological Change in Regulated Industries,* ed. William M. Capron. Washington, D.C.: Brookings Institution.

GIBBARD, ALLAN. 1973. "Manipulation of Voting Schemes: A General Result." *Econometrica* 41:587–601.

GIERKE, OTTO VON. 1868. *Das Deutsche Genossenschaftrecht.* Berlin: Wiedmann.

GLICK, IRA O. 1957. "A Social Psychological Study of Futures Trading." Ph.D. dissertation, University of Chicago.

GORMLEY, WILLIAM T., JR. 1979. "A Test of the Revolving Door Hypothesis at the FCC." *American Journal of Political Science* 23:665–683.

GOULDNER, ALVIN W. 1954. *Patterns of Industrial Bureaucracy.* New York: Free Press.

———. 1959. "Reciprocity and Autonomy in Functional Theory." Pp. 241–270 in *Symposium on Sociological Theory,* ed. Llewellyn Gross. Evanston, Ill.: Row, Peterson.

GREEN, COLIN H. 1980a. "Risk: Beliefs and Attitudes." Pp. 277–291 in *Fires and Human Behavior,* ed. David Canter. New York: Wiley.

———. 1980b. "Revealed Preference Theory: Assumptions and Presumptions." Pp. 49–56 in *Society, Technology and Risk Assessment,* ed. J. Conrad. London: Academic Press.

GREEN, COLIN H., and R. A. BROWN. 1980. "Through a Glass Darkly: Perceiving Perceived Risks to Health and Safety." Research paper, School of Architecture, Duncan of Jordanstone College of Art, University of Dundee, Scotland.

GREEN, HAROLD P., and ALAN ROSENTHAL. 1963. *Government of the Atom: The Integration of Powers.* New York: Atherton Press.

GREEN, MARK, and BEVERLY MOORE, JR. 1973. "Winter's Discontent: Market Failure and Consumer Welfare." *Yale Law Journal* 82:903–919.

GREEN, MARK, and RALPH NADER. 1973. "Economic Regulation vs. Competition: Uncle Sam the Monopoly Man." *Yale Law Journal* 82:871–889.

GREEN, MARK, and NORMAN WAITZMAN. 1981. *Business War on the Law: An Analysis of the Benefits of Federal Health/Safety Enforcement.* Washington, D.C.: Corporate Accountability Research Group.

GREENBERG, DAVID I., and THOMAS H. STANTON. 1980. "Business Groups, Consumer Problems: The Contradiction of Trade Association Complaint Handling." Pp. 193–231 in *No Access to Law,* ed. Laura Nader. New York: Academic Press.

GRETHER, DAVID M., and CHARLES R. PLOTT. 1979. "Economic Theory of Choice and the Preference Reversal Phenomenon." *American Economic Review* 69:623–638.

GRIESEMEYER, J. M., and D. OKRENT. 1981. "Risk Management and Decision Rules for Light Water Reactors." 30pp. Los Angeles: UCLA School of Engineering and Applied Science.

GUSFIELD, JOSEPH R. 1967. "Moral Passage: The Symbolic Process in Public Designations of Deviance." *Social Problems* 15:175–188.

HAEFELE, EDWIN T. 1973. "Environmental Quality as a Problem of Social Choice." Pp. 281–332 in *Environmental Quality Analysis: Theory and Method in the Social Sciences,* ed. Allen V. Kneese and Blair T. Bower. Baltimore: Johns Hopkins Press for Resources for the Future.

HAGE, JERALD, and MICHAEL AIKEN. 1967. "Program Change and Organizational Properties: A Comparative Analysis." *American Journal of Sociology* 72:503–519.

HAHN, ROBERT W., and ROGER G. NOLL. 1982. "Designing a Market for Tradable Emissions Permits." Pp. 119–146 in *Reform of Environmental Regulation,* ed. Wesley A. Magat. Cambridge, Mass.: Ballinger.

———. 1983. "Barriers to Implementing Tradable Air Pollution Permits: Problems of Regulatory Interactions." *Yale Journal on Regulation* 1:63–90.

HANEY, LEWIS H. 1910. *A Congressional History of Railways in the United States, 1850–1887.* Madison: University of Wisconsin Press.

HARNISCHFEGER, ANNEGRET. 1978. *Minority Education, 1960–1978: Grounds, Gains, and Gaps.* Vol. 1. Chicago: Central Midwest Education Lab.

HARRIS, L. 1980. "Risk in a Complex Society." Public opinion survey conducted for March and McLennan Companies, Inc.

HARSANYI, JOHN C. 1969. "Rational-Choice Models of Political Behavior vs. Functionalist and Conformist Theories." *World Politics* 21:513–538.

HART, H. L. A. 1961. *The Concept of Law.* New York: Oxford University Press.

HARTER, PHILLIP J. 1979. *Regulatory Use of Standards: Implications for Standards Writer.* Washington, D.C.: U.S. Department of Commerce. U.S. National Bureau of Standards.

HAWLEY, JAMES P. 1981. "Protecting Capital from Itself: Transnational Banks and U.S. Attempts to Regulate the Eurocurrency System." Department of Sociology, University of California, Davis.

HAZARD, WILLIAM R. 1978. *Education and the Law: Cases and Materials on Public Schools.* 2nd ed. New York: Free Press.

HELLER, WALTER P., and KARL SCHELL. 1974. "On Optimal Taxation with Costly Administration." *American Economic Review* 64:338–345.

HEMENWAY, DAVID. 1975. *Industrywide Voluntary Product Standards.* Cambridge, Mass.: Ballinger.

HICKS, J. R. 1939. "The Foundations of Welfare Economics." *Economic Journal* 49:696–712.

HIERONYMUS, THOMAS A. 1971. *Economics of Futures Trading.* New York: Commodity Research Bureau.

———. 1977. "Manipulation in Commodity Futures Trading: Toward a Definition." *Symposium on Commodity Futures Regulation, Hofstra Law Review* 6:41–56.

HINCHMAN, WALTER R. 1981. "Briefing Paper on the Evolution of Common Carrier Regulation." Pp. 45–53 in *Status of Competition and Deregulation in the Telecommunications Industry.* Hearing before the Subcommittee on Telecommunications, Consumer Protection and Finance, Committee on Energy and Commerce. Serial No. 97-29, 97th Congress, First Session.

HIRSCH, PAUL. 1972. "Processing Fads and Fashions by Cultural Industry Systems: An Organization-Set Analysis." *American Journal of Sociology* 77:639–659.

HOFFMAN, G. WRIGHT. 1932. *Futures Trading upon Organized Commodity Markets.* Philadelphia: University of Pennsylvania Press.

HOGARTH, R. M. 1981. "Beyond Discrete Biases: Functional and Dysfunctional Aspects of Judgmental Heuristics." *Psychological Bulletin* 90:197–217.

HOLDEN, CONSTANCE. 1980. "Scientist with Unpopular Data Loses Job." *Science* 210:749–750.

HOMANS, GEORGE C. 1950. *The Human Group.* New York: Harcourt, Brace and World.

HOWARD, R. A., J. E. MATHESON, and D. OWEN. 1978. "The Value of Life and Nuclear Design." *Probabilistic Analysis of Nuclear Reactor Safety.* Topical meeting proceedings, Los Angeles, 8–10 May 1978, sponsored by ANS, European Nuclear Society, and OECD. 3 vols. La Grange Park, Ill.: American Nuclear Society 2:IV.2–9.

HUGGINS, H. C., JR., and RICHARD VACCA. 1979. *Law and Education: Contemporary Issues and Court Decisions*. Charlottesville, Va.: Michie Publishing.

HUNT, MICHAEL S. 1975. "Trade Associations and Self-Regulation: Major Home Appliances." Pp. 39–55 in *Regulating the Product: Quality and Variety*, ed. Richard E. Caves and Marc J. Roberts. Cambridge, Mass.: Ballinger.

HUNTER, FLOYD. 1953. *Community Power Structure*. Chapel Hill: University of North Carolina Press.

HYNES, M., and E. VANMARCKE. 1976. "Reliability of Embankment Performance Prediction." In *Proceedings of the ASCE Engineering Mechanics Division Specialty Conference on Mechanics in Engineering*. Waterloo, Ontario: Solid Mechanics Division, University of Waterloo.

IRWIN, HAROLD S. 1954. *Evolution of Futures Trading*. Madison, Wis.: Mimir Publishers.

JACOB, HERBERT. 1971. "Black and White Perceptions of Justice in the City." *Law and Society Review* 6:69–89.

JAFFE, LOUIS. 1973. "The Illusion of the Ideal Administration." *Harvard Law Review* 86:1183–1199.

JARRELL, GREGG A. 1978. "The Demand for State Regulation of the Electric Utility Industry." *Journal of Law and Economics* 21:269–295.

JOHNSON, CHARLES A. 1979. "Judicial Decisions and Organization Change: Some Theoretical and Empirical Notes on State Court Decisions and State Administrative Agencies." *Law and Society Review* 14:27–56.

JOHNSON, E. J., and A. TVERSKY. In press. "Representations of Perceptions and Risk." *Journal of Experimental Psychology: General*.

JOSKOW, PAUL L. 1974. "Inflation and Environmental Concern: Structural Change in the Process of Public Utility Price Regulation." *Journal of Law and Economics* 17:291–327.

JOSKOW, PAUL L., and ROGER G. NOLL. 1981. "Regulation in Theory and Practice: An Overview." Pp. 1–65 in *Studies in Public Regulation*, ed. Gary Fromm. Cambridge, Mass.: MIT Press.

KAGEL, J. H., and R. C. WINKLER. 1972. "Behavioral Economics: Areas of Cooperative Research between Economics and Applied Behavior Analysis." *Journal of Applied Behavior Analysis* 5:335–342.

KAHN, ALFRED E. 1977. "Deregulation of Air Transportation Regulation." Speech given at Northwestern University, Evanston, Illinois.

———. 1979. "Applications of Economics to an Imperfect World." *American Economic Review, Papers and Proceedings* 69:1–13.

KAHNEMAN, D., P. SLOVIC, and A. TVERSKY. 1982. *Judgment under Uncertainty: Heuristics and Biases*. New York: Cambridge University Press.

KAHNEMAN, D., and A. TVERSKY. 1979. "Prospect Theory: An Analysis of Decisions under Risk." *Econometrica* 47:262–291.

KALDOR, N. 1939. "Welfare Propositions in Economics." *Economic Journal* 49:549–552.

KATZMANN, ROBERT A. 1980. "Federal Trade Commission." Pp. 152–187 in *The Politics of Regulation*, ed. James Q. Wilson. New York: Basic Books.

KAUFMAN, HERBERT. 1975. "The Natural History of Human Organization." *Administration and Society* 7:131–149.

KAUFMAN, HERBERT, and MICHAEL COUZENS. 1973. *Administrative Feedback: Monitoring Subordinates' Behavior.* Washington, D.C.: Brookings Institution.

KEELER, THEODORE E. 1972. "Airline Regulation and Market Performance." *Bell Journal of Economics and Management Science* 3:399–424.

KELMAN, STEVEN. 1981a. "Cost-Benefit Analysis—An Ethical Critique." *Regulation* 5:33–40.

_____. 1981b. *Regulating America, Regulating Sweden.* Cambridge, Mass.: MIT Press.

KENNEDY, DONALD. 1981. "The Politics of Preventive Health." *Technology Review* 84:58–60.

KIMBERLY, JOHN R., ROBERT H. MILES, and ASSOCIATES. 1980. *The Organizational Life Cycle.* San Francisco: Jossey-Bass.

KINZER, DAVID M. 1977. *Health Controls out of Control: Warning to the Nation from Massachusetts.* Chicago: Teach'em.

KIRP, DAVID. 1976. "Proceduralism and Bureaucracy: Due Process in the School Setting." *Stanford Law Review* 28:841–876.

KNIGHT, FRANK H. 1921. *Risk, Uncertainty, and Profit.* Boston: Houghton-Mifflin.

KOLKO, GABRIEL. 1963. *The Triumph of Conservatism: A Reinterpretation of American History.* New York: Free Press.

_____. 1965. *Railroads and Regulation, 1877–1916.* New York: W. W. Norton.

KRIER, JAMES, and EDMUND URSIN. 1977. *Pollution and Policy: A Case Essay on California and Federal Experience with Motor Vehicle Air Pollution, 1940–1975.* Berkeley and Los Angeles: University of California Press.

KUDRLE, ROBERT T. 1975. "Regulation and Self-Regulation in the Farm Machinery Industry." Pp. 57–73 in *Regulating the Product: Quality and Variety,* ed. Richard E. Caves and Marc J. Roberts. Cambridge, Mass.: Ballinger.

KUNREUTHER, H., R. GINSBERG, L. MILLER, P. SAGI, P. SLOVIC, B. BORKAN, and N. KATZ. 1978. *Disaster Insurance Protection: Public Policy Lessons.* New York: Wiley and Sons.

LAMB, GEORGE P., and CARRINGTON SHIELDS. 1971. *Trade Association Law and Practice.* Boston: Little, Brown.

LANDIS, JAMES M. 1938. *The Administrative Process.* New Haven: Yale University Press.

LAVE, L. 1981. *The Strategy of Social Regulation.* Washington, D.C.: Brookings Institution.

LAWLER, JOHN P. 1981. "'Whistle-blowee' Responds." Letter to the editor. *Science* 211:875–876.

LAYTON, E. T., JR. 1971. *The Revolt of the Engineers.* Cleveland: Press of Case Western Reserve University.

LEIBENSTEIN, HARVEY. 1966. "Allocative Efficiency vs. 'X-Efficiency.'" *American Economic Review* 56:392–415.

LETWIN, WILLIAM. 1965. *Law and Economic Policy in America: The Evolution of the Sherman Antitrust Act.* New York: Random House.

LEVINE, MICHAEL E. 1965. "Is Regulation Necessary? California Air Transportation and National Regulatory Policy." *Yale Law Journal* 74:1416–1447.

LEVINE, MICHAEL E., and CHARLES R. PLOTT. 1975. "On Using the Agenda to Influence Group Decisions: Theory, Experiments, and an Application." Social Science Working Paper 66. Pasadena: California Institute of Technology.

LICHTENSTEIN, SARAH, and P. SLOVIC. 1971. "Reversals of Preference between Bids and Choices in Gambling Decisions." *Journal of Experimental Psychology* 89:46–55.

LICHTENSTEIN, SARAH, P. SLOVIC, B. FISCHHOFF, M. LAYMAN, and B. COMBS. 1978. "Judged Frequency of Lethal Events." *Journal of Experimental Psychology: Human Learning and Memory* 4:551–578.

LINDBLOM, CHARLES E. 1959. "The Science of 'Muddling Through.'" *Public Administration Review* 19:79–88.

———. 1965. *The Intelligence of Democracy.* New York: Free Press.

———. 1977. *Politics and Markets.* New York: Basic Books.

LINDBLOM, CHARLES E., and DAVID BRAYBROOKE. 1963. *The Strategy of Decision.* New York: Free Press.

LINDBLOM, CHARLES E., and DAVID K. COHEN. 1979. *Useable Knowledge.* New Haven: Yale University Press.

LOVINS, AMORY B., and L. HUNTER LOVINS. 1982. *Brittle Power: Energy Strategy for National Security.* Andover, Mass.: Brick House Publishing.

LOWI, THEODORE J. 1964. "American Business, Public Policy, Case Studies, and Political Theory." *World Politics* 16:677–715.

———. 1969. *The End of Liberalism: Ideology, Policy, and the Crisis of Public Authority.* New York: W. W. Norton.

———. 1972. "Four Systems of Policy, Politics and Choice." *Public Administration Review* 32:298–310.

———. 1979. *The End of Liberalism.* 2nd ed. New York: W. W. Norton.

LOWRANCE, W. W. 1976. *Of Acceptable Risk.* Los Altos, Calif.: Kaufmann.

LUCE, R. D. 1977. "The Choice Axiom after Twenty Years." *Journal of Mathematical Psychology* 15:215–233.

LUHMANN, NIKLAS. 1975. *Legitimation durch Verfahren.* 2nd ed. Darmstadt: Luchterhand.

LURIE, JONATHAN. 1979. *The Chicago Board of Trade 1859–1905.* Urbana: University of Illinois Press.

MACAVOY, PAUL W. 1965. *The Economic Effects of Regulation: The Truckline Railroad Cartels and the ICC before 1900.* Cambridge, Mass.: MIT Press.

———. 1970. "The Effectiveness of the Federal Power Commission." *Bell Journal of Economics and Management Science* 1:271–303.

———. 1971. "The Formal Work Product of the Federal Power Commissioners." *Bell Journal of Economics and Management Science* 2:379–395.

MACAVOY, PAUL W., and ROGER G. NOLL. 1973. "Relative Prices on Regulated Transactions of the Natural Gas Pipelines." *Bell Journal of Economics and Management Science* 4:212–234

MacAvoy, Paul W., and James Sloss. 1967. *Regulation of Transport Innovation: The ICC and Unit Coal Trains to the East Coast.* New York: Random House.

MacKay, C. 1970. *Extraordinary Popular Delusions and the Madness of Crowds.* Orig. pub. London: Office of the National Illustrated Library, 1852. Reprinted New York: Noonday Press.

MacLennan, Carol. 1980. "Passive Restraints: The Political Culture of Automotive Regulation." Paper presented at the American Anthropological Association Meetings, Washington, D.C.

Malinowski, Bronislaw. 1926. *Crime and Custom in Savage Society.* London: Kegan, Paul, Trench, Trubner.

Mancuso, Thomas. 1984. "Whistleblowing vs. Proprietary Rights." Pp. 57–70 in *Science as Intellectual Property,* ed. Dorothy Nelkins. New York: Macmillan.

Mann, Patrick C., and Walter J. Primeaux, Jr. 1982. "Regulator Selection and Electricity Prices." Mimeo: College of Commerce and Business Administration, University of Illinois.

Manne, Henry G. 1975. *The Economics of Legal Relationships: Readings in the Theory of Property Rights.* St. Paul, Minn.: West Publishing.

March, J.G. 1978. "Bounded Rationality, Ambiguity, and the Engineering of Choice." *Bell Journal of Economics* 9:587–608.

———. 1981. "Decisions in Organizations and Theories of Choice." In *Perspectives on Organization Design and Behavior,* ed. Andrew Van de Ven and William Joyce. New York: Wiley.

March, J.G., and Johan P. Olsen. 1976. *Ambiguity and Choice in Organizations.* Bergen, Norway: Universitetsforlaget.

March, J.G., and Herbert A. Simon. 1958. *Organizations.* New York: John Wiley and Sons.

Martin, JoAnn. N.d. "The 'Citizen Employee' and Ethical Violations." Unpublished manuscript.

Marvel, Howard P. 1977. "Factory Regulation: A Reinterpretation of Early English Experience." *Journal of Law and Economics* 20:379–402.

Mayhew, David R. 1974. *Congress: The Electoral Connection.* New Haven: Yale University Press.

———. Forthcoming. "Legislation." In *Law and Social Sciences: An Appraisal,* ed. L. Lipson.

McConnell, Grant. 1966. *Private Power and American Democracy.* New York: Vintage.

McCubbins, Mathew, and Thomas Schwartz. 1982. "Congressional Oversight Overlooked." Mimeo: Department of Government, University of Texas.

McKean, Roland N. 1964. "Divergences between Individual and Total Costs within Government." *American Economic Review, Papers and Proceedings* 54:243–249.

McKelvey, Richard D. 1976. "Intransitivities in Multidimensional Voting Models and Some Implications for Agenda Control." *Journal of Economic Theory* 12:472–482.

_____. 1979. "General Conditions for Global Intransitivities in Formal Voting Models." *Econometrica* 47:1085–1111.

McKie, James W. 1970. "Regulation and the Free Market: The Problem of Boundaries." *Bell Journal of Economics and Management Science* 1:6–26.

McLanahan, Sarah S. 1980. "Organizational Issues in U.S. Health Policy Implementation: Participation, Discretion, and Accountability." *Journal of Applied Behavioral Science* 16:354–369.

McLaughlin, Milbrey Wallin. 1975. *Evaluation and Reform: The Elementary and Secondary Education Act of 1965, Title I.* Cambridge, Mass.: Ballinger.

Mendelhoff, John. 1981. "Does Overregulation Cause Underregulation?" *Regulation* 5:47–52.

Merton, Robert K. 1936. "The Unanticipated Consequences of Purposive Social Action." *American Sociological Review* 1:894–904.

_____. 1949. *Social Theory and Social Structure: Toward the Codification of Theory and Research.* New York: Free Press of Glencoe.

Meyer, John W. 1983. "The Impact of the Centralization of Educational Funding and Control on State and Local Organizational Governance." Pp. 179–197 in *Organizational Environments: Ritual and Rationality,* ed. John W. Meyer and W. Richard Scott. Beverly Hills, Calif.: Sage.

Meyer, John W., and Brian Rowan. 1977. "Institutional Organizations: Formal Structure as Myth and Ceremony." *American Journal of Sociology* 83:340–363.

Meyer, Marshall W. 1979. "Organizational Structure as Signaling." *Pacific Sociological Review* 22:481–500.

Michelman, Frank I. 1967. "Property, Utility and Fairness: Comments on the Ethical Foundations of 'Just Compensation' Law." *Harvard Law Review* 80:1165–1258.

Michels, Robert. 1962. *Political Parties.* Trans. Eden and Cedar Paul. New York: Free Press.

Migue, Jean-Luc, and Gérard Bélanger. 1974. "Toward a General Theory of Managerial Discretion." *Public Choice* 17:27–47.

Miles, Rufus E., Jr. 1974. *The Department of Health, Education and Welfare.* New York: Praeger.

Mills, Edwin S., and Lawrence J. White. 1978. "Government Policies toward Automotive Emissions Control." Pp. 348–409 in *Approaches to Controlling Air Pollution,* ed. Ann F. Friedlaender. Cambridge, Mass.: MIT Press.

Mohr, Lawrence B. 1969. "Determinants of Innovation in Organizations." *American Political Science Review* 63:111–126.

_____. 1973. "The Concept of Organizational Goal." *American Political Science Review* 67:470–481.

Moore, Thomas G. 1970. "The Effectiveness of Regulations of Electric Utility Prices." *Southern Economic Journal* 36:365–375.

Moore, Thomas G., and Sidney Moore. 1976. *Regulatory Reform: Highlights of a Conference on Government Regulation.* Washington, D.C.: American Enterprise Institute.

MUELLER, DENNIS. 1979. *Public Choice*. New York: Cambridge University Press.

MURDOCK, GEORGE P. 1934. *Our Primitive Contemporaries*. New York: Macmillan.

NADER, LAURA. 1964. "An Analysis of Zapotec Cases." *Ethnology* 3:404–419.

———. 1965. "Choices in Legal Procedure: Shia Moslem and Mexican Zapotec." *American Anthropologist* 67:394–399.

———. 1969. "Style of Court Procedure: To Make the Balance." Pp. 69–91 in *Law in Culture and Society*, ed. Laura Nader. Chicago: Aldine.

———, ed. 1980a. *No Access to Law*. New York: Academic Press.

———. 1980b. "The Vertical Slice." Pp. 31–43 in *Hierarchy and Society*, ed. G. M. Britan and R. Cohen. Philadelphia: Institute for the Study of Human Issues.

———. Forthcoming. "From Disputing to Complaining." In *Toward a Theory of Social Control,* ed. Donald Black. New York: Academic Press.

———. N. d. "To Make the Balance: Law and Justice in a Zapotec Town." Unpublished manuscript.

NADER, RALPH. 1973. *Unsafe at Any Speed*. New York: Bantam.

———. 1974. "The Regulation of the Safety of Cosmetics." Pp. 73–141 in *Consumer Health and Product Hazards—Cosmetics and Drugs, Pesticides, Food Additives*, vol. 2 of *The Legislation of Product Safety*, ed. Samuel S. Epstein and Richard D. Grundy. Cambridge, Mass.: MIT Press.

NADER, RALPH, P. J. PETKAS, and K. BLACKWELL, eds. 1972. *Whistleblowing*. New York: Grossman.

NAIRN, ALLAN, and ASSOCIATES. 1980. *The Reign of ETS: The Corporation That Makes up Minds*. Washington, D.C.: Learning Research Project.

NISBETT, R., and L. ROSS. 1980. *Human Inference: Strategies and Shortcomings of Social Judgment*. Englewood Cliffs, N.J.: Prentice-Hall.

NISKANEN, WILLIAM. 1971. *Bureaucracy and Representative Government*. Chicago: Aldine-Atherton.

NOBLE, D. F. 1977. *America by Design*. New York: Oxford University Press.

NOLL, ROGER G. 1971a. "The Behavior of Regulatory Agencies." *Review of Social Economy* 29:15–19.

———. 1971b. *Reforming Regulation*. Washington, D.C.: Brookings Institution.

———. 1973. "Selling Research to Regulatory Agencies." Pp. 63–69 in *The Role of Analysis in Regulatory Decisionmaking: The Case of Cable Television*, ed. Rolla Edward Park. Lexington, Mass.: Lexington Books.

———. 1980. "What Is Regulation?" Social Science Working Paper 324. Pasadena: California Institute of Technology.

———. 1983. "The Political Foundations of Regulatory Policy." *Zeitschrift für die gesamte Staatswissenschaft* 139:377–404.

NOLL, ROGER G., and BRUCE OWEN. 1983. *The Political Economy of Deregulation*. Washington, D.C.: American Enterprise Institute.

NOLL, ROGER G., MERTON J. PECK, and JOHN J. McGOWAN. 1973. *Economic Aspects of Television Regulation*. Washington, D.C.: Brookings Institution.

NONET, PHILIPPE, and PHILIP SELZNICK. 1978. *Law and Society in Transition: Toward Responsive Law*. New York: Harper/Colophon.

OI, WALTER. 1971. "A Disneyland Dilemma: Two-Part Tariffs for a Mickey Mouse Monopoly." *Quarterly Journal of Economics* 85:77–96.

———. 1977. "Safety at Any Price?" *Regulation* 1:16–23.

OKRENT, D., and C. WHIPPLE. 1977. *An Approach to Societal Risk Acceptance Criteria and Risk Management.* Report UCLA–ENG–7746. Los Angeles: School of Engineering and Applied Science, UCLA.

OLSON, C. VINCENT, and JOHN M. TRAPANI III. 1981. "Who Has Benefitted from Regulation of the Airline Industry?" *Journal of Law and Economics* 24:75–93.

OLSON, MANCUR. 1965. *The Logic of Collective Action.* Cambridge, Mass.: Harvard University Press.

———. 1970. "An Analytic Framework for Social Reporting and Policy Analysis." *Annals of the American Academy of Political and Social Sciences* 388:112–126.

———. 1973. "Evaluating Performance in the Public Sector." Pp. 355–384 in *The Measurement of Economic and Social Performance,* ed. Milton Moss. *Studies in Income and Wealth,* vol. 38. New York: National Bureau of Economic Research.

OWEN, BRUCE, and RONALD BRAEUTIGAM. 1978. *The Regulation Game.* Cambridge, Mass.: Ballinger.

PAGE, JOSEPH A., and MARY WIN O'BRIEN. 1973. *Bitter Wages.* New York: Grossman.

PANZAR, JOHN, and ROBERT WILLIG. 1977. "Free Entry and the Sustainability of Natural Monopoly." *Bell Journal of Economics* 8:1–22.

PARSONS, TALCOTT. 1960. *Structure and Process in Modern Societies.* New York: Free Press.

PASHIGIAN, B. P., L. SCHKADE, and G. H. MENEFEE. 1966. "The Selection of an Optimal Deductible for a Given Insurance Policy." *Journal of Business* 39:35–44.

PAULEY, MARK, and MICHAEL REDISCH. 1973. "The Not-for-Profit Hospital as a Physicians' Cooperative." *American Economic Review* 63:87–99.

PECK, MERTON J. 1970. "The Single-Entity Proposal for International Telecommunications." *American Economic Review, Papers and Proceedings* 60:199–203

PELTZMAN, SAM. 1965. "Entry in Commercial Banking." *Journal of Law and Economics* 8:11–50

———. 1974. *Regulation of Pharmaceutical Innovation: The 1962 Amendments.* Washington, D.C.: American Enterprise Institute.

———. 1975. *Regulation of Auto Safety.* Washington, D.C.: American Enterprise Institute.

———. 1976. "Toward a More General Theory of Regulation." *Journal of Law and Economics* 19:211–240.

PERROW, CHARLES. 1961a. "Organizational Prestige: Some Functions and Dysfunctions." *American Journal of Sociology* 66:335–341.

———. 1961b. "The Analysis of Goals in Complex Organizations." *American Sociological Review* 26:854–866.

———. 1963. "Goals and Power Structures: A Historical Case Study." Pp. 112–146 in *The Hospital in Modern Society,* ed. Eliot Freidson. New York: Free Press.

———. 1967. "A Framework for the Comparative Analysis of Organizations." *American Sociological Review* 32:194–208

PERTSHUK, MICHAEL. 1981. "The Rise and Pause of the Consumer Movement: Political Strategies of Regulation and Deregulation." Paper presented to the School of Business Administration, University of California, Berkeley.

———. 1982. *Revolt against Regulation.* Berkeley and Los Angeles: University of California Press.

PETERS, THOMAS J., and ROBERT H. WATERMAN. 1982. *In Search of Excellence.* New York: Harper and Row.

PFEFFER, JEFFREY, and GERALD R. SALANCIK. 1978. *The External Control of Organizations.* New York: Harper and Row.

PHILLIPS, ALMARIN, ed. 1975. *Promoting Competition in Regulated Industries.* Washington, D.C.: Brookings Institution.

PLOTT, CHARLES R. 1968. "Some Organizational Influences on Urban Renewal Decisions." *American Economic Review, Papers and Proceedings* 58:306–321.

———. 1972. "Ethics, Social Choice Theory and the Theory of Economic Policy." *Journal of Mathematical Sociology* 2:181–208.

POLINSKY, A. MITCHELL, and STEVEN SHAVELL. 1982. "Pigouvian Taxation with Administrative Costs." *Journal of Public Economics* 19:385–394.

POLONYI, KARL. 1944. *The Great Transformation.* Boston: Beacon Press.

POLSBY, DANIEL D. 1979. "F.C.C. vs. National Citizens Committee for Broadcasting and the Judicious Uses of Administrative Discretion." Pp. 1–37 in *Supreme Court Review, 1978,* ed. Philip B. Kurland and Gerhard Casper. Chicago: University of Chicago Press.

POSNER, RICHARD A. 1969. "Natural Monopoly and Its Regulation." *Stanford Law Review* 21:548–643.

———. 1971. "Taxation by Regulation." *Bell Journal of Economics and Management Science* 2:22–50.

———. 1977. *Economic Analysis of Law.* 2nd ed. Boston: Little, Brown.

POSPISIL, L. 1958. "Kapauku Papuans and Their Law." *Yale University Publications in Anthropology* 54.

———. 1971. *Anthropology of Law: A Comparative Theory.* New York: Harper and Row.

PRIEST, GEORGE L. 1977. "The Common Law Process and the Selection of Efficient Rules." *Journal of Legal Studies* 6:65–82.

PROTTAS, JEFFREY MANDITCH. 1978. "The Power of the Street-Level Bureaucrat in Public Service Bureaucracies." *Urban Affairs Quarterly* 13:285–312.

RABIN, ROBERT L. 1981. "The Historical Development of the Fault Principle: A Reinterpretation." *Georgia Law Review* 15:925–961.

RABKIN, JEREMY. 1980. "Office for Civil Rights." Pp. 304–353 in *The Politics of Regulation*, ed. James Q. Wilson. New York: Basic Books.

REICH, ROBERT. 1980. Review of the *Politics of Regulation*. *New Republic* 182, 24:36–38.

REISSLAND, J., and V. HARRIES. 1979. "A Scale for Measuring Risks." *New Scientist* 83:809–811.

REMINI, ROBERT V. 1981. *Andrew Jackson and the Course of American Freedom.* New York: Harper and Row.

RENN, O. 1981. *Man, Technology, and Risk: A Study on Intuitive Risk Assessment and Attitudes towards Nuclear Power.* Report Jul-Spez 115. Julich, Federal Republic of Germany: Nuclear Research Center.

RETHANS, A. 1979. "An Investigation of Consumer Perceptions of Product Hazards." Ph.D. dissertation, University of Oregon.

RHOADS, STEVEN, ed. 1980. *Valuing Life: Public Policy Dilemmas.* Boulder, Colo.: Westview Press.

RICHARD J. BARBER and ASSOCIATES. 1977. *The Interstate Commerce Commission: Application of Its Resources in a Changing Environment.* Washington, D.C.: Interstate Commerce Commission.

RITCHIE, DONALD A. 1980. *James M. Sandis: Dean of the Regulators.* Cambridge, Mass.: Harvard University Press.

ROBERTSON, L. S. 1976. "The Great Seat Belt Campaign Flop." *Journal of Communication* 26:41–45.

ROETHLISBERGER, F. J., and WILLIAM J. DICKSON. 1939. *Management and the Worker.* Cambridge, Mass.: Harvard University Press.

ROHLES, F. H. 1981. "Thermal Comfort and Strategies for Energy Conservation." *Journal of Social Issues* 37:132–199.

ROSE-ACKERMAN, SUSAN. 1978. *Corruption: An Essay in Political Economy.* Chatsworth, Calif.: Academy Press.

———. 1980. "Risk Taking and Reelection: Does Federalism Promote Innovation?" *Journal of Legal Studies* 9:593–616.

———. 1982. "A New Political Economy?" *Michigan Law Review* 80:872–884.

ROWE, W. D. 1977. *An Anatomy of Risk.* New York: Wiley.

RUBIN, PAUL H. 1977. "Why Is the Common Law Efficient?" *Journal of Legal Studies* 6:51–63.

RUFFINI, JULIO L. 1978. "Disputing over Livestock in Sardinia." Pp. 209–246 in *The Disputing Process—Law in Ten Societies*, ed. L. Nader and Harry F. Todd, Jr. New York: Columbia University Press.

RUSSELL, T., and R. THALER. 1983. "The Relevance of Quasi-Rationality in Competitive Markets." 75th Anniversary Colloquium Research Paper Series. Cambridge, Mass.: Harvard University.

SALAMON, LESTER M. 1981. "Federal Regulation: A New Arena for Presidential Power?" In *The Illusion of Presidential Government.* Boulder, Colo.: Westview Press.

SALEM, S. L., K. A. SOLOMON, and M. S. YESLEY. 1980. *Issues and Problems in Inferring a Level of Acceptable Risk.* R–2561–DOE. Santa Monica, Calif.: RAND Corp.

SAMSON, PETER. 1980. "The Emergence of Consumer Interests in America." Ph.D. dissertation, University of Chicago.

SANDERS, M. ELIZABETH. 1981. *The Regulation of Natural Gas: Policy and Politics, 1938–1978.* Philadelphia: Temple University Press.

SATTERTHWAITE, MARK A. 1975. "Strategy-Proofness and Arrow's Conditions: Existence and Correspondence Theorems for Voting Procedures and Social Welfare Functions." *Journal of Economic Theory* 10:187–217.

SAYRE, WALLACE, ed. 1965. *The Federal Government Service.* Englewood Cliffs, N.J.: Prentice-Hall.

SCHATTSCHNEIDER, ELMER ERIC. 1935. *Politics, Pressures, and the Tariff.* New York: Prentice-Hall.

SCHELLING, THOMAS. 1978. *Micromotives and Microbehavior.* New York: W.W. Norton.

SCHER, SEYMOUR. 1960. "Congressional Committee Members as Independent Agency Overseers: A Case Study." *American Political Science Review* 54:911–920.

SCHERER, F.M. 1970. *Industrial Market Structure and Economic Performance.* Chicago: Rand McNally.

SCHOEMAKER, P.J.H. 1982. "The Expected Utility Model: Its Variants, Purposes, Evidence and Limitations." *Journal of Economic Literature* 20:529–563.

SCHUCK, PETER H. 1979. "The Graying of Civil Rights Law: The Age Discrimination Act of 1975." *Yale Law Journal* 89:27–93.

SCHULTZE, CHARLES L. 1968. *The Politics and Economics of Public Spending.* Washington, D.C.: Brookings Institution.

———. 1977. *The Public Use of Private Interests.* Washington, D.C.: Brookings Institution.

SCHWALM, N.D., and P. SLOVIC. 1982. *Development and Test of a Motivational Approach and Materials for Increasing Use of Restraints.* Final Technical Report PFTR–1100–82–3. Woodland Hills, Calif.: Perceptronics, Inc.

SCHWARTZ, BERNARD. 1959. *The Professor and the Commissions.* New York: Alfred A. Knopf.

SCHWARTZMAN, DAVID. 1976. *Innovation in the Pharmaceutical Industry.* Baltimore: Johns Hopkins University Press.

SCHWING, R.C., and W.A. ALBERS, JR. 1980. *Societal Risk Assessment: How Safe Is Safe Enough?* New York: Plenum.

SCITOVSKY, TIBOR. 1942. "A Note on Welfare Propositions in Economics." *Review of Economic Studies* 9:77–88.

———. 1950. "Ignorance as a Source of Oligopoly Power." *American Economic Review* 49:48–53.

SCOTT, W. RICHARD. 1982. "Health Care Organizations in the 1980s: The Convergence of Public and Professional Control Systems." Pp. 177–195 in *Contemporary Health Services: Social Science Perspectives,* ed. Allen W. Johnson, Oscar Grusky, and Bertram H. Raven. Boston: Auburn House.

SCOTT, W. RICHARD, and JOHN W. MEYER. 1983. "The Organization of Societal Institutional Sectors." Pp. 129–154 in *Organizational Environments: Ritual and Rationality*, ed. John W. Meyer and W. Richard Scott. Beverly Hills, Calif.: Sage.

SELZNICK, PHILIP. 1943. "An Approach to a Theory of Bureaucracy." *American Sociological Review* 8:47–54.

———. 1969. *Law, Society, and Industrial Justice*. New York: Russell Sage.

SEN, AMARTYA. 1970. *Collective Choice and Social Welfare*. San Francisco: Holden-Day.

SERBER, DAVID. 1980. "Resolution or Rhetoric: Managing Complaints in the California Department of Insurance." Pp. 317–343 in *No Access to Law*, ed. Laura Nader. New York: Academic Press.

SHEPARD, HERBERT A. 1967. "Innovation-Resisting and Innovation-Producing Organizations." *Journal of Business* 40:470–477.

SHEPSLE, KENNETH A. 1979. "Institutional Arrangements and Equilibrium in Multidimensional Voting Models." *American Journal of Political Science* 23:27–59.

SHEPSLE, KENNETH A., and BARRY R. WEINGAST. 1981. "Structure Induced Equilibrium and Legislative Choice." *Public Choice* 37:503–520.

———. 1982. "Political Solutions to Market Problems." Working Paper 74. St. Louis: Center for the Study of American Business, Washington University.

SHERIF, MUZAFER. 1935. "A Study of Some Social Factors in Perception." *Archives of Psychology* 187.

SILBERMAN, LAURENCE H. 1978. "Will Lawyering Strangle Democratic Capitalism?" *Regulation* 2:15–22.

SIMON, H. A. 1956. "Rational Choice and the Structure of the Environment." *Psychological Review* 63:129–138.

———. 1957. *Models of Man: Social and Rational*. New York: Wiley.

———. 1965. *The Shape of Automation for Men and Management*. New York: Harper and Row.

SLOVIC, PAUL. 1975. "Choice between Equally-Valued Alternatives." *Journal of Experimental Psychology: Human Perception and Performance* 1:280–287.

SLOVIC, PAUL, B. FISCHHOFF, and S. LICHTENSTEIN. 1977. "Behavioral Decision Theory." *Annual Review of Psychology* 28:1–39.

———. 1978. "Accident Probabilities and Seat Belt Usage: A Psychological Perspective." *Accident Analysis and Prevention* 10:281–285.

———. 1979. "Rating the Risks." *Environment* 21:14–39.

———. 1980a. "Facts and Fears: Understanding Perceived Risk." Pp. 181–216 in *Societal Risk Assessment: How Safe Is Safe Enough?* ed. Richard C. Schwing and W. A. Albers, Jr. New York: Plenum.

———. 1980b. "Informing People about Risk." Pp. 165–180 in *Product Labeling and Health Risks*, ed. L. Morris, M. Mazis, and I. Barofsky. Banbury Report 6. Cold Spring Harbor, N.Y.: Cold Spring Laboratory.

———. 1980c. "Perceived Risk and Quantitative Safety Goals for Nuclear Power." *Transactions of the American Nuclear Society* 35:400–401.

———. 1981a. "Informing the Public about the Risks of Ionizing Radiation." *Health Physics* 41:589–598.

———. 1981b. "Perception and Acceptability of Risks from Energy Systems." Pp. 155–169 in *Advances in Environmental Psychology*, vol. 3, ed. A. Baum and J. E. Singer. Hillsdale, N.J.: Erlbaum.

———. 1982. "Response Mode, Framing, and Information-Processing Effects in Risk Assessment." Pp. 21–36 in *New Directions for Methodology of Social and Behavioral Science, No. 11: Question Framing and Response Consistency*, ed. Robin M. Hogarth. San Francisco: Jossey-Bass.

———. In press. "Characterizing Perceived Risk." In *Perilous Progress: Technology as Hazard*, ed. R. W. Kates , C. Hohenemser, and J. X. Kasperson. Boulder, Colo.: Westview Press.

SLOVIC, P., B. FISCHHOFF, S. LICHTENSTEIN, B. CORRIGAN, and B. COMBS. 1977. "Preference for Insuring against Probable Small Losses: Implications for the Theory and Practice of Insurance." *Journal of Risk and Insurance* 44:237–28.

SLOVIC, P., and S. LICHTENSTEIN. 1983. "Preference Reversals: A Broader Perspective." *American Economic Review* 73:596–605.

SLOVIC, P., S. LICHTENSTEIN, and B. FISCHHOFF. 1979. "Images of Disaster: Perception and Acceptance of Risks from Nuclear Power." Pp. 223–245 in *Energy Risk Management*, ed. Gordon T. Goodman and W. D. Rowe. London: Academic Press.

———. 1984. "Modeling the Societal Impact of Fatal Accidents." *Management Science.* 30:464–473.

SOLOMON, K. A., P. F. NELSON, and S. L. SALEM. 1981. *Utilization of Risk Analysis and Risk Criteria: A Progress Report.* Working Draft 1194–ORNL. Santa Monica, Calif.: RAND Corp.

SOMERS, ANNE, R. 1969. *Hospital Regulation: The Dilemma of Public Policy.* Princeton: Princeton University, Industrial Relations Section.

SOMERS, HERMAN M. 1965. "The President, the Congress and the Federal Government Service." Pp. 70–113 in *The Federal Government Service*, ed. Wallace S. Sayre. Englewood Cliffs, N.J.: Prentice-Hall.

SOWBY, F. D. 1965. "Radiation and Other Risks." *Health Physics* 11:879–887.

SPANN, ROBERT, and EDWARD ERICKSON. 1970. "The Economics of Railroading: The Beginning of Cartelization and Regulation." *Bell Journal of Economics and Management Science* 1:227–244.

SPITZER, MATTHEW L. 1979. "Multicriteria Choice Processes: An Application of Public Choice Theory to *Bakke*, the FCC, and the Courts." *Yale Law Journal* 88:717–779.

SPITZER, ROBERT J. 1979. "The Presidency and Public Policy: A Preliminary Inquiry." *Presidential Studies Quarterly* 9:441–456.

SPROULL, LEE S. 1981. "Response to Regulation: An Organizational Process Framework." *Administration and Society* 12:447–470.

STARK, DAVID H. 1981. "Yakoza: Japanese Crime Incorporated." Ph.D. dissertation, University of Michigan.

STARR, C. 1969. "Social Benefit vs. Technological Risk." *Science* 165: 1232–1238.

STERN, N. H. 1982. "Optimum Taxation with Errors in Administration." *Journal of Public Economics* 17:181–211.

STEVENSON, RUSSELL B., JR. 1976. "Corporate Rights and Responsibilities." Pp. 57–65 in *Federal Chartering of Giant Corporations.* Washington, D.C.: Commission for the Advancement of Public Interest Organizations.

STIGLER, GEORGE J. 1970. "Director's Law of Public Income Redistribution." *Journal of Law and Economics* 13:1–10.

———. 1971. "The Theory of Economic Regulation." *Bell Journal of Economics and Management Science* 2:3–21.

———. 1975. *The Citizen and the State.* Chicago: University of Chicago Press.

———. 1982. "Economists and Public Policy." *Regulation* 6:13–17.

STINCHCOMBE, ARTHUR L. 1965. "Social Structure and Organizations." Pp. 142–193 in *Handbook of Organizations,* ed. James G. March. Chicago: Rand McNally.

STOCKING, GEORGE W. 1954. "The Rule of Reason, Workable Competition, and the Legality of Trade Association Activities." *University of Chicago Law Review* 21:527–619.

STOCKING, GEORGE W., and MYRON WATKINS. 1951. *Monopoly and Free Enterprise.* New York: Greenwood.

STONE, CHRISTOPHER D. 1975. *Where the Law Ends: The Social Control of Corporate Behavior.* New York: Harper and Row.

———. 1980. "The Place of Enterprise Liability in the Control of Corporate Conduct." *Yale Law Journal* 90:1–77.

STRASSBURG, BERNARD. 1977. "Case Study: FCC's Specialized Common Carrier (SCC) Decision." Pp. III-1 to III-43 in *Organization Analysis of the Regulatory Process: A Comparative Study of the Decision Making Process in the Federal Communications Commission and the Environmental Protection Agency.* Washington, D.C.: Urban Institute.

SULIEMAN, EZRA. 1974. *Politics, Power and Bureaucracy.* Princeton: Princeton University Press.

SUMMERS, ROBERT, and CHARLES G. HOWARD. 1972. *Law: Its Nature, Function and Limits.* Englewood Cliffs, N.J.: Prentice-Hall.

SUTHERLAND, E. H. 1961. *White Collar Crime.* New York: Holt, Rinehart and Winston.

SVENSON, O. 1981. "Are We All Less Risky and More Skillful Than Our Fellow Drivers?" *Acta Psychologica* 47:143–148.

TAYLOR, CHARLES. 1917. *History of the Board of Trade of the City of Chicago.* Chicago: R. O. Law.

TERRIEN, FREDERIC W., and D. L. MILLS. 1955. "The Effect of Changing Size upon the Internal Structure of Organizations." *American Sociological Review* 20:11–13.

TERRIS, BRUCE J. (a panelist). 1971. "A Critique of the Agencies as Presently Constituted and of the Council's Recommendations for Realignment and Reorganization: A Panel." *Administrative Law Review* 23:445–458.

THOMPSON, JAMES D. 1967. *Organizations in Action.* New York: McGraw-Hill.

THOMPSON, JAMES D., and WILLIAM J. McEWAN. 1958. "Organizational Goals and Environment: Goal-Setting as an Interaction Process." *American Sociological Review* 23:23–31.

THOMPSON, VICTOR A. 1965. "Bureaucracy and Innovation." *Administrative Science Quarterly* 10:1–20.

THUROW, LESTER. 1980. *The Zero-Sum Society.* New York: Basic Books.

TRIBE, LAWRENCE. 1978. *American Constitutional Law.* Mineola, N.Y.: Foundation Press.

TRUMAN, HARRY S. 1956. *Memoirs,* vol. II. Garden City, N.Y.: Doubleday.

TULLOCK, GORDON. 1965. *The Politics of Bureaucracy.* Washington, D.C.: Public Affairs Press.

TURNBULL, H. RUTHERFORD III. 1978. "The Past and Future Impact of Court Decisions in Special Education." *Phi Delta Kappan* 59: 523–527.

TURNER, JAMES S. 1970. *The Chemical Feast.* New York: Grossman.

TVERSKY, A. 1972. "Elimination by Aspects: A Theory of Choice." *Psychological Review* 79:281–299.

TVERSKY, A., and E. J. Johnson. 1981. "Alternative Representation of Perceived Risk." Unpublished manuscript, Department of Psychology, Stanford University.

TVERSKY, A., and D. KAHNEMAN. 1973. "Availability: A Heuristic for Judging Frequency and Probability." *Cognitive Psychology* 5:207–232.

———. 1974. "Judgment under Uncertainty: Heuristics and Biases." *Science* 185:1124–1131.

———. 1981. "The Framing of Decisions and the Psychology of Choice." *Science* 211:1453–1458.

U.S. BUREAU OF THE BUDGET. 1950. "Project Summary, Survey of Regulatory Commissions." Washington, D.C.: U.S. Government Printing Office.

U.S. CIVIL AERONAUTICS BOARD. 1969. "Southern Tier Competitive Nonstop Investigation." *Aviation Law Reports,* docket 18257. Washington, D.C.: Commerce Clearing House.

———. Special Staff on Regulatory Reform. 1975. *Regulatory Reform: Report of the C.A.B. Special Staff.* Washington, D.C.: U.S. Civil Aeronautics Board.

U.S. GENERAL ACCOUNTING OFFICE. 1981. *Gains and Shortcomings in Resolving Regulatory Conflicts and Overlaps: Report to the Congress.* PAD-81-76. Washington, D.C.: General Accounting Office.

U.S. DEPARTMENT OF HEALTH, EDUCATION AND WELFARE. Office of Education. 1977. "Annual Evaluation Report on Programs Administered by the U.S. Office of Education, Fiscal Year 1977." Internal document.

U.S. HOUSE OF REPRESENTATIVES. 1976. *Agenda for Oversight: Domestic Common Carrier Regulation.* Subcommittee on Communications, House Interstate and Foreign Commerce Committee, 94th Congress, 2d Session. Washington, D.C.: U.S. Government Printing Office.

_____. 1979a. *Making Appropriations for the Department of Transportation and Related Agencies.* Committee on Interstate and Foreign Commerce, House Report 96-610, 96th Congress, 1st Session. Washington, D.C.: U.S. Government Printing Office.

_____. 1979b. *March Wheat Futures Trading on the Chicago Board of Trade.* Committee on Agriculture, 96th Congress, 1st Session. Washington, D.C.: U.S. Government Printing Office.

_____. 1981. *Proposed Firing of Dr. Peter Infante by OSHA: A Case Study in Science and Regulation.* Hearings before the Subcommittee on Investigations and Oversight of the Committee on Science and Technology, 97th Congress, 1st Session. Washington, D.C.: U.S. Government Printing Office.

U.S. INTERSTATE COMMERCE COMMISSION. 1975. *Annual Report.* Washington, D.C.: U.S. Government Printing Office.

U.S. JOINT ECONOMIC COMMITTEE, SUBCOMMITTEE ON ECONOMY IN GOVERNMENT. 1969. *The Analysis and Evaluation of Public Expenditures: The PPB System.* 3 vols. Washington, D.C.: U.S. Government Printing Office.

U.S. NUCLEAR REGULATORY COMMISSION. 1975. *Reactor Safety Study: An Assessment of Accident Risks in U.S. Commercial Nuclear Power Plants.* WASH 1400 (NUREG–75/014). Washington, D.C.: Nuclear Regulatory Commission.

_____. 1981. *Toward a Safety Goal: Discussion of Preliminary Policy Considerations.* NUREG–0764. Washington, D.C.: Nuclear Regulatory Commission.

U.S. PRESIDENT'S ADVISORY COUNCIL ON EXECUTIVE ORGANIZATION. 1971. *A New Regulatory Framework: Report on Selected Independent Regulatory Agencies.* Washington, D.C.: Government Printing Office.

U.S. SENATE. 1973. *Nominations: February–March 1973: Hearings before the Senate Committee on Commerce.* 93rd Congress, 1st Session. Washington, D.C.: U.S. Government Printing Office.

_____. 1976a. *Regulatory Reform in Air Transportation: Hearings before the Subcommittee on Aviation of the Senate Commerce Committee.* 94th Congress, 2d Session. Washington, D.C.: U.S. Government Printing Office.

_____. 1976b. *Teton Dam Disaster.* Committee on Government Operations, 94th Congress, 2d Session. Washington, D.C.: U.S. Government Printing Office.

_____. 1977. *Hearings before the Committee on Commerce, Science and Transportation.* 95th Congress, 1st Session. Washington, D.C.: U.S. Government Printing Office.

_____. 1979a. *Hearings before the Subcommittee on Communications of the Senate Committee on Commerce, Science and Transportation.* 96th Congress, 1st Session. Washington, D.C.: U.S. Government Printing Office.

_____. 1979b. *Department of Transportation and Related Agencies Appropriations Bill, 1980.* Senate Report 96-377, 96th Congress, 1st Session. Washington, D.C.: U.S. Government Printing Office.

————. 1979c. *Department of State, Justice and Commerce, the Judiciary, and Related Agencies Appropriations Bill, 1980.* Senate Report 96-251, 96th Congress, lst Session. Washington, D.C.: U.S. Government Printing Office.

U.S. SENATE COMMITTEE ON GOVERNMENTAL AFFAIRS. 1978. *Study on Federal Regulation.* Vol. II: *Congressional Oversight of Regulatory Agencies.* Washington, D.C.: U.S. Government Printing Office.

U.S. SUPREME COURT. 1918. *Chicago Board of Trade v. United States.* 246 U.S. Reports 231.

————. 1925. *Maple Flooring Manufacturers Association et al. v. United States.* 268 U.S. Reports 563–586.

VALENTE, WILLIAM D. 1978. *Law in the Schools.* Indianapolis: Bobbs-Merrill.

VAN DER SPRENKEL, S. 1962. "Legal Institutions in Manchu China: A Sociological Analysis." *London School of Economics Monographs on Social Anthropology,* vol. 24, 178pp.

VAN DER VALK, MARC. 1939. "An Outline of Modern Chinese Family Law." *Monumenta Serica Monograph,* vol. 2.

VLEK, C. A. J., and P. J. M. STALLEN. 1981. "Judging Risks and Benefits in the Small and in the Large." *Organizational Behavior and Human Performance* 28:235–271.

VON DER BOSCH, ROBERT. 1980. *The Pesticide Conspiracy.* New York: Doubleday.

VON DER BOSCH, ROBERT, and MARY L. FLINT. 1981. *Introduction to Integrated Pest Management.* New York: Plenum Press.

VON WINTERFELDT, D., R. S. JOHN, and K. BORCHERDING. 1981. "Cognitive Components of Risk Ratings." *Risk Analysis* 1:277–287.

WARFORD, JEREMY J. 1971. *Public Policy toward General Aviation.* Washington, D.C.: Brookings Institution.

WARNER, W. L., P. VAN RIPER, N. MARTIN, and O. COLLINS. 1963. *The American Federal Executive.* New Haven: Yale University Press.

WARREN, ROLAND L. 1967. "The Interorganizational Field as a Focus for Investigation." *Administrative Science Quarterly* 12:396–419.

WATKINS, MYRON W. 1934. "Trade Associations." In *International Encyclopedia of the Social Sciences* 7:670–676. New York: Macmillan.

WEATHERLEY, RICHARD, and MICHAEL LIPSKY. 1977. "Street-Level Bureaucrats and Institutional Innovation: Implementing Special-Education Reform." *Harvard Educational Review* 47:171–197.

WEAVER, PAUL H. 1978. "Regulation, Social Policy, and Class Conflict." *Public Interest* 50:45–63.

WEAVER, SUZANNE. 1980. "Antitrust Division of the Department of Justice." Pp. 123–151 in *The Politics of Regulation,* ed. James Q. Wilson. New York: Basic Books.

WEBBINK, DOUGLAS W. 1969. "The Impact of UHF Promotion: The All-Channel Television Receiver Law." *Law and Contemporary Problems* 34:535–561.

WEBER, ARNOLD R. 1973. *In Pursuit of Price Stability.* Washington, D.C.: Brookings Institution.

WEBER, MAX. 1922. *Grundriss der Sozialökonomik.* Part III: *Wirtschaft und Gesellschaft.* Tübingen: J. C. B. Mohr.
———. 1947. *The Theory of Social and Economic Organizations,* ed. Talcott Parsons. New York: Free Press.
———. 1948. "Bureaucracy." Part VIII. Pp. 196–244, in *From Max Weber: Essays in Sociology,* ed. and trans. by H. H. Gerth and C. Wright Mills. London: Routledge and Kegan Paul.
———. 1967. *Law in Economy and Society,* ed. Max Rheinstein and trans. Max Rheinstein and Edward Shils. New York: Simon and Schuster.
WEBSTER, GEORGE D. 1971. *The Law of Associations.* Washington, D.C.: American Society of Association Executives.
WEICK, KARL E. 1976. "Educational Organizations as Loosely Coupled Systems." *Administrative Science Quarterly* 21:1–19.
———. 1979. *The Social Psychology of Organizing.* 2nd ed. Reading, Mass.: Addison-Wesley.
WEIDENBAUM, MURRAY. 1980. *Costs of Regulation and Benefits of Reform.* Formal Publication 35. St. Louis: Center for the Study of American Business, Washington University.
WEINBERG, A. M. 1976. "The Maturity and Future of Nuclear Energy." *American Scientist* 64:16–21.
WEINER, SANFORD L. 1972. "Resource Allocation in Basic Research and Organization Design." *Public Policy* 20:227–255.
WEINGAST, BARRY. 1981. "Regulation, Reregulation and Deregulation: The Foundations of Agency-Clientele Relationships." *Law and Contemporary Problems* 44:147–177.
WEINGAST, BARRY, and MARK MORAN. 1983. "Bureaucratic Discretion or Congressional Control? Regulatory Policymaking by the Federal Trade Commission." *Journal of Political Economy* 91:765–800.
WEINGAST, BARRY, KENNETH SHEPSLE, and CHRISTOPHER JOHNSEN. 1981. "The Political Economy of Benefits and Costs: A Neoclassical Approach to the Politics of Distribution." *Journal of Political Economy* 89:642–664.
WEINSTEIN, JAMES. 1968. *The Corporate Ideal in the Liberal State, 1900–1918.* Boston: Beacon Press.
WEINSTEIN, N. D. 1980. "Unrealistic Optimism about Future Life Events." *Journal of Personality and Social Psychology* 39:806–820.
WELBORN, DAVID M. 1977. *Governance of Federal Regulatory Agencies.* Knoxville: University of Tennessee Press.
WEST, E. G. 1967. "The Political Economy of American Public School Legislation." *Journal of Law and Economics* 10:101–128.
WESTFIELD, FRED M. 1971. "Innovation and Monopoly Regulation." Pp. 13–43 in *Technological Change in Regulated Industries,* ed. William M. Capron. Washington, D.C.: Brookings Institution.
WHYTE, W. F. 1955. *Street Corner Society: The Social Structure of an Italian Slum.* Rev. ed. Chicago: University of Chicago Press.

WILCOX, CLAIRE. 1968. "Regulation of Industry." *International Encyclopedia of the Social Sciences* 13:390–396. New York: Macmillan.

WILCOX, CLAIRE, and WILHIN G. SHEPHERD. 1975. *Public Policies toward Business.* 5th ed. Homewood, Ill.: Richard D. Irwin.

WILDAVSKY, AARON. 1964. *The Politics of the Budgetary Process.* Boston: Little, Brown.

———. 1979. *Speaking Truth to Power: The Art and Craft of Policy Analysis.* Boston: Little, Brown.

WILLIAMSON, OLIVER E. 1970. "Administrative Decision Making and Pricing: Externality and Compensation Analysis Applied." Pp. 115–138 in *The Analysis of Public Output,* ed. Julius Margolis. New York: National Bureau of Economic Research.

———. 1975. *Markets and Hierarchies.* New York: Free Press.

WILLIG, ROBERT D. 1978. "Pareto Superiority of Nonlinear Outlay Schedules." *Bell Journal of Economics* 9:56–69.

WILSON, JAMES Q. 1974. "The Politics of Regulation." Pp. 135–168 in *Social Responsibility and the Business Predicament,* ed. James W. McKie. Washington, D.C.: Brookings Institution.

———. 1980. *The Politics of Regulation.* New York: Basic Books.

WILSON, R. 1979. "Analyzing the Daily Risks of Life." *Technology Review* 81:40–46.

WINETT, RICHARD A., J. W. HATCHER, T. R. FORT, I. N. LECKLITER, S. Q. LOVE, A. W. RILEY, and J. F. FISCHBACK, 1982. "The Effects of Videotape Modeling and Daily Feedback on Residential Electricity Conservation, Home Temperature and Humidity, Perceived Comfort, and Clothing Worn: Winter and Summer." *Journal of Applied Behavior Analysis* 15:381–402.

WINETT, RICHARD A., and J. H. KAGEL. 1984. "The Effects of Information Format Presentation on Consumer Demand for Resources." Unpublished manuscript. Blacksburg: Virginia Polytechnic Institute and State University.

WINKLER, R. C., and R. A. WINETT. 1982. "Behavioral Interventions in Resource Consumption: A Systems Approach Based on Behavioral Economics." *American Psychologist* 37:421–435.

WINTER, RALPH K. 1973. "Economic Regulation versus Competition: Ralph Nader and Creeping Capitalism." *Yale Law Journal* 82:890–902.

WISE, ARTHUR E. 1980. *Legislated Learning: The Bureaucratization of the American Class Room.* Berkeley and Los Angeles: University of California Press.

WOLL, PETER. 1963. *American Bureaucracy.* New York: W. W. Norton.

———. 1977. *American Bureaucracy.* 2nd ed. New York: W. W. Norton.

WRIGHT, SUSAN. 1982. "The Status of Hazards and Controls." *Environment* 24:12ff.

YUCHTMAN, EPHRAIM, and STANLEY E. SEASHORE. 1967. "A System Resource Approach to Organizational Effectiveness." *American Sociological Review* 32:891–903.

ZAJAC, EDWARD E. 1978. *Fairness or Efficiency*. Cambridge, Mass.: Ballinger.

ZERBE, RICHARD O., JR. 1980. "The Costs and Benefits of Early Regulation of the Railroads." *Bell Journal of Economics* 11:343–350.

ZUCKERMAN, H. 1977. *Scientific Elite*. New York: Free Press.

ZUCKERMAN, MICHAEL. 1970. *Peaceable Kingdoms*. New York: Alfred A. Knopf.

Appendix

List of Participants, CalTech/NSF Conference on Social Science and Regulatory Policy, 22–23 January 1982

Mitchel Abolafia *Graduate School of Administration, University of California, Davis*

Bruce Ackerman *School of Law, Yale University*

Robert C. Ashby *Senior Attorney Advisor, U.S. Department of Transportation*

Roberta Balstad Miller *Consortium of Social Science Assns.*

Barbara Bankoff *John Adams Associates*

Ronald Boster *Office of Cong. Ralph Regula*

Theodore Caplow *Department of Sociology, University of Virginia*

Eloise E. Clark *Directorate for Biological, Behavioral & Social Sciences, National Science Foundation*

Edward H. Clarke *Office of Management & Budget*

Robert W. Crandall *The Brookings Institution*

James V. DeLong *Attorney*

Martha Derthick *The Brookings Institution*

George Eads *The Rand Corporation*

Neil R. Eisner *Asst. General Counsel for Regulation and Enforcement, U.S. Department of Transportation*

John A. Ferejohn *Division of the Humanities & Social Sciences, California Institute of Technology*

Morris P. Fiorina *Division of the Humanities & Social Sciences, California Institute of Technology*

Daniel J. Fiorino *Chief, Regulation Management Staff, U.S. Environmental Protection Agency*

Lawrence M. Friedman *Stanford Law School*

Daniel W. Fulmer *Experimental Technology Incentives Program, National Bureau of Standards*

James R. Green *Chief, Policy Analysis Branch Broadcast Bureau, Federal Communications Commission*

Paul J. Halpern *U.S. Environmental Protection Agency*

Walter R. Hobby *U.S. Consumer Product Safety Commission*

Paul L. Joskow *Department of Economics, Massachusetts Institute of Technology*

Affiliations given are those at time of conference.

Marvin H. Kosters *American Enterprise Institute*

Otto Larsen *Social Sciences Division, National Science Foundation*

Lester Lave *The Brookings Institution*

Felice Levine *Law & Social Sciences, National Science Foundation*

Theodore Lowi *Department of Government, Cornell University*

Jeffrey S. Lubbers *Administrative Conference of the U.S.*

Carol A. MacLennan *National Highway Traffic Safety Administration, U.S. Department of Transportation*

Richard E. Morrison *Policy Research & Analysis, National Science Foundation*

Mark V. Nadel *Battelle Human Affairs Research Center*

Claire Nader *Washington, D.C.*

Laura Nader *Department of Anthropology, University of California, Berkeley*

Daniel H. Newlon *Economics Program, National Science Foundation*

Roger G. Noll *Division of the Humanities & Social Sciences, California Institute of Technology*

Charles Perrow *Department of Sociology, Yale University*

Mahesh Podar *Office of Management & Budget*

Lynn Pollnow *Economics Program, National Science Foundation*

Paul Quirk *The Brookings Institution*

William H. Riker *University Dean of Graduate Studies, University of Rochester*

Laurence C. Rosenberg *Regulation Program, National Science Foundation*

Frank Scioli *Political Science Program, National Science Foundation*

W. Richard Scott *Department of Sociology, Stanford University*

Philip Selznick *School of Law, University of California, Berkeley*

Kenneth A. Shepsle *Department of Political Science, Washington University*

Paul Slovic *Decision Research*

Loren A. Smith *Administrative Conference of the U.S.*

Paul C. Stern *National Academy of Sciences*

Bernard W. Tenenbaum *Office of Regulatory Analysis, Federal Energy Regulatory Commission*

Gail Updegraff *U.S. Department of Agriculture*

Mary Ellen Weber *Occupational Safety and Health Administration, U.S. Department of Labor*

James Q. Wilson *Department of Government, Harvard University*

Richard A. Winett *Department of Psychology, Virginia Polytechnic Institute*

John H. Young *Office of Technology Assessment*

James J. Zuiches *Sociology Program, National Science Foundation*

Designer: Rick Chafian
Compositor: Innovative Media
Text: VIP Baskerville
Display: Baskerville
Printer: Braun-Brumfield
Binder: Braun-Brumfield

DATE DUE